THE BLUEBELL CHILDREN

Multiple Personalities: The Art of Self-Deception

THE BLUEBELL CHILDREN

Multiple Personalities: The Art of Self-Deception

Cordelia Hannah & Godefrida Discart

ATHENA PRESS
LONDON

THE BLUEBELL CHILDREN
Multiple Personalities: The Art of Self-Deception
Copyright © Cordelia Hannah & Godefrida Discart 2005

ISBN 1 84401 431 2

First Published 2005 by
ATHENA PRESS
Queen's House, 2 Holly Road
Twickenham, TW1 4EG
United Kingdom

Printed for Athena Press

Contents

Twelve pears hanging high
Twelve knights riding by;
Each knight took a pear,
And yet left eleven there.

The Oxford Dictionary of Nursery Rhymes

What is Multiple Personality Disorder (MPD)? (or Dissociative Disorder – which is now the preferred term)

MPD is first and foremost a unique *coping mechanism*; a means to rise above certain abuse being inflicted upon the child – whether it is sexual, physical or emotional – although usually, it involves all three.

There are of course many aspects involved, as to how and why the child resorts to using such an elaborate *survival strategy*. However, the crucial aspects which seem to motivate the child, appear to be the experience of pain or fear; utter terror; feeling in danger of losing one's life, coupled with the betrayal by important others, to whom the child invariably looked up or even adored, and with the inherent shame that accompanies any such betrayal.

MPD in essence, is a *self-deception*, a *falsification of reality*, which allows the child to create the illusion that the abuse is not happening to themself – but to another. The *abused child*, in effect, feels unable to *integrate* the *bad, painful, fearful* behaviour of the adult and solves this dilemma by projecting any such badness into another imaginary child. In time, and depending on the child's environment, this *other* (imaginary) *child* may be turned into a real person – there is effectively a second beginning – when the imaginary child will be perceived as a separate person; as a real Other-Self. Thereafter, as and when circumstances dictate, this process can be repeated many times – hence why the child/adult can end up with many different (imaginary) personalities.

The book, *The Bluebell Children*, naturally, explores these different aspects, as well as the means whereby the child thereafter, diligently, maintains this self-deception and is able to switch from one (imaginary) personality to another, apparently without having conscious awareness.

What effectively began as a *way out*, a *mental escape* from the pain and distress, becomes a veritable *Art of Deception*, an *elaborate self-perpetuating trap* which only succeeds in making the life of the child even more of an ordeal than it already is, and will continue to severely complicate the life of the adult.

Godefrida Discart

Foreword

Multiple Personality Disorder implies an astonishing capacity to split and to reinvent oneself. This is the ability of someone to whom life is lived as drama and theatre, and one does not have to be traumatised in childhood to have such a characteristic, although the really troubled ones who seek our help do have histories of deprivation and abuse. The age-old term hysteria identified femaleness and sexual tensions, but recently study of the character structure of hysterics has come up with the term histrionic, which identifies the theatricality of the person and recognises that hysterical symptomatology arises from character structure and must be understood in that light if therapy is to work.

There are many histrionic people. Those who get into deep psychological trouble have disturbed childhoods and pose many difficulties in therapy. I shall quote Blacker and Tupin (1977):

> The more infantile personality organisation arises as a result of inadequate mothering and deprivation during infancy and results in chaotic, extreme and unstable behaviour as an adult which is highly resistant to psychotherapeutic psycho-analytic intervention. This is contrasted with the genital or mature hysterical personality organisation, which has experienced less early deprivation, exhibits more intact object relationships, has experienced more success in vocational, education and social areas and has symptoms amenable to the present armament of psychotherapeutic intervention.

The success that Discart describes, with the help of her patient Cordelia, is remarkable for the unusual honesty about the process, but especially remarkable because Cordelia was almost in the former category of Blacker and Tupin. Her mother hated her to the end of her mother's life; her idealised father not only died on her, but sexually abused her. The upbringing could hardly have been more traumatic within the family.

The key to success has to be in Discart's wide training and long experience of therapy techniques, in conjunction with her compassion and professionalism. Both personal qualities were sorely tried; through all Cordelia's acting out and testing, Discart had to perceive Cordelia's own qualities of compassion and honesty to stay with her therapist, who needed all her professionalism and experience to define and hold to the goal of therapy. Without the necessary qualities of long experience and professionalism there can be an endless wilderness of defeat, evasion, side-tracking and despair for therapist and patient alike. Succinctly put, the therapist has to bring the patient to remember and to re-experience emotionally her various childhood traumata. You get there, having exposed the multiple evasions and deceptions she will use to resist you exposing the truth beneath the veneers. You then take her through her anger, humiliation, outrage at broken trust, downright abuse and broken images. On the other side of this comes some personal resolution and you hope that the original person, the real Self, will emerge from beneath the emotional rubble to make a fresh start.

There are many in the legal and the medical professions who believe that we therapists have invented child abuse to account for our patients' problems; that the expectations and preconceptions that the therapist may have been taught to probe will gradually create bogus memories of incest and rape. I have to agree this may happen. Therapists must be scrupulous not to interpret, not to provide such answers. The truth, whatever it may be, will eventually out from within the patient. Although in denial and tending to resist seeing the truth, histrionic people are very suggestible and often make good subjects for hypnosis. I am concerned for instance that people purporting to find evidence for a previous incarnation on this earth may simply tell the candidate to imagine what shoes he could have been wearing in such an existence and to build imaginatively on that. A lively mind would free associate on this to shape himself a former character. We are dealing with histrionic patients with self-dramatising tendencies. We have to be very professional in our approach.

However, from my use of LSD as a resource during psycho-analysis of many patients, I know that many times the answers are there within the patient and that they often concern childhood abuse, and that becoming vividly reminded of these events is often crucial to the cure. I find I must validate the events that Discart describes by illustrating from my own experience using LSD as a 'revelatory' drug.

It was high drama that got a young married woman admitted to a mental hospital by a colleague of mine. Ostensibly unable to handle the messes produced by her first born, she had threatened to walk into the sea with him. A clue was that she had spent much time with a grandmother who was obsessional about dirt and contaminations. I was asked about taking this hysterical woman on for long-term therapy. I agreed, having had success with a mother who could not leave home without searching thoroughly for messes made by her baby. None was ever found but she had to search none the less. In her LSD session she found herself as a little girl playing with her baby brother. They were smearing each other and the wall with his faeces. For this offence she found herself being held upside down and lowered head first into a bucket of water. This one session showed her why she was so anxious about the baby's messes and her problem promptly disappeared.

But the histrionic mother I now took on did not follow this pattern. Her problem with messes was a screen that hid a profoundly dysfunctional family. She had moved with her husband close to her family home. Her father often visited her and got far too involved with advice and money for anything she needed, clashing vehemently with her husband. There was no way she would admit to a problem with her father, but in due course her first LSD session revealed that her father's close interest had a long history and involved him being excited sexually. She emerged from the session convinced that her father was responsible for her chaotic mental state and her acting out. I put her firmly on the side of therapy and into an intelligent alliance with me, although there was further working through and some histrionic crises. We were fortunate because her parents were eventually able to come clean. Seldom do parents confirm what their daughter has remembered, but in this case her mother corroborated her daughter's memories and her father apologised to her. Her husband moved his job and their home to another town. They emigrated soon after. She founded a chain of craft shops and was a successful businesswoman.

The purpose of the LSD illustrations is to validate the trauma themes that tend to be discounted in other contexts, but one cannot discount these LSD revelations from within the patients' mind that are independent of what the therapist does and says. Crucially they break through resistances to therapy and play a big part in the cure. The experience is very convincing. Ordinary remembering is distanced by time and subject to selection and censorship. LSD experience is as it actually happened with nothing left out. In fact it provides details of surroundings, objects, dress etc., that can be revisited and confirmed. It is interesting that it mostly happens this way within a psychoanalytic setting; LSD seldom provides a cure by itself, and it has to be used with great care in the selection of patients.

By 1975 researchers had identified the sites of action of the LSD molecule upon serotonin sensitive neurones whose active function is to control memories. This inhibiting action upon memories within the limbic system is essential to our survival. We certainly live by experience, but our attention must not be swamped by a mass of memories surfacing on any old pretext. There is so much memory stored there that strict inhibition is vital to our being able to act effectively in the present. Traumatic memories in particular get relegated to the depths to let us get on with our lives. The post-traumatic stress syndrome is the exception where the threat continues to haunt consciousness. LSD disinhibits by binding to certain receptors. It is removed within 2–3 hours. Only a very small amount of the oral dose reaches the brain. It is totally eliminated in the urine from the body in 2–3 days. It is not an intoxication, the effect is almost physiological; the drug is remarkably benign. The so-called flashbacks occur long after the drug has been eliminated. They are a psychological consequence of the communication the LSD establishes with the memory system; likewise dreams may become more realistic and closer to actual events.

By 1975 it had become imprudent to use LSD. The mode of action, now identified, led me to believe that there had to be a drug-free technique for accessing the traumatic memories held in check by that serotoninergic system. In 1976 I went to the USA to practise psychiatry; the problem continued to exercise me. Reading *Primal Scream* (Janov A) suggested a way of getting directly to the emotional point, shall I say. Dr Alan Jeppson in Salt Lake City demonstrated how it could be done. His patient would be recounting a memory when he would insist: 'Do not just talk about it, just get into the situation as it was; be the person you were right in the middle of it.' Generally his patient was emotionally ripe for this and he provided soundproofed accommodation for the experience to be fully worked through for as long as it took. I had my own air-conditioned and soundproofed room with carpeted walls, soft covers and light dimmer to make it easier to drop back into the raw memory as it was at the time.

Then I had a dramatic illustration of how effective this simple technique can be. A young single woman was hospitalised for a year suffering from monthly hallucinations of blood all over the place. She was regarded as a schizophrenic. In between these dramatic hallucinatory episodes she was a pleasant and friendly young woman who held court with staff and patients. I would chat with her in passing, when she impressed me as being a hysteric. Her funds exhausted, she left hospital and happened to take up residence with a male social worker near my office. Her hospital psychiatrist asked me to look after her for a while.

Hysterics break the best laid rules and sometimes you find yourself having to respond. Her partner brought her to my home, because of her wild and distraught state. It was late, she lacked funding for hospital admission, my wife and I decided to cope overnight in our home. The woman suddenly decided to escape into one of her customary self-induced trance states that she called her 'seventh heaven'. My wife told her to stop escaping and to come clean about her real trouble. 'Get into it,' we said. Lo and behold this woman, who had been in hospital for a year just being stabilised as a schizophrenic, went into an early episode of being assaulted by her father in a drunken state with broken glass and blood. She remembered being taken to hospital. This was the start of insight psychotherapy. She never again had hallucinations of blood. Anger, not blood, became her problem. Her progress was typically turbulent, but she was moving towards recovery.

In retrospect this primal-scream technique was safer to use than LSD, given the possibility of her actually being schizophrenic. In the event she proved to be a typical complicated histrionic victim of an indifferent mother and an incestuous father, showing post-traumatic stress symptoms and dissociative behaviour.

I did not know about Cordelia, when I demonstrated the technique to Discart on a male patient of mine, and I certainly was not one of her psychiatrists. Discart had taken a course in Ericksonian Hypnotherapy. I thought I could show her a *spot on* technique without the element of mind control and guesswork in Erickson's approach (1979).

My reading of the literature on MPD and my own experience forces me to conclude that the childhood relationships revealed by Cordelia in therapy are typical for MPD and that a lot is to be gained by examining such a typical causal chain. I shall start with the phenomenon of the mother who hates one of her children, because this seems to me one of the keys to understanding the peculiar childhood pressures and the consequences for behaviour in adult life.

MOTHERS WHO HATE

A family pauses in the doorway of my consulting room. Hesitatingly the mother of the children makes her entrance under pressure from the father who particularly shepherds in one of the children. I am reminded of Pirandello's play *Six Characters in Search of an Author*. Parental perceptions of one child are totally at odds and cannot be reconciled. The father seeks help for his wife because from the start she has hated this one child. He has tried to understand, but he can make no sense of her behaviour and has failed to change her. The mother does not beat about the bush. She hates this child and that is a fact of family life. The child's actual personality and behaviour, whether docile or difficult, are neither here nor there. She just hates. The father adds that his wife physically abuses and deprives this child so that he resorts to keeping the child out of her way, maybe with the help of relatives and neighbours.

You discuss her own personal history with this mother. Her theme is similar to other hating mothers. She felt intense anger and jealousy as a child herself for a younger sibling who displaced her in favour with their parents. The sex of the sibling and sometimes the position in the family will be the same as the child she now hates. It is a simple displacement. It never strikes her as unjust and somewhat evil to scapegoat this child, or as an abuse of power she wields as mother. She sees her child as the hated sibling. That is the way she started and she continues to seek her vengeance despite the innocence of any offence to provoke her by the actual child.

I offer in illustration the mother of an adult patient. Mrs B was the first born, to be succeeded by four brothers and a sister, who had no cause to remember their older sister with fondness. She disappointed her mother's desire for a feminine and home-loving girl. Instead she was a tomboy, preferring the company of boys and in her teens getting up to mischief. In fact, she was such a trouble for her mother, in the absence of her father on military service, that Mrs B was declared out of parental control and in moral peril, for which she was confined to a Church institution for such girls for eighteen months and taught laundering skills. Her mother did not communicate. Mrs B realised rightly that she had been displaced in her mother's affection by the youngest child, Mollie. Fantasising the love, clothes and presents her spoiled sister would be enjoying, Mrs B's resentment built up in hatred around Mollie. But after her marriage she had two sons before a daughter arrived. On this daughter's head all her venom about Mollie suddenly descended. When years later she was confronted by this daughter now an adult about her physical abuse and deprivations, she replied vehemently, 'I hated you. You *were* Mollie.' Hating was something Mrs B never questioned. To her, just hating was a justification in itself.

Discart's patient, Cordelia, endured similar ill-treatment and constructive deprivation from her mother, who even reminded her from the grave, in a letter with her Will, that she had been a hated daughter right to the end. Their book is the story of the uncovering of multiple abuses and of the intricate and various coping responses of the beleaguered child, which tell us a great deal about psychopathology in the adult and about the abuse of parent power.

I was lucky to have intervened successfully to end such hatred in the case of a sweet girl of nine years. She came to me from a neurologist who had assessed her for attacks resembling epilepsy, and had judged them to be hysterical. As was my custom with children, I let her imagination loose playing with puppets of family members in a doll's house. She arranged the furniture and people as she saw them in her home and she made me aware of the uneasy relationship between her parents and that only her father had love for her. In a later session she introduced a strange man into the living room. She stopped and turned to me ready to talk. The stranger had been visiting her mother without daddy knowing. She was very worried about his threat to their family life. She knew her mother had no love for her; there would be nothing to stop her mother leaving for good with this man. I confronted the mother. Yes it was true, she was on the point of leaving. I tackled her on her feelings for her sensitive and concerned daughter who had drawn attention to her fears about this threat by having dramatic episodes resembling epilepsy. She replied that she had always hated her daughter, and behind this hatred I found the usual history of jealousy of a younger sister. So I suggested that her hate had actually blinded her to the fact that she had a lovely daughter and that there had to be an end to scapegoating her daughter to satisfy long irrelevant hatreds from her past. Were she not to change her attitude she would be doing herself a tragic disservice. In better circumstances this daughter would soon grow up to be her mother's best friend and be close to her for the rest of her life. I tried to open the mother's eyes to the destruction of the very things that make family life worthwhile. My arguments worked. She announced she had sent the man packing and would now be rebuilding their lives together, realising the sincerities of both husband and daughter and needing to be part of a loving family.

CONSEQUENCES TO HER DAUGHTER

There are no half measures in this mother's behaviour. Hating is a way of life; revenge is sweet; she enjoys seeing the fear in her child's eyes; her facial expression changes when she looks at this child, who never sees any sign of love in her mother for herself. Deprivation is real; clothes are second-hand; mother does not give gifts, rather gifts to the child from others, such as the father, are made to disappear or sometimes deliberately smashed in front of the child; no birthdays are celebrated; denigration, put-downs, discouragement and physical abuse are the daily fare. There may be hints of murderous intent, such as a pillow over the child's face or being held under water in the bath.

I had a girl of five years under my care in a children's unit in Utah. She was very needy emotionally, and was apt to strike other children in jealousy or just to get acquainted. Social Services had separated her permanently from her mother because of her dangerously abusive behaviour. This mother without shame demonstrated how she would throw the infant away from her in angry exasperation. It is remarkable how hating mothers regard their hate as a natural explanation of their behaviour, as a justification in itself. When I offered the doll's house and family puppets to this five-year-old, she arranged a children's tea party in front, but circle around as she might, she could not get the invitation to join the party for which she longed. Her behaviour got more and more desperate until she crashed sobbing into the arms of her nurse who was assisting me. Her mother had shown she had been unwanted and discardable, giving her the feeling of being an outsider, who could only break into social life violently if at all. So we gave her a party and a cake, and she did the inviting.

I shall refer again to the outsider position. But before I consider the developmental consequences and the manner in which the infant and child survive to become an histrionically disturbed adult, I want to record an LSD experience that appears to challenge theories of infant development especially of the ego and of self as distinct from the mother infant fusion.

At her first LSD session a thirty-six-year-old mother with phobic anxiety found herself as an infant in her pram in the kitchen. She felt unwell and was breathing rapidly. Her mother leaned over her with a bad look on her face and was placing a blanket over the infant's face. My patient thought she would die, but suddenly two huge hands lifted her out of the pram and there was her father taking over her care. She turned away from her mother's breast believing the milk would now poison her.

When I asked her, the mother confirmed that the child had had bronchitis and that her husband had fashioned a fishtail for the kettle to humidify the air and that his efforts had got his daughter out of trouble. But she recalled the discomfort to herself of having to suppress her milk because her infant daughter refused her breast. She was adamant that this occurred at three months. This infant at three months of age sensed her mother's hatred and dangerous intentions, and not only refused further breast feeding, but distanced herself, at the same time turning to the father as the good parent. That was the turning point of decision at three months of age. This is crucial to survival; an early decision about mother being bad, resulting in distancing from mother's breast and body, coupled with a readiness of the father to respond as the loving parent.

That this decision can take place very early in life I have encountered in the transference situation demonstrated twice to me and once to another therapist in an identical way. This nineteen-year-old woman, a boutique manager, in typical histrionic way had overreached herself in fantasy promises to other pupils at a finishing school. Reality had been very humiliating. In therapy it took some time to get her confidence, then just as one felt really good about her involvement in therapy she suddenly was not there at the next appointment, without any warning or later apology. She had been fostered from birth but she had five foster mothers in succession. She was making her therapists understand how she had felt when she had begun to trust a foster mother and then suddenly the mother disappeared for ever. The experience created distress also when she had been adopted into a loving family. She refused ever to call her adoptive mother 'Mummy', and attached herself from the start to her adoptive father. An infant seems to have expectations and to make crucial decisions at a very early age.

How does one discover who one really is, that is the real person, secure in one's identity, and in touch with what Winnicott (1989) called one's psyche-soma? The discovery has to begin from the earliest relationship with mother. Having to distance oneself, as I have described, has to distort development. I had a late adolescent in group therapy for outsiders; he agonised perpetually over who he was and how he must appear to others. The unwanted infant of a single parent, he was adopted after a few months, but he refused to accept his adoptive parents as mum and dad. As an adult he was always in employment, but even in later years at the age of fifty, he still needed to question people as to how he appeared to them.

Which brings me straight to Winnicott's ideas (1971) around the mirroring of her infant by the good-enough mother that reflects back the infant's developing personality to let him know who he is. The baby knows 'I am' but 'who I am' remains to be discovered. The infant is dependent upon his mother's responses being empathic and truthful for him over time to get into touch with this hypothetical uniquely true self. The infant senses recognition and encouragement of himself through closely observing the mother's eyes and face, her baby talk and her holding and other bodily movements. The infant may sense the mother's unconscious for all we know. Their emotional relationship of body and spirit fosters and shapes the baby's knowledge of himself. So much can go wrong when the mother is unsympathetic, neglectful or just disappears. Certainly we shall expect special problems for the baby of the mother who hates.

The startling thing about the relationship with the hating mother is that the mirroring is so distorted that there is no recognition of the qualities and emerging personality of the infant. The mother sees another child, her hated sibling. Her infant is being treated as if it were someone else. There is no way for the infant to recognise itself in the mother's responses. I believe that the infant has expectations about being recognised and cherished for itself. Without this nurture the outcome can be catastrophic, but my evidence from therapy and also LSD suggests that the infant identifies the mother as bad, as a witch, and distances itself to be the better able to find a sympathetic bond with father, sister or nurse. It profoundly affects personal development making for great insecurity and defensive self-invention to get by somehow with the hating mother.

There are important insights to be learned from this critical early threat, confusion and uncertainty, from being treated as if this baby were someone else, of which the infant and growing child have no knowledge. It is a Kafka-esque situation to be treated without explanation, as if you are someone else.

So here we have the makings of an histrionic personality and of psychiatric morbidity. I shall enumerate.

1. 'I am invisible, unless I make a fuss and dramatise myself. No one will notice me at all.' This is the underlying need causing the histrionic person to be so apparently seeking attention. This self-dramatisation goes with the expectation of being ignored and put down, and is thus accompanied by a great deal of anger and emotion. 'I was a nobody,' recalls Cordelia quoting her mother.

2. 'The woman who looked after me was no mother but a wicked witch.' This generated a lot of anger and bodily discomfort from sheer emotion, which had to be controlled by surface denial of anger and by detachment from one's own bodily emotions. Hence the divorce from the meaning of feelings and the split from one's own psyche-soma, something Winnicott recognised as going along with having a false self. It is associated with 'belle indifference' the bizarre quasi-physical symptoms and other failures to recognise the obvious, to others that is. Discart makes an important use of the trance state to explain how an histrionic fails to see and to acknowledge the presence of something that her behaviour shows she knows is there.

3. But the anger is there and it permeates the whole secret thinking. Nothing is quite what it seems. An apparently highly cooperative and talkative patient is likely from sheer habit to be pursuing a secret agenda to get her own back (originally on the mother). How sweet is the revenge in its secrecy at a moment of flattery to the therapist who may see only a somewhat seductive and confiding patient.

   It was my third meeting with this married woman in her thirties. She was telling me in detail about her husband's dominance and male arrogance. She came to the point of sweet revenge for her: 'When I really hate him I pick up any man in the street and have sex with him. And then I can look at my husband and think if only you knew, how mad you would be.' I noted a gleam in her eyes and I heard myself saying, 'But you have done this to me!' Her whole demeanour changed. 'You witch,' she cried. 'How did you know?' and I was subjected to a stream of verbal abuse.

   In therapy you have to expose the secret agendas when you can, because you then get under the misleading personality to the nitty gritty of real pain, humiliation, betrayal and fantasies of revenge. This is the underlying reality. The surface appearance is the need to please and impress, to seduce the sympathy and support, and represents an act of theatre. An histrionic woman can do this brilliantly. Do not be deceived.

4. That the histrionic patient lives a life of theatre also makes her a bit of a prima donna. There is this drive to be actually visible and noticed, but there is also a drive to be number one in the family, in social situations and in the hospital milieu with other patients of her therapist. It arises from having been made to feel nobody; it is part of the fight back. (Even so, some badly traumatised MPD patients retreat from such assertion and show avoidant personality.)

    A twenty-one-year-old histrionic spinster was drawn to amateur theatricals. She had to be rebuked by the producer of a play, in which she had a supporting role, because she drew attention to herself at a critical moment for the principal. When she found she would not be given the leading role until after lengthy apprenticeship with the company she withdrew. In therapy, the histrionic woman will take care she is your most important patient; jealous scenes about some other patient may result. She has got to be number one, just as she expected to be as a babe in her mother's arms. A successful baby is the prima donna in her family. The child of the hating mother has to go on fighting for this status.

5. The mother's enduring victimising of her daughter undermines her position with brothers and sisters, one or more of whom seize opportunities to bully, deprive, injure and to satisfy sexual curiosity. Cordelia's mother uses her for her own sexual satisfaction, something which resonates in my mind with other such mothers. Hers is not an isolated behaviour. What I have heard described as family sexual games go on whereby the mother involves the children, maybe their friends and possibly her lover, if not the husband. Indeed such a mother may manipulate her husband towards a sexual act with the daughter as a final humiliation, and sweetest revenge by breaking for ever any special father and daughter relationship. This is a home of very dark deeds and of dire consequences for mental health. In her own account, Cordelia records having been locked in her bedroom, with shuttered windows and an amount of food and drink, whilst the rest of the family went away, possibly for more than a week. Her account must be read as she recalls it. It was sheer terror, to be followed by an ignominious admission to an 'asylum'.

    It is important that therapists accept that the patient's memories will be full of bizarre events that beggar the imagination and invite scepticism, for such is the wickedness within the family, where the mother hates and victimises from a position of almost absolute power.

6. Whatever saw Cordelia through to adulthood, to marriage and to motherhood? 'It was my ability to dissociate to the extreme that brought

me through. I hid inside, covered by layer upon layer of my created personalities.' These personalities were 'different persons with different names holding separate memories and different emotions' constituting 'an integral part of my coping mechanism while young,' she writes. To which one can add self-hypnosis and induced trance states, which Discart has identified as the explanation for the prominence of denial and paradoxical behaviour.

Psychiatrically we are in territory common to three diagnostic categories. There is the *histrionic personality* that sustains the typical behaviour and organises the defences and reinvents as needed. Then almost all the major traumata would qualify the victim for *post-traumatic stress disorder*. Lastly the hate and the rejections throughout infancy and childhood qualify for *depressive illness* with suicidal potential. Yet so often the suicidal behaviour is attributed to manipulative attempts on the therapist. In the perspective that I have sought to give about the nature of this disorder, I would hope there will now be no place in any therapy setting for the dismissive terms – attention-seeking, manipulative and others that the hating mother herself may have used to rubbish her daughter. Our patients are striving to be good where their parents were harsh and cruel. Most battered youngsters, such is the Social Services experience, solve their hurt by identifying with their parents and taking their hatred out on their own children or spouse. Cordelia recalls spells of identifying with her mother but found the experience very depressing. It was not her. The struggle has always been how not to grow up like mother. The legion of personalities were invented to prevent this happening and to survive as different, but there has to be at least one alter modelled on the hating mother. Reactive anger is inevitable and needs an identity for it to be controlled.

FATHERS

If the reader will turn again to Cordelia's account of her father's idealised role in her young life; of his premature death and the subsequent extinction of his memory by her mother, one will find that his treachery by raping her was the most buried of her memories. Yet the recovery of this memory was crucial to her recovery because her real self was there, on account of her being recognised and cherished by her father up to that point. He had been her mirroring and enabling parent for want of a good enough mother.

Cordelia recalls a highly significant split into two personalities from the time of the rape. Peter was the immediate injured self transformed for both safety and courage into a boy, whereas Rosalind could stay friendly with the father and not be abused. Felicity, moreover, had come into being as her father's flirt and recognised herself as such in response to meeting up with her father's male friends. This girl was a flirtatious coquette who knowingly tried to attract attention, but hers was a fragile personality that appeared and then dissolved into a depressive reaction. Felicity throws light upon a flirtatious characteristic of histrionic women that is not altogether what it seems and to which I shall now seek a better explanation.

Writers on our subject of histrionic behaviour have always remarked on seductiveness in their subjects without being able to say for certain whether this is intentional and really sexually inviting, or something that is done to attract male attention without any intention to follow through. Felicity rapidly disillusioned any suitors with a well-aimed kick. It used to be held that hysterics were flirtatious but frigid, but this is now seen to be untrue. What therefore is this seductiveness about? Is it really sexual in its intention?

Cordelia helps us to understand. She recalls how she behaved towards her father's male friends. There was an apparent precociousness about it that one might think came from the shattering of her innocence. But I have a different explanation that I believe must be the correct one.

Let us be frank. Rape is not a sexual experience. Rape is a sudden and unheralded physical assault on a most tender and private part of the child's body, that causes intense pain and shock. The rapist is the beloved father suddenly turned maniac without warning, and showing afterwards a particularly nasty and callous side of himself, that threatens and demeans his daughter to ensure her silence. So, men are dangerous, you must please them and keep them happy or else. I therefore see this so-called seductive behaviour as ingratiating and appeasing in order to ward off possible physical attack.

I was reminded of one of my first successes as a novice therapist, when I was researching essential hypertension as a possible psychosomatic disorder. This young married woman in her late twenties had documented deterioration in blood pressure over several years so that she was running diastolic pressures from 120 mms mercury upwards. She sought help beyond the research sessions, because she did everything at the double; everything had to be exactly right domestically in her home; she was an inveterate agree-er and she could not stand up to her husband on the smallest point. When she came for her therapy she could be heard running down the corridor and the same happened when she left. She would not use the couch, but insisted on a chair. She made good use of her time, but began to have difficult silences and an inability to answer questions. Throughout she flashed anxious smiles and was unnecessarily alarmed about maybe displeasing me. She grew more anxious and more winsome until suddenly at her thirty-third session she recalled as a small child coming upon her father attempting to strangle her mother, while both struggled on the floor.

Our relationship immediately changed. She accepted the couch and sought from me encouragement to establish and so be her real self. Actually she changed so rapidly that no further therapy was needed. All her driven behaviour ceased, she became calm, she stood up to her husband. She stopped trying to please all the time. She emigrated with her husband. I saw her about a year later when she appeared a confident mature woman. Her diastolic pressure was about 105 mms. (This was 1950/51. Effective drugs came later.)

This hypertensive woman went to great lengths to ingratiate herself with her husband and to put herself beyond any blame for neglecting him or the house. She flashed smiles at me all the time. The reason for this incredible behaviour was to avoid any chance of provoking male violence. I was obviously a source of great anxiety to her in the transference.

I believe this must relate to Cordelia's behaviour after the violent assault by her father. I believe it may supply the true source of the so-called seductive behaviour of distressed histrionic women, who generally have suffered incestuous interest from their fathers. Such fathers may also require risque behaviour in their daughters.

Her father was the one source for personal identity through recognition and encouragement. Her Rosalind character allows this relationship to continue; it is understandable that the associated drive for attention and personal existence reinforces the ingratiating behaviour with men in general, despite the danger. It is treading a tightrope between pleasing and pacifying men by giving them an appearance of what they apparently want in a woman, and beyond that of chancing provoking the very painful attack she is trying to avoid.

This is a conflict that may cause switching from one personality to another as a transference to a doctor, who may be seen both as male to be pleased and as a threat with power to hurt your body. I recall a withdrawn boy of eight on whom I did an admitting physical and mental examination; he seemed to be two people, the first replied yes or no, the second promptly said a contradictory no or yes as the sequence went. He had pauses and brief trance states.

FATHER'S FANCY GIRL

Although I believe I have drawn the right conclusion about the warding-off significance of seductive behaviour, there is no doubting its power. The young would-be prima donna in the dramatic society related her experiences with one GP in the Practice and also with the local psychiatrist. Both fell for her flattery and misread the signals. The GP pressed her (a married woman with children) to join him for a drink in their local; but rather more disconcertingly the psychiatrist sat on his desk in front of her and avowed that his sexual libido and prowess in the act were undiminished by middle age.

This seems to be a hazard for histrionic women that some professionals respond by putting themselves on offer. Non-medical male therapists may be even more susceptible. This is the therapist acting out his counter-transference sexually, whereas the histrionic motive is to please, to entice approval, sympathy, special treatment and to ward off rejection and anger from a parent figure. Any desired closeness would be of the hugging, reassuring, parental kind. To encounter a sexual overture when professional help is sought shatters trust. The women in question discontinued seeing both doctors. But why was she, like other histrionics, so seductive? It was taught her by her father. In her teens he took her to dances and to social functions where he was not known, so that he could pass her off as his girlfriend. 'Unbutton your blouse. Loosen your hair. Dance close to me. Look happy and smile.' She began to see a psychologist, but broke off when she was told her symptoms suggested a sexual threat. She knew that she excited her father and that it went further back in her life. But she took the point and moved away when she could. Several years later she presented with pain in her chest and abdomen – the Chest Physician finding nothing but a positive mantoux prescribed a year's supply of PAS (obligatory in USA). Later having been examined by a gynae-cologist in Casualty for severe low abdominal pain, she suddenly remembered being sexually assaulted by her father; she was probably six and it had been anal penetration. (Spontaneous opening of her anus was noted in Casualty, the sign that is said to have deceived the two paediatricians in Cleveland to identify child abuse.) He had bought her a double bed for her birthday and just joined her in it when his wife had fallen soundly asleep with a sleeping pill. These experiences were very painful, but the local tissue damage was not diagnosed as being abusive, at that age of six.

Likewise the woman who spent one year in hospital as a schizophrenic with hallucinations of blood had been trained by her father in seductive arts. He was a Hollywood agent who used his contacts and access to drape his adolescent daughter in swimming costume on the edge of film-stars' pools to attract some casting director with her erotic potential. When he took her on his business trips, he forced intercourse upon her in hotels.

During her therapy at one point she hallucinated her father on the kitchen wall and threw knives at him. This anger often appears outside the therapy session. Dramatic recall of experience, sometimes called a flashback, is a spontaneous occurrence that the therapist cannot control. It means that husbands, partners, close relatives have to be included in the wider therapy resource. Alarming as they can be, their occurrence and later working through with the therapist, is essential for the cure. As you cannot confine emotional abreaction to supervised time and place, however much you try by giving longer sessions and extra help in recovery, you may feel compelled to set limits to avoid some dangerous confrontation with a former persecutor.

VALIDATION

In writing freely about my own experiences and my interpretations, particularly in my observations on hating mothers and abusing fathers, I have done so with the confidence that I contribute to a better understanding of dissociative disorders and multiple-personality disorders with a relevance right across the spectrum of clinical presentation. My confidence comes from support studies concerning the validity of the diagnosis, the wider than previously thought epidemiology, and particularly from the close association with consistent physical and mental abuse from birth to the age of five years, an association in excess of 90%. Also validated has been the common ground, I have deduced from my clinical experience, shared with histrionic personality, post-traumatic stress disorder and depressive illness (of an experienced-based type responding poorly to antidepressives).

To my mind there are three seminal publications promoting the recent interest. The first was *Hysterical Personality*, edited by M J Horowitz (1977) and with most contributors from the University of California, that concentrated my thinking about the disorder when I was in Western USA 1976–1982. Then came an issue of the *Psychiatric Clinics of North America* (1984) devoted to MPD which obviously polarised thinking into action, because by 1991 there was a considerable harvest of research results, collected by editor Dr Loewenstein, mainly from Eastern USA medical schools. The time had seen the creation of no less than five professional units devoted to dissociative disorders. This volume is very valuable, published under the same title by Psychiatric Clinics (1991). The term 'alter' is used for a particular personality style in MPD, implying alternative, which is probably preferable to Winnicott's 'false personality'.

A PROBLEMATIC DIAGNOSIS

MPD is so little sought as a diagnostic possibility and schizophrenia is so favoured by psychiatrists that an average of eight years may pass before a succession of treatment failures forces a serious appraisal leading to a correct diagnosis. Yet it is not a rarity. Certainly the presentation as multiple personality is a rarity, but mostly the presence of alternative personalities, or alters, is a closely guarded secret, because they are a very personal and essentially secret defensive ploy to survive in a very dangerous family setting. But apart from the little people within MPD there is the evidence for post-traumatic stress disorder (PTSD) in the syndrome that may mimic a schizophrenic process.

I first encountered PTSD in 1951 in a sanatorium for tuberculosis. I was asked to see an anxious and emaciated thirty-year-old man, because he developed rashes following injections of streptomycin. I found he had been a POW in the hands of the Japanese; whenever the nurse approached with the syringe, he saw a Japanese soldier coming at him with fixed bayonet. We find it easy to accept such a genesis of PTSD after combat experience in war. What now has to be accepted is that PTSD is also a consequence of brutal abuse of a child. The Japanese soldier was not an hallucination in a schizophrenic sense, but the visual projection of a once vividly experienced danger preserved as memory. It subsided quite quickly and the man made an excellent recovery. The point is that hallucinations occur in PTSD. They are mostly visual and often intense, preoccupying and frightening. They may also be auditory, should the alters argue or an internalised parent be heard criticising, but they will be within the patient's mind and not coming from without.

Post-traumatic stress disorder is becoming very important as a diagnostic entity. The concept illuminates much of what in adult life can be related to trauma in childhood. But because it is a disorder that responds poorly to drugs and really needs psychotherapy it is probable that many psychiatrists do not take it very seriously, treating it as a lesser disorder suitable for the psychologists and counsellors to treat. But it is not a lesser disorder. It must be in a psychiatrist's mind when examining a patient with a psychotic disorder. PTSD will mimic the lot and add a bit more. But a diagnosis of schizophrenia is often made on the manifestations at interview alone, because we have been taught this way. Thus transient affective psychoses get caught in the net, for lack of enquiry, about the circumstances of the breakdown and its actual psychological significance, as the manifestation is looked on as making the diagnosis and as mandating the anti-psychotic medication. There are three bits of evidence that need to be routinely sought.

1. Was the patient *physically abused* as a child? The patient may tell you so, if actually asked. A sibling can be consulted, but this is obviously a question that will not be answered truthfully by the parents.

    A vast amount of research has been done on the childhood and infancy of schizophrenics. The most that has emerged from all this is material about patterns of communication between family members. Physical abuse has not been identified. Yet physical abuse is more than 90% present in the childhood experience of those with PTSD, so it is an important pointer away from schizophrenia.

2. Evidence of *post-traumatic stress disorder* leaves a trail throughout the life of the victim: episodes of pain without physical findings; bouts of depression; insomnia; nightmares; amnesia. (I thought it significant that the girls on the adolescent unit stayed up talking until the early hours, after the boys had gone to bed. Ten out of these eleven girls had been sexually abused in the family. Late at night was a danger time; they were programmed to stay alert, otherwise in their childhoods they had enjoyed middle-class comforts and had not been ill-treated.)

    Bathrooms and stairways may have become phobic places having originally been places where abuse and assault took place. One woman could not lie down in a bath until she recalled that her mother once had held her head under the water. Children often get kicked or pushed down stairs; as adults they will look behind them on a stairway; an MPD sufferer may say that an alter will throw him down.

    Visions of their persecutor and of abusive situations simulate hallucinations. The term flashback is a bit street-cred for my liking. We accept the term phantom pain. Maybe phantom is a better term for the sudden visualising of a real persecutor and some scene of terror from a fearful childhood. The phantom is a vision of a real person, who can be named and given a time and place, unlike images in a psychotic hallucination. Spontaneous age-regression may occur with loss of awareness of present time and place.

The clinical aspects are recorded in detail by Loewenstein (1991). First-rank Schneider symptoms regarded as pathognomonic of schizophrenia were found by Kluft (1987) to be more indicative of MPD. This finding places MPD at the centre of differential diagnosis.

3. The *pre-morbid personality* is an obvious distinguishing feature that is barely considered at the initial diagnosis, because of the prime attention paid to eliciting features of the psychotic experience and behaviour that fit a diagnosis of schizophrenia. The introduction of personality type into the diagnostic process by DSMIII has given a chance for alternative diagnosis, when this has been honestly sought and allowed to have weight. Histrionic, avoidant, borderline are distinct from the personality types associated with schizophrenia and their presence would make one consider MPD, depressive and dissociative disorders, drug-induced psychosis of course having been eliminated.

In parenthesis, concerning transient psychosis, call it a rule of thumb, but work on the assumption, that a psychosis that resolves within two weeks is unlikely to be schizophrenic.

This is a plea for a period of observation whenever practical, before making what is the favoured diagnosis, followed by the prescription of phenothiazines. The treatments favoured for schizophrenic psychosis are contra-indicated for MPD and dissociative disorders. Yet as recently as 1984 I saw case notes with the sole entry 'hysterical psychosis' and a treatment response of daily ECT for a week. This was by a senior psychiatrist and examiner for the Royal College. It had been established in 1970 by Rickman and White that hysterical psychosis is a self-limiting disturbance based on family tensions that should be addressed to expedite resolution. Therapists are in major agreement that psychotherapy should be the response to the entire group of hysterical disorders. Putnam (1993).

I cannot address here the diagnostic areas in childhood where the effects of child abuse should be a paramount concern. The theatre of survival, the alternative personalities, the trance state and the post-traumatic nightmares and hallucinations all begin in childhood and can be identified and treated by paediatric psychiatrists and their therapy teams. The abusing fathers and the hating mothers are there in positions of power within the family. This source of pain and pathology can be tackled directly, and by no means inevitably through social services and the courts. In the Multiple Personality Disorder volume (Loewenstein, September 1991), Hornstein and Tyson describe the in-patient treatment of sick children and their families.

DISCOVERY OF SELF

After re-experiencing the horrendous trauma to her body and to her personal existence, due to the abuse by her beloved father, Discart's patient found her real self in hiding under the protection of her alters. This self was true and real enough to grow and to integrate with alters and to be the basis for her own life – as it should have developed.

Finding an essential personal self to be true to has long been an objective of philosophical enquiry, before recently becoming a legitimate object for psycho-analysis. It is true that the search for a true self as a target for an analysis has been held up for mild ridicule as 'hunting the slipper', (Val Richards (1996)). In my opinion the discovery does not come from turning every stone, it just happens without warning at an unexpected moment. I have to admit that I do make a point of identifying the not-self, ego-alien baggage that accretes from all the rubbish that has been said about the patient in his childhood. It cleans up the idea of the self and helps to release energy, but I do not know who the true self may be; the patient alone can tell me that, and he will not know until the self announces its presence. You can describe identity, character and of course, personality type, but the self and the 'me' are subjective. *The Dilemma of Human Identity* by Lichtenstein (1977), examined the whole subject in a psycho-analytical perspective.

Nevertheless LSD experiences by patients have brought to light the extraordinary significance of discovering the continuity of the self from the moment of birth to the present day. Re-experiencing being born leads to the excited affirmation of having deep roots, 'I was there, it was ME being born.'

So I have also to relate one extraordinary experience related to me by one of my least educated patients with amazed awe and excitement, as I helped him put it together. He recalled emerging from a mass and having to pass through a flame in a temple-like structure to gain life. He then was the successful sperm entering the female cell, whereafter he experienced a sense of changes including being a fish that led him to becoming a human infant. This was a genuine experience and not a hoax. And why not a genuine experience in the light of present knowledge about genes. Surely the genetic material at conception has encoded the archaic memory of the stages of evolution over million of years. The development, condensed into nine months, still repeats the main developmental stages to arrive at the human infant. Does LSD access that memory encoded in the genes? Memory, the ability to encode experience, must be a fundamental property from earliest rudiments, certainly of our eternal reproduction cells.

The above is all about the exciting ME at the centre of myself, somewhere. Winnicott saw the real true self, or 'me', as a psyche-soma in full exuberant possession of the body and endowed with purpose and energy, which as a prospectus for living certainly makes it worth finding. Winnicott's idea of the false self, based on identifications and roles imposed by compromises etc. in development, is not identical with the alters in MPD. These are alternative personalities invented as characters in a theatre of survival and each able to act as front runner when appropriate and also to quarrel in disagreement.

MOVING INTO THERAPY

Coming into psychiatry from doing psychosomatic research into essential hypertension, tuberculosis and asthma, I have always been puzzled by the indifference of some colleagues to meaning and causality of symptoms and their poor understanding of psychotherapy. When you are treating headaches and pseudo-angina in hypertensives, and treating hyperventilation or other inspiratory dyspnoea as well as asthmatic dyspnoea, you have an end result to show that psychotherapy works and also you know why it worked in each case. But for psychiatrists so much of the behaviour and speech, say of schizophrenics and hypomanics, is meaningless and irrelevant to causation. Their answer is behaviour control by anti-psychotic drugs or electro-convulsive therapy. Similarly ECT and anti depressive drugs are first choice for depression; a more precise life situation diagnosis of an atypical depressive may have to wait for the treatment to fail. Their diagnostic skills are Procrustean, and the particular bed, which the patient must conform to, has the therapy label 'drugs or ECT'. It is about missing the meanings, about not understanding the theatre of communication under fear.

In illustration. I hospitalised a middle-aged, successful businessman whom I had seen a few times for unexplained anxieties. I put him in hospital because his family doctor said he had begun threatening to assault people. This behaviour sounded histrionic. My ward nurse warned me of danger as the patient was trying to strangle staff, but I saw him on his own. He did put his hands around my neck. I said, 'I think you have something to tell me. Why don't you sit down and just talk?' which he did immediately, coming to the point that he had been acting as if he had general paralysis of the insane, as the possibility had begun to prey on his mind. Twenty years before he had been treated for primary syphilis as a soldier on active service. A hidden clock had ticked away the twenty years he had believed it would take tertiary syphilis to show. A full examination relieved his anxieties.

A psychiatrist put an eighteen-year-old girl on a phenothiazine because she had concrete thinking and gave literal answers to the usual test by proverbs. As she felt worse and the disorder persisted, I was asked for a second opinion. I was quickly sure she was no schizophrenic, but the concrete ways of responding to the numerous metaphors one uses in everyday communication were most evident. Was it game playing? I recalled my brothers and I had amused ourselves by speaking in similar fashion. She had to be interrupting family life to draw attention to something, maybe. Well yes, she agreed. She was worried about her father's actions over something which had caused her mother grief. So I got her father to tell her all about it; apparently to her complete satisfaction, because she returned as a happy smiling young woman whose conversation had become completely normal. All was now well. A regrettable aspect is that although hers was an histrionic disorder her records will show a diagnosis of schizophrenia. People have an understandable fear of being seen by a psychiatrist because of the danger of being so diagnosed and never afterwards having the diagnosis corrected in medical records.

These two examples illustrate the importance of understanding histrionic communication. The girl sought attention for a problem she could not challenge her father on; she simply brought her family to a standstill. The man dramatised his twenty-year-old fears. There are many similar dramas played out by our patients and often we entirely overlook their significance. Discart makes the point that working through her patient's behaviour in retrospect it was often possible to spot underlying reasons, that in the heat of reaction had not been noticed. Behaviour has an underlying meaning. Cries for specific help take many forms. It is crass to dismiss these as manipulative and attention-seeking, even coming as they often do at times that disrupt the prescribed tempo of the therapy. The pressure from within of traumata trying to surface is no respecter of convenience of patient or therapist.

A useful rule is to realise that *traumatic memories surface backwards*, backwards in time, that is. This means that like Alice's experience with the Queen who yelled before she pricked herself, the anxiety, the pain, the urge to shout and run are the aspects that surface first, because they are the consequences, time wise, that in returning to consciousness precede the causative traumata.

Such memories present backwards, which leads to another rule of therapy that the patient is now *ripe for a regressive session*, as I have already described as being modified from primal scream therapy to reproduce an LSD experience. I strongly recommend the air-conditioned, carpet-walled, soft-mattressed and cushioned room I had constructed for such therapy. The patient readily drops into the underlying memory. Also no one will get hurt in such a room should the abreaction get physically expressive.

Clearly psychiatrists must become more perceptive. Post-traumatic stress disorder is highly relevant, now that we have realised that it is also a consequence of severe abuse in childhood; it is relevant in the practice of paediatric psychiatry and relevant in adult psychiatry when the features of the disorder appear in delayed form, but are no less recognisable. Hysteria must be forgotten, along with attention-seeking. The emerging concept of the histrionic personality at last favours understanding of expressive behaviour and opens up therapy stratagems. PTSD and HPD are now scientific disciplines that must be carefully studied and brought into clinical practice as valid and as necessary as the main psychiatric disorders.

The patient is often ripe for regressive therapy once initial trust has been established with the therapist. Transference is already in place. It does not have to develop over time on the couch; transference is already causing mayhem and the time is soon ripe for pushing the patient down into re-experiencing whatever trauma is energising her behaviour. It is important to do so without delay because the experience puts the patient into the epicentre of her troubles. She sees for herself where the problem lies in her past, indeed she emerges with a strong conviction about being on the right track. She knows what she has to do to get well and that re-experiencing is not as frightening as may have been imagined. Here then is another rule of therapy that the patient is *responsible for pursuing her own cure*. They were her traumata and she has to re-enter and resolve them herself, with help and support freely given, of course, by a therapy team and with the enduring professional skill and experience of her therapist loaned to her for the duration of the cure. Discart makes this rule all very clear amid much debate and clarification of the issues and of the stress of ensuring that it does happen. I would add that interventions that put the therapist in a dominant position must be avoided, such as IV drug-dependant interviews replayed on tape to the patient, and a form of hypnoanalysis where the therapist maintains the initiative. Hypnosis is valuable, but anything that enhances dependency is ultimately counter productive. The well know victim-persecutor-rescuer situation must be foreseen and discouraged, which is difficult because the victimised patient has no conception about a restorative healing process and just longs to be rescued from emotional chaos.

Much of the value of Discart's book lies in her discussion of counter-transference experiences and how best to deal with them. A Birmingham (England) cardiologist, for whom I worked, used to say: 'Do not let your patient deceive you; do not deceive your patient; but above all do not deceive yourself.' In therapy you keep a constant watch on yourself to maintain a professional and therapeutic relationship in a healthy state, always for the benefit of your patient. You have to survive being heavily criticised and even hated without taking it personally, unless some of it may be justified, when you have to respond honestly. Dishonesty and deception are immediately perceived and they harm the trust in which you must be held. Survival of verbal attack does wonders for the therapy as it brings honesty into the relationship and relieves the patient anxieties about destroying her therapist; you have survived!

Facilities are important. Day-hospital resource is ideal for both NHS and also private sector, where longer-term costs have to be met and insurers kept happy. Day resource allows all the extras to happen such as the nurse–mother figure and involvement of case manager. Group therapy will depend upon other MPD and HD patients being available, as only a group of people with similar problems will hold together and be useful for socialising these noisy outsiders. Discart found her patients' artistic expressions of great value; art room allows for such therapy. I think that music and songs have a lot to commend them, that is, of course, songs with significant emotional content. The needs of the spouse must be met from the beginning by someone experienced in couple therapy.

Team work is essential with regular updates and reviews. The psychiatrist may need an in-patient bed at any time for crisis, and he has to fit in his medication when needed to whatever else is going on in therapy. It is agreed that phenothiazines and other antipsychotic drugs are useless. Anti-depressive drugs may have quite a limited use, apart from MAGI's Clomipramine can allay obsessive worrying in small dose. Benzodiazepines and other anxiolytics will be demanded at times.

The patient must not take alcohol. Some are alcoholic or given to binges. This problem has to be tackled at the onset as alcohol totally negates change and renders therapy useless at the time, however forthcoming the patient may appear. The same applies to taking drugs of abuse. With some there are recurrent crises at the premenstruum.

The therapist has to be committed for two to three years with any one patient. Twice weekly is basic therapy; appointment times should be scrupulously kept and attentiveness during sessions is essential. Godefrida has shown how important is recourse to a therapy supervisor at times of stress in the relationship. These are just a few of the considerations she so ably discusses in her book. The book is a fine read with the bluebell children as an unexpected climax that deserves its prominence in the title.

John Hambling

৯

References

Blacker, KH, & Tupin, JP, *Hysterical Personality*. [ed.] by Horowitz, MJ, Jason Aronson Inc., 1977

Hornstein, NL, & Tyson S, *In-patient Treatment of Children with Multiple Personality/Dissociative Disorders and their Families*, Psychiatric Clinics of North America, vol. XIV, no. 3, 1991

Kluft, RP, *First Rank Symptoms as a Diagnostic Clue to Multiple Personality Disorder*, Amer J Psychiatry 144: pp.293–298, 1987

Lichtenstein, H, *The Dilemma of Human Identity*, Jason Aronson, 1977

Loewenstein, RJ, *An Office Mental Status Examination of Post Traumatic Stress Symptoms*, Psychiatric Clinics of North America, vol. XIV, no. 3, pp.586–593, 1991

Richards, V, *Hunt the Slipper*, Chapter 2 in *The Person Who Is Me*. Winnicott Monograph Series, [ed.] Richards. Karnac for Squiggle Foundation, 1996

Rickman, J, & White, H, *The Family View of Hysterical Psychosis*, Amer J Psychiatry 127: pp.280–285, 1970

Winnicott, DW, *Mirror-Role of Mother and Father in Child Development*, in *Playing and Reality*, Tavistock, 1971, reprinted Routledge, 1993

—, *On the Basics for Self in the Body*, Psycho-Analytical Explorations, Karnac Books, 1989

Part 1

From the Goldfish Bowl

To whom it may concern,

Mrs Cordelia Hannah

The above has asked me to supply her with a letter which might be furnished on her behalf at the time of an application to do further counselling training. I have been treating Mrs Cordelia Hannah for approximately a year with once-weekly analytic psychotherapy. She required this therapy to help her deal with the consequences of a previous therapeutic venture which she had entered as one of the requirements of a counselling course. She was unfortunate enough to be treated by a woman who lacked the necessary skills and experience to handle Mrs Hannah's problems as they emerged. A counter-transference was acted out in a highly destructive manner which provided painful and damaging recapitulation of Mrs Hannah's primary family dynamic.

In the space of one year, Mrs Hannah has done some painful but necessary work, regaining her equilibrium and learning to separate out a transference reaction to the previous therapist from legitimate justifiable outrage regarding the way she was treated. In the end, this has been a valuable learning experience for Mrs Hannah, although one which has opened up for her problems of which she was largely unaware. I feel, now that she has worked these through very considerably and given some further time to put the whole experience into perspective, I hope that she will feel able to continue the route on which she originally embarked. Since I am now leaving this district to take up a post as consultant psychotherapist elsewhere, she asked me to document my views which could be confirmed by telephone if so required.

Dr M

Introduction

This is my chance to speak out for myself. Such suffering, and the coping skills of a child, should be heard and understood. It is also healing for me to write it down and not hold it in my heart for any longer, from those who wish to share in it with me by reading this book. Thank you for attempting to do so. Still, I cannot help feeling concerned that some of the writing that follows will seem somewhat child-like to the reader – some statements are certainly disjointed, especially in my first two chapters. And yet at the time, when I first began to trust seeing my life in words, this was the only way I could write. These concise descriptions of the facts were the only way I felt able to report on the past. Feelings were still too raw, too new, too overwhelming; therefore, rather than attempt to edit my work, I have simply decided to keep those early words of my inner child intact. In fact, if I had beavered away to present the reader with a more suitably polished version of my memories, this would actually be misleading, because when I first began to write this chronicle, I was still emotionally very young indeed, even though I had of course been an adult for many years. Hopefully the reader will agree with me, that just as I matured whilst writing this book, my writing equally improved as my heart and my mind learned to work together.

As an adult I only had vague memories of my childhood, which was mostly spent by the sea. I was one of four living children and the only girl, the third in the family. I was born two months premature, along with a dead twin sister. I was given my name by my father but often I forgot that this was my name. I was called so many unpleasant things, and in my fantasies I gave myself so many other names. It was so much less painful to be someone else.

Solely for the purpose of this book, and to safeguard the future and anonymity of my family, I have adopted the name Cordelia. In fact, I have altered all relevant dates and names, including my surname, and disguised any geographical location, in order to ensure that no member of my present or family of origin can be identified. I wrote this book wishing to share my story and tell myself the truth – not in order to expose others, seek revenge or cause more distress. The sad fact that certain protagonists, should they ever read the book, will of course recognise themselves, is therefore regrettable, yet an unavoidable consequence.

When I was six years old, my father died on one of the occasions he had travelled away to attend a conference, just as my youngest brother was born. My mother struggled alone and with great difficulty to do her best for each of us, or so I believed. Others considered my family to be good, upstanding church-going people. It certainly all looked good and respectable on the outside. My father was a professional man with many talents, and I always believed he adored me because I was told he did. He had a wonderful singing voice.

My mother came from a family with an abusive father, and her cold mother preferred her sons. She was an attractive woman with many creative gifts. She spoke two other languages quite fluently, as well as English. She was always cold, silent, deeply sad and often very unwell. I was afraid of her even in death. I felt she was watching me all the time, as if she was part of me – she was me and I was her. I looked after her and my baby brother following my father's death. All responsibility for both of them seemed to be on my shoulders, and none of us was allowed to speak of our father again. I felt responsible for his death.

I had two older brothers. The eldest didn't feature much in my life because he left home as soon as he was old enough to do so. I always thought he cared about me. The second brother, Martin, featured too strongly. He took his father's place in the family soon after his death and my mother seemed to let him dominate. He caused me a great deal of sadness, pain, fear and humiliation: he called me cretin or imbecile, parasite or brainless brat. I now have no contact with him whatsoever. I came next in the family. I became the scapegoat: anything that went wrong I was directly blamed for by my brother Martin and my mother, or their frustrations were relieved by being physically violent to me. My brother Martin, for instance, frequently kicked my legs as I passed him, or swung me round in the air by my long fair hair, just for the fun of it, and as he did so, he would say, 'God, you are so ugly.'

It was nothing to experience a plate full of his dinner, after he had served himself from the dishes, thrown at me across the table, or my face pushed in it, because, he said, it was not to his liking – 'My mother had to do better.' Then his laugh, his horrible evil laugh that I can hear as I write this. Any time I had difficulty in eating because I was filled with fear at meal times, my mother force-fed me. This led me to stuff my food down as quickly as possible and leave the table to vomit it up afterwards on my own. Fortunately, my brother was happier when I was out of sight, he said, so this became the normal procedure for quite some time. I became bulimic, quite ill and thin at times, my body covered in bruises. I had periods of my childhood and adolescence when I found it just as easy to put weight on as lose it.

My youngest brother I adored, but I felt frightened by the responsibility to care for him. I became his little mother. We both lived in fear of our brother Martin, and I lived in fear of my mother too.

I was a deeply unhappy child. My childhood was spent in and out of hospital. I had a track record of many and frequent life-threatening illnesses. I remember on one of my visits to hospital, taken by a schoolteacher who rightly thought my arm was broken, they tested my blood for leukaemia because of the extensive bruising. I told the doctor that I bruised exceptionally easily. I was severely punished for supposedly telling a teacher my arm was broken. In the outside world, I was treated with indifference by my family, or I was blatantly, coldly ignored as if I didn't exist at all. I told my friends that my brother was on the same school bus and pointed him out. They thought I was telling lies because he ignored me and denied my existence.

I learnt to eat at school. I accepted sweets from others, as I was never allowed to have them. I also learnt to steal from shops, as I was deprived of books and toys. These reasons, and many more you will read about later, caused my increasing physical or emotional inability to feel pain; my body became numb, my mind split so many ways, I didn't know who I was.

My early schooldays were just as unhappy and spent in a Catholic convent, from which I was expelled for breaking a statute of Mary, the mother of Jesus. I didn't have many friends. I always felt I couldn't keep them, yet they remember me as the comedienne of the class. I tried very hard to please at home. I did not settle down to learn at school until I was fourteen. I shone at dancing and musical activities, especially singing, but I was not allowed to sing at home. All my father's records and his piano were smashed up in a fit of uncontrollable behaviour by my mother because I was showing great interest in them. I eventually achieved sufficiently academically well to train as a student nurse at one of Britain's finest hospitals.

How I got through my training, like everything else, I will never know. I found I loved learning. I thrived on the medical knowledge and skills I gained, but I was daunted by a deep depression that had steadily got worse since my teens. I battled on with pressure from my mother to go home as often as my off-duty would allow. Her letters and telephone calls were always threatening, blackmailing and disturbing. My ward reports and examination results were unbelievably good on the whole. I attempted suicide many times with accessible drugs, protected by a friend whose emergency treatment prevented these incidents being reported. I survived four years' training and then qualified. No one ever knew about the bouts of depression. I was hospitalised many times for serious illness, including temporary paralysis of the lower limbs, kidney infections and chest and throat infections to name but a few.

Along with the incongruent feelings of laughter and depression, the suicide attempts, the awful confusion, terrifying nightmares, voices in my head, intense feelings of anguish, guilt and shame and cold chilling memories that didn't belong to me, sometimes it would appear that someone had called me by a name that wasn't mine, and that there had been a period of time I couldn't account for, or else I would appear in a place without knowing how I got there or that I knew nothing about. Life constantly lacked continuity. I felt mad, yet another part of me knew I wasn't. I tried to overcome these feelings by being extrovert, by bingeing on drugs, alcohol, parties, boyfriends. Yet another part of me did not make real relationships easily. I did not connect with people. Normal environmental stimuli have always been overwhelming; they often nearly sent me crazy and resulted in dissociation which, according to Freud, is 'an unconscious defence mechanism in which a group of mental activities "split off" from the main stream of consciousness and functions as a separate unit.' Paradoxical to this, serious stressful situations allowed me to act calmly. I was good in a crisis, useful in my career.

I went out with a few medical students. One of them wanted to marry me. He was a Yorkshireman who wanted to go back to Yorkshire when he qualified. He was a super guy. My mother seemed to possess me; I knew I couldn't leave her. I married my husband, he was older and lived in my hometown. He had just decided not to continue with a career in the services when I met him. He was a stable, solid, dependable type. He too, had a beautiful singing voice. It was his voice that caused our first meeting. I heard him singing a solo one day, as I crept into the back of the church after a long hard night-duty period, before returning home. I fell in love with his beautiful voice before I fell in love with him. My husband has stood by me through the most horrendous difficulties. Life would have been more unbearable without him. He has done a great job at being my husband and friend, and the father of our two children. We lost a third baby. In fact, the guidance and support I received from my husband and the determination I had to do things differently, allowed me not to pass on my experience of life to my children. I mostly over-protected them, even if I disciplined much too harshly. I disagree strongly and reject the view that it is a forgone conclusion that you do to others what was done to you. It felt like a battle to do the opposite, a battle I think I won where our own children were concerned.

I worked periodically as a staff nurse and nursing sister in hospitals, surgeries, and in the community. I also added to my qualifications when my children started school. My mother died when I was still in my twenties, after which the depression worsened. I voluntarily resigned from nursing in my thirties, when my depression was severe. I had drugs, ECT (Electro-Convulsive Therapy); every treatment available, except no one ever talked to me or listened. In my late thirties, I had a real miraculous spiritual experience after attending a healing service in church. I got involved in my local evangelical church. I seemed to make friends more easily, and it felt as if I belonged to a family for the first time. As I got perhaps too heavily involved, to the detriment of other things, it was helping to fill a huge black hole inside me but I still didn't feel it was my life. I was still walking on the edge of life, looking at other people involved in life, watching other people care for each other.

As the years passed by, the black hole enlarged; some people started to walk away from me, some relationships became very difficult, and immediate family problems became more intense. My survival system began to break down. I became a prisoner of nightmares, memories and pain. I felt filthy dirty, ashamed, self-destructive and suicidal. I just wanted to die when the chaos inside me became frightening and unbearable. I had trouble recognising that I had feelings and, when I did, I could not tell the difference between them. If I did express my feelings, my heart pumped so hard I thought it would burst open. I developed other serious medical conditions as I fought to keep inside, memories that would pop up unexpectedly. The curate at the church lovingly tried to help. It stirred up the dirty water but I had already learned not to show the real pain. It was only knocking off easily moveable scabs that covered fiercely damaged flesh, angry, throbbing and unable to heal. There was no way I could allow outsiders into my inside world, especially those who could only stay awhile, or walked away when the going got tough, or felt trapped by my craving to be loved. Contrary to this, I often would reject what I needed most.

All of this was too much for anyone. But it was the beginning of the longest and most painful journey of my life, the journey I made of discovery and healing. Nevertheless, over the years, I learned how to deal with the voices I heard and how to hide my inner chaos from the outside world. No one suspected just how much, or how many secrets I held inside, not even my husband. I learned how to disguise the loss of time I experienced, I learned to manipulate time and use it to accomplish anything I had to do. I learned at an early age how to maintain an outward appearance that everything in life was great I learned not to show the constant pain that pounded in my heart Having said this, there was not a part of my life that was not affected. It permeated everything. So I became trapped by my own inner world.

Somehow, I felt compelled to undertake a seven-term counselling course, where students were advised to seek professional counselling or psychotherapy for themselves. Unknowingly, I engaged with an unqualified person. She was a counsellor who sought God's healing for me when all else failed. Although I became very ill, this may have been the door to discovering the truth about my life that was so deeply denied by my own internal protective system.

Dr M, a consultant psychotherapist who took over my case after the two years I spent in therapy with this woman, was angry on my behalf for the further damage she had caused; without the necessary skills and knowledge, her meddling was destructive. She had stirred a hornet's nest and made me totally dependent on her, with no appropriate boundaries. She tried to be a therapist and friend, thus destroying the therapeutic relationship, and Dr M called it 'abuse in therapy'. He tackled her, and wrote a supportive letter for me for the future. I believe she did not intentionally set out to cause harm but she would take no responsibility for what happened and totally rejected me. All this became the cause of a great deal of unpleasant and painful gossip. No progress was achieved, and I could reveal less and less as time went on.

I have often met the belief of some regular churchgoers that, as long as they pray, God will make up for their mistakes and heal them, if they ask Him to. I believe in miracles, I know God heals but we do have a responsibility for our actions, and we should never, ever assume, God will heal or do it our way. Suffering is part of this fallen world. God allowed His son to suffer, and I needed to go through yet more suffering, it seemed, to learn about my inner world and face the reality of my life. I needed desperately to be nurtured in a safe environment, I could not have reached the maturity, the understanding and the knowledge I have today, without this experience. Suffering enriches us as people. In a way, I can say it's a privilege to be able to appreciate what I now have, to feel connected to the beauty of creation around me, to have found who I am, to live in this world as if I belong, to have learnt to love without fear.

Some of our friends, many of whom were church-going, only a few years on, we never see, and some cross the road when they see us coming. The losses along the way have been enormous and have added to our suffering, not least the loss of my husband's work, which he thought was safe for many years to come. The financial loss with the increased burden of the expense of my therapy, as well as the blow to his self-esteem and the way in which and by whom it was carried out, was a devastating blow to him. Then, one of my innocent brothers chose to reject me when he knew just enough to scare him. Consequently, other members of the family do not know my story. Our fight together, to unravel the chaos and torment inside me, and the sadness it brought to us both and our children, has sometimes felt too much to bear. We are both grateful for the friends who have stayed around, not necessarily needing to understand or know what was going on. Those who were prepared to hear as much as I felt able to tell them, or as much as I felt they could believe. I was always afraid of losing them by saying too much – these friends will always be very dear, and are very special people.

One day, in an unfamiliar Catholic church, an appealing structure of modern architecture, I knelt and asked God to take this suffering from me. A beam of sunlight shone from a small window in the roof, right through the main window behind the altar, onto a stone sculptured crucifix outside the window. It seemed as if Christ descended from the cross and came through the window to my side. He told me that I had a great deal more suffering to go through, but that He would be with me through it, and the verse from Isaiah 43:2 rang in my ears:

When you pass through the waters I will be with you; and through the rivers, they shall not overwhelm you; when you walk through fire you shall not be burned and the flame shall not consume you.

From time to time, I remembered this, even in my blackest times when God, family, friends, therapist and psychiatrist, seemed to desert me. These words flashed across my memory.

I would not have gained so much without such deep suffering. It would have been easier to take a short cut but not as rewarding. I think it was God's way for me, it was my way, the only way I could do it. It was no coincidence, that the course of events that followed was the route to my final healing.

I was Dr M's patient for eleven months, before he moved 600 miles away. After the first three months he admitted me to a psychiatric hospital, in whose care I remained for six years as an in-patient, day-patient and out-patient, with crisis admissions along the way. I felt enormous pain when Dr M left. I had formed some sort of attachment, although I was not able to trust him completely; I wanted to. During my therapy with Dr M, there was a lot I felt unable to disclose. I didn't know how or whether I had got it right or whether it was really the truth. I called all my hidden secrets, 'my deeper level of disturbance' or my 'core problem'. I talked about my father's death, the pedestal I had put him on – that seemed immovable – and the unresolved grief. I also mentioned the cruelty of my mother and brother Martin, and the rape I experienced at thirteen. I mostly talked about the anger I felt over the last therapist, as well as the dependency. I seemed to be so ill and I was so confused, I didn't know what to do or say. I knew there was so much more, but the flashbacks, dreams and nightmares were increasing, I thought I was going crazy. I thought that if I dared to mention such atrocities as were in my mind, everyone would give up on me and I would be put away somewhere. I didn't want to believe any of this was true. I went through several periods of denial throughout my treatment. Dr M was a lovely man, a very skilled therapist but he knew he was leaving and could not undertake a long-term therapeutic relationship.

I urge you to read on and discover, how my inner world emerged, how my healing began, and the meaning behind the title of the first part of the book: *From the Goldfish Bowl*.

The Clinic

It was a cold grey December day in 1990 when I entered the clinic. There was a kind, warm staff nurse called Anne, about my age, who admitted me. She became someone whom I eventually learnt I could trust, who seemed genuine and fairly predictable. She consistently stood by me through some of the toughest periods, and showed me she cared when everyone else involved with my care seemed to give up, or appeared cold and dismissive.

I felt then that people who mean too much to me tend to disappear like fast-thawing snow after a night of soft snow showers that hug the earth for just a short while, so I tried not to let others matter too much.

I wasn't always in Anne's care. I attended as many groups as I could at the clinic, but I could not cope with relaxation – it made my head thump so hard, I thought it would explode. I listened at all the more formal teaching groups but I couldn't contribute much. They all made me feel vulnerable and threatened. I hated listening to other people's points of view, especially those who said, 'I know what you are going through.' They didn't, no one did, no one could. I couldn't help thinking some people's problems were so minor compared to mine, and they could not possibly understand the depth of pain and turmoil I experienced. I understood then, but more so now, that we are all different, our problems can be different and we cope with those problems in different ways – all are important to the person experiencing them. I had a physical pain in my chest and abdomen throughout all the years that passed before my core problem was fully revealed.

It was my first stress management group when I met Frieda, the senior therapist at the clinic. She was a lady who, prior to coming to Britain, lived in Europe. She was also about my age, with long dark hair. On this occasion, she had her hair pulled back in a ponytail and she wore a navy blue dress. Her eyes were dark brown, warm and penetrating. Strangely, I felt I had met her somewhere in my life before, as if I knew her. I felt safe when she was around. I also felt that she wanted to understand me and help me. I hoped she could. I didn't know then what a profound effect she was to have upon my future life and me.

It was nearly Christmas. My birthday and Christmas were always harrowing times for me. I only had one memory that returned about the time I entered the clinic, which I told Frieda about. It was one that might have clouded every Christmas but I had buried it for a very long time. My father was dead, it was the Christmas following, and my brother had planted a real Christmas tree in a pot, brought it into the house and decorated it. I remember the excitement I felt as presents were placed around it, but there was only one with my name on it, as far as I could see. There were lots of presents for my brothers. While everyone was out last-minute shopping, I peeped inside the one with my name on it, as children are apt to do. I saw with horror a red house brick. I can feel now the way my heart pumped so fast, and I tried to comfort myself with the fact that it must be a joke; my mother and especially my brother, were prone to unpleasant pranks. I always hoped for good things – there must be a lovely surprise somewhere – but I could not sleep that night, and dreaded the coming day.

Present-opening time came and I rather reluctantly opened the parcel with the brick in – and as I did so my mother said, 'That is what you are, that is what you are worth and that is all you will ever be worth, nothing more.'

Fear, pain and rage surged through my little body. I flung the brick through a large window. My little brother screamed, my older brother Martin laughed and laughed. The sound of his laughter I can hear again in my head as I write this today. However, the consequences of my angry action never allowed me to express anger again. I was locked in my room for several days after a severe beating that left me stunned and numb with shock. I heard my mother and brother talking about the brick, and how someone they knew had used the same idea to tame their unruly son. They tried so hard to break me.

I had always, from being a very small child, been partly aware that my own needs had only been considered in a very basic way – always just enough to keep me functioning, but the world I had really been brought up in, was a world where neglect, punishment, terror and pain were my constant companions, and a crisis seemed normal. I was too busy coping in my childhood to know how to play, to be happy and relaxed, to be able to learn, appreciate beauty, tenderness, affection, to make relationships, all manner of everyday things, that most little people take for granted. I was too busy coping to know what the little girl behind all the pain was really like, but eventually I found her, the child who was lost. This child, like other children who are abused, still loved her parents deeply and wanted to think the very best of them. Even her dead father she idealised – but all children are the most innocent of creatures, until abusing adults steal their birthright and violate all that is pure, beautiful and uniquely theirs.

I enjoyed art therapy in the clinic. It often allowed me to express my longings, hopes and dreams, or my buried rage, or my deep black hole. I came to love the use of paints and the freedom it gave me. The group I enjoyed the most was creative writing. It was safer to write a story – even if it did say something about me. It helped me to lose myself in fantasy or imaginary stories based on facts – even poetry expressed so much more than I dared tell anyone. Frieda asked us one day to write about colours, our favourite colours. This is what I wrote – the time given was very limited.

8TH MAY 1991. MY FAVOURITE COLOURS

A little girl whose life on earth became too painful and impossible to bear wanted to start a new life, or die and be forgotten for ever. Like *Alice in Wonderland*, the story she loved so much, she wondered if in fact something like that could happen for her. As she sat on the beach one day, dreaming of what could become of her, she wondered what the world under the sea was like, and if she could become a mermaid. As she became absorbed in this fantasy, the world under the sea opened up to her. She walked into the sea and sank to the depths very quickly. She found a new world of peace and beauty beyond compare.

It appeared to be a world of colour, the colours she loved best. The colours that she suited wearing. The deep greens of the seaweed, the turquoise shades of the water, rocks and life under the sea. The fish came up to stare at her. They were beautiful shades of mostly blue and green, with flashes of more vivid colour now and again. She reached out her arms to swim and found she could, and began to dart about up and down, in and out of rocks covered with plants and growth of various shades of green. As she swam on, to her delight she came across pretty shells, opening and shutting as if they were talking to her. They were such enchanting creatures, delicately coloured in shades of pink, they were warm and friendly. On she swam, until she came to an area of outstanding beauty, beyond anything she had ever seen, shades of coral, pink, blue and green. The fish blended with their surroundings by being clothed in colour of similar hues. She knew this was like the coral reefs her father had told her about, and wondered if she had travelled underwater to Africa or even as far as Australia. With that thought, a rather angry, dark large fish was swimming towards her, but suddenly she woke up and found herself on the beach with the water lapping around her feet; her dress was wet from the incoming tide. She felt better from her sleep and the journey she had travelled in her dream. As she walked across the sand, the sun was setting and spreading a warm pink glow in the sky and on the water. The sea was very gently coming in and sounded friendly. She felt that perhaps the world she really did live in wasn't all bad after all, and as she looked around she saw some of the colours she had seen under the water in softer more subtle shades. She continued her journey home, hoping someone would have missed her.

The many stories I wrote were usually child-like, but some appeared to be written in a more adult style. One in particular was angry, cruel and calculating.

I started one-to-one psychotherapy with Frieda. It was rather too infrequent at first for my liking. I discovered later, she didn't want to interfere with Dr M's weekly therapy with me. He eventually gave his permission for her to go ahead, as he knew he would be leaving before I was well. He thought I needed long-term psychotherapy most of the time. Sometimes he mentioned group therapy work. Difficult for him to decide, when in fact he didn't really know me. Frieda told me I was not to play one off against the other. Little did she realise then that everything in my life was compartmentalised. They were totally separate entities to me. Home was separate from the clinic – the clinic was separate from Dr M. I did tell Dr M once, because he asked, that I felt I was treated differently to others, how I felt generally, the staff at the clinic distanced themselves from me as they got to know me, and I sensed in some a definite fear of me. I've realised since that this was one thing not imagined (others confirmed this), and the observer part of me, and only that part, was very intuitive, sensitive and correct in her reading of others and her own situation.

In July 1991, after Dr M left, I found myself in day care with a nurse who was blatantly cruel to me. Another day staff nurse I had a good relationship with, but no relationship was easy. We often walked together at lunchtimes, with her dog, down the lane to the woods. Bluebell time was very special. The rest of the staff appeared kind and considerate. There were a few to whom I owe a debt of gratitude for their continuing patience and acceptance, even when it was difficult for them to understand.

The psychiatrist in whose care I was left, after Dr M's departure had not a clue from where I was coming and thought I was a hysterical dependent type. Whether under his influence, or whether Frieda independently thought the same, I will never really know but treatment and attitude towards me changed drastically. I eventually agreed to join a weekly psychotherapy group in order to please everyone. I only saw Frieda every fortnight on a one-to-one basis when this new plan for my treatment started. I had frequently and persistently, prior to joining the group, stated that I was abused emotionally, physically and sexually but I thought I could not remember very many details. I felt under pressure to get well; this forced me into stating memories that were surfacing but no one seemed to want to pick up on them. It made me feel as if I had taken all my clothes off in public. I certainly did not want to do it again in a hurry!

I learnt when I was in the group, that the clinic was in receivership but whatever happened in the future, the group would continue. This may have forced them into a quick route out of their responsibilities to me but it was not a safe environment for me to be real. In my earlier life, I had been forced into silence about the abuse and the others in the group had different problems that were more containable. Frieda and a male consultant/psychotherapist ran the group. I was treated with cold indifference by them, or that is how it felt to me, a damaged person. One lady left the group because she could not tolerate the way I was treated, so it was interesting that she felt the same. My internal observations knew that there was a definite distancing and lack of understanding. Anyone else would have walked away from it all, but I thought that was what they wanted me to do, and I desperately needed help. I didn't know where else to go, and I had by then become deeply attached to Frieda in spite of everything. The more I felt she pushed me away, the more I clung. I couldn't walk away. I hung on with grim determination to get her to see that I wanted to be well and normal, and that I needed to learn to trust before I could reveal my deeper level of disturbance.

I changed psychiatrists in February 1992, and my new doctor was horrified by the state I was in. I felt so very ill. He was a very kind man who thought I should immediately stop attending the psychotherapy group, although I should continue seeing Frieda fortnightly, Anne on the alternate weeks and return to some day care for support. The battle to survive had become intolerable amidst the atmosphere of uncertainty for any future for the clinic, the tensions amongst the staff, my angry outbursts of pain, relationship problems, my jealousy of other patients who received regular once or twice weekly therapy with Frieda, anonymous telephone calls and anonymous notes everywhere left by me. Every time I left the clinic and got to my car, I couldn't remember that I had been there. I couldn't hold on to the fact that I was now again receiving more support. I still wanted more therapy. But I think Frieda was sticking to her decision that I was a dependant type, and long-term therapy may have been impossible if the clinic closed. Maybe she also thought at that time that I was too ill and too confused for therapy. It felt as if I was disintegrating and I still didn't feel safe.

In June 1992 I also wrote a letter to Anne, the only way I could explain what I wanted to say. (I wrote letters to my mother, because I could tell her nothing to her face; she would always angrily punish me, she never read my letters.) In this letter to Anne, it was again my observer part that appeared – it was a cry from my heart. I explained exactly what was going on. No one picked up on what I had said in this letter, which went into my notes. Perhaps no one read it, or understood it.

After seeing the doctor, my mind has been in turmoil, part of me feels I am not able to have the care others have, it doesn't feel right. I'm more comfortable with being the victimised patient, the one who is treated differently, who is not liked – I wanted to tell him how frightened I am by some of the things I do, that perhaps I do have more than one personality, he spoke about this in other people. From the time I was a very young child, I had experiences which were so traumatic, they split my personality wide open. There was no way for my young mind to cope with the brutality and acts of sadism that I experienced. Instead, I completely forgot the incidents – I could not cooperate with Frieda in my therapy sessions – I didn't understand what she was trying to do. I felt six years old anyway and there was no sense of 'me' in there. Frieda could see 'me' but I couldn't. I couldn't do it, I was like a baby sometimes, I couldn't explain how I felt, then she left. She wanted me to be well and normal – I am trying to tell you how it feels to be me – I am frightened of what will be revealed, can I cope with it? Can others cope with it? Will I be rejected again? The words 'I will kill you if you tell' are thundering through my head. I also realise that I have blocks of time which I do not remember. I thought that was normal. I realise now that very few people space out and find themselves in another town, or in the midst of a conversation with no idea of what is being talked about. I've never really connected with anyone. I think if I really connected I would love too much, the kind of love a child experiences with a parent. I think I need re-parenting to heal – there is no one who could or would do that. I think it happens in the States a lot.

I want the past to be over and to begin a new future. Which path do I take? I have some memories of my own bad behaviour but not necessarily the cause of them.

Fortnightly therapy continued. It was nearly a year since I had had weekly therapy. It started again in July 1992. I was still not sure about what I could say to Frieda without the fear of her abandoning me. The memory of my attempts to tell her before were still painful and frightening! I did disclose, eventually, some aspects of the indifference versus violent abuse from my mother, and the chilling silence versus vicious and verbal attacks from my brother. I also told Frieda about my father's death and what it had meant to me, and the unresolved grief. I knew I wasn't telling the whole story sometimes; other times, I had not realised I had told her the same thing before. Every time seemed like the first time, with new information.

From December 1990 to January 1993 seemed like wasted years. When I look back, however, I no longer feel angry, only sad that I had to fight so long and so hard to be understood, for I could not tell anyone what was really wrong. I was like a screaming baby left in a cot, whom everyone became increasingly tired of and couldn't understand. I had no capacity to deal with what was going on in an adult way. Having no sense of self, nothing tangible to hold on to or to remember, fortnightly or even weekly therapy couldn't work for me. Perhaps it would have taken that long anyway for me to learn to trust. Perhaps I needed to fight them and test them with everything I slung at them?

The financial problems at the clinic obviously caused difficulties for the staff over commitment and future planning. The clinic continued in receivership for a very long time but they were hopeful of a satisfactory purchaser. All this increased my feelings of certain pending abandonment – I was likely to feel that anyway.

These past two years of excruciating agony emphasised the aloneness and imprisonment of my goldfish bowl. (Swimming always allowed me some sense of freedom; my legs were often weak, heavy and without feeling but the water held me.) I swam round and round in circles, tormented, because there was no escape from my internal chaos, no route to freedom. I only saw others in the clinic getting better because they were being helped, and others outside living what they called life. I couldn't be involved either way.

My goldfish bowl distorted my vision. I often saw everything and everyone through a mist or in a dense fog, and sometimes they were totally distorted. I would make people diminish in size or even disappear, particularly if they were in any way threatening. You would not believe how differently I view other people today, how differently they see me, respond to me. I see them for who they really are, no more distortions. I didn't know that I saw life any differently to anyone else, but now I know.

Transference and Counter-Transference 1990–1992

Transference, as many a therapy book will explain, is the tendency to express feelings and attitudes towards others, which are actually felt towards certain people in the past who still are, or were, important in one's life. It is a natural part of life and familiar to us all, able to influence our choice of partner, likes and dislikes, friend or foe, love or hate, success or failure. It is also considered to be a very necessary and salutary part of therapy, and thus could amount to giving the patient a second chance, a means to relive the past in order to correct the present. However, what most of the therapy books fail to emphasise is how painful and bewildering transference can be, especially when the intimate setting of a therapeutic relationship tends to mimic the past.

Imagine perhaps the very moment when a therapist refuses to comply with the demands for extra time, extra attention, etc. Even though the patient is usually aware that the therapist's decision was made solely in the patient's best interest, the therapist, henceforth, can nevertheless become confused; could actually appear to have merged with either the hated mother, father, teacher or sibling of old, who likewise refused to listen, who likewise demonstrated that they were unable to love the patient. What's more, any subsequent feelings of anger, fear, hate or despair are experienced by the patient, not just as very real, but are felt as intensely as the first time round. And yet at the same time, despite experiencing such negative feelings of fear and hate, such negative transference towards the therapist, this same therapist may also become an object of intense longing and love. All very confusing indeed. In fact, I believe that in a desperate attempt to redress the balance, in order to negate this painful negative transference and satisfy, or minimise the impact of the unconscious desires (as ever, tenaciously pressing to be fulfilled), the therapist, henceforth, may become exalted as the all-loving, all-caring 'important other', who is bound to love and rescue the patient!

Fenichel, (1945, p.131) when enlarging on the motives of defence in the neurotic conflict between the id and the ego, described how a 'part of the external world may be warded off: falsified' in order to 'deny that the instinctual act may be dangerous or cause pain'. Similarly, in my opinion, the patient who is experiencing a negative transference, may falsify a part of his/her world, and create the all-good therapist – the very opposite of the no-good parent, teacher, sibling – very ideal and very unreal, and thus experience a veritable positive transference, which unfortunately seems also very able to by-pass the 'reality-testing function of the ego', and henceforth can blithely go on to fool not only the patient, but sometimes also the therapist, thereby keeping them both spellbound for years. For certain patients such as Cordelia, with a history of abuse and deprivation, transference can be so severe, that it leaves the person feeling quite unable to lead a fulfilling life, unless there is access to the therapist or someone who is regarded as a suitable substitute. When transference is thus, it is comparable to travelling back in time, but without the benefit of being able to observe or learn from one's actions, meaning that when the therapist goes on holiday, for instance, and re-awakens feelings of abandonment, the past is experienced as happening all over again and the patient becomes unable to separate it from the present. Yet paradoxically, as Cordelia demonstrated again and again, despite feeling 'unloved, abandoned, abused and neglected, bruised and battered', the ideal therapist usually remains firmly enthroned.

Working through these confusing feelings, disentangling the ideal, unveiling the falsification, facing up to reality and gaining understanding of how the actions of significant others once affected the child, and continue to affect and influence the adult's thinking, actions and behaviour, is what I believe psychotherapy is all about. Although to complicate matters further, the therapist is, equally, not above experiencing what is called counter-transference, which can of course ensure that both people can be caught up in a merry dance trying to keep the past separate from the present. For an exploration of transference and counter-transference, see Eagle 1987, p.79, as well as Balint, 1952, Freud, 1939, Lacan, 1977, Lowenstein 1982, Racker, 1968, Rycroft, 1968, and Strachey 1937.

Needless to say, transference, and the subsequent attempt to help Cordelia resolve this transference, would become an important part of her therapy journey, even though Cordelia usually tended to dismiss the idea that transfer ence was a prominent issue. In fact transference, and the inevitable counter-transference it tended to provoke, had in the past caused her a lot of distress. It had certainly also been a major factor in her previous therapy and the very reason why it had all gone so drastically wrong between Cordelia and her counsellor. Hence I have started my account of this therapy journey with a description and analysis of a more recent dream of mine, a dream which indeed clearly illustrates how involved such a transference dance can be, but which also allows me to emphasise how, despite many obstacles and indeed a severe transference neurosis, Cordelia and I learned to master the steps of this truly unique dance, expend transference and finally cease to be its unhappy victim.

A dream:

I have no idea what time it was. All I knew was, that I was just minding my own business, when absentmindedly, I turned a corner, and ran smack into a vampire!

He wasn't even supposed to be a vampire anyway, just an exhibit in a dungeon somewhere!

But there he was: a glorious vampire, in all his weird and mysterious ways.

Feeling the customary fear, I was instantly alert and ready to run. Yet this time, something was different; something was very wrong.

With a shock, I noticed that the vampire was carrying a baby. The baby, however, no longer had a heart and stomach, and I suddenly realised that this phantasmal vampire, was not interested in my life, but was immersed in the life of the baby.

I began to plead for the baby's life, and to my relief, the vampire decided that he would let me keep it.

The baby would live, he said (although I wondered how it could without a heart and stomach!), provided that on a certain day, I would carefully peel a potato, and then throw the skin into the air, and let it land where it would! What a stupid condition, I remember thinking, but I accepted it without questioning, because the life of the baby depended on it.

With that the vampire slunk away; disappeared, and I was literally left holding the baby.

Always, when change is afoot, I dream about vampires! But why vampires? Surely my mind could have come up with a more benign and less drastic symbol to depict things about to happen? But no, a vampire it has to be, threatening to take away something that is precious, without so much as a by-your-leave, and with a lot of fearful and frightening *venery*; though I'm glad to say, so far I have always managed to outrun him or her. But what did the dream mean? At first, I thought that the dream referred to changes happening within my own family. The baby not having a heart, for instance, I reasoned, could be symbolic of someone having 'lost their heart', as the lyrics of so many songs proclaim. But why did the baby not have a stomach? As usual, the message of the dream was in the last few events before I woke up. What the dream was trying to tell me, I realised, was that I had to stick to the rules of the agreement regardless. (Throw the potato peel in the air on a certain day – without trying to control the outcome – otherwise the baby would die.) But which baby was it?

Again, when I let myself think back over the previous day, I instinctively knew who the baby was, for I had spoken to Cordelia on the phone in order to make an appointment to see her. The last time I saw her was six months ago, and I had been truly surprised to hear how different she sounded. Cordelia herself had been quite adamant that she was different, that since her therapy had ended, she had matured and felt certain, that I would notice the difference, even though it had been a very painful process, and 'she might well cry when she saw me again'.

Here was the mysterious baby the vampire would allow to live; here was the baby who would survive against all the odds (despite having no heart or stomach), provided I could accept that she had grown, was learning to take care of herself, was effectively in charge of her own life and she no longer needed me as her therapist.

I am glad to say that when we subsequently met, Cordelia was indeed different; feeling pleased with herself, having survived life without her therapist with no thoughts of suicide, or needing admission, or feeling that she was coming apart, even though there had been a lot of sorrow and grief about losing me. Despite all, Cordelia had grown up. The days, weeks, years of desperate longing, when she felt she would not live without seeing me, when she felt that only I could rescue her, yet hated being so dependent, seemed over. Cordelia was learning to be herself.

During the course of that meeting, I also felt able to share my vampire dream with Cordelia, and together we discussed its implications. In turn, this encouraged me to go back to our original thought: to work together on writing a book about this arduous and amazing therapy journey we had lived through, and to compile some kind of evaluation which would provide us both with a means of debriefing and (even more important), provide Cordelia with the means to dispense with the past.

Although I had originally proposed the writing of such a book, somehow it had not felt right to do so until now. When I said 'it did not feel right', I meant that I had been very much aware that if and when I joined Cordelia in writing this book, before she was able to go it alone, I would merely have been strengthening her transference, appearing to make her unconscious wishes come true. Hence, until now, I had always encouraged Cordelia to write this book by herself, and more pertinently, to write it primarily for herself. Which, in the meantime, she had started to do. (Cordelia so far had written the introduction, The Clinic, and was in the process of writing the chapter entitled Frieda.) I changed my mind after this first meeting, simply because I knew that Cordelia had conquered transference and survived the journey. Furthermore, listening to Cordelia asking me questions about her therapy, I also realised, that I owed her my memories.

When my parents died, I felt that they took a huge chunk of my life with them; their memories of my experiences, their unexpressed hopes and opinions about me just went! For instance, which one of my parents decided to name me Godefrida, and who was it who wrote Frida minus the 'e', on my birth certificate? As I only recently discovered! I will of course never know. (I mostly abbreviated my name and was in fact always known as Frieda.) Listening to Cordelia made me aware that unless I shared my memories, my opinions with her, she would equally never know. Even though I had given back to her all her own art work, and copies of the photographs I took off her drawings, as well as copies of my therapy notes (after obtaining permission from her consultant to do so), and copies of the many letters she wrote to me and others, I was mindful, that I still held pieces of the jigsaw puzzle inside my head, which, unless I gave them back to her, would forever leave the whole picture incomplete. Naturally Cordelia in her new-found independence, questioned me during my next visit as to why I had changed my mind. I gladly explained, and together with her husband we talked over the reasons for, pros and cons of a joint venture. All agreed, that it would make it, a more balanced book.

I am of course aware that in a conventional therapeutic relationship, sticking to the rules of the agreement, (as my vampire dream urged me to do) would mean that, when therapy ends, all involvement ends. However, this particular therapy journey could hardly be described as conventional. Indeed, I very much believe that therapy has been successful, because certain rules were in fact able to be broken, (whilst others were very much reinforced). Thus, another reason for writing this book springs to mind: to share with others the valuable lessons I have learned along the way, in the hope that it will encourage and promote treatment of like patients, who are normally considered too difficult, too damaged and generally believed to be beyond help (Which I feel is tantamount to adding insult to injury!). As the unfolding story of this therapy journey will clarify, sometimes those difficult, damaged patients do indeed know best, and as health professionals we can but serve them well, if we are prepared to keep an open mind and learn to listen.

If only I had known how to listen in a different way, right from the very beginning...

1990–1992

'Against all the odds, the baby would survive!' How true this was, because the odds against Cordelia just living, let alone ever achieving true independence and reaching a successful end of her therapy journey had certainly been stacked up high.

I first met Cordelia, during the stress management lecture; a new member to the group. The lecture was going well, lots of interaction, when suddenly, up she gets, clearly ill at ease, and runs out the door. Somewhat surprised, (patients did not usually leave before the end without explaining why), I duly informed the nursing staff and finished the lecture, after which I went to check up on Cordelia in order to discover why, or what had made her leave. Cordelia had one of the smaller rooms, on the north side of the house. Yet, despite the December gloom, my first impression was a mass of purple tulips in several vases brightening up the room. I naturally commented on their striking brilliance, whereupon Cordelia proceeded to tell me that they were but a token delivered by her brother, who could quite easily acknowledge physical illness but had found it impossible to comprehend that his sister might need to be admitted to a psychiatric hospital. Hence he had sent the flowers, Cordelia continued to explain, to atone, but had thereby also succeeded in subtly reminding her to keep up appearances.

I then sat down next to Cordelia on the bed (it was indeed a small room) and reached out to her, gave her a hug, and asked her what had made her leave the group; what had indeed caused her such distress?

Unbeknown to us both, transference (Mr Illusionist who will help anyone see or hear whatever they want to see or hear), stepped that moment out of the shadows, and amidst the purple blooms, started weaving his magic spell, catching us unaware, hauling us both in, hook, line and sinker. Though we would not be able to confirm this for some time to come, that spontaneous hug sealed our fate for the next five to six years; ensuring we would embark on a therapy journey together which would never fail to surprise us both.

Transference, however, knew how to play the game well and baited his hook with an account of the worthless counsellor who exploited her patient, once Cordelia had started to care. For good measure, this account was then topped up with a truly devastating, only recently remembered, childhood memory of receiving a household brick as a Christmas present, and with a description of how Cordelia's husband at times used to say that what he liked about her, was that she was solid as a brick! A mind-numbing tale of being misunderstood, deprivation and abuse, guaranteed to shock, which it did! But which, at the same time of course, also allowed Cordelia to test out the potential of this new therapist.

As it was, as Cordelia has described, I passed the test, even though I proceeded to lecture her on how she would be able to gain self-respect and peace of mind, if she could but accept that being loved in return by the counsellor or being loved by her mother was unobtainable. For good measure, I recall, I also likened her to a little girl standing outside a toyshop, bent on getting the one and only toy which was not for sale, and advised her to remember the music box, which Cordelia told me had been an earlier present from her father, rather than focus on the brick she had received from her mother. However, so thoroughly had transference prepared the ground that I left Cordelia's room feeling I had handled all this quite well, and proudly wrote in Cordelia's notes that I had encouraged Cordelia to recognise the true value of presents as well as savour the unintentional lesson the counsellor had given her on how to appreciate love from others. All she needed, I thought, was help with letting go, grieving the loss of this counsellor, and provided she could accept that searching for and clinging to ideal rescuers was not going to work, she would be well.

In retrospect, my eager summing-up was rather naive and certainly very premature, for all too soon Cordelia's determination to ensure that I would be her therapist at any cost became overtly evident, thus setting the scene for the re-enactment of the drama of her childhood, which was to follow, duly assisted of course by the opportune fact that, from then on, certain events taking place within and outside the clinic, together with Cordelia's distress and despair at not finding the kind of help she felt she was entitled to, would conspire to mimic or recreate past abusive conditions, which in turn not only enhanced transference, but clearly reinforced long-held beliefs and well-established coping methods.

DR M

As I described before, the odds against therapy being in any way successful were high indeed. Cordelia has already detailed some of the events of these early years, but I will try to list them all in order of their occurrence and their significance in relation to her therapy. To begin with, meeting Anne on admission, 'a kind warm nurse' as Cordelia has described, would prove to be both fortuitous and very significant. As we now know, this fortunate encounter not only reawakened a long lost and suppressed memory but, paradoxically, also gave Cordelia the opportunity to experience a normal healthy dependency, which had been so badly missing from her formative years. Obviously at the time, neither I nor Anne were aware of the importance of this meeting, and since the particular memory in question, and indeed the relevance of Anne's name, did not emerge until much, much later, Cordelia's need to cling (whenever the going got tough) to yet another potential rescuer (or 'insurance policy' as Cordelia called it), frequently caused great distress to Cordelia herself and to all involved with her care. Many a battle would be fought trying to help Cordelia relinquish these varied insurance schemes – whether it was her counsellor, Dr M, Day Care, Anne, myself, or her many imaginary, substitute mothers.

During this first admission, Cordelia was an in-patient for a total of twenty-one days. When Cordelia first arrived at the clinic she was tearful, anxious, complaining of headaches, and grieving the loss of her counsellor, who had left her 'high and dry' after stirring up memories of the past, which now felt more like 'newly opened wounds' (sic).

Cordelia also confessed to Anne that she was feeling suicidal, but would not say so in front of her husband, (a regular and obviously devoted visitor), thereby confirming a pattern of secrecy which had very much become a way of life. Although in those early days Cordelia appeared not to have any difficulty talking about the physical and emotional abuse she received from her mother and grandmother, nor about the sexual abuse by her brother, or the rape by a man in a uniform, when her mother had sent her abroad on a holiday, she was quite adamant that she had no intention of engaging with another therapist!

By the fourth day Cordelia had become a lot more sociable, and joined in with the varied daily therapy programme of art, swimming, stress management etc. Until then she had mainly preferred to stay alone in her room. She was spontaneous, pleasant, appearing bright and cheerful, and in the meantime, Dr M, (Cordelia's consultant), had arranged for Cordelia to be seen by a massage therapist. He hoped that a massage/counselling approach would allow Cordelia to release unexpressed emotions, which she tended to experience, as 'a steady gnawing abdominal pain'.

Dr M, would usually see Cordelia on Tuesday and Thursday, but during the second week of her admission he saw her on Monday evening. This change of routine clearly seemed to cause Cordelia a degree of distress, though she was unable to tell him so. Instead, she told Anne the next day that she had made an angry call to the counsellor, screaming at her over the phone (albeit into the answer machine). Afterwards, Cordelia had felt 'elated, giggling, over the top', but had been unable to stop herself.

On the same day Cordelia had also phoned reception saying that she was unable to cope with panic feelings, but had hung up and had not given her name. Subsequently, she talked, yet again, to another nurse about her childhood memories, but this time recounted that the rape had taken place when she was staying with her aunt, by her uncle. Later on, however, she reported feeling hurt and aggrieved, because she felt that the members of a group on anger had 'denied her anger' when they had debated whether anger is always justified. Consequently, Cordelia remained angry and distressed, (apart from during the evenings when she was again cheerful and pleasant) until she next saw Dr M, when she again settled down, having agreed to see the massage therapist.

The next day, having spent an enjoyable Thursday in open art, Cordelia again joined me for stress management, and soon afterwards started to complain that she felt uncared for. She threatened to take her discharge, and reported that she was again suffering severe headaches. When comforted by one of the nurses, Cordelia agreed to stay, and indeed saw the massage therapist that same evening, telling the nurses that it had made her think! Although, after the therapist's second visit, Cordelia confided to Anne that she would be unable to talk to this massage therapist and said that she knew to whom she could relate, and that she had been concerned that Frieda had been avoiding her. When she next saw her consultant, she in fact told him that she had felt 'invaded by the massage', and that it 'had felt more like an assault'. He nevertheless felt that she was doing fine and talked of discharge by the weekend. Cordelia subsequently approached me, stating that she was not able to be liked by others, but hoped that I would see her for individual therapy. I explained that I would not want to interfere in the treatment prescribed by Dr M, and suggested that she take her request to see me as an outpatient, back to her consultant. Shortly after Cordelia was indeed discharged as an in-patient, due to attend the day hospital twice a week.

The reader might well wonder why I have given such a detailed description of this first admission. I decided to do so because this particular admission very much set a pattern, and influenced how Cordelia would henceforth be perceived by certain members of the staff. Certainly, her frequent contradictory behaviour (one minute she could be very charming, helpful, pleasant, and next appear selective, demanding, angry, manipulative and paranoid), would in fact remain a feature of all her admissions, and obviously would have a reciprocal effect on some, thus ensuring that the apparent cycle of mood swings would continue unabated. At the time, moreover, Cordelia was of course convinced that the staff's reactions were motivated by hatred for her, and hence she usually tended to deny any part she might have had in the matter. In my opinion, however, Cordelia's conspicuous erratic behaviour only serves to illustrate how precarious the art of accurate diagnosis in the world of psychiatry actually is, and how easy it is for certain patients to manipulate a multidisciplinary team of professionals and guarantee their function as an insurance scheme. (Manipulation through necessity – that is, through unconscious motivation, I hasten to add!)

For sure, whenever Cordelia was in the presence of her GP, consultant, etc., she tended to present quite a different picture, appearing confident and reporting that she was making steady progress; so unlike the person in therapy who would cry and cry whilst recounting tales of abuse, desperately pleading not to be abandoned, and who confided to Anne, that there was a 'deeper level of disturbance', all relevant details which had of course been faithfully recorded in her notes. But how many busy consultants really read the notes, so diligently inscribed by the nurses and therapists, or pool vital opinions by holding regular case conferences? Then again, certain colleagues actually prefer not to read the notes at all, on the pretext that they do not want to be prejudiced or influenced by the opinions of others.

Being a psychiatrist, psychotherapist etc., at times is more akin to being a detective: trying to make sense of unconscious and conscious withheld clues, which tend to be expressed by the patient in an indirect way. Helping a patient make sense of this selective communication, I believe, (and now know!) would be far more productive if due communication between all concerned was given its rightful place. For example Dr M and I never actually met; we worked in different hospitals, times, commitments never coincided, although I naturally had access to his notes, and I used to send him regular reports about each therapy session. However, when it came to communication from Dr M to me, once Cordelia was discharged as an in-patient, we both relied on Cordelia acting as messenger. Of course, in the light of what was subsequently revealed, this was quite inadequate. Indeed, as I would discover to my cost, Cordelia was in fact apt to select certain parts of a sentence or an opinion, and make them fit her own doubts and projections! Perhaps, I should have insisted on regular meetings, but generally speaking, that is not how it happens in the busy and profitable world of psychiatry. Strangely enough, in the private sector, regular meetings between all concerned take place even less, since the consultant feels obliged to spend more time with each individual patient, hence less time is of course available to see the relevant staff. I suppose you can't have it both ways – although there are of course some who can. But I digress!

As far as I know, whatever Cordelia meant by this 'deeper level' was not explored at this stage, nor I believe was she ever confronted with the discrepancy in the details of the rape, or the sudden change of behaviour. Nor was she ever asked, why she was only able to tell Anne about this 'disturbance'. (All duly recorded in her notes.) Yet, as will be explained later, all these, and other varied incidents, were vital clues which could have ensured correct diagnosis and appropriate treatment, if they had been collated and acted upon.

Or would it? Maybe Cordelia also instinctively knew that to insist on revealing this deeper level of disturbance too soon would not have been productive! As Cordelia had experienced before, and has duly explained herself, approaching others with proof and tales of your madness is a risky business. Because these same professionals who are supposed to help you unravel your madness are also likely to declare you psychotic, hysterical, borderline personality, or just plain manipulative and difficult, or even more dismissive, label you as an 'iatrogenic artifact'. And then, as is usually the case with such demanding patients, having safely labelled them as suffering from a mental illness, they are prescribed a biological cure (medication, even ECT) or left to get on with it, believing that 'the best way to manage such cases is by benign neglect, which will result in spontaneous remission' (Ross & Dua, 1993). No wonder then, that it can feel far safer to maintain an 'insurance scheme' and become selective and economical with the truth!

But as far as Cordelia was concerned, so far so good. Cordelia had been referred for individual therapy, and would be seeing me once a week, though she also wanted to maintain seeing Dr M, because she did not want to 'become dependent on anyone ever again'. Hence, she opted for safety in numbers! However, all was far from well. During the next few sessions in fact, I became increasingly aware of my reluctance to work with Cordelia, though I was also well aware that my aversion was a by-product of counter-transference. Yet, because I could not stipulate precisely what was motivating my reticence, I decided to ignore it, trusting that one day I would know (which I did, via my own supervision), and settled down to working with Cordelia. However, in common with most abused people, Cordelia was very sensitive, very able to read any change of disposition, and quickly picked up my reluctance, attributing it of course to herself. In retrospect, I should have been more direct with her, even then, and explained my misgivings, but this was a new relationship, and I chose to be cautious instead. As it was, my apparent unwillingness, initially increased Cordelia's insecurity, but then seemed to act as an incentive to secure me as her therapist even more. As Cordelia quite clearly had said, she was stubborn, and would get what she wanted. Hence we struggled on, trying to form a therapeutic relationship.

The next three major events to influence her therapy, were her daughter's pregnancy, the uncertain future of the clinic, and Dr M's announcement, that he was leaving in six months' time. A very unsettling and demanding period followed, with Cordelia threatening many times to overdose, accusing both Dr M and myself that we did not care, that she had 'to buy care', and that we regarded her as just a job. One week Cordelia did indeed take an overdose, but again avoided telling her husband, believing that no one would care, even though a concerned friend had called round and persuaded her to seek help. Next, Cordelia went on a sudden trip to the town where she was born; to 'throw herself on her father's grave, and to dig him up', as she said she had tried to do as a child. (And again, on a much more recent visit, whilst accompanied by her counsellor.) Thereafter she again took extra sleeping tablets, went to the seaside to 'throw herself into the sea', and yet on another day phoned the clinic, telling the staff on duty, that she was about to drink a glass of water in which she had diluted all her medication.

During her sessions with me Cordelia complained bitterly, stating that she was not getting the right kind of care, that she felt rejected and embattled, feeling as though she had to put on her armour, every time she came to see me.

Making matters even worse, during this time, her husband had equally been prescribed antidepressants, and Cordelia had been attending a London hospital in order to investigate the apparent return of a prolactinoma (a pituitary tumour). Two quite worrisome events which were of course guaranteed to increase her level of stress.

Cordelia then contacted the counsellor, hoping to get an apology, and revealed to me that her friend had been making anonymous phone calls to the counsellor, in order to ensure that the relationship was definitely over. Her friend, Cordelia said, had pretended to be her, by staying silent and not answering the repeated hellos. This intervention by her 'friend' seemed to cause Cordelia quite a lot of distress, though she did not wish to expand on it. She merely stated that she hoped that she would never feel quite so desperate herself. When Cordelia, however, did not get the hoped-for apology and acknowledgement from the counsellor, she wrote her an angry letter instead, effectively breaking off all ties, 'Hopefully,' she said, 'for good!' Thereafter, Cordelia began to seek comfort from Anne, arriving at the clinic on Saturday and Sunday, demanding to be seen. When she was subsequently confronted by the day care nurse about her manipulative behaviour, Cordelia complained of experiencing paralysis of her legs.

Yet despite all the trauma, Cordelia was working very hard in her therapy sessions, able to reveal many details of her life, and appeared to be evaluating them in relation to the present. Nevertheless, she frequently expressed her fear, that like Dr M, I would most certainly dump her, and was convinced that once he had left, I would be cruel to her, since he would then no longer be able to protect her.

As the time got nearer to when Dr M was going to leave, Cordelia attempted suicide. She was due to attend the day hospital, and when no contact could be made, Anne phoned her GP, who informed the police, after which Cordelia seemed to resign herself to losing Dr M, even feeling positive and 'in control about coping without him'. She saw Dr M twice more, before going on holiday with her husband.

During these six upsetting months, few good events seemed to occur, apart from the birth of her first grandchild. Indeed, the arrival of this much loved grandchild would prove to be an important stepping stone in Cordelia's recovery and learning, even though it also awakened past grief, as my notes at the time recorded:

28-2-'91

> Cordelia said that caring for her grandchild is helping her a great deal, especially since it is bringing her closer to her daughter. She was surprised that her daughter did not resent it that the baby was responding to Cordelia's voice and smiles... Cordelia was able to compare her own feelings of helplessness with the helplessness of her grandchild and recognised the damage it would do to the child if it never acquired independence or needed to remain helpless in order to get care... She also spoke about the baby she lost which was a full-term pregnancy: 'he died a few days after being born, he would now have been eighteen', and how she never allowed herself to grieve over it, telling herself that it was not important... Caring for her grandchild has brought back memories of her own loss.

I am of course quite aware that just listing the facts, as I have done so far, cannot give a true picture of the very real distress Cordelia experienced during this time, and the undoubted courage with which she fought, in order to be heard. For sure, the real inspiration of this therapy has always been Cordelia's determination to succeed, despite many demoralising obstacles.

All the while, she was desperately trying to secure her therapy, whilst struggling with the devastating havoc going on inside her; reluctantly having to come to terms with the loss of her counsellor; knowing in her heart of hearts that the relationship had ceased to be therapeutic a long time ago, yet feeling unable to give up on the chance of being cared for, on the chance of being loved – even though Cordelia was of course well aware that the care and love thus promised by her counsellor was only ever meant in a Christian sense.

She was concerned about her own physical health (the prolactinoma), and the mental health of her husband, who had become quite depressed himself and therefore, so Cordelia believed, needed to be shielded as much as possible.

Dr M's imminent departure once again made her acutely aware of having missed out on a father, making her wish that she could sit on Dr M's lap and 'open his eyes as children do', or else vent her rage about being left with an abusing mother (and an apparently, disinclined therapist), whilst feeling condemned to search for her father because she was unable to believe that he was dead.

Obviously the fact that Dr M had come to Cordelia's assistance and, according to Cordelia, had rescued her from the counsellor, but was then going to leave her with a 'reluctant' therapist, was too close to the actual events of her childhood not to ensure that Cordelia would indeed experience transference. Likewise, her father had rescued Cordelia from her mother who had tried to kill her. Likewise, her father then left, died, and likewise left Cordelia in the care of a mother who did not really want her.

Therapy thus was not only stirring up memories, but events taking place in the present, as well as her therapist's counter-transference, were also unwittingly assisting Cordelia to re-enact the past, and helping her to rekindle unconscious wishes; dreams about being the beloved child, protected by loving parents, or visualising herself, as the only child, who did not have to share her mother with brothers or share her therapist with other patients! Wishes, which naturally also spilled over into her dealings with other members of staff and fellow patients and consequently led to feelings of paranoia and expressions of anger. For example, one day, Cordelia left the day care group because she felt that two other women were conspiring against her and no longer liked her, and on another day, Cordelia left the hospital, because the nurse in charge of the day hospital was not immediately available to see her. However, as Cordelia has described, battle on she did...

DR W

Dr M left, and briefed his successor, Dr W, informing him that Cordelia had used her time in the clinic well, and that he felt that the clinic staff had well complemented what he had tried to achieve, and for the most part, that we had not cut across one another. He acknowledged the distress his leaving had caused her, and therefore recommended, that Cordelia should be discouraged from substituting their relationship with a similar attachment of the same sort of intensity. The pragmatic approach, he felt, being used by Frieda, working through, going on to new things, was far more appropriate. Moreover, he also informed Dr W, that it would be extremely unlikely that Cordelia would want much contact with him 'other than the minimum which you require, to satisfy yourself as regards the clinical responsibility', and that he hoped that her association with the clinic, would in fact 'diminish and be discontinued within the next three to four months'.

Be that as it may, once Dr M left it soon became apparent that Cordelia's level of disturbance was indeed far, 'far deeper'. However, in the meantime, the financial position of the clinic had become intrusive, and dictated that no long-term therapy would be feasible anyway. In fact, it was believed that the clinic could close without any warning. Hence, Dr W referred Cordelia to the psychotherapy group, led by Dr S and myself (should the clinic close, the group would continue), whilst giving Cordelia the opportunity, to 'attach to a less personal object', and thus provide her with the means to resolve her transferences and her habitual retreat into a victim role.

Another turbulent period followed, where Cordelia accused Dr W of not taking care of her as he had promised, resenting his preoccupation with sorting out the physical aspects of her treatment: appropriate treatment for prolactinoma, which had indeed been diagnosed. She also bitterly resented the referral to the psychotherapy group, since it would ultimately mean the end of her individual therapy with me, and because she so clearly disliked the group facilitator, Dr S, whom she instantly placed into the role of her abusing brother.

By now, all concerned with her care were desperately trying to impose boundaries, aiming towards a gradual reduction of varied therapies, and replacing it with weekly attendance to the psychotherapy group only. But although Cordelia agreed to join the group, she was not really going to cooperate. After all, argued Cordelia, had not Dr M told her that whilst she was in the clinic she could behave as abominably as she wanted, use the opportunity to vent her anger, since she would never have to see those people (staff and patients) ever again! Hence angry outbursts occurred, where Cordelia threw her coffee cup against the door when she was reminded that she was no longer meant to join the day care group, and again when a mix up over her appointment with me caused her to feel what appeared to be overwhelming jealousy (in years to come, Cordelia was in fact able to correct this interpretation and explained that she threw the cup because she had felt outraged at being maltreated).

She complained vehemently that too many changes were happening at once. Yet again, she also talked about feeling pleased that she had been given boundaries, and much to her surprise, that she had actually benefited from sharing in the psychotherapy group. As usual, she also presented quite a different picture of herself whenever she met her consultant, which naturally added fuel to her being considered manipulative and disruptive.

However, all these background events, including the mix-up over the appointment for which I did apologise – only served to strengthen the transference so that more and more, I was being confused with her abusing, cruel mother. As a result, just like she used to do to her mother when she was a child, she began to write a series of letters in which she accused me of withholding treatment, of preferring others and leaving her feeling 'victimised, bruised and battered', yet insisting that she wanted to continue therapy and that she needed me, though also hated the fact, that she did!

Clearly, despite our attempts to wean Cordelia off the clinic as Dr M had advised, and prevent a repetition of her intense attachment to a significant other, we were not successful. The more I tried to assist her by encouraging her dependency on the group, the more determined she became to gain me as her therapist.

She was entitled to get help! I had become that one toy in the toyshop, which she *would* get. Whether I liked it or not, I was now a part of this battle. As Cordelia warned me, 'The more you withhold or retreat, the more I will cling.' However, to be precise, Cordelia's determination to engage me as her therapist can perhaps also be understood in view of the fact – as one of her letters described – that when she initially went for help, she had received due encouragement from Dr M who had told her, Cordelia said, that ideally she should receive long-term psychotherapy:

8 JANUARY 1992

Will you please read this before throwing away…

Dear Frieda,

Having studied various methods of therapy and some of the discoveries and methods used by different analysts, I am aware that there are various schools of thought and treatment. I think I have mentioned before that Dr M encouraged transference, and when I first went to him he said I needed long-term psychotherapy for maybe three or four years, at least twice a week. He said I needed to form a relationship of trust and basically learn to grow up and let go, as I felt able. However, he said he was only able to do crisis work with me, but he still wanted me to transfer my feelings for M (the counsellor) on to him.

Can you tell me why you and Dr S have quite different views on this? Would you treat every patient by one method, or does your treatment vary according to the circumstances or the patient's needs? How do you know, or can you be sure your method would be better, than the one Dr M suggested?

Clearly as this letter illustrates, a part of Cordelia had not only agreed with Dr M's suggestion, but had taken it very much to heart and hence was also very determined to see it happen!

DR MT

After six months under Dr W, Cordelia switched consultants to Dr Mt, and she instantly felt that she was being listened to. In fact, as Cordelia has described elsewhere, Dr Mt was horrified by the state she was in, and consequently decided, that she should stop the psychotherapy group forthwith, and that she should once again receive ongoing support from the day hospital, meaning that during the weeks she was not seeing me, she was to see Anne and be allowed to join in with certain aspects of the day care programme. Furthermore, as Cordelia had requested, Dr Mt also advised me that in due course, he would like Cordelia to restart weekly individual therapy with me.

At first, however, I felt very reluctant to agree with this change of treatment, fearing that it would only complicate matters. Since the day patients also joined me for certain groups and activities, such as swimming, art, dramatherapy and creative writing, I naturally was concerned that because of Cordelia's intense dependency, my role as her therapist and the one who also took her swimming etc., could be compromised, even though I am a convinced believer that a therapy programme need not be all work, but should also provide the opportunity to play! Yet, it seemed against all the usual therapeutic guidelines – to *need* ongoing support from other professionals in order to cope with therapy.

Nevertheless by now, despite the frequent angry outbursts and tearful protestations, I did feel a degree of commitment to this, (albeit shaky) relationship, and reasoned that with time, when Cordelia felt more secure and certain of receiving regular therapy, Cordelia would surely be able to let go of this extra support, and hence I relented and agreed with her consultant to consider increasing her sessions. But as events unfolded, this expectation would of course prove to be wrong, yet again!

In the meantime, the clinic had also gone into receivership; limping along, business as usual, gradually everything settled down again to a more secure routine, making regular therapy once again a viable option. Yet all the while, despite having achieved this extra support, the letters continued to arrive, making therapy more a test of endurance than a joint exploration, and I must admit that this particular time was a very trying time indeed. Cordelia's transference, hating me one minute, desperately loving me next, was by now so intense that I do remember reaching a point where I felt so frustrated and cornered that I convinced myself that it would probably be better for all concerned if I called it a day. However, when reading through Cordelia's letters once again, I was struck by the real determination not just to secure me as her therapist, but also to gain understanding. Moreover, whilst reading through her letters, it had of course also dawned on me that Cordelia was simply repeating patterns of old; that although she professed a desire for a healthy therapeutic relationship, she also *wanted* to be rejected. Being a victim was, after all, a much more familiar role. Consequently I felt unable to take the easy option, and during her next therapy session I duly confronted her with the consequences of her letter-writing: forcing others to reject her, thus making her predictions come true! At the same time, I also tried to reassure her that unlike her mother, I did read her letters, and that unlike her mother, I understood how desperate she felt and therefore accepted that her need for therapy was real, and that I, as her therapist, despite her angry letters, would not give up on her, provided the conditions in the clinic did not dictate otherwise. Soon after, weekly therapy was indeed resumed, and a relative period of stability followed which allowed Cordelia to begin exploring many issues of her turbulent past.

Like Cordelia, I have included one letter from that first demanding period, which I feel clearly illustrates her conflict, anger, desperation and distress, though it also gives an inkling, of yet other sides of her character to be discovered!

MARCH 1992

Dear Frieda,

It's bad enough having to wait a fortnight to see you again. Do you realise what this does to me? But one month will be impossible to bear; surely you could fit me in sometime before a month passes, you are not away all that time. Dr Mt and my doctor in London think I need therapy every week, so why are you being so withholding and cruel to me? You don't do it to anyone else – I know a victim again!

I need you very much at the moment, what do you think you are doing to me? I feel so hurt and wounded by it all. Do you want me to find another therapist or are you teaching me a lesson? Maybe I'll end up teaching you one, as enough is enough. Neutrality or clinical coldness, or whatever it is, does not help me. You do not know how injured and maimed I am during my period at home.

Have a lovely birthday at the end of the month, and I do mean it. It is very much a love/hate relationship I have with you. I wish I could run away from it. Damn it, I need you and I want to see you once a week. I would give up everything else if I could do that.

I know you will ignore me, and this letter. I know it won't do any good and I have to think again about what I can do. This is a torment so extreme. I long and pray that I might die. You have hurt me very much.

Love,
Cordelia

PS Can I come back to the group to be tortured, when I feel able?

Anyhow, despite the shaky beginnings, it seemed as though therapy was now under way, and in the next few months Cordelia would attempt to resolve her relationship with her mother and father; not an easy task, and far more complicated than either of us suspected. Indeed the following story, which Cordelia wrote when she joined me for creative writing (during the first months of her therapy under Dr M), might perhaps give the reader a better clue, as to the depth of feelings involved.

26-3-'91 THE FANTASY

I found myself on a beach, totally alone at first. I ran barefoot across the silvery sand into the water. That soothing fascinating sound of waves, rushing on to the beach and withdrawing more gently, enticed me into the fresh, inviting water. I danced along the water's edge, feeling free and happy, and as I went I asked myself what I really wanted most, and, if I had one wish that would come true, what would that wish be?

As I ran, I saw in the distance a person coming towards me. As the person approached me, I could see it was a man in long robes. He had a kindly face and a penetrating stare, but I didn't recognise him.

In his hands he carried a casket, which he opened for me to see inside as I came before him. Inside were the letters that spell F A T H E R, and I knew then that my dearest wish would be to have the father I lost as a child. Knowing this was an impossible wish, I fled from the robed man back in the direction from which I came. Again, approaching me from the other end of the beach was the figure of a man in ordinary clothes. As he came nearer to me I could see the man was my father, the young handsome, loving father who left me when I was only six. My blood surged through my body, my heart beat faster than it had ever done before and again as I came before him, he opened a casket he was carrying. I hesitantly looked in and saw before me a whole new life. Gardens flourishing with beautiful shrubs and flowers, bees humming, the fresh sounds of water flowing. I was able to walk into the gardens with new hope. I felt alive, I merged into the life around me, I did not feel so alone, I felt part of life and what it had to offer – all I had to do was to take it. With that thought the fantasy disappeared.

Amazingly, a great deal of trauma and considerable time would pass before we would know just how much of a fantasy Cordelia's early childhood actually was, and what really lay concealed in the casket.

The Clinic... continued

In January 1993, I had two weeks in-patient care. I had therapy every day with Frieda, when we explored some of the abuse by my brother and mother. Using coloured pencils, I drew some of the scenes between my brother Martin and his friend – with myself. The drawings revealed such appalling sexual abuse that I wanted to laugh about it on the outside but I felt such indescribable terror on the inside as I remembered. One of the many horrific incidents was my brother's use of ether or chloroform – I'm not sure which – placed on a rag over my face to stop my screams, although I felt the pain. Then finding myself in a pool of blood and being taken to hospital with a severe kidney infection and torn throbbing flesh, excuses being made of a bicycle accident. My brother Martin, in fact used a bone-handled sheath knife to perform what I heard him say to his friend that African tribesmen do to their women: female circumcision! My mother said nothing. My brother had not completely succeeded in what he intended to do. But I underwent some surgery at a later date, using the excuse myself of a bicycle accident as the cause of my injury. I knew every time and all of the time that I had to keep their secrets – and it felt like the truth as I told it. Until I studied anatomy, I did not realise small parts of mine were missing, and then the reason for this did not register in my conscious mind.

Thereafter, Frieda started twice-weekly therapy with me as an outpatient. Anne continued to see me once a week for support. The great black hole inside me became more noticeable, caused, I now know, by missing out on being loved as a child, particularly by my mother, and by the life-time search for someone to give me the kind of love I should have had. I felt an enormous sadness for the loss of the life I should have had. It felt as if it had been stolen from me.

The knowledge that I was one of twins, and that the dead twin sister was loved by my mother, was also explored. I realised I had been looking for her all my life, as if she was lost. I showed Frieda the letter my mother left me with her will, in which she stated she had hated me all my life. I remember it didn't feel real to me then; I suppose I didn't want it to.

The way I coped was to pretend nothing awful had happened to me but to someone else, so I could forget it. As the memories started to surface, it felt that I was going under with the pain; they invaded me the same way my abusers invaded me. The agony was so awful, and so was the aloneness, but the overriding feeling was, 'nobody loves someone who needs this much'. Hence, I could not let anyone see, because everyone, I thought, was afraid of the rawness of so much human need.

I started to remember that my mother, who ignored me by day except for the beatings, used me at night for her own sexual needs: she blindfolded me and used my little body to masturbate with. I had to sleep with her until my teens. I often left letters on her pillow, pleading with her to love me but not to touch me. These abusive acts and more, had a lasting impact on me, especially in my own marriage and in my understanding of the concept of love and my feelings about loving. I was afraid all my life to feel normal healthy, loving feelings for a woman, or a man. I could not separate love from sex.

My mother tried to erase any trace of my father's existence; she destroyed all that he had treasured and forbade me and the school to teach his daughter music or art, two of his greatest gifts. My mother dominated my thinking.

At this stage of my therapy I felt a tremendous need to grieve the loss of my father, something I was never allowed to do. I wasn't allowed to feel, and I had been told at the age of six never to cry, and that it was all my fault anyway. It would have been normal for a child of six to feel she was to blame, so this was reinforced by my mother's words. However, I also experienced, underneath the sadness, a surging rage towards my father whom I claimed to love so dearly. I thought the rage was associated with his unfortunate early death, but at times I felt his death was the best thing that had happened. I could not understand these mixed emotions. I wanted to go to his grave and dig him up, as I had wanted to do as a child following his burial. I had something I needed to say to him.

As therapy continued, I started to develop panic attacks. They came unexpectedly and they were crippling. Adrenaline would rush through my whole body, my muscles would tighten, my whole body would shake, I would sweat profusely. I would feel I was going to pass out with the pain that was crushing my chest; my vision would change and the feeling of being trapped was intense. I also felt I was going to be swallowed up by the vastness of everything around me, which was to do with lack of boundaries as a child, and not feeling safe. I had several admissions as an in-patient during this year, becoming increasingly ill and in a temporary psychotic state, which was my way of healing myself and coping with all that I had remembered. With the nightmares, constant new memories flashing across my mind, everything was too horrible, too destructive, too terrifying to hope for healing from the outside.

I had a crisis admission in July 1993 when my doctor was on leave, and Dr C attended my bedside in his absence. Dr C seemed to understand me very well and grasped the situation in a few minutes. I later asked him if I could be in his care. This was agreed by both doctors, and it felt like the right decision for me. Although the following months in 1993 were some of the worst, and the year to come one of the most difficult, I believe Dr C's decisions on my future treatment along with my therapist and the clinic manager, although harshly implemented, proved to produce remarkable results.

In September 1993, I drove my car into some trees as memories became more and more overwhelming. I wanted to die. The friend who I thought would bring God's love into a crisis was too busy. The friend, who was the real friend, went that extra mile from a human loving response. A holiday with other friends, whom I valued, caused me more pain and rejection, because there was no understanding or acceptance of how ill I was. For many weeks thereafter, I slipped in and out of a psychotic state which, despite its implications in the world of psychiatry, felt very safe and healing, but there was one period in September I became very ill indeed. I began to remember being frequently locked in a bedroom as a child, and on one occasion for a very long time indeed. To me, as the young child I was then, it seemed like a whole week. I was in fact about ten years old at the time. I was left some food and drink, the door was bolted from the outside, and the windows were barred with wooden panels hammered into place, hardly allowing any light. My brother helped my grandmother to put up the panels to stop me escaping, as the room I was in at the time was on the ground floor. (I normally had to sleep with my mother in her room.)

I recall, I constantly wet the bed as I had done for many years – and I was always beaten for it. My bowels acted infrequently anyway – two weeks was nothing.

As a result, I became distended and physically ill. Hysterical behaviour caused me to tear wallpaper from the walls and to rip open feathered pillows. I yelled, screamed, sobbed and vomited until nothing was left in me; all feeling went and I lay exhausted. No one heard: the house was detached, neighbours old and deaf, my family had gone away. I was abandoned and imprisoned in hell. On their return, our GP, a friend of the family, was summoned to the house. I vaguely remember him asking me questions but I was too weak and too afraid to answer. My grandmother, mother and brother told him I was mad, sick; all manner of untruths were told. I felt as if a rope was bound tightly round my neck; one word out of place, and the rope would have strangled me. I was taken to what I think was still called then, an asylum for the mentally ill.

One specific day in September 1993 – many years later thus, I spent the day in the clinic as memories of the asylum continually invaded my mind. I remembered being physically abused, along with other girls, by a foreign nurse, many times and particularly at shower times, and felt again the humiliation of being hosed down like cattle after a long handled brush was used to scrub the genital area on each of us, rather too profusely and for too long. I also recall that I became very physically ill in the asylum and I do remember being transferred to an isolation hospital, where no one visited me.

In the present, as the day progressed, I was admitted to the clinic, I could hear again as I did as a child the flapping of sails and clanging of the rigging on yachts in the harbour. I thought I was again locked up in the asylum. Memories were mixed up and running in together. Everyone seemed full of hate for me, except one man who seemed very special. He sat every night in my room. He watched me and smiled at me when I dared to look at him. But in the morning, he was gone. I never found out who he was.

I again escaped into a fantasy world, not always recognising those I knew in the clinic as being who they were. I learned to deceive others by picking up on what was said. For instance, when I wanted to be discharged because I was due to attend my husband's leaving party, I managed to convince Anne that I knew who she was. Anne, obviously aware of how ill I had been and concerned that I appeared not to recognise certain people, had asked 'Who am I?' Dr C, who was with me at the time, had in fact greeted Anne as she walked into my room, and being alert I therefore told her she was Anne. But I (whoever 'I' was at that precise moment), did not recognise her at all. I was skilled at fooling people, which worked against me in my recovery. Consequently, against Dr C's advice, I did leave the clinic and joined my husband at his party.

The party, however, was a sad occasion, and he told the people present how difficult he was finding the truth he had only just learnt about my life. Although he said very little, those who heard what he said did not know how to react. That evening, while he took our son to the station, I took a massive overdose of drugs. My mind had literally flipped back to the past again; I needed to escape from home or the asylum, so I had to become ill. More harrowing memories came, of being forced to swallow tablets to keep me quiet and well sedated. I felt cold, as if I was dead, and as I swallowed the pills, I felt my body was a graveyard of dead people: my brothers, my mother, my father, my little children who were part of me, were all dead, deep inside me. I felt my own heart had stopped beating because it was so broken into pieces. I thought my husband was dead, my daughter, my son and Frieda my therapist. The past and present became one.

I felt severely punished at the clinic after recovering from emergency treatment for the overdose at the Casualty department of the general hospital. It wasn't my first attempt. But this time, everyone seemed angry and distant, and my treatment was drastically streamlined. Anne was taken away, lunch and swimming with other patients and with Frieda stopped as a sessional patient. Regular therapy would continue twice weekly – but only as an outpatient. No therapy with Frieda – if I had a crisis admission. Frieda at the time thought my suicide attempt was manipulative; we both know now that I did not know what I was doing. My poor husband was stunned, confused and needing help but he found none. I just drove into complete aloneness and drove all the way through it, until eventually I was no longer afraid of the intensity of my need as a human being, but all this took a very long time. The level of distress and despair I experienced following the suicide attempt was almost beyond human tolerance. I wrote letters to Dr C, to Frieda, to Anne. I believed they wanted me to die, that being cruel was their way of getting rid of me, one way or another.

I also wanted them to understand me, to listen to me, to believe me, but no one came to me. I had to wait for discharge, and then wait until the days came for my therapy and I could return as an outpatient. Nothing changed, they stuck to their plans, except gradually Frieda and Dr C, became more understanding and recognised that between therapy sessions, life could be intolerable and I could negotiate for another session, if in crisis. Easier said than done, for I always found it very difficult to telephone and ask for help directly, since it reminded me of the demands my mother made for me to ring her every day, and I could not express my needs to her any way.

I had another emergency admission in December. I felt so ill and alone. The pain was intolerable. Memories at this stage were not so clear as to my age or the circumstances surrounding the events. This became clearer later.

Boundaries
1992–1994

February 1992, Cordelia was now under the care of Dr Mt yet, as Cordelia has explained, despite feeling understood by him, despite the prospect of regular therapy, she continued to feel very unsettled, unloved, misunderstood and insecure. As a day patient, Cordelia continued at first, to join me for fortnightly individual therapy, where we mainly explored her relationship with her parents. But although Cordelia worked very hard in these sessions, in the background was her constant distress about not getting the kind of help she felt we should give her. She felt stressed, literally lurched from one crisis to another, and when she could not come to the clinic, she began walking the streets as she used to do whenever her mother did not want her. 'I often roamed the streets, I was never missed.'

In fact, the doctor at the hospital she attended for her physical problems had actually diagnosed a stomach ulcer due to stress, yet Cordelia tended to take on more and more. She joined a Cognitive Analytic Therapy training group consisting of psychiatric nurses, social workers, psychologists etc., and reported that she had felt comforted when the consultant in charge questioned her as to why she was so troubled-looking. Moreover, much to her and her husband's dismay, Cordelia once again began to experience breathing problems, waking up at night with feelings of choking.

At the beginning of April, Cordelia decided to write a letter to Dr M. She duly informed me, that she wanted to say goodbye to him, as she intended to die. She was upset because he had asked her to write to him and when he did not reply, she took several paracetamols, which made her sick. She then wrote him another letter to tell him to ignore the first one. Yet when Dr M did reply, she felt confused, and deeply regretted the fact that she had lost him.

To make matters worse, round about that time Cordelia's daughter also underwent a major operation and had been involved in a road traffic accident. Naturally, Cordelia was very concerned and felt exhausted: worrying about her daughter, looking after her grandchild, helping with the cooking, etc. In April, furthermore, when the clinic's future seemed more certain, we also discussed increasing her therapy sessions, as her consultant had indicated. Yet, despite her eagerness for regular therapy, Cordelia also began to voice her doubts about wanting to open the can of worms, referring to a dream she had where her father injected a can of worms into her abdomen, but he did it so neatly there were no scars, so that no one could see it. In fact, after listening to another patient sharing about the sexual abuse by her father, Cordelia talked about her worst fear; wondering about being abused by her own father, stating that she would not be able to cope with the ideal father being so totally destroyed.

During the same week, prior to voicing her concern about ongoing therapy, Cordelia also rang the day hospital, distraught, sobbing, saying she had received an anonymous telephone call from someone who had said that she could no longer see Frieda. She asked Anne whether she could come in early to see her, which was agreed, and she subsequently had a one to one session with Anne in which she voiced her concern that Dr Mt should not think she is well, just because when she had seen him during the previous week she had been okay. I'm sure that today Cordelia would agree with me, that this and other so-called anonymous phone calls to the clinic, were a very believable ruse to ensure due care and attention whenever she felt insecure. It is nevertheless a testimony to her courage, and due proof that she indeed learned to trust others, when eventually, in years to come, she would be able to own up to having made other such phone calls. But at this tentative stage of her therapy journey, Cordelia was a long way from trusting anyone with such revealing, potentially incriminating details and could only make disguised attempts at telling the truth. She certainly did not feel able to trust her consultant with anything so 'mad as being a multiple personality!'

Indeed, as Cordelia has already explained in a previous chapter, at that time, the only way she could let herself hint at the truth or reveal her true distress was via a letter, written by her observer, or her spokesperson. (For an exploration of concepts such as the observing self and the hidden observer, see Deikman, 1982; Hilgard, 1984; Watkins & Watkins, 1979.)

Cordelia has in fact included parts of such a letter in the first chapter, but I have decided to print this same letter here in full, as this letter so clearly illustrates that her consultant Dr Mt had in fact introduced the concept of Multiple Personality Disorder (MPD) to her. He did so after it had been reported that Cordelia had been making strange phone calls and after I had voiced my doubts about certain contradictory aspects of her therapy. In fact, over the past weeks, I had become increasingly uneasy about the accuracy of Cordelia's diagnosis. Since I was aware that Dr Mt had actually been engaged in working with MPD, I had naturally shared my suspicions with him. Hence, he had introduced the idea of multiple personalities to Cordelia. But, as Cordelia later on was able to tell me, at the time she felt quite unable to confide in him, and simply took fright... and promptly delegated answering his probing questions to her friend.

Although the letter is in fact addressed to Anne, most letters received by either Anne or myself were usually shared between us. They were of course also filed in Cordelia's notes, though some might naturally not be read by all concerned, due to holidays, time, sheer volume of letters, etc. Then again, at that time, our collective knowledge of MPD was quite limited, and as such, these letters, which now paint such a clear picture of what it means to dissociate, were then understood in the light of conventional psychiatry, or were made to fit models of psychotherapy i.e.: seeing, hearing things, losing time, spacing out, etc., would easily fit under the label of paranoid delusions, whereas feeling like a baby who wants to please her therapist and 'come up with the goods', would be explained as mere transference.

5 JUNE 1992

Dear Anne,

After seeing Dr Mt on Friday, my mind has been in turmoil. Part of me feels I am not able to have the care others have, it doesn't feel right. I'm more comfortable with being the victimised patient, the one that is treated differently, who is not liked or loved as much.

As usual, I was controlled, sensible, able to communicate my strength and improvement. I felt I was completely convincing and utterly genuine too – yet there is another side to me. I wanted to tell him how frightened I am by some of the things I do, that perhaps I do have more than one personality. I've read somewhere about Multiple Personalities Disorder – and he spoke about it.

From the time I was a very young child, I had experiences which were so traumatic, they split my personality wide open. There was no way for my young mind to cope with the brutality and acts of sadism that I experienced. Instead I completely forgot the incidents. Before I can love myself, I have to know myself. There is one side of me that is healing fast, while the other side seems blocked off. Sometimes, I have an extraordinary capacity to cope, while other times I experience panic and fear, internal conflicts and self-destructive behaviour.

I have a terrifying fear of people at the moment. I could not cooperate with Frieda in my therapy session. I go cold when I think of those sessions in the art room, I can't go into that room now without experiencing the same fear. I didn't understand what she was trying to do. I felt six years old anyway, and there was no sense of 'me' in there. Frieda could see 'me', but I couldn't. I couldn't do it. I was like a baby sometimes. I couldn't explain how I felt. Then she left me. She wanted me to be well and normal and there is a part of me that can say, 'Yes, okay, I'm doing all right.' I wanted to please her, so I dare not say, 'But there is a part of me that is still confused, still crying out to be understood, heard and loved.'

I am telling you this, Anne, because I feel you will still accept me whatever I say, whatever I reveal about myself. You have been enormously trusting, caring, loving and loyal. You have been a friend to me throughout my long and painful journey, yet not collusive and have kept within the right boundaries, which I have respected and admired.

This letter is a cry from my heart; instead of self-destructive behaviour, I am trying to tell you how it feels to be me. I am very frightened this weekend, maybe frightened of what will be revealed. Can I cope with it, can others cope with it, will I be rejected again?

The words 'I will kill you if you tell', are thundering through my head. I also realise, I have blocks of time, which I do not remember, I thought that was normal. I realise very few people find they space out and find themselves in another city or in the midst of a conversation with no idea of what is being talked about. I think I had to be stronger to face what I have to face. I just hope I can come up with the goods, so to speak and not waste Frieda's time.

Some of my behaviour can be bizarre. I sometimes feel that if anyone touched me they would kill me. I think people are looking at me, staring at me, there are people in the trees, cameras in the corners of the rooms at the hospital and other places I go. Yet I long to be hugged and I long to give a hug. I've never really connected with anyone, not really, not completely, almost with Dr M. I think if I really connected, I would love too much, the kind of love a child experiences with a parent. I think I need re-parenting to heal completely, but I'm too old for that and there is no one who could or would do that. I think it happens in the States a lot. I want the past to be over and to begin a new future – which path do I take? I have some memories of my own bad behaviour, but not necessarily the cause of them. I am a hateful, bad person, devious, unkind, jealous and angry – not worth knowing or bothering about – that appears to be one side of my personality anyway.

Please go on being that person I have come to trust, however awful I am. I will see you next Friday, I hope. Thank you too for your interest in my daughter and in all my family, that has meant a lot to me. I do hope you are enjoying day care. At least you are professional and trustworthy, and the day patients do not know how lucky they are.

Sorry about the scrawl, sorry I had to write; it was a safety action to stop or to cope with the pain and fear.

Love

Cordelia

June came, and with it the holiday period. Cordelia went to her home town, visited the house where she was born, placed flowers on her father's grave, reporting to Anne that it had helped her. She also approached her eldest brother for confirmation of her memories, and although she said he seemed to have blocked out most of his past, he nevertheless confirmed that their mother had indeed tried to suffocate Cordelia twice, with a pillow. The first time, it was Cordelia's father who had stopped their mother, which led to a terrible row, but on the second occasion, it was her brother who had intervened. He in fact tore the pillow off Cordelia's face, which had turned blue, and took her outside, shaking her to make her breathe. (Cordelia's father by then had died.) Soon after, Cordelia said, her brother had run away to live with his aunt.

I too was due to go on holiday in August, which always caused a measure of distress, although Cordelia did not feel as distraught as she used to do, because not only had Anne agreed to see Cordelia every week whilst I was away, but we had in fact also agreed to start weekly therapy sessions when I returned. Thus, once the holidays were over, a more settled period began where Cordelia continued to reveal many details of her troubled past, recounting how she had slept in her parents' bedroom until aged six, often witnessing and hearing her parents lovemaking and how, when her father died, her mother had started to take both her and her second brother Martin into her bed. She also began revealing details of how her mother had always told her not to have a third child, and how she had retaliated to her brother Martin's cruelty and sexual experiments by throwing his favourite cat on the fire, etc., etc. Week by week, Cordelia shared her secrets, a little at the time for fear that we would reject her if we knew all!

As Cordelia has described, during these sessions she made many painful and harrowing discoveries, realising that the sexual abuse by her brother Martin and his friend, as well as witnessing the primal scene between her parents, had caused her many problems in her own sexual relationship with her husband. She also became aware that her unwavering quest for love was more akin to an addiction, effectively condemning her to perpetual anger and crippling insecurity, whilst feeling unable to love or empathise with others, let alone love herself.

This calm period lasted until January the following year, when Cordelia was suddenly admitted as an in-patient. This admission, however, came as a great surprise to me, since I believed that Cordelia was working and coping quite well with the aspects she was exploring in her therapy, despite occasional tearful setbacks. However, having since reviewed the past months and events leading up to this admission, I now realise how I had underestimated once again, the strength of feelings concerned, when a certain insurance policy becomes in danger of being withdrawn. In Cordelia's case, my suggestion, after due consultation with her consultant, to increase therapy to twice a week, to move on to a healthier therapeutic relationship, rather than constantly seek comfort from other staff within the clinic whenever her therapy brought painful issues to the forefront; to end her attendance to the day hospital, become an outpatient and only see her therapist and consultant, this sugges-tion, despite Cordelia's protestations that she would give up everything else if only she could have regular therapy with me, seems to have pressed a panic button somewhere, which I feel ultimately led to this admission.

Perhaps at the time, asking Cordelia to give up on her insurance policies, was far too soon, considering the amount of sadness and distress that had lain dormant inside her. Then again, neither Cordelia nor I were aware of the different agendas involved. Where some parts of her wanted very much to engage in therapy in order to know, other parts did not believe that therapy would do her any good and tended to sabotage her efforts. Yet other parts simply wanted to be loved and experience the care any mother should have bestowed upon a vulnerable child. Somehow, the parts who wanted to sabotage and those who wanted merely to be loved, always seemed to know exactly what to do and say in order to secure such attention or disrupt her therapy.

With hindsight of course, I now understand how this admission played an important role in the overall process and how it led to many such crisis interventions during the following year. In my opinion, this particular admission actually re-awakened a pattern or, as Cordelia has described it herself, it reinforced a 'different way of escaping' – it provided her with a 'different way of dissociating'. Being an in-patient, effectively blunted the painful truths which she had so courageously voiced during her therapy. Paradoxically, however, this second admission and the number of subsequent in-patient admissions which followed, only served to lengthen the process and ultimately resulted not only in a great deal of expense (since her husband by then was footing the bill for her therapy), but also in a lot of pain and anguish, as well as producing a baffled therapist, who had to listen to many repetitions of the same awful stories of abuse, over and over again. To illustrate this point and explain more fully, I will go through the different events prior to this important second admission.

As I described, weekly sessions started in earnest after my annual holiday in August. In the meantime, Cordelia herself had moved house and was in the process of clearing out many of her mother's belongings.

Cordelia was quite rightly pleased with herself, saying that she was making a lot of progress, finally getting rid of years of bad memories which had been safely stored away, including the bone-handled knife used so savagely by her brother Martin to maim her, which Cordelia brought to me, placing it in my care, out of harm's way. As yet, however, she felt unable to get rid of her wedding dress, which her mother had made for her and forced her to wear. Cordelia had wanted to buy her own wedding dress but had been unable to insist, and ever since, all through her married life, this dress had lived on top of her wardrobe in a cardboard box. Every time Cordelia moved to another house, the wedding dress had moved with them, and was subsequently, carefully, returned to its lofty position.

Naturally, in therapy we explored the significance of this dress and what it symbolised, and despite the sad and harrowing associations we uncovered, Cordelia nevertheless felt a lot more optimistic as to the future. She even attempted a visit to a health farm, which unfortunately evoked images of her past, being hosed down with cold water. And she had also started to reveal a lot more details of her childhood to her husband, and was beginning to feel that she could trust me. But it was not to last. At the beginning of September, Cordelia discovered that Anne was going away on holiday and would not be returning until the middle of November. At the same time, I would also be away for a short holiday in October. Cordelia consequently became quite distraught, accusing Anne of destroying the perfect mother image, and again started to talk about ending her life.

Once more we witnessed Cordelia becoming angry, tearful, insisting that whoever she loves ends up leaving her, never to return. Despite Anne's and my reassurances that we had every intention of returning, Cordelia's gloom and doom prophesies were so forceful that she managed to cause us both a fleeting degree of anxiety (not difficult to do when you are flying to your destination!), whilst ensuring that Cordelia was unable to concentrate on anything else in her therapy other than her distress about being abandoned yet again. She explained that she believed that people either left her or died because she loved them, or that they died because they loved her as though 'God has it in for me'. She also described that all her life, she has looked on as though through a mirror and watched herself perform.

Once Anne had left, Cordelia again started to test out certain members of staff, in order to discover, she later on confessed, 'whether they could cope with my pain' (sic). Thus, after an argument with her husband, she turned up at the clinic unexpectedly, stating that she knew she was taking a risk, but that her pain had been too great. Hence, she said, she had decided to risk further rejection! When the day nurse (in charge whilst Anne was away) was not immediately available to see her, she let it be known in no uncertain way (loud tearful crying and sobbing, usually in the reception hall of the clinic) that she felt rejected and that no one cared. As usual, different members of staff (including me this time) would spend some time with her, trying to console her, though it would of course never be enough. Yet all was not as desperate as before, because once she had come to terms with the fact that Anne was no longer available, she went back to exploring many painful issues in her therapy, including her excessive jealousies when she believed others received more attention than her.

During this time, Cordelia also took the courage to tell me about the rape (which she had briefly talked about and revealed to the nursing staff, during her first admission). The reason, she said, why she had not felt able to divulge details of the rape to me (though she remembered it well), was because it had taken place in the same country I originally came from, and hence she had become scared that I might not want to hear about it, or accept that it was all true. Cordelia then proceeded to tell me what she remembered, including the name of the town where the rape took place, and where her mother had sent her on a holiday for fatherless children, arranged by this particular town. When Cordelia told me the name of the town, I was amazed to hear her pronounce the name of the town where I was born and lived until I came to Britain. Needless to say, I was somewhat surprised and sceptical. How could this be? It would surely be too much of a coincidence? But, as far as I could remember (I was always proud of how well I could remember details of any therapy session), I had certainly never told Cordelia the name of my home town, and only a few members of staff would have known or could have told her so. Naturally, I confirmed with those colleagues who did know, and they reassured me that they had indeed never shared the name of my home town with any patient!

I listened to Cordelia describing details of the rape and trying to recall the location of the street and the sounds and pictures left in her mind. Although these images of the town were by now vague and of course distorted by time, I nevertheless recognised certain parts of the town, that she was describing. I felt too amazed to form an opinion either way, and decided to let time provide proof or the reason why Cordelia should have fabricated such a coincidence, if indeed she had. Later on, I myself informed Cordelia about this quite remarkable coincidence.

Cordelia continued to tell me how she had been fearful of telling me about the rape. She confessed that she had been scared of the implications, and that she had even fantasised whether I might know the family with whom she had stayed. Rather nonplussed by it all, I recall that I subsequently also asked her, if this was perhaps the reason why, she had previously tampered with the details and had in fact told one of the nurses the rape had taken place at her aunt's, by her uncle? Indeed, Cordelia agreed, she had been worried that I might feel disgusted by her and hold her to blame for it all, or that I would not believe her, as her mother had done.

After the initial shock of hearing the name of my home town, I concentrated again on what Cordelia was trying to tell me. And of course, also on what she might be avoiding telling me. Cordelia talked about how sex, pregnancy, breast feeding, etc., had always caused her distress, and how she had missed out; never feeling able to enjoy being a mother herself, as her daughter so obviously could, who by now was expecting her second child. Ruefully, Cordelia said that after the rape and the subsequent abortion, she never felt the same again.

At the time, of course, I regarded this statement as self-explanatory, but again, vital clues were missed. Cordelia was indeed never the same again, for another stage in the composition of her personality had begun. Neither of us then had any clue just how complicated this composition would turn out to be.

This particular therapy session ended and Cordelia left, appearing relieved that she had been able to tell me about the rape. However, by now the end of September was approaching, and with it her birthday, which she described as always having been harrowing, traumatic and painful; desperately feeling the loss of her father, who had been the only one who had ever bought her a birthday present: a teddy bear. Cordelia's husband had since also bought her a teddy, which Cordelia at times would bring with her to her therapy sessions, especially when she felt I would be cruel to her in some way. The teddy, she informed me rather mischievously, was called Dr M!

Prior to leaving on my holiday in October, towards the end of September, Cordelia also informed me that she intended to go and see Dr M, in order to try and say goodbye. But this time, she said, she wanted to show him that she had progressed, and wanted to say goodbye to him as the substitute father she realised he had become, during her year of therapy with him. Cordelia, moreover, also talked about having observed her grandchild coping with its mother being away. She described how the child had quite naturally turned to a substitute mother (Cordelia herself), but when the child's mother actually returned, how it had then punished its mother by ignoring her and clinging to its grandmother instead. Cordelia said that she could now recognise how she behaves just like her one-year-old grandchild, and hence agreed to use the time whilst I would be away on holiday to try and cope in a different way, and limit seeking attention from the clinic.

Yet although the desire was there, not long after, Cordelia arrived at the clinic demanding to be seen, accusing the day nurse standing in for Anne of being cruel when she insisted on sticking to the agreed appointment, and warning her that she felt like a 'raging inferno, a volcano ready to blow up'. Cordelia was in fact angry and disappointed, for despite her good intentions, when she visited Dr M she had not been able to dismiss her grief at losing him, and now worried that Frieda would reject her and be angry with her because she had not been able to let him go. Yet she also felt let down by Dr M, because he had offered her friendship instead of behaving like her therapist. Like her father, he had promised to look after her, then left her to cope on her own. Dramatically, she wished the next day 'could be my funeral, instead of my birthday', whereafter she wrote yet another angry letter to Dr M stating that she had felt betrayed. When shortly after she received his reply, she waited to open it until she was in the clinic, fearing his rejection. To her surprise, however, it was a very caring and understanding letter.

Despite these apparent setbacks, Cordelia nevertheless continued to show a steady progress; able to separate out the *ideal father* she had placed on a pedestal (sincerely believing that one day he would return for her), from the *real father* who had died. However, during this time Cordelia also learned from her eldest brother that she had been born a twin. There had been another girl, who likewise had been born premature, but who had died, causing Cordelia to exclaim, 'How much more is there to be discovered!' though she also said that she could now understand why she had always desperately wanted to belong to someone. (See Woodward, 1998. Understanding twin bereavement and loss.)

Having returned from my holiday, I saw Cordelia again on 6 November. During this session, Cordelia actually continued to challenge her relationship with her father, reading out a letter and a poem she had written to him, expressing her anger, although she also talked about forgiveness and saying goodbye.

In her next therapy session, she again confronted the image of her father (she had brought a framed photograph of him) and accused him of having left her with an unstable mother: 'He knew that she tried to kill me, because he caught me when she threw me out of the window.' Cordelia, however, surprised herself with her degree of anger, when she eventually slung his picture against the wall, breaking the glass. Although this angry outburst initially took us both by surprise, I nevertheless was able to use it effectively to help Cordelia reflect on the progress of her therapy and highlight the subtle ways in which she was inclined to sabotage herself and prevent the truth from being real – as indeed I tended to use any crisis Cordelia experienced, in order to upset her status quo *even more* (in the hope of engineering much needed change).

I'm sure that, as far as Cordelia was concerned, these timely interventions of mine often made her feel that in this therapeutic relationship, it did not just rain, but that it undeniably frequently poured! Hence, during the same session, we subsequently also discussed the need to restrict the different people she saw in the clinic (apart from her consultant), and agreed on the benefits to be gained from having twice-weekly sessions with one person only.

As I recorded in my notes at the time, Cordelia agreed to think it over and write about a) the benefits, and b) the reason why this suggestion has been proposed. She also agreed to discuss it in detail with Dr Mt and Anne, once she had returned from her holiday. When she saw Anne, however, on 11 November, she complained to Anne that no one cared. She also reported that when she tried to shut off from the abuse, a feeling of numbness had swept over her, which had scared her and that another patient had accused her of glaring at her. She ended that day by throwing a cup at the deputy clinic manager, hitting her on the back, and threatening to drive her car into a brick wall. She was given Nurofen, coffee and biscuits, and calmed down! Thus, far from discussing reducing the input of different people, it seems that Cordelia literally took fright, and once again displayed all her previous doubts and insecurities; i.e. during subsequent sessions when she saw Anne she told her that she was depressed, thought she was 'bad' and 'going mad', wondered if she was schizophrenic – she wanted to die, was numb with pain and tired of her life and said that she had been 'wailing like an animal' from a deep pain inside her.

Anne, naturally, informed Cordelia's consultant that she was low in mood. Yet Cordelia also reported to Anne that she was working well with Frieda, and making progress, and talked about having witnessed 'something awful', and having a recurring dream of seeing her mother beat up a baby. Cordelia later on also had an argument with her husband when he had to be away overnight on business. Fearing to be left alone, and fearing that he didn't believe her about the twin or about the abuse from her mother, she convinced herself that he would eventually get fed up with her and leave. Hence, Cordelia arranged for Anne to see her husband (who was in fact quite glad and grateful for the support, for he too, was literally at his wit's end). After this, Cordelia felt that he was much kinder and more sympathetic, and consequently they started talking about many incidents involving her mother, which at first, her husband said, he had forgotten; though he later on also shared that he could not understand why Cordelia could not do likewise and just forget about it all!

In her sessions with me, Cordelia complained that too much attention was being focused on the twin, angrily remarking 'as though it suddenly clarifies everything', adding that the grieving process for her father was far more important, although she confirmed that she had nevertheless agreed with Anne that it was an important aspect, and hence fully intended to write to her cousin asking for more information. As I described before, as far as I was concerned Cordelia was indeed working and coping quite well with the painful feelings of grieving her father, able to express her sadness during the session. Hence the next event was yet another unexpected surprise.

Cordelia was reported to be grief-stricken in the car park after her therapy.

But when she eventually drove home, presumably having decided that nor Anne nor myself were going to come to her rescue as she had hoped, she was stopped by the police for her erratic driving. Cordelia then informed Anne that a member of staff had phoned her at home complaining about our insensitivity, telling her that Anne was always too busy to see her, that Frieda was cold and useless as a therapist, and that we prevented her from talking to other patients, and that, therefore, she should sue the clinic for neglect. Obviously this caused a great deal of upset all round, including having to confront the perplexed member of staff, who in fact confirmed that she had phoned Cordelia at home inquiring after her wellbeing, though she said that she had not advised Cordelia in that manner at all. It was of course inappropriate for the member of staff to have phoned Cordelia at home. But then again, as I recall explaining it to the bemused member of staff, I felt that it simply demonstrated how successful certain parts of Cordelia could indeed be in securing extra care and attention from different sources.

I can of course only speak for myself, but therapy with Cordelia at times was a real obstacle course, and many a time I found myself inwardly screaming at her, or wanting to argue with her, especially when she accused me yet again of having a heart made of stone. Again and again I had to remind myself that this screaming child/adult was not screaming at me, but the mother/father/brother/grandmother substitute I, as her therapist, for the duration of her therapy, had agreed to be. I fear that I must have bored my supervisor to death with it all, and when he was not available, I would simply offload to any colleague prepared to listen, restricting names and details of course. At times, the accusations and tales of abuse were so draining and mind-numbing that I needed to get them out of my head. Writing my own notes in my personal diary and writing her official notes were a great comfort, as well as a very valuable learning process for us both. Perhaps my therapy notes were a lot more detailed than would usually be the case, but somehow I just felt compelled to record as much as I could. And, in view of later developments, I am naturally grateful that I did!

Yet working with Cordelia could also be very rewarding and enriching. Not only did we share a similar kind of humour, but her honesty and pleasure when she had mastered yet another hurdle ensured that I also stayed the course. Indeed, I clearly recall her sincere amazement when she voiced her surprise that she had realised, that the abused child she had been talking about these past months was in fact herself, and was not just another story. And I fondly remember the cheeky grin when she told me how she had discovered that she had transferred all the feelings of fear and anger about her mother onto me. It had suddenly dawned on her she said, whilst taking a bath. In her imagination, she had me sitting on her toilet, and was busy lecturing me about my neglect of her when she suddenly realised that it should not be I, her therapist, sitting there, on her loo, getting a piece of her mind, but her mother! Of course, we laughed together about the implications whilst acknowledging its due importance. This was a real revelation: allowing her to begin to see her mother for real. Exactly, how meaningful this revelation was, and how poignant to have discovered this insight whilst taking a bath, would, however become clearer and clearer!

Then again, being in Cordelia's company would at times be a real pleasure. There were parts of her who were very adept at socialising, and in the earlier days, Cordelia would often join us for lunch and duly entertain us with grisly tales of her nursing days. (Patients and staff used to eat together in the same dining room.) As one nurse remarked to me, 'When Cordelia is like this, she is a really nice person.' Of course, this marked change would encourage due speculation about the dubious quality of her tears. How was it possible that one minute she would literally be crying her eyes out, and the next be the life and soul of the party? Surely, I was told many a time, she was just manipulating us all to ensure ongoing care?

Yet, despite these apparent contradictions, something made me hang in there and defend her. Plain stubbornness, I reckon! The same stubbornness Cordelia used to complain about so bitterly when I refused to budge on the issue of boundaries? Cordelia naturally used to reflect that people only liked her when she was happy and smiling, or when she was behaving like a clown.

December 1993. Cordelia had a severe asthma attack at Christmas. Thinking she was going to die, she asked God for more time! The new year came and the subject of streamlining her sessions was once again approached, resulting in anger, with Cordelia saying we made her beg for help, stating that she was too tired, and that she might well take her life in order to end her suffering. Once again, Anne informed Dr Mt, and when she saw Cordelia two days later, Cordelia agreed to become an in-patient. The reason for her admission was to get some rest, and to enable her to feel safe enough to deal with a memory which, according to Cordelia, had been waiting to come out, though she was not sure whether this memory was in fact a true event or not.

When I was first informed that Cordelia had been admitted as an in-patient, I naturally expressed my surprise and scepticism that it had been the right course of action. In retrospect, I can now see that I at least should have stuck to my original feelings, listened to my doubts, and resumed therapy after her discharge. But at the time I felt that I had no choice but to agree, not to waste precious monies and time, and hence decided to take advantage of this admission and work with her every day so that she could indeed reveal this memory in a safe environment. But, as I described before, this admission did indeed set a pattern, because from then on Cordelia would seek admission rather than try to cope with her turmoil. I now also believe that the memory which had been pressing so sorely to be heard was in fact suppressed again. Even though, by using art, Cordelia was able to record many more details of the abuse by her second brother and his friend, and felt safe enough to reveal how she had always presented a happy, coping face to the world, whilst another face suppressed all the terror and degradation and cruelty she had endured, describing that she was split – a dual personality, hence why she thought she was schizophrenic.

Like so many people, Cordelia was naturally quite confused about the true meaning of the word. For sure, according to its Greek origins, the word 'schizophrenic' indeed means 'split mind'. Schizophrenia, on the other hand, as the Oxford Dictionary so accurately describes, is in fact, a 'mental disease marked by a breakdown in the relation between thoughts, feelings and actions, frequently accompanied by delusions and retreat from social life'.

Yet the pain inside her, stirred up by the work on grieving for her father, had, however, been successfully diverted. I'm sure that certain parts of her were quite relieved, because for now her memories were safely locked away again, even though she had indeed felt able to paint her anger and utter disgust so vividly and had let some cats out of the bag! Nonetheless, at the time, we both felt that a great deal had been achieved during this admission. Cordelia felt that she was at the start of a new way of leading her life; no longer controlled by her mother and her brother Martin. I believed that we finally might achieve a healthy therapeutic relationship: containing her sorrow and distress within the sessions – no longer seeking comfort or distraction from others; hence we agreed to start twice-weekly therapy, on Thursday and Friday. But my assumptions were wrong – yet again.

Cordelia had a total of four in-patient admissions during the next six months, before she changed consultants yet again. Each admission appeared to be triggered by feeling rejected in some way. February: finding out that I was seeing another patient she disliked. March: she was admitted overnight only, distraught because I had not given her a hug. July: Cordelia reported that she had received a phone call, telling her that her counsellor had died. When she tried to reach her by phone, she was told her counsellor no longer wished to talk to her. Cordelia then wrote her a letter ending their relationship for good.

Prior to this third admission, Cordelia was also found sitting motionless on the platform of her local railway station, for hours on end, causing the stationmaster to be so concerned that he phoned her friend, who took her to Casualty. Moreover, during this third admission, Cordelia had expected that, once again, I would work with her as often as I could, every day if possible. By now, however, I was very much aware of the negative consequences of TLC (tender loving care), and her therapist ostensibly behaving as the *good mother* during that second admission, when I indeed saw her every day! For any time I asserted myself regarding boundaries etc., Cordelia immediately seemed to be thrown into turmoil. Thus, a meeting was held with Dr Mt, Anne, myself, Cordelia, and her husband. Yet another attempt was made to streamline her treatment: Cordelia was to continue seeing me twice a week. Anne would see both Cordelia and her husband for support, aiming to gradually cut down on seeing Anne, so that her husband could take over. Hereafter, Cordelia was once again duly discharged, only to be readmitted two days later, after a difficult weekend.

During these last six months and frequent admissions, Cordelia literally seemed to have been on a merry-go-round, going from one tearful event to another, causing distress and worry all round. She drove her car at frightening speed through the fog, her husband, being concerned, following her. She attempted suicide after persuading her husband to go out. She left written messages in the art room, saying she was going to die, hinting that she had a suicide plan, and phoned her massage therapist leaving a garbled message on her answer-phone telling her that 'Cordelia... had died.' Nonetheless, good things also occurred. Cordelia had begun to grieve the loss of her life. For the first time ever, she felt entitled to feel sorry for herself, and she got confirmation from her cousin that she had indeed been born a twin, thus reaffirming some of her memories. She also discovered that she was able to love; love her husband, son, daughter and grandchildren, but in a different, healthier way than she loved Dr M and me. And, she had glimpses of 'normality'.

Her second grandchild was born, and when some weeks later the baby developed breathing problems, Cordelia was instrumental in saving its life, causing her to feel glad that she was alive, able to be there.

But of course, the major worry overshadowing all these events was the imminent withdrawal of her insurance cover. The insurance company was due to pull the plug any day now, despite frantic letters written by Dr Mt, requesting due consideration and extra care. No wonder Cordelia was feeling frantic; here she was with freshly remembered memories crowding her head, trying to make sense of them all, having regular panic and asthma attacks stirring her to remember even more, and the insurance company would almost certainly say, enough! Which in time, of course, they did: patients who appear chronic are not the insurance companies' favourite people.

However, much to her relief, her husband was prepared to find the necessary monies, desperately hoping of course, that it would give him back his wife. Unfortunately, by now Cordelia had clearly rediscovered, that being an in-patient would secure for her the same kind of care and attention she used to get as a child, whenever she was in hospital due to illness or neglect by her mother. The more she recovered and revealed past abuse and got in touch with the painful truth of her young life, the more the old coping methods also seemed to re-emerge!

DR C

During her fourth admission, Cordelia met Dr C, who was standing in for Dr Mt, and again she immediately felt that he understood her. She told him about her suicide plan, but promised to shelve it and work in her therapy without resorting to self-harm. She was again discharged after four days, but given the reassurance that she could be readmitted when needed. Cordelia then returned to day care, and I continued to see her twice a week.

However, there seemed to be no let up, for as before, Cordelia went from one crisis to another. In August Cordelia shared many more details of her sad and lonely childhood with her husband, and finally also took the courage to explain to her daughter and son some of the background to her frequent admissions and the many years of her depression, which they had of course experienced first hand. However, Cordelia did not get the loving reaction she expected from her husband, accusing him of not believing her – which he disputed – and in anger, drove her car into some trees. The car was a write-off, Cordelia herself was unharmed apart from some whiplash, although she was subsequently admitted for 'respite and TLC', and again discharged four days later. By now it was once again September, that dreaded month of her birth, which always seemed to cause her such heartache.

Cordelia began to complain that she was going mad. She also said that she had realised that she would never get the support or understanding from her two brothers, since her eldest brother had told her that he did not want to know about the past, and her younger brother had demonstrated at a recent family wedding that he clearly idolised their mother, hence would not allow Cordelia to say anything to the contrary. Moreover, a much anticipated holiday with friends only served to strengthen the feeling that no one was prepared to believe her, when a book she was reading about sexual abuse was 'confiscated by her friends', along with her diary, which she said they tore up.

On 19 September, Cordelia in fact spent the day at the clinic, feeling anxious, frequently having to vomit. She was remembering incidents of past abuse and felt compelled to 'vomit her pain away'. As the day progressed, she became more and more unwell and was duly admitted. However, she continued to seek reassurance that she was not mad, was not schizophrenic, and explained to the nurses that she was dissociating, leaving her body. During the next four days, Cordelia became increasingly unwell. She continued to vomit intermittently. She wrote a note to the night staff, describing that there was a bearded man in her room who seemed kind and caring. She began to place pieces of paper on the floor in a very ritualistic manner (just like the torn pieces of wallpaper?), and complained that her legs were going numb. She seemed to be in a trance, and as Cordelia has described herself, she again started to hear the sounds and sea noises of her childhood; or perhaps they were the noises she associated with the asylum. She certainly was in no state to concentrate in her therapy, and shortly after the session, she locked herself up in the bathroom. At first she would not respond to requests to unlock the door, but when I assured her that she would not be harmed, and confirmed that she was in the clinic and not in the asylum, she let us in. After that, she seemed to come out of her trance, and gradually started to feel a little better. She then decided to take her discharge, against the advice of her consultant, because she wanted to attend her husband's leaving party.

Two days later, her husband phoned the clinic to inform us that Cordelia had taken a massive overdose whilst he was taking his son back to the station. She was taken to the local Accident and Emergency, and afterwards was once again admitted to the clinic. An urgent meeting was held between Dr C, myself and the deputy clinic manager regarding future care. Clear, precise ground rules were drawn up, the rationale for them being that they were: 'an attempt to contain Cordelia's distress and move on in therapy, and to help Cordelia take responsibility for her own safety'. In addition to seeing me twice a week, Cordelia would also see Dr C once a fortnight for general support, and obviously to monitor her treatment. If admission was required, therapy would cease until discharge. If day care was warranted, again therapy would cease until Cordelia was once again an outpatient. Sessions with Anne, joining the programme for swimming, etc, and staying for meals in the clinic, were to end. Should Cordelia harm herself, future therapy would only be resumed at the discretion of her consultant. In due course, Cordelia would also be encouraged to negotiate for extra sessions if needed.

As we expected, when Dr C presented this care plan to Cordelia, she was not pleased. She in fact accused us of 'being cruel, we were punishing her for taking an overdose, we wanted her to die, or force her out! No one cared. No one understood her pain. A person with her deprivation was entitled to get as much love as she could find! She had never negotiated in her life!' etc., etc. She certainly gave the nursing staff a hard time, screaming at the top of her voice, running out into the garden in her night clothes; again screaming at them and blaming certain members of staff for this 'cruel plan'. When she discharged herself three days later 'so that she could attend her therapy as an outpatient', she accused the nurses of throwing her out, adding for good measure that her GP had been truly amazed at her treatment! And when, two days later her husband had to cancel the special treats he had organised for her birthday because she was so distraught, she held the nurses to blame.

For some time to come Cordelia would continue to rant and rave about the unfairness of it all, desperate to make us change our mind.

She was to have a further three admissions in a short time, before she would feel resigned and again committed to her therapy. The first admission in December was another crisis intervention, after receiving a letter from her eldest brother, breaking off all contact. But the next two in January were more an attempt to test the new boundaries when Dr C insisted they were to remain in force. As Cordelia pointed out, she was not used to daddies saying no to her. Sadly enough in June, a fourth admission would be needed when, due to illness, I did not return to work for some months. Cordelia by then had indeed engaged in a working therapeutic alliance, and was in the process of exploring her relationship with me, her consultant and the clinic, as well as continuing to discard many layers of abuse by her brother and mother. The prospect of losing this relationship after she had finally learned to trust was a bitter blow. Indeed, in her own unique way, Cordelia had recently started to show us that she was prepared to trust – just enough to allow us to begin seeing her 'deeper level of disturbance', although it would be some time yet before we would really understand the meaning of these strange phone calls. Such as the phone call in an adult woman's voice, (which we did not recognise) informing us that 'Cordelia should not be allowed to roam the streets in such a state', and asserting that 'I am bringing Cordelia to the clinic right now'. Or the little girl's voice, who phoned in requesting to know if someone called Anne worked in the clinic. When the deputy clinic manager, this time recognising Cordelia's voice, asked her if she wanted to speak to Frieda, the same little girl's voice answered, 'Who is Frieda?'

Clearly, despite her protestations, the gamble of insisting on precise boundaries had paid off. Cordelia, surprisingly enough, began to feel more and more secure; able to reveal the true state of affairs once she had accepted that we were not going to budge, and she realised that we would stick to our side of the bargain provided she did likewise. As for her therapist, I equally began to feel more secure and, for the first time felt that I would be fully supported in whatever boundary decision I needed to make to ensure a healthy therapeutic relationship. Even though the previous three consultants had in their own way fully endorsed and supported my work with Cordelia, somehow the issue of boundaries had always managed to throw a spanner in the works, which effectively had prevented the creation of a safe environment conducive to growth and risk taking.

I fully believe that the uncompromising position by both Dr C, the deputy clinic manager, and myself, with regards to the outlined plan, has been a major factor in helping Cordelia to achieve the health she has today.

Never before had anyone demonstrated to Cordelia that they cared whether she lived or died or harmed herself, and that they were prepared to take the risk of saying no to ensure her health. It was nevertheless a gamble of sorts, and there were times, as Dr C explained in a letter to her GP, 'that he feared that Cordelia might well seek another therapist with less firm boundaries.' However, deep down, I knew that despite Cordelia's provocations and vociferous remonstrations – doggedly enlisting the help of her husband to plead her case, requesting yet another meeting, in the hope of changing her consultant's mind – she was aware that this decision had been made solely with her interest at heart and that therefore, she, like us, would weather the storm.

Of course, there were other aspects involved which have been just as significant and have played an equally important role. Indeed, I am inclined to agree with Cordelia when she wrote that she 'probably needed to test us out', and even though I used to argue that TLC was not going to get her better, it has nevertheless been a very vital part of the process. As Cordelia wrote in her letter to Anne, way back in 1992: 'Knowing that others would always be there for me, regardless of what I do, regardless of what I reveal, enabled me to trust.' The reader, however, might well ask, why were these precise boundaries not set right from the beginning? The answer is simple, none of us had ever had to deal with such a clamorous patient who, despite our frequent attempts to streamline her treatment, usually managed to get her own way, often through endangering her own life. It is of course a risky business, to resolutely defend your decisions when a patient threatens suicide yet again, and naturally people are inclined to err on the side of caution. No one wants to be the one who provided the patient with a reason to act out. Maybe, if the boundaries had been enforced much earlier, we would have achieved the same result. We will of course never know.

I have decided to end this chapter with the notes of our last session prior to my absence due to illness, for I feel that they indeed sum up the value of having stood our ground, as they clearly illustrate just how far Cordelia had progressed. Indeed, whereas at one time she would only feel able to let her observer or her spokesperson write about the bizarre things she did, here she was telling me; here she was risking exposure. For sure, the events described in these notes were a major breakthrough, even though to the reader they might well seem rather strange, and I must admit, at the time, that is how they seemed to me!

WEDNESDAY, 25 MAY '94

Cordelia phoned on Monday requesting an appointment because she had become distressed after she was told by her husband that she had been making a phone call to the clinic pretending to be Cordelia's sister.

Cordelia said that she had not been aware that she was doing so, although she made the phone call when she thought her husband would be unable to hear her. Cordelia was scared that she was going mad, but said that she now remembers that she must have done this before, because at times this confident person appears who is able to assert herself and ask questions which Cordelia would be unable to ask for herself...

She said that she used to pretend to be her sister and had always felt that a part was in fact missing (Cordelia had a twin sister who died at birth.) She said she called herself Rosalind because that would have been the name her mother would have given the other baby (Rosalind was also her older sister's name).

Cordelia... identified that she had 'switched' on Friday, because the pain of losing her father was too great... She recognised that most of the weekend, she was in a dissociated state (sic) and only returned to reality when she phoned me up on Monday. Cordelia was tearful and scared because she felt 'exposed' as though she no longer could hide how 'sick' she truly was. She said, however, that she was beginning to realise that it was a positive step for she had ignored this aspect of herself over the years. She said she was only able to look at this hidden part of herself because she knew that I would be able to understand her, whereas she feels everyone would not take her seriously, and think her mad...'

As it was, sharing this hidden part with me would have to be shelved until much later.

The Clinic... continued

In January 1994, I told Frieda more about being raped at the age of thirteen years, an event I remembered well, maybe because it was not a family member and therefore easier to recall and talk about. I was staying with a family in Europe. I did not know them, and the father of the family raped me. I found it difficult at first to tell Frieda about any of this, as she actually came from the same country in which the rape took place. Some of you might think this is too much of a coincidence, but it is true. It all happened in the town where she used to live – I did not know it was her own home town until she told me. I went on to tell her about the abortion I had to have by the time I was almost fourteen years old. I was by then five months pregnant. The abortion was arranged privately by those in my family who were doctors and had suitable connections. I believe it was illegal then. I enlarge on this later in the book.

Both Dr C and Frieda often talked about losing my therapist. This invariably threw me into a dissociative state again. Constantly, throughout my therapy, losing Frieda was mentioned as if I had to be prepared for her disappearance. I suppose they didn't want me to depend on her too much, but every time it was spoken about, it was like facing the abyss. The sense of loss cut all the way down to my spirit, the centre of my being. In a letter to Frieda, I wrote and told her that my life had been beaten and suffocated out of me and that no words that I knew of could express what I went through. There was an indescribable silence over the whole of my original family – I felt powerless to change things but it felt like my responsibility. I sometimes thought that if I became very bad and committed a serious crime, I would go to prison but at least I would be safe. I had to work hard in my therapy, but it felt as though I was working towards something unknown and intangible. I didn't know where I was going, or what would happen.

I continued to battle with extremes of sadness, anger and jealousy. I tried to make myself do what Frieda expected me to be able to do, and squash jealous feelings and replace them with others, but the truth was I couldn't, I didn't know how to, I had no sense of self at the time. My feelings were overwhelming. I didn't know how to manage them, because they had not surfaced quite like this before. I had spent my life trying not to feel. I discovered I was fiercely angry about the boundaries preventing me from having the same privileges and freedom as other patients. Frieda wanted me to shift my dependency onto my immediate family and not the clinic, but I didn't know how to. With my family, it felt as though I had to care for them and protect them. But I myself needed to be looked after by someone else. Sometimes, I would take hours to return home. I don't know where I went and I didn't realise that anyone, not even my husband, would be anxious about me. I just seemed to be in a world of my own. The boundaries I found very demeaning, as if I was being treated like a child, so I continued to behave like one, although I couldn't do otherwise at this stage. I considered many times, walking out on the clinic and Frieda, but I also knew I couldn't manage without them. I do not think anyone could or did know how ill I felt, how very confused and frightened I had become.

Frieda started to help me explore feelings over other significant losses, the three babies I had lost. I was supposed to feel something? I felt nothing for them or myself at the time of the loss, neither could I feel anything in the present. I remember that at this stage, I still felt dead inside and that none of these events seemed real. I didn't feel real. All the emotions I was discovering at this time did not seem to have any connection with the past, they felt separate. I felt separate. I behaved, and felt inside, as if all these people at the clinic were making me feel bad, mad, dirty, unwanted, and it was their fault I had all these nasty feelings of sadness, anger and jealousy, although my observer knew differently.

I was increasingly living more in the past. Frieda's sister had died in the November of the previous year, and I knew this had affected her more than she could tell me. She took quite a lot of holiday in the early part of this year, and again at the end of May, during which she became very ill with hepatitis and didn't return to work for nearly three months. I was told it could be six months, so I suppose it was fortunate she recovered so soon. During this time, I experienced loss in a more normal way. I was able to feel and express my feelings without reproach or abuse, but I felt abandoned again. It was as if I was drowning, and I experienced a breakdown in physical health, as well as emotional and mental deterioration. Anne was exceptionally kind and understanding. She, as always, went beyond the call of duty and looked after me very well during Frieda's absence.

Dr C suggested another therapist, a Turkish man who knew nothing about me. I couldn't understand him very well, and he accused me of being demanding. I have never been demanding in my life, but a drowning person needs to demand to survive. I asked him not to sit looking at his watch, which he placed on the table in front of him, and to be more reliable in his timekeeping, because it increased my anxiety and insecurity. He laboured on my relationship with my father, whom I thought I adored, although the feeling and the person didn't seem real. According to the therapist, I idealised him because my father told me that I was his loved and special little girl. This, surprisingly, felt nauseatingly wrong when confronted with it, and made me angry, as if I was being accused again, and it was all my fault, whatever happened to me.

This therapist caused me more anguish and pain than I could take at such a difficult time when I felt the loss of Frieda so very deeply. So I wrote to Dr C and expressed my feelings to him, and to my surprise, he was in full agreement with my decision and agreed that I should wait for Frieda to return.

One thing I am very sure about is that I can discern very quickly whether someone understands me or at least wants to, and that they are not blinkered by their own first impressions or by what they have been told. I have, therefore, been very selective about those I give any room for in my life – it's all or nothing, although I am learning to be more tolerant and more able to accept and sift the good bits, and let the rest go without reproach. I wanted the perfect person very often, someone who would never let me down, always be there for me. I suppose like a perfect mother. I know of course, that no one is perfect, and good enough should have been enough, but such deprivation made me feel I wanted more than I could have.

My gut feeling was a recognition that in Frieda, Dr C and Anne, that there was a desire to really help and understand, even if I didn't always like the way they did it. Somehow, I sensed the expertise I needed so much, and they valued me as a person and amazingly trusted me most of the time. This was the way I learnt eventually to trust them; it was what I wanted more than anything, because it felt like caring. That is maybe why I was able to be as horrible as I dared, until fear of loss became too much again and compliance was the only route. Of course, these feelings that they wanted to help and that they cared just a little bit, waxed and waned to extremes throughout the years.

However, at the time when Frieda was first absent, nothing that anybody did for me ever seemed enough. Time with Anne seemed lost as soon as she had gone. Whatever time or attention anyone gave to me seemed to disappear faster than I could take it in. As Dr C often said, nothing would satisfy my need, all the love and care that anyone could give would never be enough. This felt hopeless, as if nothing could be done to help me, and my spirit sank to such depths, it was like falling deeper and deeper into a bottomless pit. Even now I can feel the pain of deep despair as I am reminded of that time. There was only one way to go when I reached rock bottom, I cried out to God to help me, and he did.

I received real understanding and kindness from the clinic manager and other staff at this time, which I didn't expect, and it stirred me to tap into my own power and harness the champion within. From where it came, I do not know, or perhaps I do know. No one could do it for me. I took the challenge with God's help. I knew I had to look into the bottomless pit but I couldn't look without Frieda. In the meantime, instead of throwing all the love and care I could get into this void, which would only disappear, as it could never be filled, I accepted the situation, put it aside and tried to receive the love and care I could get, instead of rejecting it because it never seemed enough; it never matched up to what I really needed. I felt I was not drowning any more after this revelation, although Dr C said I would feel like this time and time again, and even though he was right, this statement took the wind out of my sails for a while. Quite often, he expressed his doubts, which affected me more than he perhaps realised. At times, he used to tell me, that I often displayed incredible strength – but that I was a very damaged person, and that I had been subjected to a lot of misunderstanding and wrong treatment over the recent past years, because I was more complicated than most people could handle or understand. He also said that if I had been his patient from the very beginning, he would have thought therapy was contra-indicated, although he believed at this time, it was working well.

And yet as I grieved, I felt sometimes the potential within me being greater than I had ever realised. I felt like a caged bird with a broken wing that wanted to fly – I was, in other words, still in my goldfish bowl but wanting to get out! I found I had a strong desire to find out who I really was; with my black bottomless pit in view, I asked the question 'what is left; if this is not all I am, is there anyone there?' I discovered I was the black bottomless pit.

Frieda returned in early August, and I was ready to face everything, even the hopelessness and desolation, but at least I felt it was all about me and not a story I had told about someone else, about another child. I felt very touched by a gift of a book from Frieda, one she had bought in America on one of her earlier holidays this year. It was about someone else who had an equally black bottomless pit – there was someone who would understand. This man's story was different but made compelling reading. However, almost as soon as she had returned, Frieda went on holiday again for three weeks, and on her return, she told me she would definitely be going to Ireland for an extended period and leaving the hospital, although as yet she didn't know precisely when that would be. This increased my anxiety, reduced trust, and made me feel I wanted to die. Her illness, my pit, then her holiday and the news of her leaving was too much for me. I went through sheer hell in the weeks that followed.

Frieda started to go through my notes on her return. She said this was to clear up anything left undone or any misunderstandings. I could not see the point in this at the time but I was determined to make best use of the time I had left with her and face the deeper level of disturbance I knew was still there, and to discover the real me.

The transference with Frieda, the repetition of talking about events and people in the past and my feelings in the present, also helped to break the barriers and the awful silence. I found it painful going through the notes and realising what a sad and difficult person I was. They detailed the times I had asked my husband to leave me, expecting him to want to punish or hurt me, and the times I stepped over my black hole and pretended everything was okay, though when I did, although I felt competent, caring, and nothing happened that was worth remembering, I never felt a real person.

One day, on my birthday in fact, a parcel which my brother had found in his loft had been left on my doorstep. It was full of presents: books my godmother had given me throughout my childhood, which I had not received. They were still in their original wrappings and appropriately labelled. The box was sealed, with my name on it in my mother's handwriting. My hopes and my fears were stirred up by this box of gifts, and the way it was given to me had so many ways to hurt me. I became numb, dissociated and burnt the lot, as if it had never happened. However, by the end of October of this year – I was recognising that I was splitting into distinct parts, like a permanent state of dissociation but being totally different people. I slowly began to gain the courage to tell Frieda but I felt confused, distant and unable to be completely clear about what I needed to say.

At the beginning of November I talked about my friend Zillah, who had similar problems to myself. I had to face the fact that my friend was imagined and had been with me from a small child. She had a voice, and I could play with her whenever I wanted to as a child. She helped me feel able to cope with my upside-down world. I knew better than to tell anyone in my childhood of my secret friend, in case they took her away as they had done everything else. It was a tremendous risk to tell Frieda, so I told her as if I was talking about it on behalf of someone I knew, who had this friend. I also began to realise that I could experience altered states of mind, and I noticed again that I could see everyone distorted as though they were reflected in fun-fair mirrors, or make them go smaller and even disappear. This usually happened when I was experiencing severe distress. I went on to tell Frieda that I had always been aware of the 'children within me' and my husband agreed that I had portrayed many parts over the years. At times, he told me, he had felt quite envious and bewildered that I could be one person one minute, then change.

By early December, I had a devastating experience as I drove home after therapy. I saw all my past flash in front of my eyes in the sky, like some people experience in life-threatening moments, and I saw just how fragmented I was. I saw all the various parts, as if they had come unglued from each other but at least I could now talk about them and I felt relieved that it could all now be in the open – if I was able to explain it. I hurriedly drew the fragmented picture as I saw it in the sky. At Christmas, Frieda gave me a cute musical box with a teddy bear and his picnic moulded and displayed on top. It's not hard to guess which tune it played. I was as thrilled as any child would be! It certainly proved to be an important catalyst. Amazingly, and only because in due course we re-read my early notes for a second time, Frieda has since realised how I had told her the very first time we met that my father had given me a musical box as a child. She did not remember this at the time when she bought the musical box – her unconscious presumably directing the action. Much later, moreover, I was able to explain to her that it had been yet another area of make-believe – the kind of gift I had wanted the most.

By early January 1995 I was at last able to describe these other persons and reveal that they all had different names, and that they each served a separate function. They all held separate memories, and they all experienced different emotions. They had been an integral part of my coping mechanism while young, and I had suppressed them when I met my husband, who called me by a different name. I told Frieda that I did not want to scare him off, so I put them all away and became just one person – or so I thought. Together, Frieda and I drew up a hierarchy tree of the personalities in order to help the exploration into their structure. Some, as we discovered, were in fact introjections of members of my family and significant others. I explained to Frieda that I had to place them inside, so that I could be outside and lead what looked like a normal life. Although this exploration was excessively painful and caused irrational behaviour, we all agreed at the time that this had to be done if possible, on an outpatient basis. This decision was taken mainly because of the financial implications, as it was necessary for therapy now to become five times a week. Apart from my friend Zillah, twenty-two other personalities appeared in childhood, and two appeared after my mother's death in my twenties. Another one appeared as a result of my spiritual experience, but she disappeared when the buried pain started to surface. There were twenty-six personalities altogether.

As a child, my isolation at home continued into my teenage years, as did the abuse. Lies were well hidden by my abusers behind all the false façades that you can imagine. Life was not real. I was not real. I hid inside, covered by layer upon layer of my created personalities. The real me was deep inside myself somewhere, silent, almost dead but unformed. I was not a person. I had no hope, no life at all and still to this day I cannot comprehend how I survived, even though I know it was my own ability to dissociate to the extreme that brought me through. I was left with nothing but confusion, fear and intense feelings of frustration and shame. I had concluded long ago that it was all my fault that it hurt so much, and that I was not doing something right. All I had were body memories, sensations of choking, suffocating, breathing difficulties, nausea, heart thumping, numbness, loss of use of my legs, aching all over, blinding headaches on the right side of my brain, floating, looking through a dense fog, distorted vision, voices, loss of memory in time and place, feeling mildly drunk or concussed. None of these body memories connected with my brain or thinking; they continued unabated all my life, until now.

Frieda seemed to accept what I told her. I was so afraid I was mad and others would think the same. She found a way to help me discover who I am. I found a way towards this discovery by equally letting my own unconscious mind direct the process and by my relationship with Frieda, which I explain next.

Disintegration
1994–1996

I became ill in May whilst I was on my annual holiday, and did not return to work until eight weeks later. Naturally, Cordelia was distraught when she was first told the news, feeling abandoned and depressed, 'as though my life line had been removed!' And twelve days later, she did the sensible thing and phoned in requesting admission. However, although her anguish was so very painful, this sudden unplanned interruption of her therapy had a positive outcome. Three important aspects emerged which helped Cordelia to feel that all had not been wasted.

First off all, with the help of Anne, Cordelia was able to grieve the sudden loss of her therapist when she was told that I would not be returning for the foreseeable future. Cordelia recalled, that she had been quite rightly impressed with the way she had behaved:

'I screamed, cried, wailed and generally made a spectacle of myself – the way I should have been allowed to demonstrate my grief, when my father died. And, Anne let me!'

This time, the tears were for real. This time, she felt her distress, experienced her grief, rather than just acted it out, as she had done so many countless times! This time no one told her that she must not cry or that it was all her fault, but instead encouraged due expression of her feelings and accepted them for what they were.

Secondly, she agreed to continue her therapy for the time being by switching to a male colleague – though quickly realised that she felt unable to work with him. She clearly resented his way of working. (Sticking to precise time boundaries – a difficult area, one Cordelia had only just recently come to terms with!) And she was highly offended by his interpretations: telling her that she was demanding and apt to seek comfort from others whenever she felt under duress, instead of staying with, working through and resolving her feelings. When I eventually returned, Cordelia told me that she had been duly diagnosed as suffering from a transference neurosis, and that she had terminated her therapy, because there had been huge communication problems, which, she said, had not helped either of them.

Cordelia being Cordelia, she was of course quite proud to have been given a label, and I suspect that she had probably manoeuvred her therapist's observations somewhat, in order to justify her decision to stop therapy and wait until I returned. The positive aspect, however, was that Cordelia had been able to make this decision in a rational manner, pleading her case with Dr C, asking him to be allowed to make her own choices without being punished – stating that she was now, more than ever, determined to find out who she was and grow into emotional maturity, although she could not resist a dramatic coruscation by pointing out that the 4th of July, Independence Day, had seemed like a good day to make such a request!

The third positive revelation had been the discovery of what Cordelia termed her black hole. The black hole she described had been the sudden realisation that all her life she had thrown the love she had received from others such as her present-day family, her husband and children into this bottomless pit. Being allowed to express her grief, receiving kindness and understanding from varied members of staff – including those whom she usually viewed with suspicion because she was convinced that they hated her – had made her aware, Cordelia said, that the genuine love and affection she had received from others had never felt real or had never been good enough. 'All my life,' Cordelia continued, 'I had been so busy craving for the love of my father and my mother, that I had missed out on truly feeling loved.' As a result, Cordelia now recognised that she had no loving memories, no markers, no identifications which described her and connected her to other people. All she ever had, all she ever valued, were her fear, anger and longing, which somehow had sustained her over the years. Much to her surprise, in time Cordelia also discovered that anger actually made the black hole go away! This is probably why she had not been aware of its existence until now. Anger certainly had been a major feature of her life, apart from when she had felt depressed. In despair, Cordelia cried that she was fearful that she *was* the black hole, and wondered if there would ever be any real substance to her. Certainly this discovery was huge! It also proved to be a major turning point, since it made Cordelia feel even more committed to her therapy in order to discover the secret of this black hole, although initially its implications scared her. My going away had acted as a catalyst for her to discover the reality of her life, but now that she knew, she did not know what to do with it.

We returned to twice-weekly therapy, and Cordelia explored her anger and relief that I had returned, though felt that it was almost an anticlimax, since it now made her acutely aware that when therapy eventually came to an end, she would have to lose me for real. As she had done prior to my absence, she again appeared at times to be quite confused, and was preoccupied with ending. She talked about being two people, and said that she felt numb. She was also convinced that I would not be able to cope with the love she felt for me. I assured her that I accepted that she needed to love me in order to get well. At that time, as Cordelia has described, I also gave her a present of a book I had bought for her, and afterwards Cordelia decided that she was wasting the time we had left together with needless speculation. However, she was to experience more sadness, mistrust and confusion, because I too needed to tell Cordelia that I had made an important decision regarding my own future.

At the beginning of September, I confirmed that I indeed intended to leave and live in Ireland for an extended time. I had previously told Cordelia that there was a distinct possibility that I would do so, although as yet I did not have a firm date, but envisaged that it would be in about a year's time or so. Cordelia's initial tearful reaction was an instant decision to stop her therapy right there and then, exclaiming how she seemed to send all her therapists to live elsewhere! But when we explored dependency and discussed how she ultimately would have to go it alone, she consented and agreed that she did 'need to begin to lead a different life'.

Encouraged by her statement, I also proposed that we should read through my therapy notes together – analyse the sessions – so that Cordelia would be able to connect with these stories and in doing so, hopefully discover herself. Cordelia tentatively agreed with me and accordingly resigned herself, acquiesced that exploring her therapy notes might well prove to be beneficial. However, before we would do so, I naturally also informed her that I would seek the advice from her consultant first.

The main reason for my odd proposal was that whilst I was listening to Cordelia I became very much aware that she was again going over the same ground, that she was again recounting the same tales of abuse, but without appearing to experience any real catharsis or learning. It felt as though I was hearing everything again for the third time, and despite the profuse tears, I realised that she was indeed just repeating stories, and that at times she was apparently not even aware that she had told me all this before!

How then, I wondered, could I get her to see and register that they were not just stories but painful events which had happened to her? How, indeed, could I make her realise that she seemed somehow to be stuck within the stories? Using my notes I reasoned would certainly be a bold step, but might well do the trick!

Although, it was not exactly an orthodox request, to my relief Dr C faithfully supported my decision to use her extensive notes, and in due course we started reading through them, though not without a few hiccups along the way. Initially, Cordelia wrote me a letter describing how she saw herself as useless and aimed to kill herself in order to relieve her husband and her family of a burden – but, wanted to stress that my decision to go to Ireland had not influenced her in any way… 'I just felt that there was no other choice… I do it for the happiness of others… this way I can be sure of a final healing.' When Cordelia tried to make her intentions come true, she was overcome by guilt and relief. Guilt, because she intended to use her friend's medication (Cordelia had been nursing her since she had been diagnosed as dying of cancer), and relief, because Dr C had made her realise, Cordelia said, that she was not to blame for what had happened to her in her childhood and that she could not help it. Cordelia returned the medication to her friend and continued with her therapy.

At the end of the first session, after I had read a fair section of her notes out loud, Cordelia declared that she was rather impressed with herself and that despite it all, she had indeed come a long way, though she also confirmed that most of the time she had not felt anything, said whatever she thought we expected her to say, and had guessed as to the right way to behave. She nevertheless also sought my reassurance that I would not hate her, and afterwards could be heard screaming in the car park before she drove away in a hurry. Subsequently, during her next therapy time, Cordelia reported that her husband had in fact left her for a few days. He had been staying with friends, Cordelia said, because he had felt unable to cope with Cordelia's behaviour any longer, after she broke up a small table and threw it at him in a fit of temper.

However, much to her surprise and mine, as a result of reading through her notes and the many, many letters she wrote to me, to Anne, to Dr C, and the clinic staff, Cordelia began to realise that everything she had been telling me these past six months, everything she had experienced in the past years, had indeed happened for real. Obviously, I felt quite relieved, not only about my decision to use her notes but also that my notes had been so precise and painted such a vivid picture of her therapy, for it soon became apparent that Cordelia was indeed surprised to discover just how much she had actually told me.

At times, whilst attentively listening, she would make angry comments, even scrawling her disdain on certain letters, especially when I read out details of her earlier treatment. But mostly she would cry silent tears as she listened to the many painful memories she had shared with me over the years, or else she would nod her head in agreement when she realised the extent and consequences of her frequent difficult and demanding behaviour. It was true that she had written numerous letters complaining about our lack of understanding and due care. It was true that she had threatened suicide many times, though it was also true that when she took that ill-fated overdose in September, the moment she swallowed the pills, that her body had felt as though it was a graveyard full of dead people.

It was also true that she had vented and dumped all her anger about the boundaries onto Anne. And that she had written her yet another angry letter, stating that she felt let down, rejected, because Anne had promised her that it would be a gradual letting go! Although, at the time, once Cordelia had accepted that the recent drastic events such as taking such a massive overdose had of course left Anne with no other option but to support the proposed care plan of her consultant, Cordelia had immediately tried to make amends, when she realised how her angry accusations had consequently hurt and upset Anne. Cordelia also nodded her agreement when I read how she tended to rely on her husband to fight her battles for her, whether it was the issue of boundaries, insisting on due apologies from others, writing dissatisfied letters to the clinic manager on her behalf, or consoling her; when on a short holiday in Europe, Cordelia had wanted to stop when she noticed a signpost for the town where the rape took place, wishing she could confront her abuser, but had felt unable to go through with it.

Sadly, it was also true that Cordelia herself had not been aware of her husband's distress at the time when their third child died, and how she had left it to him to give the child a name and arrange its burial. And how Cordelia only recently had dared to ask him about this child, and had been told that the child had been a girl (and not a *he* as she had previously told me). Moreover, Cordelia had also told me that her husband had given this child the same name as herself, since it was due to be cremated on Cordelia's birthday.

Cordelia then sobbed when I read out how since then, she and her husband had, for the first time ever, talked about this child and how they had decided to give it due recognition.

It was also true that, since Cordelia did not know where her mother ended and she began, she had feared for this third child. Should it be a girl, she had been scared that it might be subjected to the same treatment she herself (as a third child) had received from her mother. It was also true that her mother had beaten her when Cordelia had become distraught and told her mother that she missed her father, after she had observed her uncle giving her niece a hug. Cordelia was consequently told by her mother never to talk about her father again, locked up in a room and drugged by her mother who, during the night, cut off Cordelia's hair. Cordelia again nodded her agreement when I also read how her mother had made her sit by herself to eat her meals, and only ever took the two boys out on outings, which had caused Cordelia, these many years later, to erupt in fits of jealousy, kicking over the waste bins in the hospital dining room when she noticed me sitting opposite a certain patient eating my lunch. It was true that Cordelia at one minute had felt low, and the next could feel almost manic, though it was also true that during the previous six months Cordelia had reached another layer of her memories; 'another layer of the onion', as she called it, and had begun to feel that she could be separate from her mother and 'be an individual'.

As a result, Cordelia had also discovered 'the child within', the child who needed to defy her mother, no longer be paralysed or mute, but a child that 'should tell tales'. Consequently, Cordelia had also talked about the last day she saw her father before he died, recalling that she had felt proud and warmed by his smile of recognition.

Moreover, it was also very true that Cordelia had been able to comfort her grandchild and tell the child that it was not responsible for his sibling feeling poorly and ill in hospital, as the child believed it was. Although she also told her grandchild that she understood how it could feel that way. Week by week, I diligently continued to read through Cordelia's extensive notes, and in due course Cordelia in fact expressed her surprise that I had faithfully recorded so many varied details, and also that I appeared to believe her. This was perhaps a rather strange observation to make at the time – but as we now know, because the sharing of my therapy notes had actually begun to upset the status quo, it was an entirely appropriate reaction.

To Cordelia, when she had first recounted all those dramatic events to me, it had of course all felt quite true, but as I read her notes out loud, and as she listened to her own words, healing seeds of doubt about the accuracy of certain details were obviously being sown! And, as the reader will discover, from then on, Cordelia's search for the truth, as well as the writing of this book, have allowed Cordelia's memories to 'fall into place', which in turn has enabled Cordelia to correct those details of her memories and early therapy notes which caused her to wonder and obviously set her thinking!

Just like the discovery of the 'black hole' had been so very significant, reading my therapy notes out loud to her actually proved to be yet another major turning point, since it clearly motivated Cordelia to begin asking herself 'why' questions. Indeed, as I read and Cordelia listened to many more harrowing details of her past therapy, she not only reflected on my dual role as her therapist and substitute mother (quite relieved, she declared how she could now understand and accept the importance of precise boundaries!), but she also remarked that it appeared as though she had changed in some respects, but not in others. Puzzled, she wanted to know how this was possible. What's more, she also queried, lately there had been times when she felt that she was a complete person; felt as though she was real. And yet, when she behaved as the 'competent nurse' the one 'who stepped over the black hole' and pretended that it did not exist, or when she was the needy child, that then she did not feel a real person.

Once again, however, it was September, and the spectre of suicide persistently raised its head. This time, in the form of some of her friends, who had informed Dr C that they had discovered that Cordelia intended to kill herself before 24 September – the date she took the last major overdose. When duly confronted with this information, Cordelia explained to Dr C that she had been misunderstood by her friends, and that September always made her feel preoccupied with death – considering that it was the month her twin and her baby had died.

On a more positive note, in her therapy session with me, Cordelia also shared that despite her distress about the trauma of her childhood, despite discovering such unpalatable truths about her life, she was feeling nevertheless, very much alive and could now even see herself reflected when she looked at others, though she was still fearful that others might not want to see her – in the same way that her mother had always avoided looking at her. Three days later, Cordelia phoned the clinic, requesting an earlier appointment to see me. She had 'gone cold' she told me, and had three dead babies inside her. Cordelia, however, remained vague during subsequent sessions, not really wanting to talk about unhappy things, preferring to concentrate on the forthcoming concert in which she was due to join her husband on stage. She did, however, report that she had opted out, had been God knows where, sometimes in the present and able to feel, but most of the time that she had been in a dissociated state! Music, said Cordelia, 'had allowed me to come back, as well as thinking about me!'

Cordelia nevertheless decided to talk about the impact of the rape and the sexual abuse by her brother and mother, and revealed how she always sees the faces of her abusers whenever she attempts to engage in love-making with her husband – though she added rather defiantly that she knew that her father would encourage her not only to sing, but also to enjoy her life, including having a sexual relationship with her husband.

As an experiment, Cordelia then decided to observe herself making love, and described how she had discovered that she could split into two distinct persons. One had been a fearful frightened child, the other a sneering person who laughed at her attempts to have sex. Cordelia furthermore also described that these two parts of her were not aware of each other, and that until now, she had not been cognizant of when they emerge, though knew, that they 'could each talk with their own voice!'

During this particular session, Cordelia also reported that she was in fact conscious that these two parts of her were now present during her therapy, yet that she did not feel as though she had dissociated. Cordelia, understandably, was quite amazed at what she had uncovered, but also mindful of how bizarre it all sounded. Indeed, as I recorded in my notes at the time: 'Cordelia said that she recognises that the only way of making progress is to talk about this, although she fears that it may sound very crazy.'

I therefore duly reassured Cordelia that dissociation is a mere survival technique, and encouraged her to recognise the importance of having become aware of these various parts of herself. Nevertheless, we were both somewhat nonplussed about the significance of these parts and what their function could be, and I recall that we tried to explain them away by discussing them in terms of the id, ego, and super ego.

The exploration of these 'mysterious parts', however, would be shelved for a while, whilst Cordelia concentrated on 'defying her mother', whom she said had always undermined her singing, even though her music teacher had encouraged her and praised her singing voice. (Certainly, on the rare occasions that I had heard Cordelia sing, whilst she was an in-patient, I had been amazed at the almost angelic, childlike beauty and clarity of her voice.) As Cordelia recounted, her mother had not only promised and then had not turned up for a school concert in which Cordelia was due to sing – which had greatly upset her – but after her father died, her mother had actually forbidden her to sing in the house. Cordelia described that there had been a battle going on inside her, but that her father had won, and hence she was determined to be on that stage and sing!

Both Anne and I had accepted Cordelia's invitation to witness this event, and along with her daughter and son-in-law, we very much enjoyed and applauded the performance. There she was, singing on stage! Afterwards, Cordelia appeared to be quite euphoric and pleased with herself, though I suspect that the presence of two substitute mothers might well have had something to do with it. Of course, Anne and I talked over whether our presence at this concert would be advisable or not. But we both agreed that it would help Cordelia rather than harm, even though, strictly speaking, it was in breach of boundaries. I can of course not speak for Anne, but today I am inclined to think that we went to this concert probably as much for ourselves as for Cordelia. Having been on the receiving end of Cordelia's anger and denunciation for so long, it felt right to be good mothers for once, and thus assist Cordelia in building up a store of positive memories. Apart from the fact of course, that we were both also quite proud that this fledgling of ours had come this far! Cordelia's husband and daughter naturally shared our appreciation of her achievement. However, whether our decision to go was right or wrong, the next events which took place simply made our breach of boundaries seem immaterial!

As Cordelia has briefly described before, a parcel had been left on the doorstep by Cordelia's brother. A note was attached, explaining that he had been clearing out the loft and had discovered that this box belonged to his sister. Cordelia had instantly recognised her mother's handwriting on the label and had eagerly opened the box, only to discover that it contained birthday presents from her godmother, which Cordelia had of course never received. They were still sealed up in their original wrapping. Cordelia was distraught, not only about the casual way her brother had just left this parcel on the doorstep, but also about the implications that her mother, all these years, had hidden these presents from her. However, her distress soon turned to anger. Her husband offered to help, to phone the hospital for her in order to request an earlier appointment, but Cordelia insisted on doing so herself. When she was told, however, that I was not available to see her, but that she could come in to see Dr C instead, Cordelia slammed the phone down, started screaming, and in her anger burned the box of presents – though she did come in later to keep her appointment with Dr C.

When she came for her therapy two days later, Cordelia told me that her husband had 'left [her] to it' when she had started screaming at him, and that she now hated everyone in the clinic, including me. She said that Dr C had told her that everyone there was afraid of her, although when I confronted her about the accuracy of this statement, Cordelia reluctantly agreed that once again she had selected parts of a sentence and turned them around to suit her projections and expectations. Dr C had in fact complied with her own suggestion, Cordelia conceded, and had agreed that it might well be true that certain members of staff were indeed scared of her. Cordelia consequently calmed down and talked about her despair when she had discovered what the box contained, and how she had felt so very disappointed.

The moment she recognised her mother's handwriting, an irrational surge of hope had flared up: perhaps her mother had loved her after all. But when she realised that the presents were not from her mother but instead, that her own mother had kept these tokens of love hidden from her, year after year, she had wanted to destroy the box and its contents. She just wanted to destroy everything, Cordelia said, partly because she could not believe that her mother had done this and wanted it not to be true, and partly, because she also wanted to end the control her mother could still exert over her. Cordelia explained that she had gone into shock, and compared the feeling with the moment when she had been told by her brother that her mother had died. The box and its contents had seemed like the final insult. Here was proof that her mother hated her, here was proof that the black hole was for real. No wonder Cordelia wanted to burn the evidence!

I'm sure that the reader, like me, can but reflect on the so-called sanctity of motherhood, and how we are all conditioned to see mothers as all loving, all caring. A visit to any art gallery will clearly illustrate this point. Being confronted with the reality that some mothers can and do hate and harm their children, for whatever reason, tends to upset the equilibrium of most, let alone when that particular mother should happen to be your mother! All I could do was support Cordelia through it, and encourage her to realise the opportunity this box of presents had given her; to sever the links for good and finally allow herself to begin grieving the loss of her mother. Much to my surprise, however, Cordelia was to sever those links sooner rather than later.

Although, Cordelia has already described how she next introduced me to her friend Zillah, I have at this point decided to use the notes I wrote at the time, in order to convey the series of events which followed and led to the most important part of this therapy journey yet. I wanted to use these particular notes in order to ensure that the reader can share in the importance of this event, and because they clearly illustrate how, step by step, Cordelia finally took the risk to trust her therapist. But first, how she also needed to test me out before feeling able to reveal yet another layer of the onion. After all, as Cordelia said, it was a tremendous risk and a lot was at stake. Would I too be scared of her? (As clearly Cordelia had become quite scared of herself – having approached Dr C for corroboration that certain members of staff were indeed scared of her.) Would I declare her mad? Would I feel unable to cope with what she had to reveal? And above all, would I believe her?

THURSDAY, 10 NOVEMBER 1994

Several phone calls were received during the week requesting admission but when offered a bed, Cordelia refused to come in on the grounds that she would not be able to see me. On Wednesday evening, however, Cordelia arrived at the clinic at about 8 p.m., believing that she had had an appointment with me at 4.30 p.m. that afternoon but had missed it! (Cordelia of course knew that, on a Wednesday, I would be in the clinic at that time for the psychotherapy group.) When the group had ended I briefly talked to her, whereupon Cordelia offered her apologies for missing her appointment. Moreover, she also appeared to be rather confused, asking me whether I was better yet, because she knew that I had been ill.

I naturally confirmed that she did indeed not have an appointment that day, but assured her that I would help her to sort out whatever seemed so obviously to be going astray, during her next therapy time. Visibly relieved, Cordelia duly accepted that no one from the clinic had called her or talked to her on the phone to arrange an appointment. After this, she left the clinic and she appeared somewhat less confused. She was asked to report, to phone the clinic on arrival home, which she did.

On Thursday (during her regular therapy session), Cordelia again asked me if I was better, and said that she had not seen me for six months. She then proceeded to talk about a 'friend of hers' who had similar problems to herself, but this friend could 'feel' and 'knows' that she has to give up on searching for love from her mother and her therapist, but is afraid to do so, because without this search, without the hatred of her mother, she would be 'a nothing – there would be nothing of her left'. Yet she (this friend) knows, that this other person (her therapist), whom she loves, can help her solve her problems. She, (Cordelia) was here today because she wanted to help her friend solve her problems, and because if her friend could solve them, she would be able to solve hers as well!

Cordelia said she did not know 'who' she was, and that she felt dead. She also said that they called her Delia. Sometimes they called her Cordelia, but that she did not like this name because it was connected with hatred.

At first, Cordelia could not accept it when I pointed out similarities between herself and this 'friend', i.e. they had the same therapist. But gradually Cordelia began to accept this, and agreed that they did indeed have the same therapist, though, remarked that she was not jealous of her friend, whereas she is jealous when her therapist sees other patients.

Eventually, Cordelia began to remember the parcel left on her doorstep, her mother hiding the presents away in the attic, and agreed that the friend *is* herself! She then revealed that she (Cordelia) often speaks to her friend, and that this friend tends to be by her side and looks like her, but is much younger.

Cordelia then confirmed that during the past week, she has been 'spaced out' (sic) 'out of this world', and that she can often experience altered states of mind, i.e. she can walk along the road and everyone will appear distorted as though they are reflected in funfair mirrors.

Cordelia subsequently also said that she was now 'feeling again', and that she *now* realises that 'this other part of her' comes to the foreground when she is in severe distress, in order to help her cope.

'I started to grieve for my mother at the weekend, the way I had never grieved before, but I could not cope with it.'

Cordelia also described that this part comes to the foreground whenever we talk about the abused child, though that at some level '*it* does know that Cordelia has to relive these events of abuse in order to redress them'.

Prior to the end of the session, Cordelia said that '*she can see four people* – but also, that there appears to be *one who keeps them all together!*'

FRIDAY, 11 NOVEMBER 1994

Cordelia read out her observations about having revealed that she has a separate part of her which she identified as her friend. She also said that she has discovered that there are four children within her, aged six and a half, seven, and eight, and one who is a teenager.

I have encouraged Cordelia to realise that it is quite normal for children to have an imaginary friend, for example, and especially so if they are in distress and have traumatic childhoods, and hence that this 'friend' is but a coping mechanism.

Cordelia continued to describe the differences and similarities between herself and the 'friend', and how it has mostly been the 'friend' who has come for therapy, whereas Cordelia would sit in the corner and listen. But today, she was sitting in the chair, and the friend was sitting in the corner.

Cordelia is concerned as to how others will view her, and whether we will consider her to be crazy, the way her mother and brother used to say that she was crazy. I reinforced that splitting (herself into parts – dissociation) is a coping mechanism which allows her not to feel, and does not mean that she is crazy.

Cordelia said that she has always been aware of 'the children within her', but when Dr Mt talked about multiple personality, she said she took fright and was not able to talk about them again.

What my notes can of course not convey is the range of feelings I experienced, listening to Cordelia describing this imaginary friend. Certainly amazement, a sort of 'how do I handle this?' kind of feeling, but also a feeling of joy and love. For I just knew that Cordelia had taken a very important step towards her recovery and health and, therefore, I felt quite privileged that she had been able to do so. Many a time, when I used to work with certain patients, whenever they reached a point of catharsis, a moment of real spiritual healing, I would get a strange tingling sensation running along my spine. I can only suggest that, at the moment a person reveals the truth to themselves, they perhaps experience some kind of energy which others can sense.

Certainly I have not been the only one to have experienced this, for some of my colleagues at the hospital have described a similar sensation. During this particular therapy session with Cordelia, I had many such sensations, and although I initially felt perplexed as to what it all meant, I knew that what Cordelia had been revealing to me was true. All I had to do now was help her make sense of it! Little did I know that there would be many more such emotionally laden events before we would reach the end of the road.

Equally, what my notes can not impart was the careful delicate negotiating which took place, allowing Cordelia not only to begin remembering the parcel left on the doorstep, but also to feel safe enough to admit to herself and to me that Zillah and Cordelia were one and the same person. Somehow, using my words carefully, I managed to reassure Cordelia that I could cope with what she was telling me, and above all, that I was not scared (which, incidentally, I never was, even when it became apparent, that some parts of her were indeed borderline and inclined to be somewhat unpredictable). Instinctively I just knew that, whatever else I said or did, it was important to convince Cordelia that no matter what it meant, whatever else she would uncover, we would be able to fathom it all out and that she was not crazy or abnormal – even though I agreed with her that it sounded far from normal.

Cordelia, however, was once again in crisis, though she refused to seek admission because she would not be able to see me and work things through. She insisted that she now knew which kind of care she needed!

Her husband, however, feeling rather desperate by now, phoned the clinic. He could no longer cope. He no longer understood what was happening with his wife, because she refused to talk to him. Feeling so very frustrated, he had been very angry with Cordelia, which somehow seemed to have brought her back. His main concern, however, was that it appeared as though the boundaries were now counter-productive, since they prevented Cordelia from seeking help. Hence I invited them both to come for a joint session, in the hope that it would enable Cordelia to explain to her husband precisely what was amiss – and assured him that in the meantime, I would indeed discuss the boundary issue with Dr C.

Although a bit apprehensive at first, but as courageous as ever, Cordelia told her husband about the children within and about the friend she has heard and talked to these many years. She also revealed that she had discovered that there was a fifth child who was, Cordelia said, 'very deceptive and not very nice'. To her surprise, as Cordelia has explained, her husband actually confirmed that Cordelia had indeed portrayed 'many parts over the years', causing him at times to feel envious though also quite bewildered that his wife could be one person one minute, and then change so drastically the next. Cordelia was most certainly surprised but also quite relieved, for she now felt free to openly explore these parts.

In the next few sessions she especially talked about the 'deceptive part', which gets her needs met, she said, in an indirect way, either by using others or by pretending to be someone else. Cordelia said she has no awareness of when this part is out or what it gets up to, and feels that it is sick. She now suspected that it had been this part which had left the anonymous note in her car some months ago, written in a very childish hand, and which had caused her so much anguish at the time, for it had seemed to be so cruel:

> We are intrigued to know whether you have learnt to hate F, or whether she is still precious to you in spite of her blatant coldness and cruelty to you in the days we enjoyed all the drama. We hear she is leaving you soon.

This part, said Cordelia, along with the other parts, had always maintained the false hope that one day her mother might be able to love her. But whereas most parts of her, by now, had accepted the truth of the parcel and the birthday presents, this part had not, hence why 'it' had burned the box. I pointed out, however, that in the act of trying to destroy the evidence, 'it' had also demonstrated that 'it' knew the truth of her mother. As a result, Cordelia there and then allowed me to see how she can so very easily go into a trance, and again became very vague and distant. When I asked her what was happening, Cordelia replied that she was under the sea, and that I had grown very small and that I was a long long distance away. I asked her to return to the here and now, which she did, after which she explained that the deceptive part would not give up on this hope so easily, and that it was very cunning. Clearly, Cordelia was feeling more and more at ease discussing the why and wherefore of these parts, as well as introducing me to yet others. One part, Cordelia said, tended to be quite mischievous.

In the meantime, however, we had also returned to reading through the notes. Although Cordelia angrily wanted to know whether I had become 'bored' with what she had disclosed about the various parts. I'm sure that my decision to continue reading through the notes was probably just a means of giving myself some space, so that I could try and work out precisely how I was going to continue working with these mind-boggling revelations. Nothing in my career so far, had prepared me for this. But as usual in this most unusual therapy, events soon seemed to indicate the way, and continuing to read through her notes actually proved to be a vital step in the right direction. As Cordelia has explained, one day on her return home from therapy, she 'saw' every part, and 'saw' how separate they all were. Like a giant tableau in the sky, Cordelia 'saw' the truth of her life. What, then, had caused such insight?

During her preceding therapy session, Cordelia had in fact confirmed that certain parts of her notes were indeed new to her although she had also observed that she knew that they related to her. She had furthermore also agreed that each part needed to listen to the truth of her past and no longer just think of these notes as mere stories. We had ended the session with Cordelia seeking my reassurance that I accepted all her parts, and in turn I had encouraged her to equally accept that they all belonged to herself. Obviously, Cordelia had subsequently decided that she could no longer go on denying that she knew that they existed, and hence she had seen every part of her displayed before her mind's eye.

Just how significant and devastating this experience had been for Cordelia is, however, difficult to convey. She complained bitterly that she had felt 'smashed into a thousand pieces', that she had come 'unglued'. Although she had managed to scribble down every part she had seen on a piece of paper, hurriedly writing down the very words which described each one of them. At first she had been rather fearful that I would give up on her when I saw just how many parts there were. But eventually, she had felt able to explain the meaning of those hastily inscribed words – finally giving them all their long overdue recognition.

Perhaps by including a poem Cordelia wrote at the time (borrowing some verses from well-remembered, well-loved poems) as well as a list of those miscellaneous words with which Cordelia had tried so desperately to paint the past reality of her life, the reader might well get a better indication of how important and daunting it all was.

The clouds gather
Dark and threatening
Whipped up by the winds of my fear
Mists of my own making
Blotting out the light
And warmth that is around
So easy in mouth-dry anxiety
To feel alone, abandoned, unprotected.
I roll in nettlebeds of shock
The pain spreading as vision contracts
Until my horizon is described
By the jangled nerve endings of my despair.

Angry or depressed
Self-abusive, self-hatred
Lost, dead, empty, nothingness, sad, pain,
Fatigue, aching muscles, back pain, skin disorders
Stomach and headaches, huge aching void in pit of abdomen
Pituitary problems, eating disorder, asthma, bronchitis
Chest pain, susceptible to infectious illness
Loving, caring
Panic, dependent
Cold – critical – controlling – manipulative
Crying, despairing
Anxious, loss of bodily functions and reflexes,
Secret, deceptive, jealous, possessive
Partial amnesia, numbed, frozen, let down feelings
Jokey and giggly
Independent, strong, reliable, dependable, loving, sensitive
Agitation, fear, phobia, nightmares, flashbacks, fantasize
Sleep problems, weight fluctuations, crisis, mania,
Chronic pain, nausea, vomiting, choking, bed wetting,
Unexplained sensations, genital and anal pain
Never feel part of what is happening, even when aware of it
Sometimes totally splitting, I feel like another person
Rejection, grief, abandoned, desolate,
Courageous, capable, sensible, coper,
Lack of concentration, social alienation, terror, ill at ease,
Constant worries, babies, children.

1.   The child.
2.   The life and soul of the party.
3.   Weight of the world on my shoulders.
      (The three main aspects of her which her husband 'had seen'.)

All of these – he said – can be divided and subdivided.

But what did it all mean, and who, I could not help wondering, was this 'he' who seemed to know so much about the structure of her personality? Cordelia, however, was quite rightly overwhelmed by it all, and hence I advised her to seek admission, arguing the point that for a while she might need a different kind of care. But yet again she insisted that it should be left to be her decision, and full of distress she continued exploring the meaning and various functions of these parts – a truly immense task, as the following excerpt from her diary clearly illustrates:

> I am caught within such a muddle. I do not know whether I am coming or going.
> In a desperate effort to hold on to something, I think I delude myself – split.
> One person within me conveys to the other that she should do something, and at the same time conveys on another level that she should not, or that she should do something else incompatible with it. Then another person or child forbids her to get out of the situation, or dissolves it by commenting on it. I therefore cannot make a move without catastrophe. This complicated mess seems to arise because I was always given false/true or double messages: 'Will you do something for me/don't come near me to do it.' I, having read the message 'don't come near me', am then told 'I am too mad, or too ill, to be near anyone anyway'.

By now it was Christmas. Cordelia coped with the festivities and the break in her therapy, by distributing her sadness and pain around various parts. Obviously this was something she had done all her life, but until now had not been aware of doing so. Although yet again this technique made her feel unreal and 'inclined to do strange things'. As we later discovered, the deceptive part, especially, had been very active over Christmas, and had convinced Cordelia that she had travelled forwards into the future, and that, therefore, it was best if she forgot all about the clinic and me! Cordelia subsequently had phoned the clinic in order to discover whether I was still working there, and as a result, her husband, who heard her making the call, quite rightly had insisted that Cordelia should seek in-patient care.

In the meantime, I had of course discussed the boundary issue and recent developments with Dr C, and we had concluded that it would indeed be counter-productive to insist on rigid application of the set boundaries. We agreed that, as we expected Cordelia to change and adapt, we equally needed to be able to review our stance when required. In due course Dr C also explained to concerned members of staff that our decision to admit Cordelia and explore the recent events would not undermine the validity of the boundaries, since this admission would be a planned event, rather than a fight or flight reaction.

Naturally, Cordelia's husband was quite relieved, that his wife would at last be looked after, though unfortunately, the clinic at the time was quite full and Cordelia would have to wait until a bed became available. I thus proposed that in the meantime we would continue on a sessional basis and begin to allow each of these alter egos to be identified. I also suggested that should long-term in-patient care be required but not be feasible due to financial constraints, that we should increase therapy to five times a week, in order to monitor the frequent switching from one part to another, which now seemed to take place so regularly. (Or maybe Cordelia was simply allowing us now, to see it happening?)

However, I also pointed out that this way of working, would only be safe enough provided that Cordelia was prepared to involve her husband more and explain to him the reasons for her distress. At first, Cordelia was quite understandably reluctant to share more details with her husband. Not only because her husband had not been feeling too good himself (his own GP had suggested counselling for him), but also because, as Cordelia has explained elsewhere, when she originally met her husband, she placed all the various parts inside her, in order to be able to have as normal a life as possible and not scare him away. To be asked to reveal these parts to him now, to trust him with her secrets, was a major decision. Yet, having come this far, rather than wait for a bed Cordelia felt she wanted to go ahead and discover as much as she could.

During the following week, Cordelia actually managed to draw up a hierarchy tree of those parts who had been willing to reveal themselves so far, though as yet, she felt able to identify them only in terms of their respective functions. As Cordelia told me, there appeared to be the following:

1. A willing child,
2. A rejected child,
3. A withdrawn child,
4. A mad, ill child.

Yet others were:

5. Mischievous
6. Frightened
7. Anxious
8. Misunderstood
9. Paranoid/mistrusting
10. Compliant – copies acceptable behaviour

11. Demon/revenge
12. Pretending
13. Loving/caring
14. Puppet
15. Numb
16. Analytical thinker
17. Doubting
18. Grandiose

A week later, however, Cordelia would feel able to give them their proper names. At last, Cordelia confessed, they were out in the open – '*the mists of her own making*' were beginning to disperse, and one by one 'the children' would attempt to tell their sad tales. Before I describe the process which facilitated such disclosure, like Cordelia, I want to explore relationships.

Frieda

To Frieda before Therapy

I have not seen
I have not known
When morning breaks across the sea
And hungry seagulls cry,
I have not felt the summer's gentle breeze
A frozen embryo in a bowl of lies

After Therapy as Frieda Leaves

I shall not see
I shall not beauty know
Without remembering what in my heart I hold,
These things I keep, O' wings unfold
As you, your splendid way do go.

From a secure child's view point, a real mother cares when no one else does. A mother cares when you are completely unbearable and as horrible as you know how to be. She cares when you are angry, sad and very jealous; when you want your mother all to yourself; when you want her love and you want to be the most special person in her life. She cares when you can't bear her to leave you. A therapist can't be a mother. But the pain I felt as an adult, in my relationship with my therapist, was because I had engaged in an intense transference, transference meaning (according to Freud) a displacement on to the therapist of feelings, ideas which derive from the introjected figures acquired in the patient's past life. The therapist's detachment creates a new problem, where the patient behaves as though the therapist were a parent or brother. The conflict is worked through, by unconscious patterns becoming conscious to the patient.

I felt like the child who had never had a mother's love, whose mother was cruelly abusive and yet demanded a lot, but after meeting Frieda, I was experiencing a taste of what vaguely resembled the possible fulfilment of the need for mother's love I had had all my life. Frieda gave me time, she listened and worked with what she heard and perceived as a rational adult who had worked as a professional therapist for a number of years. I fully understood that this was a therapeutic relationship that should resemble nothing more than a process of discovering myself with a genuine empathic therapist. The child within me had suffered severe deprivation and damage. She needed to express her childlike absolute love and wanted desperately to receive love, before she could begin to grow into a balanced, emotional mature adult.

My child within was very young when I first met Frieda. The transference was immediate and it grew into a painful, very intense, emotional bonding, but sometimes, a warm loving diversion from the reality of my life. I think it was so spontaneous because I felt like a baby exhausted from screaming, picked up from a soaking wet and dirty cradle, who suddenly felt the possibility of being cared for, although I didn't know what was wrong, or what was happening. Frieda was the first person in my life I really connected with emotionally, certainly the first woman, a very necessary process for any child.

The relationship was a battlefield in which I fought my therapist as if my life depended on it, trying to win her over; she remained resolute and strong throughout, often appearing cruel, cold and dismissive. I do not think Dr M or Frieda realised that I had only regressed – or more precisely – had only matured as far as babyhood in the two years with the unqualified therapist, and that I was indeed emotionally that young when first in their care. Dr C, when he took over my case, saw exactly how young I was emotionally, although by then, I had moved on a little; no one seemed aware that I was a more independent person before I saw the unqualified therapist and that I had a co-dependent relationship with my husband. I was crying out for someone or something, I didn't know what, to fill the empty void of pain, that had been so stirred up by the previous therapy. And yet, at the end of any therapy session, Frieda always seemed to change from the therapist who held me so tightly to someone quite different. Her enormous hug then never made me feel better. I either longed for more or I found her touch threatening. Every time, as the end of my therapy time approached, she changed into someone cold and hard who I was afraid of but wanted to please in case she dropped me completely, which I expected to happen. I reasoned that, like my mother, a bad therapist was better than no one.

There was a period of time when I was constantly picking up vibes that Frieda did not want to be my therapist. She deliberately gave away my appointment on one occasion, for which she later apologised, but I felt for a long time that in some way I had forced her into being my therapist. I had come to terms with the fact that, at one stage, she did feel reluctant to go on for all sorts of reasons. Some I have already mentioned earlier in the book, such as the threat of closure of the clinic. One reason, which Frieda later on told me herself, was because she felt I had chosen her, and she preferred to do the choosing and be in control.

Nonetheless, I battled on regardless, because my need was so great. Frieda was just as much of an enormous challenge for me as I was for her, when she finally decided I was worth it. Again, a bit like with my mother, I battled on, always hoping that one day I would make her love me.

I felt like an unwanted patient, as well as an unwanted child. I needed much more help and much more love than I could get from anyone – but the more I felt pushed away by Frieda, the harder I clung. The more I wanted, the less I got, and it constantly felt as if I was clinging to a cliff edge by my hands, with my feet desperate to find a firm, secure foothold. Then Frieda stamped down hard on my fingers. Whether she meant to hurt or not, it hurt like hell, and I would fall into the abyss and dissociate, because it was too much to tolerate and it was an alternative to suicide. If I hadn't learnt to dissociate as a child, and was still able to do so as an adult, I would have succeeded in an attempt to kill myself at some stage. Dissociating kept me alive.

For a long time, neither Frieda or the consultant or myself knew which way to turn. I seemed to go round and round in circles. I realised I was presenting too much of a problem. I did not have the ego strength and development to always take the struggles and concepts of psychotherapy. I had violently angry outbursts when pushed too far. I wrote angry letters, almost wanting Frieda to reject me, yet not wanting her to at the same time. But she decided to stay with me for as long as she could, for which I will be eternally grateful.

After Dr C and Frieda worked together with stricter boundaries enforced, I began slowly to trust more. Although the boundaries seemed cruel, it strangely began to feel more secure. However, I kicked against them time and time again. I pleaded with Frieda to see me when I was once an in-patient in crisis because I felt so desperate, but she resisted. I remember this with enormous pain. Others didn't have these boundaries, and to me it all seemed so unfair. I resented, even hated, those who had therapy with her when I couldn't. I was intensely jealous of others who were her patients; I wanted her all to myself. All feelings were denied me as a child. Hence, I did not understand the feelings of jealousy, or Frieda telling me to replace it with another feeling. Apart from the angry letters, pleading letters, there were many expressing my love for her. Most were child-like and too personal to put into print, some I was never able to let her see. Many were left on the windscreen of her car, although the letters amounted to more than two hundred in the five years and six months of my therapy.

1995, as you will see later, was a year of amazing discovery for both Frieda and myself, and in that year I wrote a little more maturely about my feelings for her, sometimes in poetry or prose. I quote now extracts from some of my writings, which I called 'Love for my Therapist.

I never know what will happen next, it seems like one big struggle to keep going. I love you with all my heart and soul, yet that love has to be kept under strict control. You cannot be mine, yet I ache for your love and to have you in my life forever. I can't see very far ahead, maybe that's just as well; if I knew what was coming, it would change too much in the present. You have helped me put one step in front of the other, amazingly I follow your lead. You have come with me on the most painful journey of my life. I thank you for all you have done for me. Thank you for what you are, for being the strong ground in which I saw my true self and who I am. Please help me gain the courage to live your freedom, to think for myself, to strike out into the unknown, confident, although I don't know the way.

When I'm feeling unsure in my first steps, let me take your hand in my imagination. I don't feel quite ready yet but my goal is to seek the wide-open spaces of liberty when all restraints are gone and I can grow.

You are going to leave me for ever. My anger with you is now really fear, I rant and rave but you just sit there and raise no objection, perhaps you haven't heard?

The shock, the truth, now sink in, no love returned, no contact, nothing certain except the loss. Pain and protest rise in my throat, I choke, become breathless, full of fear, suspense and panic, that horrible hollowness, as I remember my hopes and dreams of what might have been. When you have gone, I will nowhere find your face, your voice, your touch; how can I face the loneliness of your absence for ever, when one day, one week, one month seems like the same thing? Through my deep anguish and my doubt, I reach out to you, before you go, I look into your eyes and we meet again. I find comfort in that you know me better than myself. One day I shall stand in peace.

In the same year, Frieda asked me to write a letter to my dead mother and tell her exactly how I felt about her and my life. It helps to explain the relationship between Frieda and myself, as I experienced it. What follows is part of the letter to my mother, 5 November 1995.

Mother,

Nothing would delight me more than if I could write a letter to you full of gratitude and loving memories. I wish I could tell you how much I miss you, how much I miss the closeness, the sharing and caring of a thoroughly dependable, faithful, loving mother. No relationship is more important than that of mother and child.

How my heart aches when I hear my friends talk about their mothers with affection and sadness at their losses. My sadness is deeply painful, I had no real mother, no unconditional love. I was cruelly deprived of everything I needed to be secure and stable, to grow to maturity valuing who I am. Instead, I was viciously abused. I cannot share in my friend's conversations. I cannot say anything, because in the world I walk in, mothers are good and well-intentioned, not perfect, because no mother is. I cannot tell the truth, no one would believe me, because in spite of everything, I have made a reasonable impression on those I meet in my world; no one would know the truth, I've hidden it all so well.

My grief and pain is so well suppressed, most of the time, that the occasional outburst of unreasonable behaviour shocks even my therapist. She would not believe what I hold inside sometimes, and I know she would leave me if I let it all out. I would like to be able to scream at you, and sometimes at her too. I've never known anyone, certainly no female, who would go that extra mile for me, who would forgive me anything, who would love me, even when I am objectionable and unreasonable – this is never to be an experience of mine but it's one I long for.

Yes, Mother, I have a therapist, with whom I work through the pain and the damage you and my father have caused me. In fact, I've had to engage in long-term therapy to try and resolve all this pain, anger and damage that my appalling childhood and adolescence caused me.

Consequently, I have been forced to trust and love very deeply, someone who was a total stranger, someone I met in a psychiatric clinic. You wouldn't understand this but I love this lady, my therapist, so intensely it is sometimes embarrassing as well as totally consuming.

This is one of those times, Mother – if you had been able to love me and allowed me to love you, respond to you, connect with you, I would never have had such an intense need.

My therapist, whom I love as if my life depended on it, like you, cannot return my love, so the heartache of the past is resurrected. This is cruel to the extreme, because the heartache I experienced as a child was of the most traumatic and damaging kind.

My therapist doesn't intentionally abuse me. But when she tells me she cannot return my love, or she cannot be part of my life, the pain surges through me, I go cold inside and shake. My legs feel achy and wobbly, my heart races, my head spins, I feel sick and don't know where to go or what to do. This is how you made me feel, but I learnt not to feel, in order to survive.

My therapist thinks it is good for me to hear the truth; truth is better than lies but it frightens me so much I want to die. The truth is, she does not return my love and never will, she cannot ever be part of my life, and when she moves to Ireland, she will never think of me or ever want to see me again. She loves reinforcing this truth, in case I have a grain of hope that it might one day be different. Why do I waste my precious, locked-away feelings on someone who cannot appreciate them or value them, or even want them? It makes me feel my love is not good enough, or I am completely unlovable. All this is your fault, Mother. It used to make me cling more, and sometimes still does. At present I just want to run away from those who cannot love me.

This is, of course, exactly how you made me feel. I wasted my love on you, as I am wasting my love on my therapist. I cannot change my heart; I am locked into this unfruitful one-sided love affair with my therapist. This love affair is totally degrading and leaves me painfully powerless in an unresolvable situation, and it's all because of you. I needed so much that longed-for unconditional love and to express child-like, absolute love. You made absolutely certain that I grew up the most damaged person from the most deprived childhood anybody has ever heard of or read about. Unbelievable how you covered up such a multitude of badness and madness. The truth is out, Mother, I've told my therapist and my husband and I think they believe me. I am going to write a book, to state the truth in black and white for all the world to read, if they want to...

I felt like running away from Frieda many times, but as I did with my mother, I always came back. I sometimes needed to avoid her but needed to see her at the same time. The harder I tried to run away, the more I was pulled back towards her she was like a gigantic magnet. As I felt her determination to help me, so I became less afraid to remember; the trouble was, I had no solid foundation on which to begin recovering or growing to wholeness or maturity.

I had to start from the very beginning and intuitively I knew this, but someone had to believe in me wholeheartedly, and eventually Frieda took that challenge, risky though it was, and I knew others were not convinced she was doing the right thing. Some staff at the clinic told me that I should not love my therapist. There is no should about it; I did because I needed to, I did what I had to to reach wholeness, my unconscious directed the process most amazingly. My unconscious produced and directed the drama, and has been the artist who painted the picture all the way through. As for the actual ending of my therapy, I feel that the following poem I wrote at the time will speak volumes (Frieda left end of May 1996).

May is Here

I wait now in inconsolable dread
To hear the cuckoo cry. Knowing that spring has gone
And May is here.
Not even bluebells in the wood
Can comfort such grief
Tears might wash away the past
But May is here.

In fact, there was a lot of work to cram into the last weeks before Frieda left. I had been very seriously physically ill at the beginning of 1996 and although I did return to therapy as soon as I could, I was too weak to concentrate and work to a proper ending. My therapy had to be rushed and felt unfinished, and because it was ending, it had to reduce fairly quickly. This illness and the major surgery the previous year were in their way very symbolic, since they actually engineered my escape from my entrancing transference spell, which will be explained in a later section of the book.

Of course, this does not mean to say that in the breaking of the transference, in the struggle to let go, I suddenly stopped loving Frieda. I will always respect and love her, she will always be special – but the intensity, the awful wrenching pain and struggle has abated. Indeed, I wrote the following on 3 January 1997, seven months after Frieda left the clinic. She had seen me once, at this stage, on a return visit for Christmas.

Take away the intensity of the transference, I am left with the raw reality and sadness of my life. I have been through my life in a world of make-believe in order to cover up the truth. The transference felt like the only thing in my life that was real, whether it felt good or bad.

In some ways the transference was like a diversion from the complete horror and awfulness of my life, and now I feel only the cold penetrating pain of the truth as I stand alone.

The smoke screen has lifted, I know for sure I am out of the goldfish bowl in every sense, and as I fully draw back the curtains, I can see the complete and whole canvas of the most appalling agonising drama ever painted – that drama is my life. It's not a story, it's not about any little girl or any woman, it's about me, and I am writing it completely for the very first time.

I own it unashamedly, no one can take it away, it's mine for ever, but the stark cold reality penetrates every part of my being that feels more alone than I have ever felt. Alone but so much more able to cope with these feelings, because I know who I am and I can feel love even for myself.

I am now a woman who will always remember with gratitude the time, patience and commitment Frieda gave, to help me towards being born again, to a life worth waiting for. This sort of therapist's love is tough love, and got me well – I had to give up the search for mother love. Transference is something we all do, all of the time, quite unconsciously with our relationships, but apart from not being aware of it, it would hopefully never be on this kind of scale. It has been for me the most necessary, the most painful yet rewarding journey I have ever had or will ever have again.

Objects Relationships

Some time ago, I read a research report which suggested that the most important aspect of any therapeutic journey is the relationship between therapist and patient, irrespective of technique or method used. Although I would agree with this, like most research summaries this statement makes it all sound so very easy and straightforward, as though all you need do is to engage in a relationship and a positive outcome is assured! But, as Cordelia in the previous chapter so graphically depicted, a relationship with a therapist can be full of traps and diversions which can so easily ensnare both.

Truly, a patient and therapist can go round and round in circles, sometimes for years on end. Even those alliances which appear so wonderful and healthy on the surface can nevertheless mean that the patient is simply stuck, either by pleasing the therapist, always guessing the right response, or anticipating the therapist's every move. As a result, however, the patient is unable to grow and achieve true independence, and like a mother caught in a symbiotic relationship with a child, the therapist and patient may be bound together, literally for better or worse, for richer and usually poorer, since such therapy can be addictive and hence comes at a costly price. Indeed, as Cordelia has explained, the relationship with a therapist can be like a 'gigantic magnet'

When Cordelia in fact wrote those words, she was no longer my patient. Therapy had ended seven months prior, although she continued to see her consultant, Dr C, once a fortnight. At first, the loss of her therapist had caused, as Cordelia had feared, 'inconsolable dread'. But gradually, as she mourned my loss and continued writing the story of her life, Cordelia let go of me, let go of the substitute mother and the transference, and began to relate to me as an ex-therapist – someone who would answer her letters and share her opinions and theories, someone who would visit Cordelia and her husband to discuss details of the book, someone who was very different from her therapist, yet was the same person.

Whereas before, the relationship with her therapist had been all consuming, a true re-enactment of the past, slowly it shifted to one of mutuality, though we both agreed that the relationship with an ex-therapist would always be unlike any other she could have, such as with a friend or with a colleague. Nonetheless, Cordelia was quite clear that the relationship today was far preferable to how it had been.

As I have described before, I believe that Cordelia's therapy achieved a positive outcome because certain rules were strictly reinforced, whilst others were in fact broken. Maintaining contact after therapy ended was one of those rules which were broken. I must admit that, before I agreed that Cordelia could write to me in Ireland, I checked out the usual position, wishing to ensure that my rebellious decision (I had already decided to say yes) would not cause Cordelia untold harm. To my relief, I subsequently also discovered that other colleagues usually replied when patients wrote to them, which in turn of course reinforced my decision to stay in touch.

I could have argued that maintaining contact was necessary when we intended to collaborate on writing a book. But that would not have been totally accurate, for I genuinely wanted to keep in touch with Cordelia, if she herself so wished. Besides, I simply had a feeling that it was right to do so. Indeed, as time progressed, I need not have worried, because once again it would seem, that the conventional rules in this therapy would not have been a reliable guide anyway, and instead of causing harm, the opposite appears to have happened. As a result of staying in touch, and the more her therapist became distant and the ex-therapist remained, the more Cordelia has been able to integrate the good and the bad parts of me, helping her to relate to me as a whole person who continuous to exist even though Cordelia was no longer able to see me every day. Previously, as Cordelia has described, unless she could physically see me, she tended to believe that I had died. In turn of course, Cordelia has equally grown to accept more and more that she too is 'real' and is 'one person with many parts', as indeed we all are.

Breaking the rules thus need not always be disastrous. This, however, should not be read as meaning that all rules can be done away with. Therapy, as I described earlier, can be a precarious adventure, and therefore, both parties need the security rules can provide. But I am inclined to agree with Nini Hermann (1988, p.160), who wrote that the concepts we as therapists are taught, 'can only serve as scaffolding for our own observations and working creativity'. Sometimes I feel we simply need to take risks and follow our intuitions about what is right for a certain patient.

When in due course Cordelia gave me the previous chapter to read through, I could not help but wonder about the many different aspects involved which have gone into the making of this therapeutic relationship. Was it, I queried, my training as a dramatherapist, as a health psychologist, the years of clinical experience, my own therapy and my own relationship with my parents, siblings, husband and children? Was it the relationships I had with my colleagues, my supervisor, other patients, or Cordelia herself? The more I explored relationships, the more I discovered that it was all of these and others beside. When I previously wrote that 'nothing so far in my career had prepared me for this', this was not exactly true. Not only, had I encountered Multiple Personality Disorder before but NLP (Neuro Linguistic Programming) had also taught me how to work with parts. What's more, I was equally no stranger to the many diverse and wondrous ways, in which the mind learns to cope with utter powerlessness and severe trauma, or any trauma for that matter.

I was first introduced to this cornucopia of imaginative solutions when I worked in a large Victorian mental hospital, not long before they were bulldozed flat and replaced with castles in the air: the so-called community homes. Some of the patients at that time had been in this lunatic asylum (as the bronze plague by the front door used to call it), for fifty years or more and lived there quite comfortably in their own hierarchy, their own routines, and of course in their own inner world. Now and then, some would share this inner world with me, and time and time again I would be surprised at the inventive and creative ways in which they explained and coped with their predicaments and amazing life events. I will always remember, and still feel humble when I think about, the Polish lady who had survived Hitler's concentration camps by believing that God had forbidden her to feel pain. Nor will I forget the once boisterous, sensitive lad from the West End – a patient for fifty long years – who explained to me that he initially fought with another youth and smashed his skull with a hammer, because he had been possessed by an evil spirit who had invaded his brain which had transferred itself via his hands one day whilst he was practising healing.

Looking back on those days, I can now see how they shaped me to keep an open mind and taught me to value any disclosure. On the face of it, these tales could of course so easily be dismissed as so much nonsense or just madness. Yet when you consider them in the context of their lives, it becomes obvious that initially they served a real purpose and represented a means to survive, or a means to rise above the situation, and with time simply became part of their inner belief system. In essence, these explanations were no more far-fetched than the writings of many authors who project their own fears and unconscious wishes into imaginary characters who engage in battle with weird and wonderful foe and friend alike. Of course, the significant difference was that my patients of old truly believed every word! But then, if your very survival depended on not feeling pain, you would probably believe it too.

Although at first Cordelia's imaginary friend took me by surprise, the fleeting relationships I had with those long-term patients had nevertheless equipped me to feel at ease about entering the world of another and join his or her frame of reference, whilst at the same time staying firmly anchored in my own.

As such, I was quite charged, you could say, to try and discover the exact meaning behind Cordelia's imaginary friend. Yet when I approached others for information and feedback, my energies were soon flattened. For instance, when I subsequently asked one of the consultants if he had ever experienced one of his patients telling him that she had an imaginary friend. His first reaction was quite logically to ask me how old this patient was. But when I replied that she was an adult woman about my age, his immediate hearty laugh and response was to declare her 'crackers, barking', and he advised me to forget it and send her home.

From then on, quite often when I discussed my observations about this remarkable therapy with different colleagues, I would either meet this kind of humorous response, or else be told in no uncertain way that the patient was taking me for a ride. The concept of multiple personalities it seemed was for some indeed too far-fetched. Thus all too soon I realised that I would be quite alone with this therapeutic encounter, and that somehow I would have to learn to navigate around a number of misgivings and considerable reservations. First of all, when I approached Dr C about the possible diagnostic implications of the growing number of revelations Cordelia was now sharing with me, he passionately remarked, 'As you know, Frieda, British psychiatrists on the whole tend not to believe in Multiple Personality Disorder.' Unfortunately, at the time when this concise statement was made, we were both rather busy and were only able to have a brief, snatched meeting between patients and groups. This meant that we of course never fully discussed the implications of Dr C's reply. As such, this apropos observation had the unfavourable result, as far as the multiple aspect was concerned, of creating the impression that I would indeed have to rely upon my own resources and find such a way of working with Cordelia which would ensure a healthy outcome.

Be that as it may, my rather premature conclusions should not be read as meaning that I did not receive ample support either from Dr C or other members of staff. Certainly, any time I was stuck or had a problem, I knew that I would always be able to seek out my colleagues for guidance or a listening ear. Which is why the important role of the staff structure within the clinic at that time and its significance in Cordelia's therapy will be explored more fully in my next chapter. In fact, since then, Dr C has written to me explaining the different way in which British psychiatrists tend to conceptualise this 'very real phenomenon', and with his permission, I have decided to quote his words in full.

Most psychiatrists use the conceptualisation of 'dissociation'. Thus a child dissociates easily in all sorts of circumstances. Children always will survive somehow, sometimes by using a dissociative mechanism of bringing in other personalities to cope with the situation that they are in. Under stress, either then or later in life, these coping strategies using a different personality type may occur involuntarily and unconsciously. This will occur in a range of stressful situations, and where resonances of previous experience occur. Thus, the different personalities that are exhibited, would be seen by those of us in the UK who use this model, as being real; not a fabrication, but as a real way of coping, which reflects one part of the person's mental make up. After all, what is personality? The only definition which makes sense to me, is that it is the product of a person's behaviours persisting over time. Cordelia's 'personalities' were definitely real, as they were consistent over a period of time and were a real reflection of her. The fact that I and many of my colleagues do not choose to use the term Multiple Personality Disorder does not mean, that we do not believe our patients or do not have an interest in the deeper levels of psychic functioning of our patients, but that we feel that in labelling in this way, something is lost by the risk of losing the basic truth that all of the persisting forms of behaviour belong to the one real person who has created them.

As it turned out, despite our initial lack of discussion, we both approached Cordelia's personalities from the same perspective anyway. Throughout her therapy, in fact, I never used the label of *multiple personality* and certainly never reinforced the *disorder* aspect. On the contrary, I was always quite convinced that it could all be broken down to normal mechanisms, which sadly enough, Cordelia had needed to employ in extreme ways. Taken literally, Cordelia was of course not a multiple personality. One person cannot become two or three, let alone four or more. But, as Cordelia's therapy would reveal, one person can most certainly have a divided mind and as such, employ different as-if personalities; become each one as and when required, and switch from one to the other, apparently without consciously registering the fact that he or she has done so.

Indeed, as I wrote in my reply to Dr C, I most certainly agreed with him that labelling a person as a multiple can side-track the truth that the personalities are after all just survival creations of a child's mind. Only towards the end of her therapy, when Cordelia had fully accepted that each and every person was a part of herself, that they were all parts of the one personality, did we begin using terms such as multiple personalities.

Regretfully, however, as I explained earlier, at the time when Cordelia first revealed any of this to me, we never got around to dissecting Dr C's reply to my diagnostic questions, and as such his correct observation only served to increase my sense of bewilderment and sense of isolation. For sure I did know that in Britain a diagnosis of MPD was frowned upon.

'Not a single unequivocal case of multiple personality existed in the UK literature,' asserted Aldridge-Morris (1989, p.108). Yet here I was being told by my patient that she had several children within. Each with a different name and demeanour. Great, I remember thinking at the time, but what do I do, and how do I continue working with Cordelia? I cannot tell her that in Britain, the psychiatrists do not believe in her condition! Secondly, the clinic at that time seemed to have had its fair share of admissions who had indeed been diagnosed by their respective counsellors and psychologists as 'multiples'. This of course tended to fuel those who believed that the condition was iatrogenic: caused by the therapeutic relationship and no more than an elaborate collaboration between the therapist and the patient. The first one, the therapists, so the comments rang, were obviously 'hooked on this interesting phenomenon', whereas the second one, the patients, were thereby conveniently 'guaranteed long-term care'. Nor were they the only voices to raise objections, for similar criticism could be found in varied books and articles. (See Fahy, 1988, Hilgard, 1988, Merskey, 1992, and Piper, 1994.)

Even today, despite the fact that some excellent books have been written about accurate diagnosis and succinct treatment of MPD, the same dismissive comments are still being printed, regardless: 'Many critics have persuasively argued that the phenomenon of multiple personality is almost invariably an artifact of therapy, produced by the therapist's expectations and the suggestible, vulnerable, attention-seeking client.' Although the author of this observation, Mark Pendergast, writing in *Victims of Memory* (1998, p.137), pointed out that establishing whether there 'have been instances of true MPD' was in fact outside the scope of his particular book! Equally at that time, False Memory Syndrome (FMS), and its controversial companion, Satanic Rituals, had begun to be quite newsworthy, and many new cases were regularly dramatised in the newspapers, thus adding their pennyworth to the mixture of disbelief (Merskey, 1995, Spiegel & Scheflin, 1994).

Then again, an earlier letter written by Cordelia in March 1992 also sprang to mind, in which she catalogued a list of character defects and personality traits, concluding that she was untreatable and wondering if I had considered that I might simply be wasting my time! All this was so much fuel to the fire which was quickly burning up my erstwhile confidence.

Dear Frieda,

I have a great instability of personality organisation. I have polarised relationships into idealised or abusive. I have primitive defences, a lot of splitting and projection. Instability of self-image, e.g. bored, empty. I have great difficulty tolerating aloneness. I have mood shifts from anger and aggression to anxiety and sadness, impulsivity and explosiveness. I can be self-damaging, and the enormous stress I am experiencing at the moment leads, as before, to loss of contact through numbness and depersonalisation. This I feel is due to long-term emotional neglect and abandonment, and this is the way I construct an escape from it. This situation in a client or patient cannot be cured, so you may be wasting your time, have you thought about that?

Moreover, those colleagues who did support me were nevertheless cautious, since some of the more popular literature on MPD available at the time tended to depict a rather involved therapeutic alliance which had a habit of becoming all-enveloping. In one book for instance: *The Flock*, (Casey & Wilson, 1993), the therapist had clearly taken reparenting to extremes and had taken the patient home with her, with the intention of providing her with a substitute family. I recall how one of my colleagues advised me to read this particular book, since it clearly depicted 'how not to conduct therapy with someone who claims to be a multiple personality'. Although that particular therapy in fact seemed to have ended quite successfully. Even breaking such rules did not necessarily mean dire consequences it seemed. Nevertheless, I heeded my colleague's advice, read the book, and duly took note on how to avoid getting overwhelmed.

(See also: *Prism*, (Bliss & Bliss, 1985), *When Rabbit Howls*, (Chase, 1989), *René*, (Confer & Ables, 1983), *The Five of Me*, (Hawksworth & Schwarz, 1977), *The Minds of Billy Milligan*, (Keyes, 1995), *The Final Face of Eve*, (Lancaster, 1958), *Through Divided Minds*, (Mayer, 1992), *Christine Beauchamp*, (Prince, 1906), *Sybil*, (Schreiber, 1974,) *I'm Eve*, (Sizemore, 1977), and *The Three Faces of Eve*, (Thigpen & Cleckley 1957).

Yet, notwithstanding the support I did receive, my predicament was as I had feared: I was on my own. I would indeed, have to find my own way of working with Cordelia's dramatic disclosures, for as far as I was aware, none of my past or current colleagues, save one, had ever worked with Multiple Personality Disorder. What's more, this one colleague, the only consultant in the clinic who was engaged in working with MPD, had regretfully confessed to me that he too was in fact just learning as he went along, since it was all quite new to him also. Besides, his main method of working was using hypnosis and ideo motor signalling (posing questions and asking the patient to lift up a finger to indicate a yes or no reply), thus eliciting a response from the various personalities in turn, which I did not feel qualified to do, even though I had been trained in Ericksonian hypnosis.

However, in retrospect, I do owe him a debt of gratitude. Certainly, for sharing his extensive knowledge of hypnosis with me but also for the many discussions we did have, which clearly have helped me to avoid falling into certain traps, such as getting caught up in the novelty of it all, or unintentionally colluding with the patient's frame of reference, thereby giving each personality due substance and an added reason not to integrate and give up believing that each personality was separate and therefore very real. Likewise, the response from my supervisor, who confirmed that in his long outstanding career he had never encountered MPD and hence preferred to talk in terms of depersonalisation or a hysterical reaction etc., has ensured that I kept my feet firmly on the ground. Even though he could not really help me with the day to day management of Cordelia's chaos. His willingness to listen to my eager theories and his cautious yet open-minded scepticism, ensured that I did not get caught up in making each personality even more real than they already were to Cordelia. Something Cordelia later on divulged that she would like to have experienced, meaning that I would have got to know each personality in depth as a real person, rather than as an *as-if* person. Moreover, since leaving the clinic I have been duly encouraged by former colleagues to formulate my wild thoughts and commit them to paper. Their helpful comments and morale boosting assistance – such as sharing their own theories with me, sending me articles or precious books to read etc. – have made the decision to stick my neck out and risk being challenged by the experts (as Cordelia so aptly warned me), a lot easier.

But at the time, I don't mind admitting it, I felt quite lost. Where indeed was I going to find the necessary guidelines to understand this phenomenon of MPD? Nothing can be so daunting to a patient, I feared, as a therapist/practitioner who does not know what to do next. Realistically, it would of course just be part and parcel of our humanness. In my own days as a patient (as part of my training as a dramatherapist), I well remembered that sinking feeling when I realised that one of my tutors did not know what to do with a particular student's reluctance to disclose, and hence proceeded to cover up her own distress with an aggressive exposure of her student's pain. I recall thinking, 'Far better if she had just left her alone!' But I could not really just leave Cordelia alone, could I? Somehow, I needed to find the know-how to help her win through. Yet I was also well aware that my anxiety was being generated by a long-standing need to 'come up with the goods', to be useful to others – which incidentally I thought I'd laid to rest. It certainly goes to show that as therapists we constantly need to work and update ourselves as well.

The obvious solution, I reasoned, was knowledge: books, and more books, and I consequently read as many as I could find, though the market at the time was not as great. I also re-read one of the few books published in Britain at the time on MPD. I had discovered it one day whilst browsing in the bookshop of the university where I was studying for my MSc., long before Cordelia had revealed any alters. Even though the title appeared anti MPD, I had been intrigued about its implications. It was *Multiple Personality: An Exercise in Deception*, (Aldridge-Morris, 1989). Who, I wondered, was deceiving who? This book was then newly published and promised an objective look at MPD. The author described how he had been duly concerned that MPD seemed peculiar to America, and virtually non-existent elsewhere in the world. Although three years later, as reported by Pendergast (1998, p.155), when the author subsequently conducted a survey of British psychotherapists treating multiple personality disorder, he recorded a total of 53 cases.

Initially, Aldridge-Morris had send 680 anonymous questionnaires, and had received 140 replies. Fifteen of these had indeed diagnosed and treated patients with MPD; the number of cases being seen by one therapist ranged between one and three, and two therapists who had each seen ten and twenty MPDs respectively.

Pendergast consequently has attributed this marked increase ('this disturbing trend'), to an earlier publication of another British book by Hellmut Karle (1992), which is a detailed account of his treatment of an MPD patient. Although Pendergast described the book as 'remarkably honest', he also called the book a *follie à deux*, in which doctor and patient collude to produce an 'iatrogenic illness', and asserts that it has given a 'tremendous boost to recovered memory, hypnosis, and MPD in England'. If, as Pendergast claims, this book, *The Filthy Lie*, now hailed he writes, by some 'as *proof* of repressed memories and multiple personality disorder', is indeed responsible for the increase in cases of MPD in Britain – rather than insinuating that all those therapists are mere enthusiastic voyeurs who collude with their patients – might this increase in MPD diagnosis not simply be because, in Karle's book and many others like it, patients and therapists alike have taken the risk to expose themselves, risking ridicule, rejection and professional alienation. But in doing so they have encouraged due dialogue and disclosure, which in turn would surely have facilitated learning and encouraged innovative and specific treatment?

It is no easy feat, as I discussed earlier, to approach another with tales of your madness, let alone broadcast it to the world. Certainly, as far as Cordelia is concerned, the constant fear has always been, 'Will I be believed?' Anyone who, likewise, cannot actually provide proof of their memories, proof of their innocence, yet knows that they are, will understand her fear and recognise how such fear can ensure that you do not insist on an accurate diagnosis, seek out the appropriate treatment, or set out to gain due recognition for the years of suffering and confusion.

Contrary to propaganda, a diagnosis of MPD sounds as mad and implausible to the patient as it might seem far-fetched to the consultant, which in turn can of course condemn the patient to inadequate treatments such as drugs, ECT and frequent in-patient care (including admissions for surgery or numerous investigations of mysterious ailments). Certainly, as Cordelia's lengthy therapy has illustrated, sometimes it can take years before the patient will find the necessary courage, or trust an objective listening ear and reveal all. And yet, most MPD patients will subsequently confess that they have been aware since childhood that they 'switch' from one personality to another, 'lose time' (sometimes months, or whole years), can find themselves in strange places and not know how they got there, 'hear voices' commenting on their behaviour and actions, discover clothes in their wardrobe which they do not remember buying, frequently end up wondering why someone will insist that they met before, and constantly 'feel besieged' as they do not remember making certain promises or spending their money etc., and 'have to guess' about their own role and the role of their colleagues, friends and family members. Indeed, most MPD patients will in fact describe themselves as empty, as having only a fleeting sense of self but mostly that they do not know who they are. Hence, they change like chameleons and act out the appropriate role dictated to them by others and circumstances. Yet at the same time, MPD patients will valiantly struggle with life. In my experience, they display a great deal of courage and a remarkable ongoing resolve to rise above their trauma.

Despite the odds, despite life being a perpetual mad guessing game, they know that they are not crazy, and often have quite successful careers and have lasting marriages (though obviously not without due drama and painful reconciliations). They achieve this remarkable Herculean task, because they do not add up these discrepancies, those lapses of continuity of self, of time or memory, since they also firmly believe that the same happens to all people. Until a life event happens, which invariable forces them to take stock! Though even then, there seems to be no guarantee that they will be listened to – as Cordelia's lengthy treatment and different diagnoses have illustrated. Nor, it appears, are they really understood when eventually they do take the risk to reveal their secret world, as Cordelia so aptly described:

> When I approached Dr M about my *deeper level of disturbance* and told him that there were many dead people inside me; that I had a switch inside my head which made me change; could actually feel a click and then knew (though only sometimes) that I was someone else – he listened, but he did not hear!

However, I also did not hear at first. Nor, I believe, would most health professionals have heard anything, other than the appropriate psychiatric labels or analytical jargon: the dead people, clearly, were the introjected parts of all those who were important to her, and now perhaps lost. And as for changing, having a switch inside her head, surely this could be read as an oedipal wish: a desire to be the coveted daughter able to dispatch the mother with the click of a switch and duly take her place, or else usurp the dead father's place and thus secure the love of her mother. All very well, but what about the children Cordelia could actually see and hear, and who told her such devastating stories. And how can one explain the autonomous actions of those introjected parts, which invariably tended to get Cordelia in so much trouble?

But at this point, I need to remind myself that this book is not about whether MPD exists, nor about the validity of repressed memories, but is instead an account of Cordelia's therapy journey and gradual unveiling of her past – though as such, it will of course add its own special ripple to the pond and fuel the debate about recovered memories, which by all accounts appears at present to be splitting the profession of psycho-analysts into two opposing camps, without leaving room for grey areas.

Many times of course, I was asked, 'Do you believe the stories of abuse Cordelia is telling you?' My approach to believing Cordelia has been throughout one which steadfastly has maintained a belief in her integrity to tell me the truth whenever she could, or whenever she would uncover it – even though at times certain details tended to stretch one's imagination, as Cordelia has been able to demonstrate so courageously by recording Gillian's history.

I once read an account of a therapist's appraisal of treatment with sexually abused survivors, in which the author described how he tended to believe 'everything and nothing'. It struck me then as an appropriate way of describing the special kind of believing which is necessary when working with MPD: a certain fluid open mind approach, which instils confidence in the patient, yet allows the therapist to be ever vigilant on her patient's behalf. In fact, I would describe it as a focused and informed believing which takes into account the possibility that certain outrageous anecdotes may have another, far more important meaning – or that the past and present of an MPD patient at times tends to merge and that certain memories may well be mixed up between the real person and a carbon copy personality, and how each personality held only certain fragments of a particular memory, and that, therefore, the narration of a certain memory would be influenced by whichever personality was telling the story.

Even so, those part memories tend to be repeated (by the same personality) in the same manner, with the same content, without any variation, and appeared, quite remarkably, to be very intact (as though they had been carefully wrapped in tissue paper and were preserved in their original state). But they were only a part of the whole picture (a very *real* part nonetheless) and when in due course therapy restored continuity, they sometimes needed to be appraised and updated. For sure, as the reader might remember, those early seeds of doubt sown when we began reading through my therapy notes ensured ongoing scrutiny and appropriate correction as therapy continued, the book progressed, and Cordelia's understanding of her multiple personality system increased. For instance, it was true as I reported earlier on, that Cordelia's third child had died shortly after birth. It was also true that her husband had threatened many times to leave Cordelia. But when we compared our notes and certain chapters of the book, Cordelia was able to correct certain details. For example, it was not true that the baby was a boy and had been full term. The baby was instead a girl born two months premature, as indeed Cordelia had been a premature baby herself. Neither had her husband given the baby Cordelia's name, or had taken care of the cremation. Instead, Cordelia had told the hospital staff to 'dispose of the child', and her husband had never even seen their child. It was equally not true that her husband had 'left, gone away to stay with friends', though he was supposed to be away overnight for a few days in connection with work, and Cordelia had indeed broken a small table and thrown it at him, injuring his knee. But considering the poor state Cordelia was in at the time, her husband had decided to travel back and forth instead.

Obviously Cordelia has been able to correct these two discrepancies quite easily, since she could seek confirmation of her doubts from her husband. She nevertheless always maintained that the way she remembered being left by her husband '*felt* right', but agreed with him that she was probably quite heavily sedated (something she frequently used to do whenever her distress was too great), and hence fast asleep in bed when he returned home in the evening. Whereas in contrast, she is now quite clear that her husband's version of the death of their third child, the fact that he never saw the child, is accurate. However, other variances were not so easily amended, since they could of course not be corroborated, and appeared to be due to the vagaries of the multiple system. For instance, when I read out my therapy notes to Cordelia, describing how her mother cut off her hair during the night, she immediately responded, saying it did not feel accurate but she did not know why. All she could say was that it just felt wrong and that it caused her to feel a sudden immense headache.

Much later, Cordelia would of course understand and come to realise that these immediate curious reservations did make sense, and that her gut feelings had actually been a very powerful tool in her quest for truth. Indeed, when Cordelia eventually remembered that, although her mother 'was always styling, curling, messing about' with Cordelia's hair, her long fair hair had actually been cut off in the asylum on the day she was admitted, Cordelia was able to appreciate not only why she had suddenly experienced such unease when she heard me recounting the wrong version, but also how she could quite easily have mixed up her memories and protagonists – duly taking into account that one of her internal people was modelled on her mother, had the same name as her mother (Bryony), wore the same brown clothes as her mother and behaved like her mother, who in the past had indeed cut off her own hair. In turn, this new information clarified why Cordelia, during an earlier therapy session, had told me that she had always believed that it was Bryony who had been admitted to the asylum. Likewise, in time, the now amended memory of her husband naming their child and giving the dead baby Cordelia's name and arranging its cremation, equally began to make sense when Cordelia was able to confirm that this particular memory had always felt as though it was a dream, but also that it felt as though it had happened for real.

As my therapy notes confirmed, at the time when Cordelia first talked about the death of her child, Cordelia had become preoccupied with her dead twin. Once again, when we take into account the significance of the loss of this twin, (one of the personalities had the same name her mother would have chosen for this child), it is not difficult to appreciate how, in this instance, the past and present could have merged, and how her own premature/dead child could have been confused with the premature/dead child of her mother; the one her mother had wanted to live; the one who was held up as a shining example, and caused her mother often to scold Cordelia with the phrase, 'Why are you not the dead one?' Thereby, of course, burdening Cordelia with a prodigious paradox: only by dying would she ever be able to please her mother, yet if she died (killed herself), she would never know whether her mother might one day love her for real.

Under those conditions, it is easy to understand, how Cordelia frequently toyed with the idea that she was dead or wished to be dead (one part of her certainly always felt as though it was dead), and, that when her own child died, the role of her husband could have been confused with her father's actions at the time when Cordelia herself was born, since he did choose the name of the baby, and almost certainly had been involved in the internment of the dead twin, since her mother was quite ill after Cordelia was born. Then again, Cordelia's dream/reality feeling might just as easily be read as a symbolic communication, since her father had indeed buried Cordelia on her birthday, as the next chapter will reveal.

I am of course well aware that the previous explorations will enable some disbelievers to have a field day, especially those who want to sink recovered memories and MPD without a trace. But rather than dismiss it out of hand, surely these apparent distortions are a valuable tool to help us understand how memory does work, since we still know very little. MPD especially, I feel, offers us a rare opportunity to explore how the mind deals with its memories, and how it manages to keep some events so fresh and clear, as though they only happened yesterday, thereby inflicting such immense pain whenever they are activated, whilst other memories are clearly disposable? Certainly as a therapist, MPD has taught me many valuable lessons and instilled in me a deep respect for memory and its confusing paradox: how it can be so accurate, yet can also so easily mislead, though always with a certain purpose which it seems we seldom can fathom straightaway or usually will bother to try and comprehend. Yet when we consider how an MPD patient compartmentalises her or his memories, dividing them around the system: the beginning of an episode of abuse with one personality, the ending with an other, suddenly the mysterious workings of memory do make sense. Clearly, it becomes a case of why put all your eggs in one basket when distributing them makes it easier to bear? Memory, it seems, aims to please, though unfortunately at a cost, since it often tends to hide the key, the secret password, as well. Thus, leaving the afflicted person with nothing but apparently unrelated snapshots of a memory, quite unable to see the whole film.

I am therefore also quite aware, how devastating it must be to be accused of abusive behaviour on the basis of recovered memories, whether those memories are a lie, a deliberate falsehood or only a part of the picture. Yet sooner or later those lies will out, irrespective of whether this so-called lie had been suggested by an eager therapist or whether the patient gladly embraced it since it so conveniently explained everything, exonerated those dreadful feelings and reaffirmed the more familiar victim role. Again, what MPD has taught me, is that we find it very difficult to ignore that we are lying, or that we are blatantly denying that we are remembering only a select part of the truth, once the True Self is allowed to speak. What's more – and even though the True Self respects that we have a choice to override its voice – it also tends to give us a recognisable sign that we are in fact doing so.

The reader might recall how, earlier on I described how Cordelia complained of a sudden severe headache, when she heard my description of when her mother cut her hair during the night. Of course, this headache could be explained in terms of mere suggestion or a hysterical reaction. We were after all talking about cutting her hair under dramatic circumstances. But from then on, whenever Cordelia was untrue to her Self, the same headache seemed to manifest itself, telling us both that we were off beam with our explanations, or that I had better curb my own imagination and stick to the facts whenever Cordelia had rather eagerly agreed with an interpretation of mine. A very valuable therapy tool indeed! Counter transference, (when the therapist gets the headache) can obviously serve the same purpose!

Thus, as a therapist, MPD certainly taught me to trust the process; learn to be patient and not read a memory before it is completely revealed. A memory, like a negative, needs time to develop, and any pre-emptive interpretation will only blur the real truth. For instance, when I previously wrote how I had suggested that Cordelia had perhaps tampered with the details of the rape (telling the nurses it had taken place at her aunt's by her uncle) because, I surmised, Cordelia was scared to lose me if she told me it had taken place in my own country. This sensible explication was not quite true. This was my explanation, quite a logical deduction, I thought, but wrong. Yes, Cordelia was scared to lose me, scared that I would be disgusted by her, fearful I would not believe her, but the reason she had said at her aunt's by her uncle, only emerged later on, and was quite different from the interpretation I had ascribed to it.

As Cordelia's memories grew clearer and developed fully, 'at her aunt's by her uncle' had in fact been a reference to the abortion which had followed the rape. When Cordelia eventually confessed to her mother that she was pregnant, Cordelia's mother had duly enlisted the help of her family, her brother and his wife, who had rallied round and organised due admission to a private hospital for an abortion, a rather taboo subject at the time, and something Cordelia at that stage of her therapy could only talk about in a roundabout way.

Thus, my eagerness to make sense of it all did not exactly help. A part of Cordelia of course knew the real truth, but did not feel confident enough to assert herself, since its memories were still so fragmented, and hence Cordelia accepted (albeit reluctantly I remember) my logical interpretation. With hindsight, of course, I should have listened, not only to Cordelia's reluctance, but also to my own inner voice, since it clearly told me at the time, that I was making things fit. Likewise, when a part of Cordelia (Martin) drew a graphic picture of a certain memory which had 'occurred many times and involved many people', she (he) said. At first glance, this drawing had all the hallmarks of satanic ritual: a bonfire on the moors, people singing and dancing round the fire, little girls tied naked to stakes, girls being tortured. Indeed, it would have been so easy to interpret this drawing and make it fit preconceived ideas, especially since Cordelia again had a feeling that something was very wrong with this picture and hinted that it contained a dark secret. But by then, I had learned my lessons, and duly waited until the process would enable Cordelia to reveal its true meaning, which in due course she was indeed able to do. Far from being a memory of satanic ritual, this picture simply depicted a child's attempt to reach out to others and speak about her abuse in an indirect way.

As for repressed memories, MPD clearly teaches us that we can most certainly keep unpleasant events out of our conscious mind. Unfortunately, because so many of those memories depict sexual and physical abuse or tell tales of neglect and abandonment, they immediately seem to become 'unbelievable', whereas when someone recovers a memory which throws light on his/her phobia or anxiety, no one makes waves or asserts that the therapist must have suggested it, or obviously just wants to make money out of her client's suffering. Over the years I have worked with a number of people who suddenly, in the course of their therapy, remembered for instance, how they froze as a child when climbing a high tower, or saw themselves shooting a gun which nearly killed someone, or felt again the sensation of powerlessness when a sudden flashback began to make sense of their fear of travelling. All these were memories which the patients had somehow forgotten, yet were traumatic enough to leave a lasting imprint on their behaviour as an adult.

Some would argue that abuse, which tends to be repeated, cannot be forgotten. Familiarity breeds contempt, and in my opinion repetitive actions are in fact easier to forget: one burnt meal may stand out, but if your daily fare was nothing but charcoal offerings, it would just become the norm and thus quite easily pushed into the background, especially so when imagination rallied round and helped to compensate by visualising a wonderful meal instead.

Yet I also believe that we cannot forget a memory completely, though it tends to disguise itself. Memories are not set in stone; details can be vague and distorted, although the principal event of a memory, once the person has allowed themselves to remember it, tends to be preserved in its original state. Cordelia's therapy journey, for example, clearly illustrated how the month of September in itself was a yearly trigger reminding her that she must forget again – that once again those disturbing dreams, those mysterious flashbacks, those feelings of utter despair and seething anger needed to be repressed and delegated around the system. Any such yearly effort, however, tends in itself to be a very effective way of ensuring forgetting, since it is so draining and frequently results in the person becoming depressed or seriously ill. Consequently, help is sought from others who usually will rally round and help the person (to forget) by various means such as holidays, moving house etc., or else assist them to snap out of it by encouraging treatment and directing all their attention and energies solely towards getting well again.

Paradoxically, when a depressed person struggling thus with unconscious memories seeks help from a GP or consultant, the help he or she receives in the form of drugs or hospitalisation, for instance, can often ensure that memories are safely locked away again, only to plague the victim over and over. In my experience, when a patient is prescribed medication only, it is extremely easy for that patient to get stuck in a closed feedback loop of distress – medication – illness – distress, and to shift his/her focus from the cause of his/her distress onto illness; to become a model patient instead, rather than sort out painful memories and feelings.

However, this is not to say that medication, such as antidepressants for instance, do not have a vital role to play. In fact, I am inclined to agree with Dr C, who regards antidepressants as an essential aid and certainly when it concerns a clinical depression, which is after all, he stresses, a chemical illness and entirely different from the emotional feeling of being depressed. As Dr C explained in his subsequent letter to me, antidepressants, in his view, should be regarded as a first aid – the first stage to enable those individuals who have been under considerable strain for a very long time, and have experienced what Dr C termed as loss of – either loss of sleep, appetite, energy, enthusiasm, concentration, memory, confidence, self-esteem, sex drive, enjoyment, patience, feelings, optimism – one could insert almost any word here, he wrote, to become well enough to be accessible for therapy – in order that they may proceed to address the underlying issues.

There are some patients, he asserted, who suffer from an endogenous depression, apparently without a background reason for their depression.

However, he continued, in the majority of people, there are a range of psychodynamic factors at play, which lead to them being under sufficient strain for a sufficient time to become clinically ill. Hence, and although antidepressant are often quite effective in causing resolution of the loss of symptoms, they will return in the future if the psychodynamic issues underpinning the clinical depression are not resolved. Most of his colleagues in fact, according to Dr C, tend to embrace this particular model: antidepressants as first aid – though there are quite a few biological psychiatrists, he added, who minimise or ignore the effect of psychodynamics, and a few who do the same with biological factors. Sadly, as Dr C also described, psychotherapeutic resources within the NHS tend to be rather scarce, and hence the opportunity to explore psychodynamics is rarely available, which is why, he argues, in recent years, there has been an increase in cognitive therapy and short-term, supportive advice giving types of counselling.

Be that as it may, many patients still do not get beyond this first aid. And of course, they were even less likely to do so at the time when Cordelia first approached her GP, and consultant. Medication in those days was generally regarded not as a means to an end, as Dr C phrased it, a way of getting someone to a point where they could indeed begin to address those underlying issues, those buried feelings, those suppressed memories. Instead, medication was often prescribed as the main method of treatment, and any memories which did surface were frequently considered to be counter-productive. Certainly, when we consider the treatment and the long list of drugs Cordelia had been prescribed over the years to help her with the distress of her memories, we can but be amazed that she has in fact remembered anything at all. As Cordelia herself wrote in an earlier chapter, 'I received lots of treatment but no one ever talked or listened to me!'

For sure, ever since the death of her mother, which effectively lifted the lid of the pressure cooker containing Cordelia's memories, Cordelia has been prescribed a most impressive list of medication.

To begin with, she was of course prescribed antidepressants, since she was at that time indeed quite depressed. However, this diagnosis and its allied biological treatment were in fact the beginning of a very slippery slope. Following the diagnosis of clinical depression, a subsequent diagnosis was made of manic depression, and lithium carbonate was given, followed by MAOI, yet another type of antidepressant, topped up by a course of twelve ECTs (Electro Convulsive Therapy). All interventions which were of course guaranteed to disrupt remembering, and duly reinforced Cordelia's 'goldfish bowl' – a condition perhaps akin to the feeling of being behind a 'glass wall', as Peter Breggin in *Toxic Psychiatry* (1993, p.218) has so passionately illustrated, by including the extremely unusual research by three psychiatrists who actually administered lithium carbonate to themselves in doses within the therapeutic range, *for relatively short periods of one to three weeks*:

The subjects often had a feeling of being at a distance from their environment, as if separated from it by a glass wall... Intellectual initiative was diminished, and there was a feeling of lowered ability to concentrate and memorise... The assessment of time was often impaired; it was difficult to decide whether an event had taken place recently or some time ago.

Twelve years and many pills later, as a result of raised levels of prolactin (caused by the antidepressants), Cordelia developed a prolactinoma (a pituitary tumour) which, although of course traumatic and an added stress, could in a perverse kind of way also be considered to have been a so-called blessing in disguise, since it ensured that any psychiatric medication thereafter was kept to a minimum for fear of exacerbating the tumour, thus making psychotherapy a viable option. Nonetheless, since the life event of losing her mother, which opened the door to remembering, Cordelia has been struggling to keep this door open, somehow knowing that she needed to sort out her memories, in order to be whole before she could close the door for good. Medication, in my opinion, has only made this struggle harder, even though at times it has been a necessary and welcome evil. As Cordelia herself told me, 'I believed they gave me all this medication, in order to stop me thinking clearly, and now I depend on them in order to survive. Today, drugs, equals comfort.'

For sure, my erstwhile query when I first read Aldridge-Morris's book, who deceived who, certainly seemed to have taken on extra meaning. Drugs by now clearly represented the care Cordelia never experienced in her childhood and young life, but instead of setting her free and giving her peace of mind, they trapped her in this mad, disjointed world where she had to be many people and the Self was effectively tied up with unresolved vestiges of memories. My initial interest in Aldridge-Morris's book, however, was actually motivated by a recent turn of events, when a patient I had been working with for some time informed me that she had always been aware of having at least seven personalities. As I wrote earlier, I had indeed been exposed to multiple personalities before, so why was I panicking?

As usual, the answers we seek are often already within us. Not only had I at the time, explored with this patient the implications and reasons for her MPD, but she had also felt safe enough to let me see one of her internal children. At first, when this mischievous child suddenly appeared during a therapy session, I had been most concerned that she could get stuck, and that I would not be able to restore the adult personality. But much to my surprise, the patient seemed not at all perturbed and easily complied with my suggestion, when I asked her, to let me talk to the original person again. I certainly learned a valuable lesson that day, and realised that in this kind of therapy, I would be required to be a pupil and teacher at the same time, sometimes leading, but most of the time just walking side by side.

Sadly, I was not able to continue working with this patient. Like many others, she became a victim of the insurance companies' stance on chronic illness, though likewise, she found ways of maintaining her therapy and whenever we subsequently met in the clinic, she has continued to be an eager and informative teacher. Again, I am aware that those critics wishing to insist that MPD is just an artifact of therapy will point out that as a therapist, I was obviously primed to listen out for MPD and hence could quite easily have influenced Cordelia's subsequent revelations, or else would have been fertile ground – eager to receive Cordelia's so-called ingenious manipulations. All I can do is refer the reader back to the earlier chapters, and allow them to speak for themselves.

Thus, re-armed with knowledge, I re-affirmed my trust in Cordelia's integrity, strengthened my belief in her desire to be well, and took my own omnipotent child part firmly by the hand and told it that success or failure was not just up to me, but that Cordelia and I together would find the way to unravel the meaning of this imaginary friend. My one-sided relationship with books of course continued and I was especially relieved to have access to a comprehensive assessment and treatment book (Bloch, 1991), which some friends of mine had sent me from America. I once lent it to Dr C when I could bear to part with it, but I don't think he ever had the time to read it, since I asked for it back quite soon as new twists in Cordelia's treatment occurred. Besides, and though the books were indeed a valuable source of information, I soon realised that I had other, more potent strings to my bow. As a dramatherapist, I was of course familiar with the notion of stepping in and out of role. And more pertinently, I was not scared of facilitating catharsis and abreaction (it never fails to amaze me that someone can work in psychiatry and feel intimidated when a patient displays emotive feelings). Furthermore, had I not also trained to be an Ericksonian hypnosis and NLP practitioner? And was I therefore not familiar with establishing dialogue between patient's parts? And, as a health psychologist, had I not been taught to work systemically: to consider the body as a whole and not confine myself solely to its parts? Indeed, I admonished myself, there really was no need to feel deskilled. All I needed to do was apply and adapt the skills I already possessed. However, Cordelia was pressing me for an explanation. What did it all mean? How could she be so fragmented? Clearly, the picture in the sky of the many pieces of her personality had scared her, even though it had also rekindled hope and the possibility of finding answers to the untold questions which had littered her life.

The answer, I tentatively explained, seemed quite straightforward. Somehow, the original personality, the Self, as and when required, created copies of itself, which it sent out into the world as delegates, thereby leaving the Self secure, in charge, able to observe, mediate, and direct the battle, (just like a beleaguered general safely ensconced behind the lines). And somehow I continued, this normal process seemed to have gone awry with MPD. Did we not all have many parts I argued? Did we not all constantly update or create new parts to help us cope and adjust from student to colleague to partner, parent, grandparent? Could we not all switch from an efficient adult into a sulky child, from a caring partner to a self-righteous manipulator, from a competent mother or father to an insecure daughter or son, and from an assertive colleague to a passive patient? Indeed, did we not all surprise ourselves whenever we behaved out of character or when we discovered parts we did not know we had? Surely we only needed to listen to the language we used and it would confirm that being many parts was a very common feature. I am not myself today; it's the devil in me; it's the other side of me; I've lost myself; a part of me won't cooperate when I am in this frame of mind; let me put my other cap on; I'm not feeling myself; I am a wolf in sheep's clothing; I'll snap out of it; I am very good at fooling myself; I cannot trust that side of me; I'm bound to make a fool of myself, etc., etc.

So, what was the difference between most people and MPDs, insisted Cordelia? For a start, I replied, most people know what their parts get up to. They do not have amnesia. They also have continuity, know exactly when they switched, and that they have switched, i.e. from a careful driver to a manic one, from a thoughtful colleague to an avenging employee – perhaps because they felt unduly criticised, though mostly, they might not always know how or why. In fact, most people are not usually surprised by their parts, they come and go without being noticed unless a certain part behaves in an extreme way, i.e. sudden uncontrollable tempers or impulsive actions. Most people's parts, however, do not act independently, and if they do there is still some awareness that a certain action is against the overall welfare of the person, i.e. dangerous stunts, crimes, overeating, excessive drinking. In fact, most people's parts communicate with each other, debate before taking action and have a constant but silent inner dialogue going on inside their heads, unlike MPDs, who experience their inner conversations as voices belonging to others, as someone constantly butting in or commenting on their behaviour. Most people's parts will usually attempt to work as one. Indeed, most people's parts do not think of themselves as existing for real, as though they are the only one who is alive in the body, or regard the other parts as other people quite separate from themselves. Most people's parts are just that, parts of a whole, together they make a person, one personality, a Self with ego parts, and are not, as appears to be the case in MPD separate, where each part is a whole (false) Other-Self, who in itself, can display different parts.

Some people's parts, however, do appear to be kept separate, though are not considered to be another person. Instead, they are pushed to the peripheries of the personality in order to maintain the illusion of overall health. For example, one only has to think of the SS officers in Auschwitz who could be moved to tears by the haunting music performed by the prisoners' orchestra, only to return to their duties, and proceed to kill indiscriminately. Indeed, we only need to consider the paedophile, the father who can justify his actions: fondling, perverting, abusing, teaching his children about sex and intercourse, and still regard himself as a caring parent, since he would never force a child to have sex.

So, if having a Self in charge of many parts is normal, what went wrong? How did the parts take over, and what happened to the Self? Cordelia demanded to know. Back I went to the books... The answer, I felt, had to lie in the study of children, since Cordelia had so clearly illustrated that the creation of parts seemed to take place very early on in life. To my surprise, I found the answers in the theories of Melanie Klein, Wilfred Bion, Donald Meltzer, Michael Fordham and in Fenichel's book, *The Psycho-Analytic Theory of Neurosis*, as well as in the *International Journal of Infant Observation and its Applications*. Melanie Klein's therapeutic observations over many years working with children led her to formulate Object Relations Theory (ORT), where she described how a baby becomes aware of an object (one of the first objects would of course be the mother's breasts) after which the baby learns to distinguish part objects: two separate breasts, a good *or* a bad breast, one that feeds him and one that stops feeding him, and a whole object: the mother with two breasts, with a good and a bad breast. However, not only will the baby become aware and proceed to split the object (the mother) into good objects or bad objects, but it will also introject those opposites via projective identification: first the baby projects itself into the mother and then identifies with what it can see in the mother (like standing in front of a mirror), whereupon it copies the split so that the baby's Self, equally, becomes split into good and bad parts (Klein 1932, Mitchell, 1986, Segal, 1973). According to Klein, the manner in which the baby, the child, is able to move from part object (what she called the paranoid schizophrenic position) to whole object (to the depressive position) will influence the child's healthy functioning in the world. She estimated that this process from part to whole object started roughly when the baby was three months old, and that by the end of the first year of life, the baby would usually have mastered it.

Meltzer (1978) on the other hand, describes this same process as follows: the developing, omnipotent baby suddenly, rudely aware that there are others in its world, will experience both gratifying and frustrating events, and henceforth will construct an 'internal world of objects and parts of the self', where the 'unconscious fantasies and dreams' give meaning and emotional significance to these events, which in turn, will provide the baby with guidelines: 'a model for subsequent behaviour in the world'. Moreover, he asserts, the bad part of the self is immediately segregated, since it is perceived as the 'persecutor of the personality', and hence needs to be kept away from the good and the idealised parts, 'which come together to form the core of the personality'.

All very well I thought, if the baby/mother relationship is a healthy one. But what would happen when there are few or no gratifying events, no good breast, but only painful and frustrating experiences, only one bad breast? What would happen when the bad part of an important other, and hence the introjected bad part of the self, is so bad that it cannot possibly be viewed as belonging to one and the same person? As Cordelia used to argue, 'How can I be good, when I am so bad, so ugly?' It is not difficult to comprehend that a child thus plagued by such a confusing ambivalence, might find it extremely difficult to move from part object to whole object and negotiate a successful transition from this paranoid schizophrenic position to the depressive position? Indeed, what choices are there available to the baby, to the developing child, to cope with this kind of truth? Fight or flight, evade or confront?

As far as the baby is concerned, wrote Caplan (1998), recording her findings in the *Journal of Infant Observation and its Applications*, Freud (1911), actually suggested that the frustrated infant, as yet totally dependent on its mother to help it resolve its frustrations, has but a 'limited number of choices available'. In fact, whenever mother does not fulfil its needs, the distressed baby can either choose to 'increase its actions', (cry and flail its arms and legs), or else it can opt for 'dissociation from its unpleasurable internal reality', literally 'fly away with the birds' as Cordelia would describe it. Whereas Klein, added Caplan, is of the opinion that such a child 'may take flight to an idealised internal object, and may even hallucinate the longed for pre-natal state'.

Caplan herself, after lengthy observations of a young baby boy who was 'clearly loved and very much wanted by its parents', has supplied the following account of how the baby was nonetheless able to 'visibly withdraw' whenever its feeble protests were misinterpreted: 'His gaze, initially so focused, disintegrates, and his parents worry that he might be blind.'

When I first read this description, I could not help but recall the often empty look of Cordelia, especially when she appeared to have gone into a trance in the course of her therapy whenever painful memories were about to engulf her, although it never felt like the usual trance I had witnessed in other patients. In fact, I often had the notion that at that critical moment, Cordelia had equally become blind even though she continued to look at me and appeared to see whatever she was observing. But to me, it seemed as though she had simply retreated into what I used to call the blind spot in her eyes. She only saw what was safe to see. She appeared to see, without registering the meaning of what she was seeing. Sometimes she would actually reach out and touch the object she was looking at, in order to help her see it. Needless to say that I felt duly encouraged to trust and indeed 'believe my own eyes', when I found confirmation of this strange phenomenon in yet another description of infant observation – this time, in a paper entitled *Learning to Be: Observation of a Premature Baby*, by Ross Lazar, Christine Ropke and Gisele Ermann. The author in fact had ended his report with the following observation:

> His eyes, at first open only a little, have this quality: in himself he is like a mere glance, a relaxed open eye, he looks neither inwards nor out, but holds the light within him and seems relaxed. *He seems to have the possibility of an inner space in his eye, in which he appears protected from both internal and external* stimuli... it is now as if he is simply there... yet, if Mother arrived, he would certainly let her into his eyes.

But what happens when mother does not come, or clearly hates the baby? What if father's attention, standing in for mother, invariably results in pain and moral conflict, and only succeeds in widening the gap between the child's internal good and bad objects? Attention seeking and the ability to dissociate may indeed assist the child for quite a while, and thus, effectively, allow it to 'modify its frustration and distress' – something we all have to achieve. But for some children, as Cordelia's history has illustrated, there might eventually be no other option left, but to 'evade' the reality of their world, and to make the truth of their parents 'more digestible' as Bion described, and in addition, resort to creating 'a mechanism for modifying the truth; establishing an object which assists them to un-think, to misunderstand, to establish lies and hallucinations' (Bion, 1962).

Nevertheless, as I described earlier, in the case of MPD, despite having 'modified the truth', as adults they frequently do lead successful lives and have gainful careers, functioning to all intents and purposes as a 'whole object' – provided of course, they can continue to keep their memories firmly at bay. Certainly, what often used to amaze me is that despite such severe fragmentation, those patients who had revealed their multiple systems to me also left me with an impression of great ego strength. How could this be? Or was it the Self, I wondered, which appeared so strong? For sure, when I thought about my Self, my ego, I was aware that they were two different things. My Self seemed to be fairly constant and reliable, whereas my ego, in common with most people, would at times go off the rails.

Michael Fordham (1994) equally has spent many years working with children, and described a similar process whereby the child learns first to come apart, then reforms. In agreement with Jung ('The Self is the organism as a whole of which the ego and the archetypes and the body are aspects' p.72), Fordham also proposed that the infant at the start of its life is primarily a unit or a Self. At birth, this Self becomes duly flooded by stimuli, both from within and without, which causes it to feel prototypic anxiety and to deintegrate, which in turn could lead to the infant experiencing such horrors as 'nameless dread, catastrophic chaos or terror of a black hole', especially, asserted Fordham, 'when it is not reintegrated'. However, on the whole, he argued, reintegration tends to follow birth quite quickly and will certainly be made easier 'when something tangible and reliable is found by the baby after birth, such as skin contact with its mother' (p.85). From then on, the baby will continue to experience this bewildering process of initially coming apart, (a part deintegrates out of the Self) and thereafter reforms, (the part reintegrates within the Self), thereby creating the ego, i.e., when it first encounters the bottle or the breast, weaning, potty training, walking, playing, speech, separation, birth of a sibling etc.

As maturation proceeds, the Self and the ego, (which is usually in evidence by the time the child is two years old), will endeavour to work together in order to ensure productive 'interactive structures'. The Primal Self thus will effectively become 'the sum of parts (conscious and unconscious) systems'. Furthermore, continued Fordham, this process of 'deintegration and reintegration' is not confined to childhood, but continues all through life, whenever circumstances dictate the creation of new parts. (See also Jacobson, 1964–65, *The Self and the Object World*.)

Moreover, asserted Fordham, all too soon the baby will in fact develop infantile omnipotence, meaning that within the inner world of the baby, – only the baby can rule, and its mother's breast, for instance, will henceforth be perceived as belonging to the baby, until such time as the baby, the growing child, learns to differentiate between itself and others. 'In this state of mind,' writes Fordham, 'there can be no breast out there' – the breast, then he explained, has in fact become a Self-Object, a Self-Representation' (p.86), which in my opinion, would in itself, of course facilitate due reintegration.

However, what would happen when reintegration is prevented, when there is no tangible anything available to the baby? Might the 'black hole' become all too real? What happens when the omnipotent infant is prematurely forced to become aware of others? What indeed would happen, as I queried before, when the growing child is confronted by an extreme bad part of the mother or the father, which is asking the Self to betray itself? Would the prospect of such a betrayal, perhaps force the child to become overtly Self-conscious, overtly narcissistic in order to preserve its perfect inner world? And if so, might it not be possible that the inevitable feelings of shame, might make it impossible for this child to assimilate that this bad object, may be a part of the beloved mother or father, may be a part of the Self? Would the omnipotent, narcissistic child not refuse to integrate such Self-Objects, such Self Representations? How indeed can a very young child accommodate such a persecutor of the personality when 'segregation' clearly is no longer an acceptable solution? How can the Self integrate such an unpalatable part? A perplexing paradox for sure! One possible outcome, I believe, could be the subsequent creation of false Other-Self Objects. Just like the omnipotent baby who refuses to accept that the breast belongs to another, the omnipotent, narcissistic child may refuse to accept that the shameful, bad introjected part of the mother or the father could be a part of its inner world: this bad breast, this bad penis, cannot possibly be a part of my inner world, they must belong to someone else!

Indeed, as Fenichel described:

> So long as the line of demarkation between ego and nonego is not yet sharp… the offensive, nonedible object may be projected – spit out – and is then perceived in another person, instead of in one's own ego (p.146).

As such, I propose that a distressed, deintegrated Self who is confronted with many such unpleasant and painful 'nonedible objects', and whose ego has not had sufficient time to be formed, may have no option but to deceive itself in a desperate attempt to restore the balance. And henceforth, instead of establishing its own ego, may go on to create false other-selfs, as and when events in the real world dictate – thereby of course creating not 'interactive structures', as Fordham suggested, but quite separate, competitive structures, existing along side each other in one person. These false other-selfs then, whilst jealously guarding their specific unpleasant knowledge – isolating it from the rest of the personality, as Freud suggested, (1928, 1941) would not only proceed to isolate themselves from each other (thus split the personality as Fenichel described p.157), but, as Cordelia's experiences seem to indicate, in time would also become autonomous, acquire their own ego, and delegate the True Self to a cloistered space (since it would threaten their independence), from which it would only (be allowed to) emerge now and then. Plausible hypothesis? Perhaps! Surprisingly enough, however, Cordelia herself described such a process taking place when she first began to recall the abuse by her father:

> Not only did I keep the head of my father separate from his body and his penis, as though they belonged to two different people, but I also kept myself separate from myself: I could see what was happening to me on the bed by looking at my reflection in the mirror of the dressing table, which clearly captured every vile action of my father. I used to pretend that it could not possibly be happening to me, since it was happening to the little girl in the mirror, and with time I actually learned to go behind the mirror so I could be certain that it was definitely not happening to me. It reminds me now of a dog I once had, who could not comprehend that the image he saw in the tall upright mirror was himself, and therefore began to walk around and around the mirror, looking for the other dog.

Refusing to acknowledge a part, again I feel is a very common trait; I can't believe I did that; that wasn't me; I must have been out of my mind; just ignore that part of me; I'm going crackers; I can't help it; the fairies are playing tricks on me; I can't believe I can be so bad; it must have been my double; God alone knows why I did that. Those children, however, who needed to create multiple other-selfs only seem to make this refusal absolute: It *is* not I, but he, she; it *is* another person; it *is* the 'trickster', he, she, (the persecutor of the personality) '*is* a real person' who 'will give me a hard time!' For sure, according to Ogden (1979), we are all capable of 'depositing unwanted parts into another person' via the process of projective identification. However, whereas most people, after being contained and modified by the mother (or therapist), will in time reabsorb these parts. The use of projection only will make such repossession very difficult, since the ousted parts tend to be 'disavowed; evoke no kinship; are seen as foreign, strange, frightening'.

As for placing the True Self in a cloistered space, we all tend to secure the Self behind our ego, within its 'armour', within its shell, from which it will emerge periodically. With MPD patients, however, this emerging, seems to be more poignant and highly significant since it occurs so infrequently and marks important events in their lives, often taking place in their early life, as the list drawn up by Cordelia clearly depicts:

1. In church one day with my father, before I was six, he sang a solo.

2. The day I went to see my baby brother in hospital after he was born.

3. The day I was confirmed.

4. The day I was married.

5. Occasions when the beauty of creation reaches my soul: beams of winter sunlight through the trees, in early mist or early morning frost; sunsets – I remember one I experienced in an aircraft, as if I was flying through it; not just looking at it; an African sunset, the best I've ever seen! Flying in a tiny aircraft with the pilot over an African landscape in a thunderstorm; rough sea over rugged rocks; a carpet of snowdrops or early spring crocuses or a host of golden daffodils, then I know who I am. Best of all are bluebells; music that searches out the depths of my despair, e.g. meditation by Massenet; solo violin or cello – simply wonderful.

6. The spiritual experience I had in my thirties.

And as for those separate structures becoming autonomous? As therapy progressed and more and more memories were falling into their rightful place, it also became apparent that a second beginning had occurred in the history of each personality, which had secured its role and independent existence, as well as its particular ego-strength. But which mechanism, I subsequently wondered, would have allowed the growing child to maintain such a deception? Indeed, which psychological skill would have enabled the child not only to ratify these separate structures, but in time also give them a name, a set of behaviours, a specific image, characteristics, a set of clothes, and truly believe that each one was a real person? True, by dividing the ego in many separate pieces, the reality testing function of the ego may have been prevented from operating on behalf of the whole person, and may only have been able to affirm the specific inner world of each other-self. Yet sooner or later, I speculated, the divided ego would surely have come together? The answer, I felt, could be found in a different discipline: hypnosis.

It is well documented that MPD patient are very hypnotisable, and that a close relationship exists between naturally occurring dissociation and hypnotic phenomena. Some authors, as Aldridge-Morris has pointed out, actually regard dissociation as a form of auto hypnosis (Bliss, 1984, 1986, Braun, 1979, 1983). Moreover, he explained, MPD patients have usually been using dissociation for years, clearly developing strong skills, which enable them to change their state of consciousness. Consequently, he added, they tend to suspend 'reality testing' and adopt a more 'autistic' creative and fantasy orientated mode of thinking; using the right hemisphere of their brains in favour of the left (Hilgard, 1977). In fact, when we consider the circumstances which promote altered states of consciousness as described by Ludwig (1966), it soon becomes obvious that the abusive environment of many MPD patients will almost certainly ensure that they do become very skilled at this dissociation/auto hypnosis:

Sensory deprivation (long periods left on their own).

Overload (constant scolding and inner conflict). Increased alertness (listening out for the approach of the abuser).

Reverie (escaping in daydreaming). Hyperventilation (pain, living in fear of one's life).

Medication (in Cordelia's case, the drugs her mother used to give her to keep her quiet).

What then are the effects of auto hypnosis/altered states of consciousness/dissociation? According to Ludwig, the characteristics are as follows: altered thinking – especially logical reasoning; a disturbed sense of time, a sense of loss of control, mood swings and affective blunting; distorted body image, depersonalisation, perceptual distortions; sudden magical 'ineffable' insights, rejuvenation and hypersuggestibility.

Certainly an impressive list guaranteed to disrupt many a life, when used in excess! Yet dissociation, although it can of course 'also be manifestly pathological', is once again a normal skill which we all employ, apparently from an early age onwards. For instance, writes Aldridge-Morris (p.71), how else could we cope with the 'tedium of motorway driving?' A 'part remains in control', while another 'splits off and indulges in vivid fantasies'. Indeed, suddenly (as I have experienced myself) we can be many miles nearer our destination, without remembering how we got there.

How then would auto hypnosis/dissociation help the child to maintain the deception that abuse is not happening to him/herself, but to another child, thereby giving credence to those separate structures? Cordelia herself supplied the answer when she described how she used to see other little children sitting in the corners of the room. Like her, these children were immensely sad, were hugging the walls and were trying to press themselves into the corners for safety and comfort. Cordelia in fact recalled how she could not only see these other little girls, but could also talk with them. Obviously those children were not real, so what was occurring?

I remembered a certain lecture by one of my tutors in university, explaining hypnotic concepts such as negative hallucinations (not seeing something which is there), positive hallucinations (seeing something which is not there), and trance logic, (making the illogical, logical) (Orne, 1959), concepts which I will explain and explore more fully later on. Could these be the mechanisms which ensured ongoing deception? Could trance logic especially, embody Bion's 'Fiendish Friend – the Liar in oneself – the shark within' who helped Cordelia to distort the truth, who helped her to continue hallucinating and continue to 'see' her Other-Selves and her imaginary friend Zillah well into adulthood? I believed so, and in time would become even more convinced, when another adult patient I was working with equally revealed a multiple system and shared like structures and marked similarities.

Certainly, in terms of auto hypnosis/dissociation, they both seemed able to go in a trance whenever the real world of their past impinged and whenever they felt threatened by what they needed to remember. They simply withdrew from the world, residing in a 'black hole', a 'black box' (the blind spot in their eyes?), either by 'imploding', going backwards into space, as though 'travelling through a tunnel' or else, by making others smaller; shrinking them, and making them move a considerable distance away. In contrast, however, they both also found it very difficult to partake in relaxation, and hated the feelings of losing control.

They both were also extremely good at not seeing something. Cordelia especially could instantly not see i.e., a picture on the wall, whenever she focussed on it – likewise she would also see things which were not there, especially when a certain paranoid part of her (Geraldine) came to the forefront. Cordelia furthermore could also make me disappear completely, or else, in her mind's eye, she would frequently go under the water, usually in the sea somewhere. In addition, both patients would certainly classify for Spiegel's (1974) Grade 5 syndrome: reaching a high score on a 0–5 hypnotisable range as measured by the Hypnotic Induction Profile – which incidentally, according to Spiegel, would certainly prime them to become the 'so-called hysterical patient' whenever they were severely stressed (Aldridge-Morris p.80), an observation which, I am sure, would find favour with my supervisor, who frequently used to complain: 'Why must you complicate matters by calling it multiple personalities, why can't you just call it hysteria?'

Those high scorers, explained Aldrige-Morris, are in fact a very select group of people, only 10% of the population – which, no doubt, will find favour with those diagnosed as MPDs, since they tend to regard themselves as rather unique and quite unlike others. In itself of course, a useful mechanism, which can ensure ongoing deception, since it effectively prevents them from having any real friends who might well see past their smoke-screens of normality at any cost. Certainly at first, Cordelia tended to resent it whenever I compared her MPD behaviour with like patients, jealously guarding what we had discovered together, not even wanting other patients to benefit from her experiences. Initially quite an understandable reaction, I feel, considering that it would be so easy to approach the whole concept of MPD as an interesting phenomenon; studying the disorder, reducing the patient to a guinea pig rather than engaging in therapy. Nor did Cordelia want to read any books on the subject of MPD, as she did not want to be influenced in any way by what she might read. So far, Cordelia informed me, she had only ever read one article on multiple personalities!

However, continued Aldridge-Morris, those high scorers certainly have specific behavioural and personality traits which in themselves, I feel, could well assist accurate diagnosis. To begin with, they have a 'high eye-roll' (ER).

Although I never actually observed ER (eyes moving upwards), Cordelia would often move her eyes from side to side (as though she was checking out voices), whereas the other patient would continuously blink whenever painful issues were discussed (as though trying not to see, trying to stay in a trance). They lack (healthy) 'cynicism' and despite a background of abuse, have a 'beguiling innocence', an expectation that others will support them, hence they also fervently believe that 'therapy is good for them', even when it becomes obvious, it seems, that the therapist is exploiting the relationship, i.e. Cordelia used to recall how her counsellor would request her to make dinner and take her on car journeys, yet felt unable to terminate their relationship.

Because of their unwavering belief in their therapists/doctors, they are also quite willing to replace if need be, 'old premises and beliefs with new ones', without thinking it through first. Hence, their 'metaphoric inner world is often in disarray', leaving them without due guidelines, i.e. Cordelia often used to complain that she could not please everybody, despite trying so very hard to be a good patient. They are very empathic, readily absorb the pain of others and easily 'affiliate with new events', and in turn frequently become unwell themselves. Cordelia tended to become absorbed in caring for others; suffering for and with them, then becoming ill herself – even displaying the same symptoms as the patients she was nursing.

They also re-experience their past as though it is happening for real, 'as though it is happening now', which of course isolates them from 'current decision making'. For example, when Cordelia, in the course of her therapy, heard the sounds and noises of her home town, felt the sensations of the asylum, Cordelia was in the asylum. Cordelia was the little girl trapped by her abusers, making herself small or larger in order to evade them (paradoxically a most useful therapy tool which has allowed Cordelia to undo the past).

In addition, they also tolerate trance logic and passively accept logical inconsistencies and contradictions. (An amazing contradiction in itself, since in my opinion, their incarceration in a multiple system was manufactured by not being able to accept opposing concepts such as good and bad); i.e. both patients readily accepted many discrepancies and illogical events and behaviours, such as loss of time, without ever really questioning it.

Those same high scorers, however, tend to learn by rote (repetition), have an eidetic (visual) memory and total recall, which reinforces their ability to regress under hypnosis, i.e. a part of Cordelia (Mary) would speak Arabic which a teacher once taught her in bible classes. Moreover, they also have an intense capacity for concentration and concurrent dissociation, i.e. both patients were dedicated artists, displaying an intense concentration, yet also tended to assert that their art somehow, just 'formed itself'. Yet, they also tend to have 'role confusion' and a 'reactive sense of inferiority', i.e. despite the fact that they do achieve, they never feel as though they have. Both patients were indeed often surprised when other people admired their work or gave them credit for achieving.

And finally, wrote Aldridge-Morris, according to Spiegel, they also have a 'fixed personality core', i.e. as I described earlier, despite being so changeable, despite fragmentation, their core appeared remarkably strong and was very adamant about its role. Certainly, whenever it was given the chance, it would patiently guide the system towards health, from within, proving itself to be a truly remarkable trustworthy and valuable ally to the therapist.

Again this is a most impressive list of characteristics, which in due course we were able to utilise as tools, in order to undo the harmful effects of this auto hypnosis. Indeed, thus armed with a set of attributes, a theory and certain proof that this MPD phenomenon had a recognisable pattern, Cordelia and I set out to unravel the meaning of those hallucinations, those separate structures, those alter egos, those internal people, those Other-Selves. Call them what you may. The fact is, that the next phase of Cordelia's therapy required that I should form a relationship of sorts, with each part, with each personality, so that finally, they would be able to tell their stories and help Cordelia to put together this giant jigsaw puzzle she saw in the sky.

Since I actually started this chapter with an exploration of the importance of the therapeutic relationship, I want to end it by sharing a dream Cordelia had shortly after she wrote the next chapter. Cordelia recounted this dream to me on one of my visits to her, after we discussed the process of the book and analysed the implications of the next chapter, and after we explored this particular theory of mine, of Self versus Other-Selves, of Bad versus Good Objects.

I decided to include this dream for several reasons. First of all, as the reader will be able to verify, this dream clearly affirms that in this teacher/pupil relationship, Cordelia at times would indeed be a step ahead, although she would not always appreciate it or recognise that she was. Secondly, in view of the fact that the main focus of this chapter is concerned with trying to make sense of it all, trying to find a plausible explanation. The dream, in a round-about way, actually highlights what I believe is an important aspect of the therapeutic relationship, namely, that the therapist might propose as many theories, quote as many experts as he or she likes, but that ultimately, it is more important to be alert, observe, and truly hear the patients, or else we may equally just 'feed them from a single breast'. Indeed, the ability to be 'scientists together' aptly proved to be a major asset in this particular therapy journey.

Thirdly, I wanted to include this dream because it is a fitting delineation of the important step Cordelia has achieved by writing the next chapter, and because it so clearly defined the immense task ahead: accepting that the bad as well as the good, idealised part of her father belonged to one and the same person.

Until now, Cordelia had coped by splitting her father, splitting her mother and splitting herself. Now she would attempt to mend this split; for sure no easy task, as Cordelia duly discovered and her dream so clearly predicted. Even as we were discussing the implications of Cordelia trying to mend this split; to end the deception that her father was either all good (according to Rosalind), or all bad (according to Peter), Cordelia in fact, began to 'see things'. Indeed, whilst we were discussing the all-good father versus the all-bad father, Cordelia suddenly asked me if I could equally 'see a man standing at the end of her garden', whereupon, she wondered if this man could be her father.

I naturally encouraged Cordelia to look again, to test out the reality of what she thought she saw, and to realise that giving up on Rosalind's father was obviously far more traumatic than she had so far allowed herself to register. When Cordelia consequently did look again, she saw only the trees, and by the time I left, she said she now knew that the so-called man in the garden was but a 'different colour on the tree', though it naturally distressed her that she would have had such a reaction to 'just talking about giving up on her ideal father'. Shortly, after this last visit, however, I received a letter from Cordelia in which she informed me that she had needed an emergency appointment with Dr C. He had prescribed Melleril for her, she said, used in schizophrenia and emotional disturbances, because she was seeing things and hearing voices. 'They seem to come from an empty large jug, that's what it sounds like.' Cordelia also wrote that she was adamant that she did not want to take such a powerful drug and said that she had negotiated to remain on an increased dose of her regular medicine, promazine. Nor did she want another therapist. In fact, she wanted to sort it out herself: sort out Rosalind (representing the good, idealised part of her father) and Peter (representing the bad, abusing part of her father). 'When I have the words, I will tell you what Rosalind and Peter and Cordelia feel about their father.'

Splitting the good from the bad and employing dissociation had kept her sane in a mad world. Now, in attempting to mend this split, Cordelia appeared to be travelling back in time, experiencing perhaps, what she should have achieved as a young child: finding a way through this paranoid schizophrenic position to stable health; able to cope with contradictions, ambivalence, and the perplexing paradox of life: that good and bad go hand in hand; that her beloved father could be evil, as well as show her the beauty of the world; and that the Almighty Father, in which her father so fervently believed and prayed to, asking for due guidance, could be all loving and all withholding? A maddening task indeed, which is perhaps the reason why Melanie Klein said that all children are psychotic, and that the blueprint for mental illness and psychotic breakdown in later life, originated in those early days.

A dream:

I can see a mother feeding a baby. The woman looks like me but I did not really want to look at her. The scene never changed. I am looking at myself, I am being fed and feeding the baby. The baby is only ever fed from one breast only… I do not want to recognise… Yet it feels as though I was looking at the problem: *only fed from one breast*. It didn't feel as though I was stuck, because I was looking at the problem…

I did not recognise the mother… like I did not recognise the face of my father.

My Father

My daily battle for survival didn't come without major cost. My inner child survived but I was sentenced to my own brand of protective custody, I grew up with many secrets. The most deeply buried secret was almost the last memory to return in therapy, and it turned out to be the key to eventual health and wholeness. All my life, I treasured the memory that my father was the best in the world and that he loved me more than anyone else. That idealised image became the way I survived against all odds. To have that memory shattered, or so I thought, would destroy me, so I hung on to what turned out to be nothing but a false memory. Through my painful journey of therapy, I wanted to be able to tell my father how it felt to live my life without the one person who I knew loved me. I wanted to tell him how let down I felt that he could not keep his promise to look after me and to come back to me every time he went away, as the last time he did not return.

As a child, I had split my father into two people, the good and the bad. After his death, I remembered only the good, so my few memories became just simply wonderful. I put him on the biggest pedestal I could find. I seemed to always minimise the bad things and enlarge the good things. I imagined he had given me something so precious, something so beautiful in those short moments of seeming truths from which I believed my inner strength came. Walks along the beach holding hands and singing love songs together, sitting on grassy headlands watching the angry sea lash out at rocks that seemed to hug each other below, fleetingly left with white foam spat at them from the mouths of fiercely mounting waves. Or watching the sun sink over the horizon, leaving its warm glow to light our homeward path, but leaving my heart so sad as it meant goodbye again. To express how I felt each time I saw a sunset with my father, I wrote a poem during my time in therapy, from which I take just one verse:

> Poor aching aching human heart
> What fitful fever breaks you now
> The earth's most lovely things depart
> What are you and how?
> Your spring, than earths, does sooner fade
> To sorrow born, for suffering made
> Poor aching aching human heart

I often expressed to Frieda in my therapy session how I had missed this wonderful father all my life, and that part of me died with him. I always wanted to die, to go to him wherever he was. I believed he had gone to be with his heavenly Father. He always took me to church with him when he was home. He told me about his faith in Jesus Christ, he read me Bible stories and gave me his Bible on his last visit home, which I still surprisingly have today. I have often asked this heavenly Father, of whom my earthly father spoke so lovingly, 'why oh why did He take away the only person who showed me love as a child and whose love I could return without fear? So often my prayer during therapy has been:

> Please God forgive me for loving and needing love so deeply, my heart is swollen with the pain and sadness of my life. Heal my broken heart and show me your love and compassion before I die. Restore my faith and trust. Help me find myself and give me back my life again.
>
> Amen

He answered my prayer, because I have found myself and I do have a life, although I will always hold a great deal of sadness in my heart.

I realise as I look back over the letters I wrote to my father during therapy that I was very, very angry with him. I thought then I was angry with him for leaving me to survive my family and life without him. I wrote that, 'Loving you and losing you, has been like a heavy brick tied to a short rope around my neck, while I've struggled most of my life to swim free from the bottom of a goldfish bowl, or sometimes round and round in circles, either hoping to die or longing to be saved.' Another statement expressing my need of love and care came in the words 'I needed you like roses need rain.'

In my teenage years my mother occasionally mentioned my father, although she had never done so before. She used to delight in telling me stories of how my father always saved me from dangerous situations. One such occasion was when she flung me through an open bedroom window as a baby, because I would not stop screaming; my father apparently caught me as I fell. Also during my teens, I can remember the pain inside when others on the school bus talked about their parents warmly and the welcome they would receive on returning home. I knew home for me was cold and unwelcoming. I had to prepare the evening meal for everyone on my return. I can also remember the feelings of distinct contradiction to the longing, with thoughts that life is indeed better without my father, but I did not realise then where these thoughts were coming from.

When I remembered all the truth, it felt like this, 'Am I ever going to smile again?' I feel such despair inside. I am in a dark black pit, it smells like a sewer and I cannot see the light of day. Why did I remember all this? It's like coping with an army of demons inside me, an army of horrific memories, one goes and another comes to haunt me. I feel angry with myself for opening up this huge can of worms that I don't know what to do with, except to deny myself the truth and run away. I know the anger is about the truth and the grief will heal my deep black hole, or so they say.

Never was grief like mine.

Grief for the little girl who never was.

Grief for the little girl who was not to blame.

Grief for a lost childhood and the whole of my life deeply affected.

To be a healthy adult, I have to find Cordelia, I need to be this child again. I have to feel like Cordelia to find the softness, gentleness and innocence of this small child. I have to cry the tears this little girl was unable to cry. I have to feel what happened to her. She feels separate from me, even when I've told my therapist as much as Cordelia can remember. I want to remember what it felt like to have a little body, to be vulnerable, trusting, dependent, and then full of fear – I want to get under her skin if possible.

It was autumn, and I know it was near my birthday. It might have been the very day. I remember my father telling me I would have a big surprise. I had the greatest and most violent of all shocking experiences; I was raped. I was abused emotionally, physically and sexually, it was total violation, it was worse than the most violent of deaths, because I had to exist without identity, my life had been snatched away. Everything I was, anything I ever had, my hope, my joy, my spontaneity, my wonder, my trust, my feelings, my enthusiasm for life, my discovery – all stopped. The little girl died inside herself.

On this terrible day, the usual bath time had taken place. I remember I didn't want to keep playing my father's games, and on this day he was wanting me to touch him and kiss him a lot. I kept saying no.

He dressed me and put me in his bed to sleep, he kept touching me between my legs. I fell asleep, only to be woken with my father's penis in my mouth; my head was pushed back, I couldn't breathe, I was choking, suffocating, I thought I was going to die. He took it out and began raping me vaginally; I was violently sick but didn't speak. He split me open and as he entered my tiny body I wanted desperately to scream but he stuffed something in my mouth to muffle the sound. I now understand my silent scream that lies deep inside me.

The splitting, burning pain of his penetration and the manner in which he wrenched my legs apart, the sheer pressure of his body and the fierce movement, caused me temporary unconsciousness. When I came round, he had gone and my mother was standing over me. She started to scream when she saw the vomit and blood and the awful state I was in. She called me a bad, mad, evil child. I started to scream back, 'Daddy has done this, he did this to me, it wasn't me, it wasn't my fault!' She started to hit me violently and continually, she could not stop, and as she did so, she called me a liar and a dirty, filthy child.

I still carried on saying, 'I didn't do it, I didn't do it, he did.' I knew then I was innocent, but this changed. My mother left me still screaming, and my father met her on the landing. I heard him shout at her and hit her. He wrapped me in a blanket and picked me up and put me in his car. He took me to a hospital. He said, I was to tell no one what happened. I remember a large, fat, kind nurse taking me into her arms and saying, 'Poor, poor, little darling, who did this to you, what has happened?' I looked at my father, and then the nurse; I said, 'Nothing, it was my fault.' I then split, properly, for the very first time, and watched from above the proceedings, as they repaired the damage. Mask, trolley, swing doors, doctors, nurses all rushing around.

When I woke up, I had splints on my legs and a terrible pain between and at the top of my legs. My father insisted he would look after me, and he took me home; as he laid me back into bed, I felt I was a very bad girl for the trouble I caused. The next morning, my father was gone, even my mother had gone and the lady next door, Mrs Foster came to wash me and get me up. I told her, 'I hurt too much to move, what happened to me?'

She said, 'Pretend it didn't happen then it will go away.' She was kind to me, and she said I was to forget all about it, so I forgot. Memories of further abuse from my father are returning. After a long period away from home, whilst my mother ignored me except for repeated washouts, my father returned and the abuse continued. The first rape burned so deeply into my brain I was never, ever the same person again.

Now as an adult, many years later, the only way I could come near to confronting him was by writing a letter, which will explain the depth of anguish and pain I held inside.

Dear Father,

I now know why I have always wanted to dig up your body from its grave, as I tried to do a few days after you were buried. The only reason I would want you to be alive right now is so that I could say what I need to say to your face. 'Why, why, oh why, did you do this to me?' The hardest thing for me is to accept the fact that someone I loved and cherished so absolutely for so many years – you, my father – could have violated me so deeply, damaged my body, my emotions, my soul and worst of all my spirit.

I have experienced absolute isolation in my life, even within a happy marriage. I have felt absolute aloneness, and the world and everyone in it was the most frightening thing.

The scariest part has been the panic, which feels as if I am dissolving and there is nothing to hold on to.

There has always been this terror, with an incredible impulse to do something about it, but there has been nothing I could do. I only knew you for the first six years of my life and you lied to me the whole time. The deception is the thing that hurts the most, and in return I gave you nothing but pure innocent absolute love. You told me you loved me, you told me, a small vulnerable child of three, to stop you doing what you knew was wrong. You told me you would die if I didn't love you, you told me to tell no one, to keep our secret safe.

Our secret no longer exists. I have told my therapist all I can remember. I have journeyed through agonising pain, facing reality slowly; the worst has been to discover the truth about you. I was an innocent child not really wanted by my mother, clearly already at risk when you traumatically caused me terror, damage, pain and a deep, deep sadness that has stayed with me all my life.

You robbed me of my childhood, my health, my happiness, you robbed me of my roots, my family, my inheritance, you robbed me of my sense of self, of freedom, of opportunities, of achievements – you put me in prison.

The punishment, the pain and the shame should have been yours. The man who gave me life, took it away almost before it had started. Can you understand, that bottled up inside me all these years, has been a continual festering of unexpressed rage?

With no help from you I did marry a fine man, who has been a wonderful husband and father, far better than anything you were capable of. It hurts so much to discover you were not worth loving all those years, and it will take a long time for me to reconcile my loving feelings with the most appalling abuse of all time. My disillusioned broken heart needs time to come to terms with all this and I don't know how I will feel in time. I should say I hate you, but I can't, I'm only glad that you died when you did, something I thought I could never say.

Goodbye, Daddy,
Cordelia

My father's love was my reason for living, for holding on. I thought it was the reason I had the strength to withstand the most horrendous torment, because I knew the father whose death I had never mourned, loved me, and in death he could be all mine. No one, nothing could match up to him. The truth was devastating. I thought I would fall apart, and nearly did as, added to this, some months later, was the final betrayal of my mother, and I became very seriously ill with atypical double-sided pneumonia and nearly died.

The terrible shock about my father, which I experienced only the autumn before, coupled with yet another inescapable realisation when, in the following winter, I burned my badly made wedding dress to symbolise the ending of the hold my mother had on me. The two things together were just too much, and I experienced a near death experience after being taken to the Accident and Emergency department of a large general hospital. I had a rigor and the GP said I had labyrinthitis! I had lain in bed at home for six days with a fever of 104.5 rising rapidly to 105. I couldn't walk. I lost all strength and control.

I drifted in and out of consciousness. My husband could not convince the GP's surgery how ill I was becoming. I vaguely remember a bell ringing and an oxygen mask, then being on a bed in the A & E department. The flowers on the curtains round the bed would not stay still, they turned into ugly gargoyle faces, insects crawled across my body and dogs growled at my side. All this, of course, being caused by lack of oxygen to the brain. Then, everything stopped, and my bed appeared to start moving, it sped swiftly and silently towards a very powerful white light in front of me. Fountains of cool, gentle water fell on me, and I felt the heat from my body go, as the bed travelled through exotic gardens with lush green plants and beautiful flowers of every kind and hue, glistening as they hung with drops of sparkling, clear dew. Either side of my bed were full orchestras, so close it seemed I felt a violin bow touch me (an instrument I love so much). Beyond the orchestras, reaching up as far as I could see were choirs of angels singing such heavenly music, which I recognised, even the words seemed familiar. I longed to reach the bright light, then I saw my husband, my children, my grandchildren and my therapist.

My therapist looked at me and said, 'You aren't going to die, after all you've been through, you haven't lived yet!' My grandchildren were teenagers and young adults; some were not yet born. I then knew I had to live, I wanted to live to see them grow up, I wanted to live for the first time ever and I said no to death. The bed stopped moving and the doctor appeared to be shaking me, and she said, 'Keep the oxygen mask over your face, you have a severe atypical pneumonia of both lungs, they have stopped working altogether but we hope to get you better. The IV drip has a powerful antibiotic in it, and potassium, your potassium levels are nil.' My husband was standing next to my bed. He told me afterwards, he thought I had died. I will never forget the look of relief and his smile as I recognised him.

It was a long haul back to reasonably normal health and one day, seven months later, listening to an old tape of Brahms Requiem; I recognised the heavenly music, it was a section of the music where the words come from Isaiah 35:10.

> And the ransomed of the Lord shall return and come to Zion with songs and everlasting joy upon their heads: they shall obtain joy and gladness and sorrow and sighing shall flee away.

Brahm's idea was that his music and texts from the Old and New Testaments would mourn the dead and give comfort to the living. This experience was marking an ending as well as a beginning. I have never wanted to take my life since; I really wanted to live for the first time. Life didn't have the same importance before I extricated myself from the hold my parents had over me and all the awful deception.

The shock and horror of this realisation of the truth about my father brought a degree of relief too, that the silence was broken, the block removed. I could at last grieve for real the whole of my miserable existence. My parents should have loved and nurtured me, the tiny entity that I was when all this began. Gradually, their love would have built up layer upon layer, forming me into a separate being with a lustre all of my own, much in the same way a pearl is formed in nature. In so doing, my psychological sense of self would have been born. Likewise, other family members should have reinforced my joy for life, if they had allowed themselves to respond warmly, but they all let me down; the deficit was huge, so huge it is not completely repairable.

I can go on living because I now recognise unconditional love in whatever proportion it can be given but I cannot deny the struggle is enormous, sometimes I fail, sometimes I get it right. One definition for forgiveness that I think I can accept is to grant relief from payment; I do not really have a choice in the circumstances but to do otherwise. Dr C always talked to me about tearing up the IOU. I could only do it when I was ready, but I remember telling him when I knew I had done so. His response was one of being delighted for me and this encouraged me to go on.

To write all this about my father has been one of the most difficult and painful exercises I have had to do. I am also not satisfied that I have been able to find the words to express the depth of my feelings or to give understanding to the reader. I feel disloyal to the good father, disloyal to the child who remembered only the good father, and completely shattered as an adult that my longings, my dreams, my memories of being loved – upon which I based my strong centre and some degree of stability and hope – were in fact nothing but my own deceptions. However, on a positive note, the words of Celine Dion's song 'I'm everything I am, because you loved me' would have been so empty for me before, because the realness of love was missing. Now I can say these words do have meaning, everything good I have received from anyone since I discovered the truth, dare I say, has felt like some sort of love.

As I write on, the pain of the truth I am more able to leave on the pages and less in my heart. The most amazing significant change is that everything around me seems clearer and brighter as if, gradually, the people around me and my surroundings are being slowly unveiled and I become more real. I can appreciate what I have so much more, I can see genuine love and response for what it is, it is like coming alive and being part of the real world, no more looking through the glass of my goldfish bowl at others living their lives. I now feel I can join in with those who accept me.

Part 2
Out of the Goldfish Bowl

To whom it may concern,

Mrs Cordelia Hannah

I can confirm that Mrs Cordelia Hannah has been under my care, suffering from chronic depression over the last three years. She has been under psychiatric care since 1968 and since that time has been prone to recurrent episodes of depression which have rendered her unable to work. Since that time, according to her history and her records she has not been medically fit to return to work and certainly I would not see any significant prospect of her being able to work in the foreseeable future.

Dr C

Bluebell Children

After many years working with a number of abuse survivors from all walks of life, I have sadly had to come to the conclusion that the violation of trust, especially by important others, ranks as one of the most enduring invasions and injuries a person can sustain, and certainly so if the abuse was coupled with mortal agony – literally feeling in danger of losing one's life. What so many abusers fail to recognise or will not acknowledge is that their act of betrayal is for life. It cannot be undone, let alone be forgiven, even though ultimately, forgiving what was done is the only way real health can be achieved. But what does it mean to forgive? It certainly cannot mean that we can ever condone or agree with abuse. Cordelia herself has described how she views forgiving and I want to quote her definition, since I will not be able to put it in better words:

> Forgiveness. One definition: to grant relief from payment.
> It seems appropriate to fight back but it keeps me trapped.
> I cannot ever forgive my father.
> I cannot forgive my mother's extreme cruelty and sexual abuse but I can understand her better now.
> I've even begun to understand my brother better.
> I cannot forgive anything until it comes naturally but I have noticed tiny glimpses of compassion for others, very occasionally, rising up inside me, which may mean I can feel compassionate towards myself.
> That is where my healing lies: forgiving myself.
> Hating myself makes me hate others, the world – everything. Also fighting, holding on to anger and hate is avoidance of the extreme sadness I feel. I want to see a break in the clouds. I want to see myself separate from the struggle, now I am one person.

Fighting back – wanting payment from the abuser – 'keeps me trapped'. How ironic and paradoxical those words are, since the justifiable urge, for sure, would be to exact payment for what was done – 'an eye for an eye'. How immense the step then, when the abused child-adult can allow compassion and love to enter a heart so cold. How lonely the world of the abused child-adult was, is, and usually remains until forgiveness can let others in.

Yet, outwardly, the child, the adult, may seem unaffected. But if only the abusers and those who would minimise the effects of abuse could enter the body, mind and soul of such a child or adult, they would be able to confirm the tremendous suffering and the long-term effect. Not only would they hear the constant self-criticism and self-doubt, but they would also see the hate for the defiled body – now useless, a canvass for self abuse – or else they would feel the driving urge to be perfect, nothing can ever be good enough; or witness the shame that they are the offspring of such a father, such a mother; or that they were unable to prevent the abuser from injuring them. Indeed, if only the abusers would let themselves feel what their victims had to endure – still endure – they would experience the never-ending mind-numbing search for an answer, ponder the same recriminations over and over again: I am to blame. I should have fought harder, I should have said no, I should have died instead – Why me? – How can anyone do this to a little boy, a little girl – I never could – could I?

But above all, they would be able to observe the excruciating sadness, the all-pervasive powerlessness. They would literally taste the fear: that stifling fear that they will get hurt even more if they do not comply – that heart-stopping fear that they will be killed if they dare to reveal the secret – that shameful fear that they will be disowned by the family (as the abuser might tell the child), if the family knew what this bad child did. Moreover, they would also be able to observe the very real, yet illogical fear of being abandoned by the abusing father, mother or both, which tends to be a frequent threat. Illogical of course, but only to an outside observer, since being abandoned by such a dysfunctional family might actually free the child of abuse! However, for the child who is trapped in a nightmare scenario of powerlessness and abuse, there are no alternatives but to endure and to suffer.

In my opinion, the most crippling aspect of abuse is the sad reality that the victim invariably ends up being conditioned to learn to please, to adapt, to accommodate and accept abuse. Long after the actual abuse has stopped, or the abuser has died and the child is now an adult, such terror, such powerlessness, such dependency continues creating havoc, causing depression, ill health and troublesome relationships for the rest of the abused person's life. Frequently, the various books will highlight that of course not everyone is affected by abuse to the same degree, depending on the level of abuse, and the support the child might receive from its family when the abuse comes to light, etc. However, this grading, I feel, often tends to do the abused person a disservice, since it can create the impression that some abuse is not as bad as others. To the abused person, it may sound as though the books tell the world that it is okay, for instance, to chop off a finger but it is not all right to chop off an arm. All abuse hurts the child-adult even though some can undeniably be more traumatic and produce a more dramatic outcome.

Indeed, the fear of being killed, shunned or abandoned as a child, can be so intense that the child actually learns to disappear, and puts in its place a selection of marionettes who will feel no pain, do as the abuser asks, even instigate more sex, more abuse, in order to be in some kind of control or receive some token of love, a glimmer of remorse. Or else the child may become mute, silent as the grave, or 'fly away with the birds'. With time, these escape strategies simply become unconscious mental processes whose sole function is to avoid conscious conflict, anxiety, more pain, and to survive. Thus, the very defence mechanisms the child employs to cope with the abuse only serve to entrap it even further. Needless to say, abusers will readily exploit such apparent agreeable behaviour, justifying their actions on the basis that the child 'was willing, did not get hurt, seduced them, provoked them, or did not protest', etc.

The child-adult, who learns to disappear, talks, eats, works, plays, reads, sings, laughs, cries, marries, has children, and appears to succeed at this task of living. But the real Self is but an observer. It watches, it notes, it survives. It is the lost soul of the child-adult. It is locked away for safekeeping. The price of this incarceration, however, is so very high: the true Self does not grow, the true Self does not experience, the true Self is as good as dead. How painful and difficult the journey, trying to find the real Self again. Especially when life was ticking along and the knowledge that the Self was lost was carefully confined to periods of depression, was only really visible at night, during nightmares, dreams or in drawings or creative writing, etc.

As Cordelia has described elsewhere, prior to her engaging in counselling and therapy, to the outside world, and to a large extent to herself as well, all was as it should be. She had a good marriage, healthy children, all things considered a remarkably loving, sexual and reasonably interdependent relationship with her husband, even though throughout their marriage, the burden of dependency did rear its head in the form of her severe clinical depressions and her suicide attempts. And of course, also in the act of cooking and caring for Martin, her abusing brother, whenever he came to stay with Cordelia and her husband during his holidays and at Christmas time. As Cordelia recalled, she felt sorry for him being so alone. Not only did her brother frequently outstay his welcome, but he would also aggressively insist on being thoroughly pampered by her, and would subsequently express his resentment, whenever her husband tried to assert himself on their behalf. Also, when, later on in life, Cordelia experienced a religious conversion, 'belonging to a family' was the added inducement which ensured, as Cordelia has described, that she became 'perhaps too heavily involved, to the detriment of other things'.

Can an adult ever escape from the legacy of abuse completely? In my experience, all those I have worked with in the course of my time as a therapist, and who took the important step of wanting to rid themselves of unwanted residue, have grown as individuals – though for some the battle goes on, and probably always will. In fact, shedding the inheritance of our parents and teachers can be a lifelong task for most of us, certainly as far as Cordelia is concerned, although at this stage of the book she was quite well, having survived the trauma of writing about her father's betrayal and her subsequent brief sojourn into psychosis 'when she was hearing and seeing things'. Traces of dependency – fearing abandonment, wanting to please, etc., periodically do continue to rear their heads, landing her as usual in deep water. For instance, after Cordelia wrote to me telling me that her consultant had wanted her to take Melleril, she wrote me yet another letter, saying that she might well have misled me because the decision not to take Melleril had in fact been a joint resolution between her and Dr C, after they had both explored pros and cons, taking into account the danger of interfering with her prolactinoma. Since Cordelia is quite aware of my opinions about undue medication, elements of transference, wanting to please an ex-therapist, had obviously crept into the way she had initially reported this decision to me. All would have been well had it not been for the fact that Cordelia had given Dr C the chapter on Objects Relationships to read (as I had advised her to do, so that he might know where she was at). And naturally, he had objected to being portrayed, so it appeared, as a cynical consultant who prescribed neuroleptics willy nilly, prompting him to write to me, in amongst other aspects related to Cordelia's therapy, in order to put the matter straight.

However, and though it might indeed be impossible to shed the legacy of abuse completely, colouring the truth somewhat certainly does not compare with the way Cordelia used to feel compelled to manipulate her world. Whereas today Cordelia was able to discuss and defend herself against the fall-out of all this letter writing, in the past, such feedback would certainly have produced a very different reaction. Not only would she have been unable to admit that she might have misled someone, since the responsibility for doing so would have been passed around the system, conveniently getting lost in the process, like Chinese whispers, but such appraisal indeed from a significant other such as Dr C, would in the past have been interpreted by Cordelia as a 'deliberate rejection' and would merely have entrenched her in the familiar victim role. Be that as it may, in the year 1995 Cordelia was still very much a victim!

In January 1995, Cordelia and I began to work together five times a week. We would in fact continue to do so for the following nine months, apart from when Cordelia and I were on holiday of course, (Cordelia's husband usually tended to arrange his holidays, so that he could take Cordelia away at the same time as I would be on leave). Whence her therapy sessions were then reduced to four times a week, whereafter, come February, we gradually decreased the sessions even further, prior to my leaving towards the end of May 1996.

As it turned out, it would be a remarkable seventeen months, a time of major revelations, a time of painful learning, but above all, a time of real growth. In the whole scheme of things, it would seem that the previous arduous five years, had been but the introduction to these amazing seventeen months where the real work took place. However, those painful, chaotic years, I feel, have been as important as the final stretch, even though Cordelia used to feel that they had been wasted years. Indeed, the shaky beginnings of Cordelia's therapy, the uncertain future of the clinic, the temporary loss of her therapist and the involvement of so many different health professionals all served to set the scene for later revelations – because throughout those years, the ongoing and enduring care and patience of all concerned with Cordelia's therapy and treatment ensured that eventually trust was restored. All (in addition to her consultants of course) meaning the clinic manager, the deputy manager, the nurses, night staff, bank staff, therapists, the reception and kitchen staff, etc. Indeed all of us, to some extent, had become involved in Cordelia's treatment over the ensuing years, and each one henceforth had coped as best as they knew how with Cordelia 'acting out' her transferences and her frequent subsequent desperate behaviour.

Such 'acting out' as sitting in reception with her coat over her head, not wanting to attract attention to herself, believing that we rather not see her at all. Leaving numerous notes, cards, letters (once a bunch of nettles), on the windscreen of my car as well as writing love messages on the walls of the art room, running out of groups and accusing certain nurses of hating her (especially those in authority, who tended to be a trigger for Geraldine). Such desperate reactions as having severe asthma attacks whilst sitting waiting in reception or turning up unexpectedly at the clinic demanding to be seen. Or else she could be found crying, wailing, screaming in reception, the dining room, in the car park and the driveway. Or else she would cause anxiety all round by going missing for hours, by taking extra medication, leave suicide notes in the art room, as well as periodically writing angry letters to the clinic manager, accusing her staff of neglect and discrimination.

Yet, as Cordelia so clearly has protested elsewhere, as far as she was concerned she did not regard herself as demanding in any way. But of course, certain personalities were indeed anything but, whereas others, at times, certainly led us all a merry dance and I must confess that, in the early years, when the boundaries were so flexible, I was very grateful indeed for the involvement of Anne and the other nurses, for I doubt whether I could have coped with Cordelia on my own during that time. Then again, the encouragement and care Cordelia received from all the nurses whilst I was absent due to illness ensured that she was able to gain considerable insight into her pathology, her painful longing to be loved.

For sure, discovering that certain members of staff did not hate her as she thought they did, proved to be an important turning point. Of course, as explained before, treatment would have taken a very different course if circumstances had been different. Or else, as Cordelia has described, psychotherapy would not have been regarded as appropriate. Indeed at one stage, Cordelia and I actually talked it over and drew up a list as to why treatment had been so lengthy, prior to having revealed the different people within.

REASONS WHY IT TOOK SO LONG:

1. The Clinic: Financial difficulties – no long-term therapy. Frieda could only offer ten sessions.
2. Offered alternative = long-term psychotherapy group.

3. Dr M: Started, did not finish – what had been revealed was lost. Parts of Cordelia felt betrayed, having revealed and having to start again. Expected to be better having told all?

4. Cordelia's history: Dependency – beginning a new relationship, with new potential rescuers, then ending it when she felt that they could not deliver – repeating history over and over, again and again.

5. Many health professionals = insurance policies. Resenting boundaries – acting out.

6. Cordelia's husband: Fighting Cordelia's battles – his protection helped Cordelia to cover up (lapses of memory, lapses of continuity). Parts of Cordelia could be very persuasive as well as devious, and would not have allowed her husband to reveal the true state of affairs at home.

7. Multiple system: Secrecy – system's prime concern was to hide the truth.

8. Therapist's training: Occupational Therapy, dramatherapy, NLP, health psychology = lack of knowledge of a multiple system. Knowledge gained from books.

Indeed, quite a telling list, and credit must surely go to Cordelia for being so tenacious and clearly committed to her therapy, but also I feel to the nursing staff, who often had to cope with Cordelia when she was at her most desperate and despairing. In fact, in my opinion, the dedication of the nurses as well as the unique, empowering staff structure at the clinic has played a vital role in allowing Cordelia to achieve the health she has today. Whereas in most NHS hospitals a more rigid hierarchy structure tends to dominate, with the usual effect of squashing spontaneity and initiative, in the clinic, every regular member of staff would be encouraged by the clinic manager to operate quite independently and be responsible for a certain workload, thereby making their particular and unique skills readily available to all the patients whilst maintaining the important structure of working as a team: pooling ideas, providing regular feedback during the handovers, sharing certain workloads, as well as covering for each other when someone was ill or on holiday. The majority of the staff in the clinic at that time would, I'm sure, have described their work environment as providing due job satisfaction.

All the regular nurses and therapists in fact knew every patient very well, and despite my previously expressed views on the matter ('unravelling the covert, selective communication of patients would be more productive, if due communication between all concerned was given its rightful place'), the day to day communication between all the staff was in fact excellent and I, believe, was responsible for the high quality of care. Moreover, the ready availability of the varied consultants whenever difficulties arose or a different treatment needed to be considered, ensured optimum attention and due regard.

Admittedly, the clinic at that time was quite small, catering for about twenty in-patients as well as a number of day patients, and the ratio of regular staff to patients was certainly higher than it tended to be in the NHS. Nor did the nursing staff feel inclined to leave as frequently as they seemed to do in the NHS (it's the only way, I have been informed, to ensure promotion), still, all in all, the excellent staff and the close working relationship which existed in the clinic at that time certainly provided a secure background (despite concerns and worries about receivership), conducive to the development of trust and healing, as well as providing the opportunity for innovative and challenging work. Since I was the only full-time therapist, I was responsible for most of the daily therapy programme as well as seeing patients for individual therapy and providing supervision for certain members of staff. The design of my workload, however, was mainly left up to me. Naturally, any major changes would be discussed prior to being implemented with the clinic manager, her deputy manager, the respective consultants and the nursing and therapy staff, such as the feasibility of working with Cordelia five times a week.

I proposed to increase the sessions because it would enable me to observe switching between personalities and challenge Cordelia's amnesia, as well as provide due time to each personality and its particular story – considering that there appeared to be at least eighteen of them, and I had given myself a kind of deadline of when I intended to leave. This, incidentally, acted as an extra incentive for Cordelia to finally take the risk and let me into her secret world. As Cordelia told me, time was running out, and if she did not take the chance now, it might never come again. Yet, although the intention was certainly there, I still did not really know how I was going to proceed, although as usual, Cordelia would provide the answer.

To begin with, Cordelia had been able to write yet another list of some of her personalities, describing this time their characteristics as well as giving them their rightful name. As Cordelia wrote in her diary that day:

> On my return home (from an evening appointment with Dr C), I seemed to develop a clear picture in my mind, like another revelation, of all the personalities I have inside me, and I wrote them down with such ease it even amazed me afterwards. I didn't realise I knew so much about them. I had a wealth of prior knowledge about all the people I could be! I gave them the names I remembered from childhood. The whole exercise caused me a great deal of anxiety, yet I thought I should feel relieved.

Here then is the list, as Cordelia composed it on 11 January 1995.

As a child these separate personalities developed – some before the age of five years.

Cordelia – sad child, not appearing to be here – tries to hide all feelings, guilt, shame, etc. Became secretive and deceptive. She must not remember anything or must not tell anyone how she feels or what is going on. Dislikes herself. She is afraid and rather prim and proper. Always compliant and cooperative. Very alone. A weak smile.

Stephanie – (Cordelia's twin sister). Very sad, despairing, full of hopelessness, frail, always ill, wants to die.

Elizabeth – throws things, behaved badly, screams, hurts herself, feels trapped, panics, is jealous and angry.

Victoria – confident, academic, strong, adores company and parties. Dresses smartly, can be attractive and interesting. Denies the truth but knows all the other children. She has a good memory. Achieves.

Bryony – (mother's name). Cold, sarcastic, cruel, also indifferent to others. Demands, abuses, seeks self-gratification in all things. Can be creative. Her flip side is 'Poor Me Syndrome.' Schizophrenic.

Esther – swimmer, tennis and hockey player, loves the outdoor life. Dancer, can be graceful and strong.

Rosalind – (another sister). Singer, pianist, lover of music, actress. Not always confident, but gentle.

Angela – carer of little brother and mother. She became a good nurse, able to cope with a crisis. Defender of others. Firm but kind.

Felicity – flirtatious, extrovert, daring, passionate, likes to be the centre of attraction.

Geraldine – (grandmother's name). Argumentative, defends herself. Can be paranoid, strong, aggressive, and selfish.

Gillian – giggly, fun-loving, plays jokes on others. Likes telling funny stories, can be a real clown. Laughs in a serious situation.

Peter – dependable father-like, protective, kind, caring, capable. Not around very much, especially when most needed.

Martin – (brother to Bryony – second brother's name). Kills, experiments, dissects and inflicts pain. Smells of chloroform, ether and rubber gloves. Sometimes smells of cider, plum wine and chemicals he mixes. He is sly and very critical. Grandiose ideas about himself and his achievements. Uses threats, deceit and other weapons to get his victims. Shouts. Very sadistic nature. Abuses. Viciously strong in word and deed. Demands attention. Cold and cruel. No friends. Great achiever academically but hopeless at sport. Violent temper. Well dressed and clean.

Mary – (Magdalene), age 13 years. Feels injured and dirty. Doesn't eat, or makes herself vomit. Dislikes herself intensely. Feels full of guilt and shame. Fearful.

Zillah – (shadow friend); Always with Cordelia, everyone liked her. She had the same experiences in life as Cordelia but coped better.

Delia – (age 19 years). Had met future husband. Felt loved and fell 'in-love' – despairing, hopeless/strength, courage, depression, suicide, amnesia. Thought the past was behind her. She didn't feel worthy of being loved, and became afraid and suspicious of feeling good inside, but being loved gave her the freedom to express her dislike of her Self, found life all too much. The other children kept appearing but she tried to push them away and become someone new. Depression worsened over the years. Life was a huge struggle. She always felt alone.

Secondly, on the Monday of the second week in January, the nursing staff reported to me that someone had been phoning them up during the weekend, not speaking or responding to their questions. All they could hear was the sound of music, produced by what appeared to be a music box. When I confronted Cordelia with this, (the reader might remember that I had given Cordelia a music box as a Christmas present), at first, she denied that she had made such a call. But when I encouraged her to realise that playing the music box over the phone was in fact a very positive step, since it meant that whoever had made the call had wanted to be found out, as the caller would know, not only that the nurses would inform me, but also that because I actually gave Cordelia the music box, I would of course recognise the tune.

Young Cordelia hardly ever spoke, and appeared not to have a voice. She was the one, Cordelia said, who had played the music box over the phone. Now, since I had uncovered her, found her out, she began to talk about her life with her mother and how the badness and sadness of her mother had stuck to her. Cordelia explained, that she had been terrorised into silence by her mother telling her that she would be killed if she ever told anyone the secrets of the family. Cordelia, small child that she was, had of course believed that her mother would keep her word. During that first Monday session then, Cordelia graphically told me about the abuse of her mother, the hot baths, the disinfectant, the colonic lavages, hanging her to dry in the loft. Here was Cordelia, telling me more precise details of abuse which she had not told me before. Yet, the astonishing part was to follow. The details of the abuse were bad enough, but towards the end of the session, she suddenly sat upright and in a different, more abrupt tone of voice asked me, 'What has she been telling you?' She was clearly intimating that she did not know what had just been revealed. As it was nearly time to finish, I replied that tomorrow we would talk about it further. Cordelia then said goodbye and I was left behind wondering what it was all about.

Was it all true? Obviously, I reasoned, anyone who has read *Sybil*, would make instant connections and would likewise question whether Cordelia had in fact simply copied Sybil's accounts of being hung upside down by her mother? Then again, I contemplated, if she had not, could these mothers really be that cruel? In point of fact, would it not be preferable to believe that Cordelia and Sybil had made it all up, otherwise it must all be too painfully true! And if it was all true, could Cordelia really not have known what she had just been telling me? I certainly had never encountered such amnesia before, yet, I had to admit, something about Cordelia's demeanour had also told me that her question had been genuine, for I had undeniably heard the fear in her voice that young Cordelia might well have let the cat out of the bag. Hence I concluded, come what may. If I was to get to the bottom of things, I would first of all have to find a way of working with this phenomenon of amnesia, or else come next year, I would be no further than I was today. This juggling with the truth, I realised, could go on forever.

On Tuesday, therefore, I asked Cordelia (Delia) if she would ask young Cordelia whether she would draw for me the details of what she had told me the previous day. I reassured her that the drawings were not meant to be masterpieces but rather just an expression of her feelings and of what she remembered. I then provided her with a stack of loose drawing paper, felt-tip pens and crayons. There was a desk in the room, an office chair and a comfortable armchair. Patients usually sat in the armchair opposite me, the desk was by my side and spare chairs were stacked up by the wall. In order to enable Cordelia to draw, I would invite her to come and sit at the desk next to me.

Young Cordelia then produced her first drawing: a stick figure, with her eyes covered by her hands, no face, no features, but a head full of smog and her legs splayed open at a very unnatural angle. She did not talk, just drew. In quick succession she then drew the outline of another stick figure in a bath whose legs were tied to a rope hanging from the ceiling, and a second larger figure standing at the back of the bath, who had attached some kind of hose or tube to the stick figure in the bath. As I said, Cordelia did not speak, she just cried silent tears and in the corner of the second drawing wrote: vaginal and colonic lavage – disinfectant – scalding water. Cordelia then did a third drawing of some pointed rafters and someone wrapped in what appeared to be a cocoon hanging upside down by a twisting rope attached to the rafters. On the edge of the paper was another figure – not a stick figure this time but a well-rounded figure with a defined head, although it still did not have a face or arms. Cordelia sat back, and after a while responded to my question asking her if she could tell me what the drawings meant. Cordelia then printed the words 'bathroom – don't tell anyone – threats' on the third drawing, after which she seemed to find her voice again and while she added the words 'kill – die – terror – numb – evil – bad – sick' she began to reveal the meaning of the drawings, steadily replacing sadness with anger, repeatedly circling the word terror. Finally, she added the name Zillah to the round figure and explained that originally, she had been the tailor's dummy, which stood in the loft but hence had become her friend Zillah. Cordelia did no more drawings that day but instead wrote about her mother masturbating her and then using her tiny body to masturbate herself with, concluding with the words, 'She stinks.'

On a second piece of paper, Cordelia then wrote 'I'm very lucky,' describing how she used to believe it when others said that she was indeed lucky to have a mother who made all these pretty clothes for her, angrily retorting that her mother was in fact lucky she had Cordelia to look after her all these years and that her mother was the devil's daughter, and 'not me'.

Cordelia had also written the words, 'deaf in one ear', but had crossed them out. At the time, I obviously noticed her doing so but did not inquire as to why she had done so, since I assumed it was just a mistake. However, time would teach me that there is no such thing as just a mistake when dealing with a multiple system, because later on it would become clear, that 'deaf in one ear' was a remark which actually referred to another personality, Elizabeth (the angry one), who came (was created by Cordelia) in the loft in order to help Cordelia fight back – 'screamed the place down' – and for her pains got hit by her mother round the head so often that she became 'deaf in one ear'.

As I described, when Cordelia (as the young Cordelia, the silent one) at first began drawing, she was sad and did not speak, but steadily became more and more upset whilst sketching the image of the loft, and ended up by drawing angry circles around the word terror. Obviously, Elizabeth had been waiting in the wings. But who then crossed out her words? Who held Elizabeth in check? Who decided that it was too soon to let her loose? As I duly discovered, within a multiple system, there would usually be a reason of sorts for a certain action; some long-term goal to be achieved. Indeed, I swiftly realised, that there truly was design in this madness, and with time, I simply learned to trust the system as well as respect its ingenuity and deviousness.

The next day, Cordelia in fact brought her wedding dress with her. She wanted, she said, to get in touch with her feelings about it all. She wanted to experience the sadness of it all, which anger (in the shape of Elizabeth) would normally prevent her from doing so. Although Cordelia loathed the dress, since it reminded her of the mother that was, she had also treasured it. Not only because it was her wedding dress, and thus symbolic of a new way of life, of being loved and cared for, but also because it represented the mother that could have been. However, when we in fact examined the dress, we discovered that in the making of it, an error had occurred which her mother had covered up by adding a piece of lace. As Cordelia had always believed that her mother's dressmaking was flawless, this glaring mistake in so important a dress came as a great shock, 'As though even this special day, she had to spoil somehow!'

Cordelia then produced another set of drawings, depicting the emptiness of her mother, the ray of friendship she got from Zillah, the anger of Elizabeth who was burning with rage, as well as detailing how Cordelia would dissociate: become one with the bath, her body expanding, filling the bath, after which, she would float up to the ceiling where she would be safe and able to observe her mother. Cordelia, in addition, also painted how she felt hounded by three abusing devils, felt shattered in many pieces, trapped in her mother's web, and sketched how her mother was the worm, the snake, which had invaded the apple (now rotten to the core, though still appearing whole and sound). Cordelia ended this series of drawings by depicting how her mother in reality was no more than 'a heap of dung steaming in the sun'. After this, we explored certain implications of these drawings, i.e., who exactly were the three devils? I also tentatively introduced the idea of Cordelia having created various as-if personalities in order to help her cope with such distress. Cordelia said that she could accept that this might well have been the reason why her inner people came into existence. She nevertheless insisted that when she was very young, they were very real and very separate, and that she never knew when or into whom she would change, recounting how she suddenly would begin throwing things around in school, behave abominably, and once, even got herself expelled.

The following morning, another phone call was made to the clinic. This time, it was someone speaking French, although the caller did not really hide the fact that she was indeed Cordelia. In fact, she (Delia) told the nurses that Young Cordelia had been crying all night, and that she was concerned about her, but that she would make sure that young Cordelia would come to her therapy that afternoon. Cordelia's first reaction, when I asked her about the meaning of her call, was again to deny that she had made such a call, but then confirmed that Victoria (the efficient one – who came to help Cordelia be 'grown up about the abortion') had made many such calls, though in the past she would have made certain that she would not be recognised. Cordelia then talked about her distress discovering the botched up wedding dress, and how she had driven to the seaside afterwards (which, as it turned out, Cordelia tended to do quite frequently whenever she felt distressed), but how this time, she had actually felt connected with nature: as though by allowing herself to experience her suffering, as though by virtue of actually having suffered, she had in fact been able to connect with nature, with God, with others.

Naturally, we also explored the implications that like Cordelia, Victoria, so it seemed, now equally wanted to be found out, and what exactly this meant in terms of Cordelia and her inner world. On Friday, thus, not only did we continue exploring the different personalities in terms of as-if people, creations of Cordelia's mind, but Victoria also began to enlarge on what her function might have been and how she had maintained 'the others' by preferring to believe that the abuse did not take place. 'That sort of thing does not happen in white middle-class homes, and certainly not when they belong to a profession.'

Although she (Victoria) declined to enlarge on what she meant by 'that sort of thing', Victoria, however, agreed with me that something was certainly amiss, if according to her drawing of Cordelia's past, Cordelia was no more than 'a delicate flower who had safely weathered a few storms in her life'. Then why, I pointed out, did Cordelia experience such levels of distress, need to come for therapy, and why indeed was Victoria so concerned about Cordelia, and why did Victoria herself need medication to help her sleep?

The first week of working with Cordelia every day had ended. I remember feeling rather optimistic, as well as relieved that my suggestion to increase the work to that level had paid off. Not only did Cordelia feel that she was able to cope with daily therapy on an outpatient basis and wanted to continue (far cheaper of course, and less inclined to encourage her dependency and habitual flight into the sick role), but we had also, for the first time, been able to work with some kind of continuity, where material brought to one session could be enlarged upon in the next. Furthermore, we had also clearly established the immediate task ahead: to unravel the cause, to listen to each peculiar story of why each personality had been created, as well as confirm their subsequent function and the role they had each played in Cordelia's life.

To the reader, all this might sound perhaps rather obvious and straightforward. To Cordelia, however, this task ahead, this unravelling, had severe implications and consequences. Indeed, whereas Cordelia quite resolutely had always perceived herself to be but a victim at the mercy of her mother, brother, grandmother and father, here was this therapist, encouraging her to think in terms of cause and effect, to realise that she had in fact created a coping mechanism which had enabled her to escape from her abusers, albeit in her mind only. Today, she could no longer go on denying responsibility for the way this coping mechanism now behaved.

To Cordelia, it must have been comparable to a teacher suddenly discovering that a class of unruly children were in fact her very own. And that, when the school bell would ring, she could no longer send them all home to their respective parents, but that from now on, she had to take care of them and teach them the ways of the world, for real.

No wonder then that when eventually all stories were told, all children revealed, Cordelia wanted to give them all to me, saying that she felt as though they belonged more to me, the therapist who had 'brought them out of the woodwork', than that they actually belonged to her. No wonder then that Cordelia would rather be declared mad or bad, and frequently engineered events with such an aim in mind, since it would allow her to claim that the abuse had all been a figment of her mad mind. No wonder then that during the following weekend, Cordelia would run scared, and cry for help in her own inimitable way. On the Monday of the second week, Cordelia revealed that, on Saturday, she had called all the various emergency services, who had arrived at her door together. She said that she didn't really understand why she had done so, other than that she had been lonely, and that 'one of the children must have made the call'. Luckily enough, she had 'switched' again before the services arrived, and she had been able to talk her way out of the situation and out of trouble. Yet all was not as desperate as before. Although Cordelia had called for help in this manner before, this time she said – much to her surprise – she had actually felt guilty for doing so. But this was not the only revelation in store for me that morning, for when we subsequently looked through the drawings of the first week, Cordelia refused to believe that the drawings were hers. She said that she did not remember drawing them, and that she certainly did not recognise the one which I said had been drawn by someone called Victoria. Although by the end of the session, she had again changed her mind and had once again 'switched', as I wrote in my therapy notes that evening: 'When I assured her that the drawing was hers, she was able to recall that she had indeed drawn it, and once again realised, how a large part of her wants to deny the abuse and maintain her mother's secret.'

Naturally, from then on, I always made sure that Cordelia duly signed and dated each and every drawing. However, continuity was indeed producing results. Not only did Cordelia, that evening, write down certain details of the abuse in black and white, but during the rest of the week Cordelia stayed with the subject of denial, depicting it as a giant snake who had hypnotised her family and certain personalities, especially Victoria, who despite being able 'to empty her head of the abuse during the day' would nevertheless be troubled by harrowing thoughts at night. She produced a long list of bewildering thoughts such as:

1. I've remembered horrific circumstances.
2. I feel crazy for having such thoughts.
3. I feel I will be punished.
4. I feel no one will believe me.
5. I feel disgusting and dirty.
6. I feel bad, so bad things happen to me.
7. My mother may have been right about me, and no one else has the courage to tell me the truth. Dr C just says I'm damaged.
8. I am frightened to feel the full implications of the secrets I've told.
9. I feel responsible for what happened.
10. I feel shame, guilt and despair about it all.
11. I feel helpless and powerless to stop these thoughts.

During that same session, Cordelia also drew a picture of how the abuse momentarily, deceptively, could make her feel very much alive; how receiving such 'false tokens of love' felt better than nothing; felt like a 'bolt of lightning' before the pain of the abuse, as usual, would make her 'fly away again' and thus enable her to escape from this 'iceberg of deceit'. Equally, during this therapy session, we also discovered how the various parts can and will communicate with each other and with the therapist, when you pose a question or make an observation and subsequently invite them to comment on what has just been revealed or has been learned. A most useful strategy, which we would of course employ again and again, and provided both Cordelia and myself with valuable feedback. For example, alongside the drawing of the snake which had hypnotised her family, Cordelia also wrote down the following dialogue between Cordelia (so we assumed) and Victoria – each part giving their point of view, when I asked them how they each explained the abuse.

The abuse was stifling, and crushing, life threatening. This was done by the most sick, sadistic of mothers. Victoria can't cope with unpleasant truth. Time she did.

Victoria: This is vivid imagination. Cordelia is prone to panic and imagination of the most dramatic tragedies of life. Okay, I'm learning.

Cordelia consequently ended that week by drawing how she was halfway up the hill of recovery and had arrived at a crossroads, though the way ahead was blocked by a high wall. Yet she also depicted how 'people are urging her to go on', and that she was beginning to recognise that the various personalities – if they were linked together – could provide her with the metaphorical rope which would enable her to get over the wall, to where life was waiting for her. Two weeks were gone, and despite some reservations and Cordelia's initial refusal to recognise her drawings, Cordelia clearly seemed to have taken the plunge and was no longer unduly concerned about introducing me to her people within. In fact, by the end of the third week, Cordelia had also introduced me to Rosalind, the willing child who only likes to talk about nice things, likes to sing and originally came to help Cordelia cope with the abuse of her father. And to Stephanie, who usually felt 'half-dead', was named after Cordelia's dead twin, and came in the hope, that her mother might love her. I also met the two adult parts of Cordelia which we later on would call Delia I and Delia II, and who each came when Cordelia was nineteen, 'in order to control the children and not scare her husband away'.

Delia I, we agreed, embraced Esther, Angela, Rosalind, Felicity, Rebekah, Gillian and Victoria, whereas Delia II we thought was an amalgamation of Stephanie, Peter, Elizabeth, Martin, Bryony, Geraldine and Mary, although each list – as we would subsequently discover – was at that time far from complete. Delia I moreover, was also the person who, since having met her future husband, had been the one who had been in conscious control of Cordelia's mind and body most of the time, and thus had lived Cordelia's adult life for her. By the end of the fourth week, Cordelia furthermore also introduced me to Gillian, the giggling child, who came when her brother was performing a female circumcision on her and helped Cordelia to 'laugh in the face of severe trauma'. And to Felicity, the flirtatious girl who came to protect Peter and give her father's colleagues at his place of work 'what they were really after', and who subsequently, after the rape on holiday, helped Cordelia to get her revenge for the rape by encouraging many boyfriends, teasing them, encouraging their sexual advances but then withdrawing and 'kicking them'.

As before, Cordelia produced a number of drawings. Some were vivid pictures of the sexual abuse by her mother and the mutilation by her brother. Others depicted her desire to be separate from her mother; a person in her own right. Yet others recorded a dream, what it meant 'to be Elizabeth', and the words of a lament:

I hate the way you glare at me
Your cruel eyes burning down upon the tiny child you see
Battered and kicked into the ground
Neglected, betrayed
Crushed the life from me
Washed me out, turned my life into a torment so extreme
Fear and terror invaded all my being
Why was no one there to save me, no one to be angry for me?
Support and protect me from the cruellest and most wicked of mothers
I longed to die
Trapped, imprisoned in the darkest Hell.

Where was love?
I looked for it everywhere
Wanting to be special to someone
Who should have loved me
I was that someone's child.

At that time, who drew what was not always very clear, as Cordelia was still quite reluctant to put a more precise name to each drawing, signing them all as Delia. Certainly, when we read through my therapy notes again towards the end of Cordelia's therapy, it was quite obvious that in the early weeks there were times when we had in fact used the wrong name. However, the value of the drawings as a therapeutic tool was by now becoming quite clear. Not only did the process of committing the many secret mental images inside her head on to paper enable Cordelia to literally reduce her horrific memories to a much safer and more manageable drawing, thereby making them accessible and able to be scrutinised. But the drawings also allowed me to challenge Cordelia's denial, and affirm that the content of those revealing drawings did relate to her, since she naturally had to admit, whenever she disputed that the drawings were hers, that she had indeed signed and dated them.

Likewise, the fact that I also read out my therapy notes of the previous weeks to her ensured that amnesia became less of a handicap, less able to dull the waters, as more and more details of the abuse were now becoming available to many more personalities. In the past, Victoria, it seemed, would in fact have filtered any such incoming information and would only have allowed certain details to be common knowledge. Since Victoria was older than the others, (she came after the abortion), she could of course quite easily deny that the earlier abuse by the father, brother, grandmother or mother had in fact taken place. Victoria could after all (legitimately) only remember the later sexual abuse by her mother.

Therapy thus was producing a shift in the way the system had been controlled. Whereas before, Victoria had been the one to monitor the information – 'She knows everything' – and Delia II especially had controlled the children within, whilst yet other parts had painstakingly ensured that

Cordelia would not reveal too many secrets, now there was this therapist to contend with who would insist on showing 'every one of them these vile drawings'. Of course, certain parts (Bryony, Geraldine, Martin) who did not believe that therapy would do her much good in any case, began to fight back. First of all, they made Cordelia believe that I would be angry with her for 'sitting crying in reception with Anne'. Secondly, they made anonymous phone calls over the weekend, both to the clinic and to me at my home, hoping that such disregard for the boundaries would get Cordelia into trouble with her therapist – having obtained my home number by dialling 1471 after I had phoned Cordelia to confirm an appointment.

Thirdly, those same parts, I presume, also tried to persuade Cordelia to disappear (dissociate), making her believe that she was once again locked up in the asylum and was quite mad, and that therefore she had best stop with this therapy lark, since it would be just a waste of time.

In addition, they subsequently also began to stir up her anxiety, focussing on loss and on the end of therapy, convincing her that I would end her therapy because I might have had enough of her. Finally, when all else failed, they seemed to withdraw, leaving Cordelia to 'wake up in the morning as Stephanie', the one who tended to feel overwhelmed with the many dead children within her, and hence would take the medication in order to try and kill herself. Naturally, every side-tracking manoeuvre resulted in considerable time spent reassuring Cordelia that therapy was not about to end, that she was not mad, that neither Anne nor I were angry with her, etc., although I of course advised her that having obtained my phone number via devious means was not acceptable.

However, the majority of the system appeared to accept the authority of this therapist, helped I'm sure by the fact that Cordelia and I actually did some trust exercises together, Cordelia literally putting her safety in my hands. And because, I had enlisted the help of Victoria, who from then on became a valuable ally, after I had suggested that Cordelia ask Victoria to help her access her memories by going 'inside' and simply ask her what happened. Discovering that Victoria was prepared to cooperate with her and allow her access to her memories was of course a major step forward, which made Cordelia feel that she was no longer quite so much at the mercy of those parts who had always appeared to wish her ill. Furthermore, in the course of the past weeks, Cordelia had also become aware that she 'clicked' into another person-ality and then 'clicked' into yet another one, realising that she could have a measure of control over this multiple system and thus might be able to monitor its eccentricities as well as discover why in fact those parts were bent on sabotage. As Cordelia recorded in her diary that evening:

> Gillian remembered her pictures from Monday, then a click happened as Frieda started to read and Stephanie, cold and numb, appeared for a short while. Frieda got out the drawings and when the ones of the bath and the loft were held in

front of me, another click happened and Cordelia was there with Frieda.

Cordelia feels very sad and feels the pain, sees the faces, hears the water and the creaking of the rope on the wooden rafters, hears her mother's voice. Then Frieda wanted me to talk to Victoria because she is the one who denies the suffering. Victoria is quite clever and won't show herself if she is to be challenged. The quick clicking from one to another is new and felt very strange and confusing. It felt like feeling new emotions, yet they were emotions that are only compartmentalised into the different personalities and were being felt at a faster rate in succession. This feels as if I am writing about someone else, not me. I often feel I am my abuser, or my abuser is inside me. I felt these feelings as I went to sleep.

In addition, the fact that Cordelia was now keeping a diary also meant that she was engaged in a tremendous amount of really courageous homework which was producing remarkable insights – such as the realisation that she had made herself adore her abuser because she had been desperate for closeness, love, attention and affection. And how she had actually preferred to think of herself as bad and responsible for the abuse, rather than accept that she had been powerless, wholly unable to prevent the abuse, or to change what had happened. As Cordelia so poignantly wrote, 'The thought of being so powerless makes me weep.'

However, Cordelia was actually writing in a number of different diaries. One had been written in a large round, more childlike hand, and another in a more spiky, frenzied hand. This of course caused a measure of confusion as we often had to try and work out who wrote what. Nonetheless, Cordelia's homework was also producing vital guidelines and the means to get out of this multiple system, since it was making her acutely aware of the danger of continuing to employ dissociation indiscriminately. Again an excerpt from one of her diaries will explain it better than I could:

When I awoke on Friday I felt I was becoming disconnected. My world and everyone in it was becoming more and more distant. I felt tremendous fear because this time, I didn't want to go into my psychotic state to a safe place. I knew this time, that if I did, I would stay there for ever. It seemed more serious, or I was more aware of what was happening. I had to do something to stop myself being sucked into my black hole. It felt like an experience of being pulled into the abyss. I sat up, then very firmly I talked to myself about not splitting off or disconnecting because it achieves nothing and could have serious consequences. I had the feeling that if I let it happen this time, I would be very seriously ill and maybe for ever. It felt final and loud warning bells were sounding in my head. I have never been so certain before that I had to fight to stop this happening.

Naturally, we also used Cordelia's homework during her therapy, both of us, in turn, reading out loud the previous day's writing, or any letters I had asked her to write. My narrations of course, were mainly for the benefit of Cordelia's children within. Thus, despite the earlier attempts by certain parts to sabotage her therapy, Cordelia nonetheless appeared to have gained some measure of control, as well as due awareness, of the very real need to switch off the automatic pilot: to fight her habitual way of coping with the world, and no longer select to split off, or disconnect at the least sign of distress. What's more, the recent hiatus had equally not prevented her from producing a number of important tell-tale drawings, i.e., Cordelia had explained her dread about loss by drawing yet another sunset, (a metaphor for losing the ideal father). She had also depicted how Stephanie is no more than a 'thinking head', and that her whole body is quite numb. In addition, she had also managed to draw 'Stephanie's many children contained within her body', as well as record a recent realisation that she needed to somehow 'integrate Stephanie's children, and replace them with better objects'. Motivated perhaps, by now understanding a recurring dream Cordelia said she had experienced at different times during her therapy:

> I inhabit this large black hole. All these children appear and they are very strange and unrecognisable to me. I see a female uterus, ovaries and fallopian tubes before me and these children are being pulled back into the uterus by a pair of large hands.

During the same session, Cordelia also drew an image of her mother burning at the stake. Once again it seemed that Elizabeth and her anger were never very far away! But even more significant was the fact that during the following week, Cordelia would come to realise that, as well as the covert attempt by the 'three devils' to sabotage her therapy, yet another agenda had perhaps been motivating her actions; as usual, secretly, resolutely directing her from behind the scenes. For sure, some of the strange phone calls we had received at the clinic over the weekend and during the past week had been made by someone speaking in an Arabic tongue. At first, when I questioned Cordelia about whether she had in fact made the calls, Cordelia, as usual, denied hotly a) that she could speak Arabic, and b) that she had made any such calls. But once again when she felt encouraged and reassured, she confessed. Yes, she had made the calls, although she quickly added that she 'was truly nonplussed as to why'. However, after due discussion, and taking the previous week into account, Cordelia consequently ventured the following explanation, duly wondering whether since they (the three devils), had made her believe that she was back in the asylum, she had in fact been impersonating the woman in charge of the girls in the asylum (whom Cordelia believed spoke Arabic – although Victoria later on told her that the woman spoke German).

By the end of the week, however, Cordelia in fact remembered that Mary Magdalene, (the sad one who *came* to prevent Felicity from being raped, and thereafter helped Cordelia by being the sexual partner of her husband) could indeed speak Arabic: 'A scripture teacher had once taught the class Arabic and Hebrew!' Consequently, the strange phone calls suddenly made sense; the cloak and dagger subterfuge had, once again, had a real purpose! Yet another personality, it seemed, had finally felt able to reveal itself. And just like the Young Cordelia and Victoria before her, Mary Magdalene had obviously decided to allow herself to be found out, surreptitiously, via the telephone. This meant that Mary Magdalene could now tell all, and draw the pictures of the rape.

I'm sure that by now, the reader is wondering, as I did, can it all be as involved and complex as it sounds? The answer I'm afraid is yes. To Cordelia, each child, each part had since childhood not only been very real, but had also been very separate and had been created for a specific function. Each part was in fact quite independent, and each part in turn was able to take control of Cordelia's conscious mind and her body as and when needed, duly behaving according to its particular design. How then had Cordelia achieved this? The set of drawings by Mary Magdalene clearly illustrated that for each child/part, a certain beginning had occurred and that their creation by Cordelia as well as the selection of their name, etc., had not just been a random affair but had in fact been well thought out.

As Cordelia was able to tell me later on, after all the stories had been told and collated, when she went abroad for that ill-fated Easter holiday, Elizabeth had in fact hoped to find a new loving family who might take her in, adopt her and care for her. Whilst accompanying the father of the family with whom she was staying on day trips and visits to his place of work, Felicity, reminiscent of her days in the recreational lounge at her father's place of work, had taken over from Elizabeth and had begun to flirt with this potential brand-new father and of course also with his colleagues. When this man afterwards began to rape Cordelia, Felicity at first had struggled indignantly, since being raped had not been her brief. She was after all meant to be the one whom her father would only allow to marry a 'damn fine man'.

Even though she might indeed be a 'gorgeous little thing', she was certainly not for general use, or 'just a catch for someone when she grows up' as her father's colleagues had joked.

Elizabeth then came to help Felicity, struggling even harder, kicking, biting. But of course she could not match the man's strength. Then, feeling utterly powerless as Cordelia described in her diary, 'I left my body.' Just as she had done before when her mother washed her out, her brother mutilated her, Cordelia floated up to the ceiling and observed herself being raped, and in the process created yet another person to help her cope with what was happening to her. Thus, once again, the magic mirror of her mind allowed her to see another child lying on the bed being abused; allowed her to create yet another other-self. Mary Magdalene would become her name, and from that moment on, like the prostitute who found acceptance in the eyes of Jesus, she would dutifully play her part in Cordelia's life, eventually becoming her husband's sexual partner, because he was so different and asked her permission to have sex. 'No one had ever asked before!' Indeed, as time went on, what had originally been just an as-if person created by Cordelia's mind, seemed to become a person for real. For sure, as we would discover much later, there was usually a second event which seemed to allow every as-if person to be born for a second time and become autonomous in its own right. But how, repeating my question, did Cordelia achieve such deception?

The reader might remember how I briefly described positive and negative hallucinations as part of a hypnotic trance. It is quite clear of course that when Cordelia dissociated in the bath, when she was being raped and floated up to the ceiling, that she had once again gone into a trance state, which enabled her not just to create these Other-Selves with her mind's eye, but actually begin to see and hear them. All would have remained just a fabrication of her mind, a 'neurotic falsification of reality' as Fenichel would describe it – a means to 'digest yet another nonedible object', had it not been for shame and trance logic, which seem to have allowed Cordelia to continue fooling herself and accept the illogical aberration, that she was indeed no longer there in person (a negative hallucination), but that there really was someone else who was being abused instead of her (a positive hallucination). But I had better explain precisely what I mean.

Whereas in time Cordelia might well have been able to challenge her perceptions and reason that Other-Selves could not really exist (in the same way a child may grow out of an imaginary friend), I believe that the shame of belonging to such a dysfunctional family and especially the shame about joining in with the vile games her father asked her to play, the shame of being this dirty child, in truth prevented her from doing so. Shame, writes Fenichel (p.139), is in many ways connected with guilt feelings; 'Shame of oneself.' Moreover, he explained, 'I feel ashamed' means 'I do not want to be seen.' Therefore, persons who feel ashamed hide themselves or at least avert their faces. However, they may also close their eyes and refuse to look. This is a kind of magical gesture, arising from the magical belief that anyone who does not look cannot be looked at.

For sure, as Cordelia's very first drawing of the stick figure holding its hands over its eyes so graphically depicted. From a very early age onwards, Cordelia had indeed closed her eyes, and had refused to look. Not only did she no longer see her father (she only ever saw his eyes), she equally, no longer saw herself, but saw all those other children instead. However, whereas shame might indeed have closed her eyes and allowed her to go 'behind the mirror', trance logic, in an attempt to keep her integrity and belief in her self intact, would allow her to keep them shut and stay in this never-never wonderland, where each one of her make-believe playmates, longed-for sister, brother, ideal mother, grandmother and much needed Other-Selves would adroitly be turned into real people.

Trance logic, I believe, motivated by shame, simply allowed her to reason that these as-if children just had to be for real, otherwise Cordelia herself would be this evil child who behaved in such a wicked way. Cordelia herself would be as bad as her father. As Cordelia described, she simply could not be that child. She was after all prim and proper! She just could not be that bad, but Peter could! Elizabeth certainly was!

And thus the trap was sprung, for once Cordelia had decided to make Peter a real boy, give him a name, a role to play, all the Other-Selves which were to follow equally had to be for real. For if they were not, Peter couldn't be real either, which meant that the child in the mirror had to be Cordelia. Thus obligingly – as and when required, as and when events in the real world dictated – each other-self was duly born again into a real person with its own name and specific function. For instance, when Cordelia, at the age of (almost) fourteen, went to have an abortion five months after being raped, five months after she had initially created Mary Magdalene, trance logic, once again motivated by the same feelings of shame, allowed her to reason that Mary Madalene just had to be for real, otherwise it would have been Cordelia who had been the dirty, filthy child her mother said she was – otherwise it would have been Cordelia who would have had to cope with 'the nurses and doctors glaring at her, for destroying a life'.

Indeed, as Cordelia had done many times before, she simply convinced herself that Mary Magdalene was real, that she was a separate person with her very own name, characteristics, peculiar history, pertinent memories and specific function. Thus, yet another other-self had become a truly separate autonomous structure who from then on, in the role of Mary Magdalene, would cope with all the sexual demands Cordelia might encounter.

The reader might well say oh yes, obviously! However, trance logic is such, as one of my lecturers explained. It allows us to distort the truth, it allows us to explain the illogical. For example, imagine a hypnotised person who has been told that he can no longer see a table standing in the middle of the room. He will of course walk in a circle around the invisible table when he is subsequently asked to cross the room. When he is then asked why he in fact made such a detour since nothing stood in his way, the hapless person, rather than lose face, rather than lose self-esteem by stating the obvious, because the table was in the way, will fabricate an explanation, such as, 'I thought I saw a penny on the floor which is why I walked in a circle.' Such is trance logic! It helps us to preserve our self-esteem, it helps us to make compromises, it helps us convince ourselves and may indeed deservedly be called the liar in oneself. Moreover, trance logic in my opinion most certainly also helped Cordelia to make sense of a senseless world, and more precisely, helped her to survive it by maintaining this unique, creative, life saving deception of being many different people.

As I described before, some can indeed hypnotise themselves and tolerate trance logic far better than others, as I have experienced myself. Once, as a volunteer demonstrating hypnosis to a group of dentists and GPs, I was asked 'not to see' a certain doctor sitting on a chair, and to throw a newspaper on the (apparently) empty chair. The hypnotist in fact wanted to demonstrate negative and positive hallucinations to his audience. I knew that I was in a hypnotic trance, as I had experienced a trance state many times before, but a part of me was somehow unable to comply with the request. The hypnotist then switched to a positive hallucination, which he said most people find much easier to do, and asked me 'to see' a candelabra on the vacant chair next to him and to go and pick it up. Again I found it difficult at first to comply with the request, but wanting to cooperate, I duly visualised with my mind's eye a candelabra. But when I picked it up, to my surprise I exclaimed, 'It's a plastic one!' Thus I realised afterwards, trance logic may indeed have helped me to see a candelabra but it had obviously also reached a compromise with my internal observer and made it a mere plastic one – one which was not real – thereby allowing me, although in a very different way, to keep my integrity and belief in my Self as intact.

How then did I approach Cordelia's Trance Logic during therapy? To begin with I encouraged each personality to tell their particular story as though they were a separate person, as though they had led an independent life. We then pasted together all the various tales so that they began to form an ongoing history of Cordelia's life. In fact, the drawings by Mary Magdalene had given us yet another tool with which we were able to unravel this deception. Simply by asking Cordelia to draw or describe the very first thing a certain personality can see or hear, taste, smell, touch, etc., we actually began to get access to the moment of their creation and their subsequent coming of age. As a result, the fragments of stories Cordelia used to tell me were beginning to form a complete account of a certain event. Whereas a certain memory had always been cut off at a crucial point, cut up like pieces of a jigsaw puzzle, now the different personalities were each providing either the beginning, the middle or the end; i.e. since Mary Magdalene came halfway through the abuse, after Cordelia had floated out of her body and was looking down at herself from the ceiling, the very first thing she saw and therefore sketched, was the top of the other (four poster) bed which stood in the room, whereafter she drew her own empty besmeared bed and the basin full with blood in which Cordelia had washed herself. After which, Felicity drew the beginning of the rape: his huge hands tearing at her body, ripping her nightdress, and Elizabeth depicted the middle: his leering eyes, his panting, the penetration, ending with Mary Magdalene again describing the end product: 'His Semen – His Saliva – His Baby – Her Blood – Her Tears – Her Shame.'

Secondly, having told their tale, we also explored the specific function of each personality in Cordelia's life, and I literally began to reason with them all, attempting to shift Cordelia from a fixed dogmatic belief system to a more open hypothetical one, gradually introducing her to a flexible system, which facilitated and encouraged her to ask herself a series of pertinent questions such as, had each as-if person fulfilled the reason why they had been created? Did they need to update their manner of protecting Cordelia? Did they indeed serve the better good of Cordelia, rather than just think of themselves? Had they in fact remained a child living in the past, instead of in the present? Should each personality continue behaving as though they were separate and lived alone in the body? If Stephanie succeeded in killing the body, would it not mean that they would all die?

These questions were obviously geared towards enlarging her cognitive framework and freeing herself from this enduring trance, literally forcing her to begin using the analytical left side of her brain in equal proportions, whereas the imaginative right side had obviously been the favourite tool with which she had decoded and interpreted the world. (The reader might actually remember how Cordelia described that she tended to suffer from immense headaches on the right side of her head. Perhaps it is no wonder that she did so.)

These questions also forced Cordelia to examine and appraise the actions of her internal system; i.e. after Elizabeth had drawn the pictures of the rape during her therapy, she actually went to the local Casualty department to report that she had been raped, but left before it was her turn to be examined. Although during her next therapy time I naturally commended Elizabeth for 'having found her voice' and having realised that today 'she need no longer be powerless', we also explored the wisdom of her actions in terms of Cordelia and her present day life and how she (Elizabeth) could so easily have managed to get Cordelia into trouble, which surely had not been the reason Elizabeth came? Thirdly, by indeed encouraging the personalities to think in terms of the reason why each of them had been created, they gradually also began to accept that they were not real, not separate, and began to accept the notion of working together as one. However, at this point in time of Cordelia's therapy, we were a long way away from achieving such a goal. During the sixth week in fact (after we had started to work together five days a week), Cordelia announced, that 'Victoria was not feeling too pleased and did not feel like cooperating and answering any more questions.'

Cordelia described how Victoria's 'veneer' had started to break and that she felt quite lost. Yet when I encouraged Victoria herself to tell me the sad tale of her life, she told me that her mother had told her to lie in school about the abortion and pretend that all was well. Victoria subsequently drew a set of pictures depicting the reality of her life; how the inside of the house was always a mess, which she had to clear up, but that the garden and her mother's clothes were always beautiful. Victoria also described how the sexual abuse by her mother had continued until she found a woman friend, after which she treated Victoria with total indifference. She furthermore also revealed how she had in fact been her mother's shadow, modelling herself on her. She spoke French as her mother did, and became very efficient when dealing with strangers, and was in fact very two-faced, and at times quite unrecognisable.

The following Monday, Cordelia at first reported that Victoria had been relieved that she had disclosed the truth. Victoria, moreover, had also been quite surprised, Cordelia said, 'about how much the children had been able to tell their therapist already', and had felt concerned that she had disbelieved them, 'whereas it must all have been true!' As for herself, Cordelia described that she too had been amazed that Victoria had revealed as much, but that ever since, she had begun to feel so sad, sadder than she had ever felt before.

Victoria it seemed had in fact played a very vital role in keeping up appearances, and now, having revealed the cracks beneath the surface, the whole system appeared to be collapsing. Not only did Cordelia subsequently report that Victoria apparently had 'disappeared', but the children who had relied on her for guidance were all at sixes and seven's. After one particular therapy session, Cordelia returned to the clinic feeling confused, complaining that she had been unable to find her car in the car park. She also appeared not to recognise certain members of the kitchen staff, whom she had of course met several times before. The car park was too small to prevent anyone from finding their car, and Cordelia in fact confirmed, that this had happened before but that Victoria would normally have come to her assistance. Victoria's disappearance really seemed to have caused a major upset, and I must admit that I was equally as perturbed and anxious on Cordelia's behalf. She had obviously reached a serious impasse in her therapy: if the abuse was true, then she had to let herself feel what it meant, which would surely send her mad. 'To grieve is to discover home!' Yet, if she did not grieve, did not 'discover her home', then she had no choice but to go on believing that she was many people, which would truly send her mad – since she now knew different!

We naturally discussed the various options: she could either run back into the multiple system, deny everything – give up on her therapy, or else continue fighting and allow the truth to be heard. I also encouraged her to let the strong part of Cordelia (Delia I) once again take control, and proposed a third option, to freeze – take a break, and suggested admission as an in-patient. However, before I could actually confirm whether a bed would be available, Cordelia had obviously made up her mind and left the clinic.

For the next four weeks, Cordelia would feel unable to draw any more mental images, or freely put her thoughts on paper, and some of the old responses and grievances became once again the main focus of her therapy, of course side-tracking her as before. She saw the face of her dead mother at the window and wanted to deny the abuse so she began using TCP once more, trying to disinfect herself as her mother used to do, and again left notes on my car, whereas she had begun to feel able to give them to me in person. Her sad, poignant notes as usual expressed her shame and dislike for herself and apologised for being!

> Sorry for being so frustrating
> Sorry for being so difficult
> Sorry for being such a burden
> Sorry for being me
> I hate myself too.
>
> Cordelia

She again made numerous telephone calls to the clinic, some anonymous, some in different voices, and again came to the clinic outside her normal hours and sat crying in reception, hoping to meet up with Anne and be comforted, but also hoping that I would respond to her tears! Her behaviour, furthermore, became once again overtly dramatic, reckless, or just plain scared. She drove her car at 100 miles per hour. ('I'll prove to the reception staff that my car can go as fast!') and was of course stopped by the police (who believed her excuse that she was suffering from diarrhoea). When she arrived for her therapy, she sat on her knees, head on the desk, crying, exclaiming in a dramatic way that she might as well end it all because no one understood her. Yet at other times, she wanted to sit behind the big armchair in the corner, feeling too scared to face me, in the same way she periodically used to do in the early days of her therapy.

Thus it became quite apparent, that she was switching fairly rapidly from one personality into another, both at home and during her therapy, which caused her to feel quite lost and really scared that she was 'coming apart'. Whereas one minute she had sat on the floor of the therapy room, crying, she then said she had 'clicked' and began rather angrily to throw the tissue box around. She 'clicked' again, and then took out of her pocket a strip of pills, (which turned out to be vitamin pills), and swallowed four of them, one after the other, after which she 'clicked' again and wanted to know what she had just been talking about. She also began challenging the boundaries again, requesting that Dr C give her credit for having worked so very hard. But when I confirmed that the boundaries still applied, she insisted that she just knew that he would tell lies. Her paranoia thus became quite marked again, accusing us all of planning to send her away because 'we were fed up with her', or else saying that we would punish her for having suicidal thoughts.

One morning Cordelia actually arrived at the clinic at half past eight in order to 'check out a dream in which the deputy clinic manager had told her that she could no longer see Frieda'.

She also began to hear things again which had not been said, and thought I was trying to make her out to be 'really mad' when I reminded her that she had experienced such delusions before, i.e. she overheard two women in a supermarket talking about her, saying that she (Cordelia) was mentally unstable. At the time, Cordelia had immediately retaliated and told the two women that she was not mad! However, Cordelia subsequently was able to tell me that a certain part of her she called Geraldine, (which was her grandmother's name) was in fact extremely paranoid – just like her grandmother, who always thought that people were talking about her.

Cordelia's impasse and the apparent disappearance of Victoria certainly seemed to have caused a major shake up within the system, although the fact that the Easter holiday season was near naturally helped to stir up Cordelia's anxiety. Yet all was not lost. Not only had Cordelia reasoned with herself that her dream could not be accurate, since 'Frieda would not have behaved like that', but she had also agreed to start monitoring her loss of time, her so-called blank periods and the frequency of her switching by keeping a daily diary and recording the sequence of the ordinary everyday events. Furthermore, she had also accepted my request not to leave any more notes on my car but to hand them to me in person, with seemingly good grace, though I remember her asking me what I would do if she did not comply. The next day, rather like a naughty teenager who just had to defy Mother, she had in fact left a card on my car, with the inscription, 'Frieda – this is not a note or a letter! So, yah boo shucks!'

Moreover, Cordelia had also produced a very important piece of homework describing the paradoxical role illness had played in her life: allowing her to escape from the abuse, yet at the same time trapping her in denial. And she had also began to talk to her daughter, bravely revealing certain details of what she had endured as a child, feeling quite emotive and touched by her daughter's care and affection. In addition, during her therapy, Cordelia had also quite willingly complied with my request to begin telling me the exact moment she felt herself switching – felt the 'clicking' – which naturally enabled us both to keep track of each personality and make sense of the feelings and the dialogue which ensued, as well as piece together an ongoing history, although by now I had actually begun to recognise the signs, the idiosyncrasies of certain personalities, such as the mannerisms, the facial expressions and the change of posture. Some personalities apparently could read without glasses, whereas others very much needed them.

In fact, now that Victoria was out of the way, the coast seemed clear for Cordelia to start revealing even more secrets from her internal world, and accordingly she introduced me to the three 'hard nuts', the three voices which had persistently plagued her head: Bryony, Geraldine and Martin. Bryony, Cordelia subsequently told me, was based on her mother; Geraldine, on her grandmother; and Martin, on her abusing brother, in the desperate and misguided hope, that if she was more like them, they might perhaps love her just a little. For example, Cordelia said that the moment she met her grandmother she had created Geraldine, hoping to have a caring/loving relationship with another woman, but had in fact achieved the opposite.

Cordelia described the functions of the as-if Bryony, as-if Martin and as-if Geraldine in her life and revealed some of their internal dialogue. They certainly appeared to be as desperate as their original role models. Not only would they give Cordelia a hard time, but they also clearly despised her for needing therapy, care and affection. Frequently when Cordelia went for a massage, she would leave her body, observe herself being massaged, and become aware of Bryony, Geraldine and Martin urging her to forget the past, telling her that she should not allow 'other people' to upset her – that she did not need other people, that she did not need to be massaged. And that she should 'pull herself together'. The only means of silencing them, Cordelia said, seemed to be via admission to hospital for ill health. However, most of the time they sneered at her, mocked her sadness and, just like Victoria, they also denied the abuse. And they certainly did not agree with Cordelia keeping a daily diary, and would obstruct her whenever they could, since it might reveal far too much and could expose them!

All three of them in fact, as Cordelia had subsequently discovered, were actually convinced that they were a part of the body of the mother, the grandmother or the brother respectively, and hence firmly believed, that they most certainly did not belong to Cordelia. Consequently, they were quite indignant; refused even to entertain the idea, saying that they had certainly never been abused, and therefore, they had no reservations in being cruel and horrible to Cordelia, and felt totally justified in wanting this weak, snivelling, pathetic, Cordelia dead.

In the meantime, however, Cordelia's husband had also begun to attend the clinic for his own counselling, since he was feeling so very low and had suggested, Cordelia told me, that they jump off the cliffs into the sea together. When they talked it through, Cordelia said, they had decided to 'continue battling'. Naturally, her husband's distress caused her a lot of anxiety, worry and concern for him. It also made her feel very guilty, since she felt that she must be the cause of his emotional pain. In due course, her husband's therapy began of course also to create its own ripples (helping him to express his anger, on his own behalf). This caused Cordelia, as before, to phone the clinic requesting to speak to Anne (I was on holiday). Anne as we had previously agreed, advised Cordelia to continue using her diary and bring it all back to her therapy. It certainly came as no surprise to me that Cordelia thereupon instantly switched into Elizabeth. She retaliated by stopping the diary and accused Anne yet again of deserting her, preferring others, etc., and ended up having emergency treatment for a severe asthma attack in the local hospital. However, whereas not so long ago Elizabeth would have remained in angry control of Cordelia's consciousness, creating her own particular brand of carnage, this time, Cordelia actually became aware of the extent of her anger and the usual damage it left in its wake. Hence, shortly after I returned from holiday, Cordelia once more, religiously, started keeping her daily diary. The diary was in fact producing remarkable results. Not only, as I described before, had it allowed Cordelia to recognise the depth of Elizabeth's anger, but she was also becoming very much aware of how often she tended to use dissociation in order to avoid feeling. Sometimes by switching frantically from one personality to another, at other times, by simply retreating from reality, 'going into her goldfish bowl'; literally disappearing into a trance.

Nevertheless, just like a shift had occurred in the way the system had been controlled, likewise Cordelia was experiencing a difference in the quality of her dissociation. Whereas before she would have vanished into her black hole, (the Self had closed her eyes), she now began observing herself dissociating and was no longer any one of the personalities in particular (the Self had opened her eyes); i.e., when Cordelia did a further two drawings about the abuse by her mother and her brother, recalling a most distasteful memory, she was aware that it was not just Bryony or Martin who did the drawing, but that 'all of her' was in fact present whilst she was doing the drawing, which is why, when we looked at them again the next day, she had no problem recognising each drawing, even though by then she had 'switched' again.

The diary, furthermore, was also beginning to upset another status quo and causing dissension between two opposing camps; between those parts who remembered about her father as he had asked her to do, and those parts who forgot about him as her mother had ordered her to do. Every time I insisted that 'everyone' listen to Cordelia's diary (and my therapy notes), unwelcome information of course reached reluctant ears! But as a result, Cordelia not only began experiencing her sadness instead of distributing it around the system as she used to do. She also began to feel that she was no longer mad! Indeed, Cordelia was beginning to feel that she was not weird, nor unnatural and no longer believed that she was 'an alien' or that she was 'sick', but rather that her 'complex life' and the way she had tried to organise it, in fact made sense.

Writing her diary thus enabled her to sort out her many jumbled memories. This in turn, encouraged her to realise why she had 'switched' so drastically all her life. Writing her diary, furthermore, also clearly helped her to feel that she was indeed a separate person, and was very different from her mother. For sure, as her drawing depicted, all her life Cordelia had in fact felt as though her mother had 'consumed' her, swallowed her up like the big bad wolf in Red Riding Hood, making her believe that she resided inside her mother's body, or that her mother lived inside hers. Moreover, during these past weeks, Cordelia had also begun to feel that she was no longer afraid to love and show her feelings, and duly confessed that she no longer felt compelled to get something in return. An important revelation, which I of course duly recorded in my therapy notes that day:

> I thanked Cordelia for the flowers she had bought for my birthday... We continued to explore what it means to be an adult and the various ways of expressing that you love and, or like someone... Cordelia said she had bought the flowers because she wanted to express her feelings and not because she would like something in return, the way she would have done in the past. Cordelia said she has realised that you cannot make someone love you, and certainly that she was never able to make her mother, grandmother or brothers love her, although she continued to try to do so for many years. Cordelia said she was very sad at the thought of how much she has missed out on – if only she had understood all this many years ago!

Obviously a very important change had occurred, one which naturally brought a lot of pain and sadness to the surface, but one which also made Cordelia feel quite pleased with herself, reporting that she had in fact achieved 'being herself', that she had actually 'felt together', and that the past therapy therefore 'had all been worth it'. However, as-if Martin, as-if Geraldine and as-if Bryony still needed to tell their particular stories.

By now it had become apparent that, although Cordelia had originally created each one of them in order to help her (i.e. Martin came on the moors when a bonfire was threatening to get out of hand. He then ran to get help and phoned the fire brigade), in time each one of them seemed to have 'turned on her' and instead of protecting her, now appeared to persecute her. Furthermore, I had also discovered that whenever we talked about a certain personality, this particular person then tended to become very much in evidence, and would usually remain in conscious control over the body. For example, after Cordelia had been talking about as-if Martin during her therapy time. That same evening, Cordelia (as Martin) subsequently threw the dinner (which her husband had cooked for her), at her husband – in the same manner that Martin (Cordelia's brother) used to throw his dinner (which she had cooked for him) at Cordelia. Martin the brother and Martin the as-if person, so it appeared, truly seemed to have merged and become one and the same, and clearly had remained in conscious control after therapy had ended.

Naturally, from then on, I became much more aware of the part I played in the appearance of a certain personality, and would usually ask a more considerate one to come forward towards the end of therapy, although Cordelia would of course not always be so obliging. However, I also began to use this apparent power to call a personality forward by just calling its name, or by inviting its appearance – in order to enhance communication between the various parts, set up dialogues, exchange information or allow them to draw the relevant images, and of course also in order to encourage them to listen to Cordelia's diary and my therapy notes.

However, when I previously said that as-if Martin, as-if Bryony and as-if Geraldine 'appeared to have become persecutors', I am in fact referring to the moment when Cordelia discovered that the part of her she called Martin – instead of wanting to kill Cordelia, as she had always believed he might do, would actually do anything to ensure her survival, including killing others, he said. This of course turned her previous beliefs about him quite upside down, and also made her wonder whether Geraldine and Bryony might, equally, have had her best interest at heart, although the manner in which they tried to achieve it tended to cause more pain than it cured. Thus, bit by bit, we were able to negate the hold as-if Martin, as-if Geraldine and as-if Bryony used to have over the system and turn them back into some kind of helpers – although it took Geraldine, especially, far longer to give up on her acquired position, since Geraldine mistrusted all people, especially other women, and especially therapists!

How then did Cordelia and I achieve this? First of all, by challenging their belief that they were in a separate body, and convincing them that if they succeeded in killing Cordelia they would also succeed in annihilating themselves. Secondly, by confronting them with the evidence, the drawings, the writing of the other children, as well as by recognising their distress and encouraging them to tell their own sad story. Also by helping them to cope with the realisation that they were in fact all abused; that whatever had happened to Cordelia, or to one of them, had in fact happened to them all.

Thirdly, by reinforcing that they had in fact been created by Cordelia, and encouraging them to behave according to the reason why they had been created in the first place, effectively enlisting their help for the greater good of them all.

Fourthly, we described the advantages of working together as one, as well as highlighting the disadvantages of staying fragmented and keeping the Self locked out, using the familiar image of an orchestra without a conductor, where each person played whatever tune they wanted, producing of course nothing but a cacophony of sounds, (this is a popular metaphor used quite frequently in many books on MPD, as I have since discovered).

Finally, we reassured them that working as one did not mean that certain parts would be 'killed off', as they believed they would, but rather that they – and every other part of Cordelia for that matter – were all needed to contribute their unique insight. As usual, however, just describing a process, assisted with hindsight, makes it all sound so easy and straightforward. It certainly was not! Each achievement was like a stepping stone in a foreign river, where the unknown current could just as easily sweep you away as allow you to reach the other side. But maybe the following piece of writing/internal dialogue between Cordelia and the part she called Bryony might perhaps give the reader a better idea of how involved and demanding it all was:

'It is hard to leave my mother's body.'

'But you are not in my mother's body, you are in mine and a part of me. I need your help, to help me grieve the loss of our father.'

'I do not know how to help but, I will try to express all the pain I carry inside. I feel to let it out, will cause me to fall apart and die.'

'We will all work together to put it right. Everything about me and within me is round the wrong way or upside down?

'Most important, all the parts in me, are coming together.'

Then again, turning a persecutor back into a helper was of course not without its dangers, as we discovered in due course, and my notes at the time recorded:

I received a phone call at home from a distraught Cordelia, saying that she felt she had no other option but to phone me because she was feeling compelled to stab herself with a knife, with which she had previously also threatened her husband, who had left, convinced that she meant it, saying that Cordelia was mad. Cordelia said that during their exchange of words, her husband's face had turned into the face of her abusing brother, and hence her rage and threats to kill him. Cordelia said that she had become very scared of her own murderous intent, and that she now intended to kill herself because she must indeed be as mad as her husband said she was.

I remember telling Cordelia to go and put the knife in the kitchen drawer, now, and then come back to the phone, after which I arranged for her to come to the hospital where I would meet her. As I suspected, her current work on the abuse by her brother had triggered her erstwhile persecutor, as-if Martin, to defend her – as he said he would – when Cordelia and her husband had been arguing, resulting in this outrageous and potentially dangerous reaction. However, once Cordelia had calmed down, she wanted to go back home. She said that she did not require admission as I had suggested and wanted to go and sort it all out with her husband, although what had occurred had obviously shaken her considerably. I naturally informed her consultant, who endorsed Cordelia's decision to go back home, provided she would monitor the situation and seek admission if needed.

Consequently, I also invited her husband to come for a joint session, which proved to be very positive and resulted in a frank, open and honest discussion, very much in contrast with their previous way of protecting each other by withholding information. We also agreed to have joint sessions much more frequently, in order to avoid a similar build-up of emotions. Nonetheless, I also informed Cordelia and her husband that it was not advisable for her to regard phoning me at home as a viable option in the future, because I could not guarantee that I would be able to assist her, and that a far safer option was to phone the clinic (whose phones are manned twenty-four hours,) and to persevere and explain to whomsoever was on duty what her needs were, even though, as Cordelia protested, she found it difficult to talk to certain members of staff because she felt that they did not take her seriously, or did not know what to do with her. Cordelia, quite understandably, immediately saw my concern as rejection, as telling her off for having called me – she said she was now 'wishing she had not called me', now 'wishing she had killed herself', although she eventually accepted my explanation, albeit reluctantly.

In the course of reflecting on what exactly had occurred, once again I assured Cordelia that it was indeed commendable that as-if Martin now appeared to want to protect her. But I naturally also stressed the fact that it was imperative that he learn to defend her in a more adult and less threatening way, since it would definitely be counter-productive to kill someone, or land Cordelia (and all of them) in jail. Nonetheless, despite the trauma and distress this particular incident had caused, we learned some very important and vital lessons.

First of all, triggers in the present seemed to instantly transport Cordelia back into the past (her husband's new, short haircut, had reminded Cordelia of her abusing brother Martin, whereupon her husband's face had instantaneously become her brother Martin's face). Secondly, feeling the familiar fears, she then would re-enact a scene from the past, relying solely on known and tried methods of solving a problem, behaving according to whichever child she had become, apparently unable to behave or think as an adult. (Cordelia threatened her husband in the same way [having switched into as-if Martin] she had once threatened her brother Martin with a knife, who had indeed 'coldly and calmly' walked away from her, saying she was 'mad'). Thirdly, Cordelia then felt unable to separate the present from the past, and would normally accuse those present – such as her husband – of having abused or threatened her. Although her husband agreed that in the past he had indeed said, 'You're mad,' he did not say so on this occasion, and he had in fact left because he was due to go to a meeting. Such scenarios had of course happened many times before. But this time, when Cordelia recorded the event in her diary, much to her amazement she had actually been able to keep the past separate from the present, and had observed that she might have been mistaken. 'My husband has in the past – a long time ago – blamed me, told me I was sick, sometimes mad and I needed treatment, he doesn't do that now – and perhaps I was wrong.' In the past of course, no such appraisal would have been possible, since Cordelia would have been convinced of the accuracy of her feelings and reactions. 'Perhaps I was wrong?' Just a few short words, but oh so important a change!

Week fifteen! The first of May. Victoria had returned! But with a difference. Cordelia said she now knew that Victoria was pretending. What's more, Cordelia explained, in a recent dream, she had actually been able to retaliate and had told her mother and brother that she no longer intended to be abused by them in any way. Consequently, she had decided to allow the adult Delia I and Delia II – to work together, whilst she was away on holiday. In fact, as per usual, we were both due to go on holiday. Only before we set out, yet another important and amazing incident was to take place. On that last Friday, Cordelia would see all her internal children for the first time together. During the week – once again utilising any crisis – we had been able to talk about loss, about the need to learn to comfort oneself, but whereas in the past I only had to mention the word loss for Cordelia to either switch madly from one personality to another or else go into a trance. That week she was able to approach the subject in a much more rational and adult way. As a result she had made the startling discovery that her internal children, despite their clamouring to be comforted, actually pushed people away when they did try to comfort her.

We consequently practised being held and feeling at ease about reaching out to others – after which, I also encouraged Cordelia to begin seeking comfort from within the system, to begin recognising each other and regard each separate personality as belonging to one family. Therefore, I suggested that she call up all the children, all her various parts, and ask them 'to have a conference' and discuss tactics to help her cope whilst on holiday. To my utter surprise, Cordelia then proceeded to describe a most vivid and colourful scene: all Cordelia's internal children appeared one by one in the bluebell woods (the same bluebell woods Cordelia used to play in as a child, and where she first began to visualise her imaginary playmates). Gradually, they all began emerging from behind the trees, gingerly stepping into the clearing, cautiously beginning to form a circle. Peter came first. They were all there. They were all different sizes. They were all different ages – none were adult, except perhaps for Delia I and Delia II, who were each nineteen. Some of them were very small indeed, just small toddlers, and two were boys. The others were all girls. All were wearing different clothes.

When I also suggested that they all hold hands, Cordelia said that in her mind's eye, that was exactly what they did, and for the very first time they looked at each other, and realised that they were all one – belonged to one person.

Needless to say, the whole description felt very special, and I can assure the reader that I felt quite spellbound and very inspired by this vision. It was as though I could see with my own mind's eye all these children amongst the bluebells, just as clear as Cordelia could see them. Moreover, I also felt very moved on behalf of Cordelia – acutely aware of how important this visualisation was. For the first time in her life, Cordelia could actually see herself – Cordelia was beginning to find her soul! True, she had of course looked in a mirror many times, but she had never really recognised herself, because – as I described before, and her very first drawing of the stick figure, covering both eyes with its hands, had so poignantly endorsed, her Self had indeed, a long, long time ago, decided that it no longer wanted to see and be a part of this painful and shameful world. Ever since, it had kept its eyes resolutely shut (residing in its very own black hole), or else had periodically looked at the world, other people and itself as though through a 'fog, a smog, a window, a set of lacy net curtains – or from within a goldfish bowl', as though in a trance?

Anyone who has not experienced mortal agony, deprivation and terror as a child, and hence felt compelled to disappear, will find it extremely difficult to understand how someone can actually go through their life without having at least a certain sense of Self. Indeed, all of us who were lucky enough to see ourselves reflected in the eyes of loving parents, and who therefore can recognise our-selves and know who we are, cannot comprehend the utter devastation involved when a child does not encounter such recognition.

The nearest experience I can compare such darkness with, such a void, such nothingness, is when in the course of my work, I have looked in the eyes of patients with their minds still stoned on drugs, or looked into the eyes of those who have chosen to withdraw from the world into psychosis, or else, when I looked into the eyes of those patients who suffered from a biological illness such as dementia or Alzheimer's.

They all looked at me, but they did not see me. They did not recognise me. They did not see a specific individual. They just saw another person, like so many flowers in a field! It was almost as though they looked through me. Hence I could not find myself in their eyes, for their eyes (those so-called 'mirrors of the soul') did not reflect me!

Anyone who has ever lost a beloved person to such depredation will confirm that it is a most disconcerting and painful feeling. How much more devastating such an experience must be when as a child, the eyes of an important other are just as dark and empty or reflect nothing but lust, depravity, anger, hatred, terror, insanity, religious fervour, boredom, duty or indifference. Or, as in the case of Cordelia, your mother actually makes you wear a blindfold, so that she cannot see you and you cannot see her. By seeing all her internal children together like this, it was as though by visualising them, Cordelia could now see herself – it was as though all the children, each representing a piece of the jigsaw puzzle had come together to form a face, which belonged to a head which was attached to a body that had arms and legs, etc., and which Cordelia could now recognise as herself. Indeed, whereas in her recurring dream some months ago Cordelia had said that she 'did not recognise the various children who had appeared', today, she had no difficulty in either identifying them, or claiming them as hers. They were no longer 'strange', they were rather beautiful! And wistfully they enticed Cordelia out of her 'black hole' into the light, lovingly giving her a taste of freedom and harmony.

Needless to say, that from then on, Cordelia's internal children, which she now clearly had accepted as her very own unique survival system, would collectively be known by us both as the bluebell children. Cordelia left to go on holiday. She gave me a card, together with a huge grin, feeling sure I would approve. She felt amazed, sad, fearful but also determined that she was going to cope, as well as somewhat relieved that she could maintain her contact with me via letters, and was intent on practising writing normal letters about the weather, the scenery, and her everyday life as I had suggested.

The holiday would turn out to be normal enough, but not the memories it called forth!

The Personalities:
Before the Death of My Father

According to my therapist, my childhood was not unlike that of many other multiple personality disorders, and until now I have not wanted to know about others before telling my own story, but I am very unlike many people who enter therapy. A multiple has no solid foundation on which to begin the struggle towards wholeness, and I had to start from the very beginning, hence it was necessary for me to bond with my therapist and you will see why.

CORDELIA

Although I was born prematurely I had survived, but not my twin, who was to be called Stephanie. My older sister Rosalind also died a little later. My mother seemed angry and disappointed with the only daughter she was left with. She told me she had tried many times to dispose of me, once throwing me from a bedroom window, but my father caught me. She also said they argued continually about many things, and after I was born my mother would not agree upon a name for me. My father, consequently, made the decision alone, and gave this much longed-for daughter the name he wanted her to have. As I have explained elsewhere, for the purpose of this book I decided to choose the name Cordelia, which means 'daughter of the sea'. For it is the sea from which I gain my inner God-given strength – and strength I had if nothing else – also the sea is very important to me. At the same time, I am also reminded of Shakespeare's Cordelia in *King Lear*, his third, youngest daughter. She too needed to be truthful to herself as I have needed to express the truth on the pages of this book.

My mother neglected me as a baby. I have memories of lying in my white cot being cold, wet, hungry, sometimes sick, sometimes exhausted from crying, but no one came. Both my older sister and myself were dumped on the steps of a children's hospital. We were both sick and my mother couldn't cope. She told my aunt what she had done. Rosalind died, I survived against all odds.

I, Cordelia, was pale and thin with fair hair and blue eyes. I was expressionless, silent, frightened, insecure and compliant. I wanted to please. I craved love and saw my parents as all-knowing, all-seeing and very powerful; they shaped my life. My days were filled with lonely play; the only attention I received seemed to be when my father was home. He spent long periods of time away from his family, I was told on business when I was old enough to understand.

As I grew, I craved companionship and started to create in my mind other children to help me; their cries in my head would sometimes break the awful silence and loneliness of my goldfish bowl. As emotional and physical pain and sexual perversion invaded my life, I created more and more children inside to help me. I let them survive what I no longer could. I did not experience anger, for it was kept firmly locked away inside, only being expressed by one created personality. I did not experience pain any longer, for it was held by some of my other selves. Eventually, I only experienced total isolation as I split away from the other personalities, who I sometimes watched through a fog below me. I could float above them, peeping down from a corner of the ceiling, watching their poor little bodies being tortured. I eventually learnt not to see very much at all. My belief was, I was anything but human. I was ugly, rotten, evil and thoroughly worthless.

When my mother told me my father was dead and I was not to cry, I can remember feeling as if all my blood had drained from my body. I was cold and numb. She coldly and cruelly reinforced the feeling that I was responsible for this tragedy – as children feel anyway at that age – by saying, 'It is your fault he is dead and never speak of him again. You must grow up now and look after me and your baby brother.' My mother did not cry; I don't believe she could. I felt excessive loss at the news of my father's death, and some disbelief as he had promised to be back for me. I also felt some degree of relief – if it was really true. I was never sure what was the truth. I was full of mixed emotions I could not understand or express. After my father's death, I would leave letters on my mother's pillow as soon as I could write. Every night before I went to sleep, usually suffering from severe exhaustion, I would write words such as:

> Mummy please love me but please don't hurt me any more. I love you so very much, please will you love me. I am so sorry I am bad. I will try to be good. I will help you and look after you, and always and for ever, I will do anything to help you love me just a little bit. I am sorry I do make you so unhappy, I will try harder. Please do not die, Mummy.

I would cry silently into my pillow, I hated the night. Often I could not sleep, but lay awake listening hard for threatening or invading footsteps. I was sometimes afraid to sleep as I wet the bed every night (enuresis) until I was at least ten years old. I was beaten every morning for this demeanour. After my mother beat me with her leather strap or my father's cane, she would throw me into a dark attic room where I would stay for hours. I learnt that if I pressed my little body into the corner of the room, it felt as if the walls were hugging me and they gave me comfort and strength. Into the other three corners I placed more created children for company and it wasn't long before they became autonomous along with the others.

At quite an early age, I developed an ability not to feel physical pain as well as emotional pain. I did this quite unconsciously, by allowing my body to only feel numb, especially my lower body and legs, and this often developed into long but temporary emotional paralysis, often confusing doctors. I was diagnosed as having poliomyelitis as a child, and probable multiple sclerosis as a nurse in training. In fact, I am left with some degree of weakness of the limbs and no reflex action of the nerves down one side of my body.

I did not make friends easily at school; the teachers could not understand me, so they said. I was punished for not paying attention, forgetting things, not doing my homework, playing truant and telling lies, or so they thought. I could not sit at my school desk for long, my knickers hurt too much, and school dinners made me sick. I was glad I had a uniform to wear to school as on any other occasion I was overdressed like a doll. I felt conspicuous and stupid with frills and bows, and other children laughed at me. Everything looked too good on the outside but underneath I was not properly cared for.

If I wasn't being punished for something or looking after someone or helping around the house, I escaped and spent time alone, but not free, in the big outside world. I wandered along the beaches collecting pretty shells, crabs and other small sea creatures washed in with the tide. I wandered through the woods kicking the leaves that rustled at my feet. I always made for my special clearing in the woods where bluebells bloomed in May and where my imaginary children played hide and seek with me. I now remember my 'bendy' tree, the trunk leaned over enough for me to climb on and I sat astride the trunk and travelled in my mind to a new place, a new land where everyone was kind, and a fairy princess with a wave of her magic wand transformed my mother and father into fairy-story beautiful and loving people. I held on to the hope that one day I would be granted my wish. Hope always kept me going somehow. The other thought that often came to mind was that, if there really was a God in heaven, the God my father often talked to me about, would He hear the cries of my heart and make things better for me? I learnt at Sunday School that God the Father or His son Jesus would answer my prayers, but He gave me strength, not release. I often used to think that He took my father away because He knew that was best for us all.

My mother only improved towards me in my later teenage years but by then immeasurable damage had been done. My mother played games with my emotions, promised to be somewhere for me but never turned up. She took no interest in my achievements as she did in my brothers. She showed them some affection but never to me. She always laughed in the face of my adversity, many times creating the situation herself. She would walk behind me and push me hard for the fun of it, then blame me for scraping my shoes or for blood staining my clothes from a grazed knee. She would say in a shop that she was going to buy some sweets for me and then eat them all herself. Running for a bus, she would jump on and leave me still running with my arms stretched out – still hoping. She often locked me in a room for days until she needed my help. My brothers became demanding as my mother did everything for them, and I became a slave to my brother Martin, as did my mother for the rest of her life.

One event sticks in my memory. I had been in hospital, very ill after my brother's abuse. I was badly cut and bruised, and infection had spread to my kidneys. My mother never, ever came to see me in hospital but she was asked by the hospital staff to pick me up when I was due for discharge some weeks later. The doctor saw her alone before we left, and she arrived at my bedside very angry and blamed me for being ill, causing her so much worry and work. I was weak but she made me walk two miles home and pushed me hard when I lagged behind. I fell many times but tried not to cry and to keep going. I collapsed on arrival home and was immediately sent away to my aunt's for several weeks (my uncle was a doctor). She often sent me away when I was ill, she hated illness, she hated me and I was no good to her in such a weak state. She had instilled into me that, never ever, should I tell anyone anything that happened at home, because they would know it was lies and she would die with the shock of it all.

It was of course at my aunt's home that I discovered all girls were not treated like me; she had four of her own and she was firm but kind. It hurt so deeply that I didn't have the same loving family. I was sent home sooner than expected on this occasion, because I cried and cried as I have never cried before, but I could not tell them I wasn't homesick, as they believed. On the one hand, I wanted to stay with them for ever if they could love me and yet on the other, I wanted my own mother to love me. The more she pushed me away, the more I clung. I often wore my mother's clothes, which seemed to please her. In fact I used to think I was my mother and she was me, she had reached so far down inside me it was hard to know where I began and she left off. I loved her and yet she repulsed me, sometimes she made me physically vomit, her smell, her perfume left its trace on me. I grew to dislike my own sex and my own sexuality. I was frightened and threatened by my mother, my brother Martin and my grandmother. All three of them thrived on their hatred of me, and particularly the emotional abuse they inflicted, which seemed to give them pleasure.

I had very few toys, in fact, my only doll was given to me by an aunt, and my one teddy by my father, but it was taken away and burnt as a punishment. I used my brothers' bikes and read their books. I never had any of my own. My father bought me a puppy but that died, I fear through neglect. I dreaded my birthday and Christmas every year, holiday times and sunny days, hearing other children's laughter and fun. I dreaded life so much as I grew older. I awoke every morning wishing that life would stop for me, for it was too much of an ordeal and a struggle.

The lonely, fearful and anxious Cordelia remembered very little of her horrific abuse in her life, only the fear of her family and others. She spoke very little, she appeared most of the time to have no voice. Life was not real for Cordelia, Cordelia was not real. I lost my sense of self.

STEPHANIE (TWIN SISTER'S NAME) 1–2 YEARS

I pretended to be Stephanie in order to please my mother and to cope with the awful depression my mother seemed to experience, some of which at this time may have been postnatal depression, as well as grief at having given birth to a stillborn child.

She told me, when I was old enough to feel hurt but not old enough to understand her disappointment, that I could not give her the joy and love Stephanie would have given her. She said she used to shake me senseless and shout at me 'why were you not the other one?' She also told me she was too ill to look after me. I knew at a very early age that I could do nothing to please her. Stephanie, the child I wanted to be and eventually pretended to be, was a sickly baby. I could not tolerate milk. I did not grow properly for a long time. Much of Stephanie's childhood was spent being ill, with many admissions to hospital with life-threatening illnesses. Being ill was the only time I was shown kindness by others but my mother had a fear of illness and would shout and scream at me for being ill, sometimes even beating me until I could no longer feel. I remember, when she was forced to get a doctor because she realised I was very ill and this frightened her. She was told by the GP that I needed to be cared for, I remember her anger with me afterwards when she was told my hair and body needed a good wash. I once had gingivitis (inflammation and infection of the gums) when I was ill with neglected tonsillitis. She was again told that I was a physically neglected child and the doctor sent a nurse to train her to care for me.

I am not recording a story of a child being reared in the slums of Victorian London but the story of a child whose family and home looked good on the outside, a middle-class family with good clothes, well educated, church going, a family of achievers.

My mother preferred that I be sent to hospital when ill, so she could ignore me until I was better; someone else had the responsibility. She never visited me and I was rather glad, as well as frightened, because she always blamed me for being ill and causing her more work and worry. Her bathroom made me feel so nauseous, it smelt horrible, it was horrible, she never cleaned it. Although the bathroom was dirty, the smell was a strong disinfectant smell, the like of which makes my stomach churn even today.

From the age of about three to four, Stephanie became autonomous – meaning she became a separate little girl, because the abuse she received was beyond belief. It was Cordelia's only escape.

I think fairly regularly my mother placed me naked on a large wooden board that was kept covering one end of a strangely shaped bath, like an old-fashioned tub with a seat. My legs were tied up to a washing or airing pulley over where the bath stood, long rubber tubing and enamel funnels were filled with warm disinfectant smelling water and the tubes went into my body. I now know of course that one went into my rectum, the other into my vagina. I was sometimes dunked into a very hot disinfectant bath afterwards, beneath the board, but never properly washed. I remember the first time, it hurt to be touched but I was never touched with tenderness, only force.

I remember very little about how I felt, I only remember that I believed my suffering would soon end because I would die, and the thought always comforted me. The room always seemed filled with steam and my legs went numb, then paralysed – something that happened throughout my life when I was deeply unhappy or trapped in a situation I wanted to escape from. I felt no pain after the initial trauma. I have always been able to tolerate a lot of pain.

After the washing out or bath, my little body was wrapped tightly in long strips of towelling or sheeting, bound round and round my body. The sound of tearing towelling or sheets, would always make my body go numb straightaway. There were canvas straps hanging from the washing pulley in the attic room, which was like a washroom. My little body was tied to the washing pulley by the canvas straps, then hoisted to the roof rafters. Sometimes I was hung up one way and then the other, like a joint of meat in a butcher's shop window. The attic-room door was shut, I have no idea how long I was left there but I can remember my head hurting sometimes so very much and then not at all. I cannot imagine why any mother should even think of doing such appalling acts to a small child, but Frieda told me that similar activities have occurred to other abused children.

These rituals of physical abuse began to increase as time went on, always following the mornings after my mother had used my little body to masturbate herself with. I had no idea what she was doing at the time but it felt wrong and filled me with fear. I remembered more clearly when I started to look at the drawings I did for Frieda. My mother's large body compared to mine, how I saw her, the positions she put me in, the feelings that surfaced, the things she made me do, the blindfolds she wore and made me wear when she was doing these things. As I write these words, the feelings of revulsion are returning and I cannot go into the graphic detail even of my drawings. I am now, only too aware of the extent of the damage my mother caused me.

I went through awful periods of denial over these sadistic acts, thinking I was going mad to see such scenes flash across the screen of my memory, hear my mother's voice, the creaking of the pulley swinging on wood, smell disinfectant, feel my legs go numb. Sometimes I was very afraid to admit, even to Frieda, just how bad things were, because I still wanted to think the best of my mother and I didn't want to believe these awful things happened to me – but I know they did. During my time in therapy, whilst on holiday with my family, I visited my old childhood home, which was empty and up for sale. As I walked into each room, the pain inside me grew. However, memories did not return immediately, only strong physical symptoms, but nightmares occurred, night after night, until I was eventually able to draw for Frieda what was held in my unconscious mind.

As I grew older, my mother eventually stopped all this; it may have coincided with my father's death or I guess I became too heavy to hang up, but she continued to cut large strips of soap and insert them in at least one hole every week. I began to think of myself as dirty, and these places not being very nice places, especially on me. It was only Stephanie who heard the creaking of the ships masts in the wind or maybe the creaking of the rope on wood as she hung in the attic room, I do not know. Stephanie always saw everything through a fog. She was pale, thin, weak, always ill. She felt lifeless all the time as if she wasn't really in this world. She was the personality who attempted suicide many times, who was silent as the grave, withdrawn and undemanding. She found comfort in the thought of death, an escape from this cruel world – and if she died, she knew her mother would be able to love her.

ALICE (LIKE ALICE IN WONDERLAND) 18 MONTHS–2 YEARS

Alice was the first imaginary person created to help Cordelia cope with her father's behaviour. I started to dissociate at a very early age; I gave myself the ability not to be there. Alice could disappear – I could not disappear! Although so young, there seemed even then to be an awareness of make believe. I made myself believe that my father was not asking me to do certain things that felt instinctively wrong. He played games in the bath with me, his penis was the harbour around which I had to line up the boats and plastic ducks, I had to kiss the ducks and then his penis. His fingers and toes were often between my little legs, poking me. I tried to push him away – and when I couldn't, I made myself disappear. He also used to sing to me, 'Only make believe I love you. Only make believe that you love me, Couldn't I, Couldn't you, Couldn't we?' I maintained the ability to make myself smaller, make others small and even make them disappear. A small child often shuts her eyes, thinking that if she can't see then others can't see her. I went a stage further; dissociation allowed me to feel unreal and not actually there.

It was when my father died that Alice became autonomous. She was given her name for real and developed the ability to make herself not only smaller, but larger too. My mother said I had to grow up and look after her and my baby brother, and I was never to cry again. With a child's logic, if Alice could be larger, so could I. I added another six years, because that felt 'big enough' and thereafter, Alice was always six years older than Cordelia, which meant that she never knew her father at all. This felt safer; also, it would please her mother as she didn't want him spoken of again. I, Alice, was able to observe all that was going on around me, I sensed that many things that happened were morally wrong and I tried to protect myself by either disappearing or by being so big no one would want to harm me. They might even respect me.

I tried to control the behaviour of my family instead of them controlling me; this was a way I could protect myself and prove to all the other internal children that they could do the same, they could control all horrific circumstances by not seeing them or not letting them happen. I knew about all the other children but they seemed completely unaware of me. Only Felicity and

Victoria, who came later, knew about me. There was an emotional control switch inside me somewhere and each personality appeared according to the need or the trauma. I used to feel the click in my head and then I was someone else, different in appearance, voice, feelings, behaviour and experiences. To explain this process, I will now refer to the incident that led to my admission to the asylum written in more detail in a previous chapter. I will have to use names of two other personalities not yet described in detail – they all became to me completely separate people, not parts of the same person.

When Cordelia was locked in her room while her mother and family went away, she was abandoned alone in a darkened room. I switched, and Elizabeth appeared and screamed and went completely wild, tearing wallpaper, splitting open feather pillows, then Stephanie came and she was very weak and lay helpless wanting only to die. On the return of the family, Stephanie was seen by a doctor and taken to an asylum. I, Alice, then came into action in the locked room at the asylum. I made myself smaller, to avoid my jailers, and larger, when I was needed to protect the other children at the asylum, particularly at communal shower times. It wasn't long before Stephanie was taken to a hospital because she was so ill, a place she felt safe.

I spent my entire time coping; I used to get so tired and despondent. I've spent a lot of time writing all my life, writing letters, poetry or some other disguise, like a story about someone else who was really me, telling the story of my life and what was going on. I would write on my arm or hand at school, help! But no one took any notice and if they had, I could not have revealed the truth. The letter to Anne at the clinic was a vital clue and so important to me, it told of my dilemma, but everyone ignored it. Alice took all responsibility in her life for relating to others in situations where control of feelings but correct concise reporting of her situation was necessary, i.e., consultant, doctors, hospital and GP appointments, interviews and form filling. She consequently only reported on information as Alice saw it, everything being correct as far as she could remember, except sometimes her year of birth, because she believed she was older than the other personalities. She had a dull, unexpressive quiet voice, her gift was only in her writing. She could not easily look someone straight in the eye.

As I write now, the need to express how I felt then is very strong, the child in me needs to tell anyone who will read and hear the cries of a child's heart and wants to understand the numerous coping skills she was forced to develop and use in order to survive – however simplistically explained. Alice felt disloyal having to explain to Frieda what had happened to her, because she wanted to believe her parents were good and lovely people, and even then, it was easier to write it down or draw with coloured pencils but it always felt so shocking – could it really be true?

I had many periods of denial but I always felt so ill at these times, more confused and totally disorientated. Relief only came when it felt safe to pour out to Frieda; safe to tell the whole truth without fear of punishment or desertion. Alice was one of the last personalities to reveal herself.

PETER 2–3 YEARS

After writing about Rosalind and Peter, I suffered a great deal of denial about the reality of my father's abuse (as the subsequent analysis of Rosalind will clarify). Horror surged through my body, guilt, remorse. 'Have I made it all up? I will have to write to Frieda, and tell her, and ask her forgiveness!'

I was due to visit the area of my original family home and I wanted to go for many reasons, but not least that I may discover the truth. Finally, I hoped, this visit would reveal all. Sitting on old familiar rocks, watching the sea and all its moods, walking the paths I trod long ago, watching the sunset in the very place I watched it with my father, history came flooding into the present – I knew for sure and would not doubt again. Amazingly, I coped so well with the pain inside. I was glad to have the family of the present; my love for them and their love for me. I went home with hope for the future and a degree of acceptance in my heart.

My father spent time teaching me the scriptures and when he was at home I was made to accompany him to church. I gradually became familiar with Bible stories, and one of the disciples of Jesus, called Peter, I seemed to latch on to; his name meant rock, a dependable character. At the beginning of his existence my Peter was a small thin pale and frightened boy with callipers on his legs, whose heart ached with sadness. He was a personality I had created in order to cope with the horrific abuse of my own father; the father who claimed me for himself and declared his love for me so passionately. He was the little boy whose mother ridiculed him for not being able to walk properly – 'I was a weakling!' Yes, you might well wonder, why a boy? I, too, wondered how I was going to tell Frieda about Peter.

To my child's mind, it was because I was a girl that I was used and abused. Being the only living girl in my family, I thought bad things didn't happen to boys. Of course I now know that for me to become a boy in my imagination at the worst moments of abuse meant the abuse didn't really happen – it couldn't happen – because I was a boy after all. Whether one or maybe two of my brothers also experienced abuse of one kind or another, I can of course only speculate about, since my brothers would not feel able to reveal such intimate details to me, if it was true. Sadly enough, the reality of my original family is such that they do appear very unhappy adults, and we all live separate lives with little or no contact with one another.

Peter carried the excruciating pain for that little girl. For me, life would have been too unbearable, so I saved myself unknowingly from madness by my own childlike creativity. Now, as I look back on the Peter I created, I would want to love him to bits and look after him. It is only now that I have a picture of him in my mind's eye that tears me apart inside, as I see the pain and anguish, the forlorn, sad pale little boy, looking ill-kept and unloved with no one to turn to. It has taken me all this time to feel anything for him because that child was me. I dared not feel, it was too risky; I could not love myself under any circumstances. The horrible rape scene I described in the section on my father was the moment when Peter first appeared, as I floated on the ceiling above the hospital bed and watched Peter's legs being straightened and repair work being done to the torn areas. Nurses and doctors were rushing around, a mask was put over Peter's face and then the pain went. No more could my father hurt me, because now I was a real boy. Peter thus almost instantly became autonomous.

After my father's death, Peter was given his name and became my protector, always kind and friendly. He rescued me from potentially dangerous situations; he became my rock, my defender, so I named him Peter. Eventually he was around less often and as time went on it appeared he deserted me when I needed him most. I suppose the need for him had gone away, but he had become like a friend or family member who I wanted to talk to. I felt sad inside that he had distanced himself from me. At my saddest times, when I was thrown into an empty room after a severe beating, I can remember pushing my back into the corner as tightly as possible because it felt like I was being held. In the other three corners I sat other children from my imaginary world. Usually one of them was Peter, I always wanted him there. I talked to the other children and they talked to me but they were never aware of each other.

Peter always appeared on my visits to my father's recreational lounge at his place of work. It was a very frightening experience for me to be taken there, a little girl clasping her father's hand among so many strange, large men, who seemed to think I was somewhat of a prize to be sat on a table and laughed and joked about – or that is how it felt? I had to be Peter when I went out alone with my father, or when I was alone with him at home, depending on which father he was, the good or the bad. If the men in the recreational lounge were friendly and enjoyed me being there, for whatever reason (I did not always understand their remarks or laughter), I changed into flirtatious Felicity. In fact, I remember my father calling me Flirtatious Felicity on one such visit. I can only remember smiling back at one handsome man who had smiled kindly at me; he didn't seem to be the same as some of them, my smile was misunderstood as I remember but I was, after all, only a child.

Peter was pushed around by other members of the family but he never seemed to mind, he coped with anything, or so I thought. He eventually gave up rescuing me, I guess he had had enough! Remembering Peter was very painful, because I now really know that little boy who dared to be me; consequently I find it strange that I saw him first as the children of my inner world emerged from behind the trees in the bluebell wood in my therapy session, because I could not have told Frieda about him then.

My legs have always been the weakest part of my body; they would often go numb or I would experience paralysis many times and sometimes for several weeks at a time. I now know this was an emotional effect of the inner turmoil. Even to the present day, my legs ache a lot when I am tired or under a great deal of stress. When I was fourteen, I was sick with a viral or bacterial infection, including increasing weakness of my legs and loss of movement. It was thought at first I had poliomyelitis but this was never proved. I used this probable reason for my weak legs from that day forward.

ROSALIND 2–3 YEARS

Just twenty-one months after my therapy finished with Frieda, I had just completed the section in this book about my father, which had made me feel utterly disloyal as well as angry, sad and despairing. Frieda wafted in one day, about ten days before she returned to Ireland after visiting family. She stirred up old feelings, having tried to sort out the denial that was fast taking hold of me, concerning the memories of my father's abuse. Unintentionally, she left me in somewhat of a mess, and the weeks that followed were confusing and painful. I started to hear voices and see my father everywhere and in everything. I felt disorientated, yet help was unobtainable, even Dr C's clinics were full, then he was away on holiday. I also knew that it was the wrong time to see him, because if I was dissociating then I could not be real, and the session would be a waste of his time and mine as he does not do therapy with me – as he frequently used to point out to me.

Consequently, I allowed myself to go into a dissociative state. I have since discovered it was my way of escaping pain and coming to terms with my memories. I had split my father into two people as a child and as a result there were two separate personalities I created within me to cope with the two sides of my father's personality. I now realise I was going through a process of integrating the two separate personalities as part of the healing.

One of these personalities was Rosalind. The name, I was told, had belonged to an older, dead sister of mine. I also remembered it was a name my father loved. Rosalind (my personality) was told by her father that she was beautiful. She was a happy and pleasing child, well-mannered and well-spoken. She had a sweet, melodious singing voice, she played the piano, went to ballet lessons and performed on the stage at a very young age. She was everything her father wanted. Rosalind rarely showed herself after her father's death, because her mother did not want music in the house again. Consequently, Rosalind rarely showed herself to Frieda and has remained very much a separate part of Cordelia, her story not told until now. This is the first time Rosalind has been able to express her long-held secrets.

Apart from her father, Rosalind was separated from the family she lived with; they treated her with total indifference, as she did them. Nothing was important to her except her father, so the others could do nothing to hurt her. She led her life as if she was an invisible ghost, like a spirit of perfection, only her father had eyes for her. She was as unaware of the other personalities as most were of her. I, Rosalind, remember my father only as a good man who was traumatised by wartime experiences. He told me something very shocking had happened to him during the war. I do not know what it was or where it happened, I was too young to remember the detail, but I do know that it caused him a great deal of mental pain and distress and that he did try to explain it had left him very scarred. He used to sit me on his lap and tell me tragic stories that made him weep so bitterly as he related details that I could not comprehend. Neither did I know how to respond, but I do have memories of these awful scenes that made me so anxious, and it was all about the war. I also remember him telling me he was a very sick man, not long before he died, and asking me to forgive him for hurting me so much. I always replied that he had never hurt me.

Rosalind became autonomous at this stage, as she felt very special to her father. He had a strong Christian faith but believed what he had done was unforgivable; he often prayed aloud with me and those times were clouded by a strong sense of his guilt and remorse, which made them feel like unhappy times. His heart, as well as mine, was completely broken and when he died, I felt as if I had died with him. I tried so hard to dig him up from his grave. I never ever recovered from the loss of this good father. I walked and talked, sang songs with my father and watched the sun set over the sea and consequently, because the rest of my life was so painful and damaging, these small moments, however infrequent, became enormously important and totally out of proportion. I carried a torch for him all my life, I tried to keep him alive in my heart. I carried on going to church after his death, usually quite alone, because I always sensed his presence beside me so I did not feel I was so completely alone, although I was only six. I sang the hymns from my heart as he did; it was as if my father, who had a beautiful voice, was singing through me. I wanted to go on singing for ever but my mother tried, and mostly succeeded, to knock that desire out of me. I've had periods of my life where singing was important again but unfortunately the periods of my life when it seemed wrong to express myself this way, strongly had the upper hand.

There has been so much need within me to express myself through music that I encouraged my children in these gifts they inherited, and just enjoyed them and my husband's beautiful voice. Now my youth has gone, I am saddened by all the opportunities lost, but deep inside me I still have longings to find a way to sing, to dance, to act, but it all feels too late. I would burst with happiness if this longing could be fulfilled! My father was very artistic in other ways and I am told he had a natural talent for painting and calligraphy. I amazingly discovered during my long, lonely days in the clinic that I enjoyed art therapy, and only recently found enough courage to join an art group.

I find it more difficult and more painful that I remember now that my father did feel remorse for all his wrong-doings. It may have meant we could have sorted things out in time, if only he had lived. But it definitely means I can't hate him or write him off as just a bad lot. As the person I am today, I realise I never really knew my father, after all, I was only six years old when he disappeared from my life, and he hadn't been around much anyway. But what a dramatic effect he caused in so short a time. I am aware that the mixed messages I received from both my parents left me confused and mistrusting of my own loving feelings as well as the feeling of others.

REBEKAH 2–3 YEARS

I had almost finished this book before I remembered how the personality Rebekah began her life and in remembering this, I am now able to complete my writing about the personality system. Following the rape by my father – I cannot be certain how small I was – but I was hospitalised for longer than I realised until now. Although I remember my father wanted to take me home, I stayed in hospital for some time, both traumatised and eventually quite ill. My mind had split into many parts already, and I realise now that this was the only way a small child could cope. At this stage I remember very little except my father shouting, crying and exclaiming he did not want me to die. I do remember the cot I was put into, and sometime later a transparent tent. I can only imagine this may have been an oxygen tent. I learnt later in life that this was the first time I had pneumonia. I only remember the injections I had, and drifting in and out of sleep, and sometimes watching a hazy outline of my father who sat for long periods by my cot, reading to me, telling me he loved me and praying for me to be healed. I also remember the feeling that I wanted him to go away.

After what seemed like many days or weeks, a kind fat nurse and a man in uniform asked me again what had happened to me. I do not remember replying but at some stage in my life I had heard my father say it was an accident on my brother's bicycle, which was too big for me. Whether I heard this then or at a different stage of my life I cannot be clear, but I do know, however, that I used the same explanation right through my life every time anyone medical asked what had caused my injuries, and I truly believed this explanation.

Rebekah knew and Peter knew but no other part of me could ever remember what it was that had caused me so much bruising and bleeding, and pushed my little legs apart until the pain was so bad that I disappeared into unconsciousness. The other parts only remembered my father's words – that I had done this to myself because I was disobedient.

Eventually, I learnt to walk again with callipers on my legs and returned home. It must have been almost two months later when I was put back into my parents' bed on my return home whereupon I created Rebekah. I remembered, as if it had just happened – that bad, black day, and I saw in my mind's eye the blood on the sheets, vomit on the pillow and felt again the searing burning pain inside. I screamed with sheer terror and my father brought the old lady who lived down the lane to look after me. No one told me where my mother was, and I did not ask. I had not seen my mother for a very long time and my father went away after my return home, leaving me in the care of the old lady. The old lady might not have been so old but her cheeks were as red as the apples on the trees in her orchard, and she was kind to me. I spent Christmas with her at her house and it should have been one of the happiest Christmases I was to experience, but I felt my parents had abandoned me, although I didn't really want to see them. I enjoyed being special, and the old lady pushed me out in an old-fashioned pushchair, dressed in a red coat and hat she had given to me. (Amazingly, quite some time before I allowed myself to remember precisely why I had created Rebekah, I found myself one day buying a red hat and gloves, where I had always avoided wearing anything red.)

We watched the sea crash against the rocks, a sight I still find thrilling to the present day. She read lovely stories to me and told me to forget the bad and painful things, and to pretend everything was wonderful and it would soon become wonderful. I told her my daddy had hurt me and she said she knew – but it would all go away if I forgot it. She knew, she knew. But still did not protect me. She believed me but she did not want to speak about it to me, or to anyone else. I remember now what hurt most was that she was not angry on my behalf. All my life I have wanted someone to be angry on my behalf; not just believing me but also acting in my defence. I knew as I grew up that the day someone acted on my behalf unconditionally, no strings attached, then and only then would I know that I was really loved. I would not have to pretend that bad things had not happened, or that I was someone else. The old lady knew, she believed, but she could not speak about it, and from that day on I felt I would never really be believed.

I created Rebekah about two years before she became autonomous; she could not speak about her feelings or the facts and knew in her heart that no one would believe her enough to want to help her. I suppose most of us need a positive response of understanding and belief when telling a painful true story but I not only needed this, I almost craved action on my behalf. Although it is now too late for action on the past, and it would be unreasonable to expect it and impossible for anyone to do anything about it, I do long for action when treated unjustly in the present. Although I am quite able to defend myself, it never seems enough. I am sure that the reader can now understand how difficult it was to trust a therapist who seemed reluctant to help me at first. Then, when that hurdle appeared to be overcome, I never really knew what went on in her mind, but I do now.

At the age of four years, I would imagine that a child is becoming more aware of what is going on around her, and more able to read the moods and reactions of others. Rebekah, however, was a little personality who became my own internal observer. She knew all the personalities, she knew how to protect herself, how to avoid trouble and manipulate situations to rescue herself. Alice was the personality I would call the external observer who interacted with the world in quite an adult way. She wrote good explanatory letters, interviewed well and dealt with authority in a composed confident way, stating her needs when necessary.

This is how and why, Rebekah became a real girl: Elizabeth, who was very angry one day with both her mother and Martin, displayed her jealousy of Martin's love for his cat by throwing the cat on the drawing room fire. The cat fortunately leapt off very much quicker than she went on. Martin and her mother both reacted in the same way; the encyclopaedia my father had bought me and other books I cherished, although they were not directly my property, were thrown on to the fire. The fire got totally out of hand and the chimney caught alight, filling the room with smoke. Fear filled my heart, whereupon Rebekah walked into the room; she was then instantly banished by her mother but on leaving the room asked, 'Is there a book I can take with me?' My brother Martin, amazed by the remark said: 'She's mad, she doesn't even seem to know what she's done, she's totally insane!'

The dear old lady who lived further down the lane lived alone, and she often gave me tea and cakes; she read to me and helped me to learn to read. I told the old lady it all had to be a secret. Rebekah was the child who grew fond of this old lady and her secret was very special. Books became an escape for Rebekah, and she gave herself the name from a story the old lady read to her, *Rebecca of Sunnybrook Farm*. She, however, used the spelling from the Old Testament of the Bible, because she felt that would protect her.

The day of the fire Rebekah became autonomous, banishing the fear out of the situation and escaping that day without punishment, only leaving both mother and brother unable to acknowledge her presence and clearly convinced she was far from normal. Rebekah told the old lady about the fire in her home but she never spoke about the cruelty she experienced.

One awful day a few years later, the old lady had gone away (I did not know then that she had died), and new people came to live in her house. I can remember thinking that nothing good ever lasts for long and wondering why she had left me. She had, however, left me with a hunger for knowledge and also fed my desire to disappear into an imaginary world when the real world was too hard to bear. All through my childhood I made attachments to older people in whom I found comfort, affection or refuge at times of trouble. Instinctively I found what I needed most to survive. Rebekah knew when Frieda had become aware of the multiple system and also knew she was the one to help her. Nothing would stop her holding on to the hope she had of being understood and helped. Rebekah helped the system of personalities to slowly reveal themselves, as and when it felt safe to do so. Rebekah was intuitive; she certainly knew when she had met with a situation or person which was good for her. Likewise, she could discard what she felt was a waste of time. Rebekah was a useful tool at the clinic and a help throughout my therapy journey, although she was always on the alert for signs of disbelief, always looking for a response or reaction, to confirm she could still trust this therapist.

FELICITY 3–4 YEARS

This personality was born out of visits to my father's place of work; she actually came to protect Peter. Felicity came when my father referred to me as 'Flirtatious Felicity'. Ironically the name means happiness, an emotion I had not really experienced. I was so young and yet so aware of the affect a small child can have on an adult, and I used the power of my sexuality at a very young age. I knew I was giving them what they were really after by taking my clothes off. I was only responding to their remarks, e.g. 'What a beauty – what a cracker she will be when she grows up.' Whereupon my father said, 'It will have to be a damn fine man I'll let her marry.' Felicity didn't appear when the rest of the family was present. Very few knew her, and those who did, either strongly liked her or disliked her. Felicity grew into a flirtatious extrovert, who was at times daring and passionate. The other personalities knew her, and she knew them. She played the part of keeping them safe from abuse. I enjoyed the few times I was the centre of attraction, I liked men noticing me and being attracted to me. However, as a teenager and young adult any unwanted pursuer, if they took liberties, would receive violence from me beyond my normal strength, usually in the form of a kick, having sometimes encouraged their advances in the first place. Dealing with it this way, I felt as if I was in control. In later life, my husband said he often felt jealous of my vivaciousness and the way I could attract all the men around me at a dance or party.

Felicity only appeared when needed. She usually only lasted for an evening, for on my return home I would fall into a depressive state for days, but thankfully I was safe at home with my husband. Felicity always felt more unreal than the other personalities; it felt as if I was acting a part that I couldn't help being when in the company of men. On one occasion, I remember feeling I was acting at being happy and full of fun but aware of being deeply unhappy underneath, when a gentleman I was dancing with said, 'Your mouth smiles but your eyes show deep sadness.' I changed into Cordelia in a flash and had to go home. Felicity, who appeared to be strong, was not as strong as she liked to believe she was, nothing like the impression she gave to others, but she played nonetheless a necessary part in getting me through the struggle of my life.

Felicity became autonomous at nearly six years old after she experienced the most horrifying ordeal of being used by her father to demonstrate the parts of the female body to her older brothers, and precisely how the sexual act of intercourse takes place. As Felicity, I took all this in my stride – it is only today, as I remember more clearly, I cringe at the humiliation and embarrassment, and of course I wonder if my brothers remember too.

ELIZABETH 3–4 YEARS

This personality appeared to come from Stephanie. Stephanie was compliant; she put up with too much from her mother in order to be loved and accepted. She did not complain, only remained silent when her mother washed her in the bath and used the tubes and funnels to cleanse her inside. She did not complain even when she was tied up to the washing pulley in the attic room. From Stephanie then came Elizabeth, who held all the anger, sadness, pain, frustration and jealousy, which she expressed vehemently in uncontrollable outbursts throughout her life, even into adulthood. Hanging from the washing pulley, she felt sick, dizzy and trapped, and wanted to kill her mother, even burn her, so that she knew what pain felt like. She was so mixed up, she strangely and perversely felt angry on her mother's behalf at times. She knew her mother and father were not happy and her father caused her mother to do these sadistic things to her, or that is what she concluded.

Her mother usually carried out this physical abuse in total silence except for occasionally laughing. She looked angrily at Elizabeth, and it was as if Elizabeth read the pain in her mother's face and did not want to believe her mother hated her. She so wanted her mother to stop hurting her and would forgive her anything if only she could love her. She loved her mother as deeply and passionately as she hated her. Elizabeth loved and hated Frieda in the same way. I recall the pain that caused me to shout down the driveway at the clinic after Frieda, 'I hate you.' It could so easily have been 'I love you.' Elizabeth looked angry and hurt, she sometimes walked along clutching her abdomen which held a deep harrowed gnawing pain inside that sometimes made her bend over, it was so severe. She cried a lot, threw things, ranted and raved, which resulted in a panic attack or exhaustion and weakness from such emotional stress and trauma.

Elizabeth wrote letters to her mother, leaving them on her pillow at night, expressing her love and pleading with her not to hurt her anymore, always asking for her forgiveness and promising to try harder and to be a good girl. The letter that follows is one Elizabeth wrote in therapy in a child's handwriting.

Dear Mummy,

You don't hate my baby brother, so why do you say you hate me? I try hard to please you, to be a good girl and to keep out of your way. I don't want you to be ill or unhappy, and I will look after you, as you want me to. I want more than anything for you to love me, to comfort me when I am hurt, please love me, please try hard to love me.

When someone hurts me at school, when I feel sad and lonely, I want you to be at home waiting for me. I want you to be interested in me, in how I think and feel. I don't achieve much because you don't think I can or want me to.

I want to climb onto your lap, like I've seen other children do. I want you to tell me that you do love me, that I am everything you ever wanted, that I am special because I am your little girl. I want to be precious to you. How could you hate me? I didn't ask to be your little girl, I was given to you as a special gift or so my father said. I need you to care for me, to wash my clothes and my hair. I need you to cook my meals, to care for my baby brother; he frightens me because I am too little to look after him. He cries for you and I have to try and comfort him. I am very afraid to be left alone with him, you leave me so often and I am afraid of the dark and afraid that you will never return. I would rather you return and beat me than never return at all. I am frightened to lose you as well as my daddy.

I watch other children skipping and playing in the street. They look so happy and carefree I long to join them but I can't feel happy whatever I am doing. I spend my days working for you or locked away for hours. I miss the daylight and sunshine for so long it seems almost painful when I am exposed to it.

During my days at school I am disruptive or very sad and quite often play truant. When you are tired of me being around, you tell me to get out of your sight, so I go as far and as fast as I can on my eldest brother's cycle. Sometimes I am away for hours and it is nearly dark on my return, but you don't seem to care where I have been or worry about me at all. If only you cared about me. There is always another beating on my return before I am sent to bed. I am used to your beatings; I go numb in my body and head until it is all over.

I go to bed every night aching all over, I sit in the corner of my room, pushing myself against the walls as if the walls were hugging me, swallowing me up, protecting me, holding me together, comforting me, they seem to give me strength. I sometimes fall asleep in the corner – sometimes I crawl to my bed. I wish you would wash and change my bedclothes; our bedclothes. I am so often sick and every night I wet the bed in my dreams. I don't know why I do it but I am ashamed and afraid, it also means another beating the next morning and locking me in the cupboard or the attic room

Perhaps I am silly to think you will one day love me, that one day you will change.

I watch you cuddle my brothers and even kiss them. You have never touched me except to be physically cruel. Your favourite child is Martin. I hate him, I am afraid of him but I cannot tell you why, because you will not believe me and you will beat me again for telling lies but they are not lies, you do not see what you don't want to see. Will anyone rescue me, will anyone believe me?

You love your sewing machine more than me. I used to find comfort in the sound it made, it meant you were at home, but now the sound means 'go away I am busy, get on with the chores or you'll have another beating.' I am never sure whether I am meant to stay in and help you, or go away for as long as possible, I always feel confused, I never seem to guess your will or mood quite right, I am always wrong. You never speak to me unless it is to reprimand me, you glare long and hard at me. I never know quite what I have done wrong.

Surely, you do love me just a little bit, say that you do please, please Mummy. I love you, I need you, please love me too. I want more than anything for you to hold me and tell me that you love me. I would give all I have, all my love and trust to get that love I need from you.

Why do you want to hurt me so much? I will do anything for you if only you will love me.

Please, please love me.

Your ever loving child

Elizabeth wrote letters to Frieda, leaving them on the windscreen of her car, expressing her love for her and in the same way pleading with her to help her and not to make her suffer any more, asking always for her forgiveness. I can remember the relief I experienced by writing a note to Frieda and leaving it for her, carefully covering it with polythene, if rain was threatened or when it was indeed raining.

Elizabeth became autonomous at around the age of four years, six months, when her mother dropped the heavy part of her sewing machine that lifted up to reveal a storage compartment. Elizabeth was invited by her mother to put her fingers on the wooden base of the machine and her mother deliberately dropped the machine back on her fingers, laughing as she often did when she caused her pain. Elizabeth noted that her brothers were not treated in the same way, they received more kindness and more attention, even affection at times, but that didn't come easily to their mother. The hurt that Elizabeth experienced by not being treated in the same way, grew into jealousy. The emotion of jealousy is very painful and confusing in a small child, and she never learnt what it was she felt or how to deal with it. She was always rejected and made to feel different, she was not allowed to show her feelings, she was not supposed to have any feelings, because she was considered to be the lowest form of humanity (this was often said to her) and therefore not equal to others.

Painful jealousy was displayed when Frieda spent a lot of time with another patient I didn't like, and this patient was always telling me how to behave and what I should do. In fact, no one ever believed that this woman was often very spiteful and cruel to me. I punished her with similar childish pranks to those I played on my brothers. I used to put things in the pockets of her coat when she visited the clinic. Her coat was hung in the cloakroom area. I remember filling them one day with snails I had collected from the garden. I now also remember how snails were my playthings as a child for a long time; I used to have races with them as I had very little else to play with. Elizabeth was the personality who expressed the rage and jealousy of this deeply hurt and injured child. It made her behaviour intolerable and misunderstood. This child was me.

ZILLAH (IMAGINARY FRIEND)

Elizabeth, who was the personality who displayed all the anger, frustration and passion, was hanging in the attic room of her family home. She had to find a way to cope with her predicament because no one heard her cries that quickly turned to terrified screams, especially the first time she was there. The blood rushing to her head made her dizzy and nauseous, silenced her. She saw a tailor's dummy standing in the loft but saw it first upside down. After a period of time, she did not know how long, she was turned to hang the right way up, and as she looked at the tailor's dummy, it spoke to her. 'Don't be angry, don't be sad, I am your friend, I'll always be with you, I've been here a long time, I am lonely too.' At first, Elizabeth thought it was the water in her ears and wondered if she was hearing properly, then she so wanted it to be real. Zillah said, 'I'm over here, it's all going to be all right, I shall always be your friend.'

As Elizabeth grew older she gave her friend the name Zillah. Her mother had a friend called Zillah and she told Cordelia that her name meant shadow. Thereafter, Zillah indeed became Elizabeth's 'shadow' and went with her everywhere. She was more attractive and more confident than Elizabeth, and spoke up for her when she was too angry or too sad to speak for herself. She trailed along with Elizabeth all her life; they were never separated but the other personalities were not aware of Elizabeth's friend. Elizabeth was a difficult girl and could not make real friends, so her imaginary friend brought some degree of comfort to her. They played for many lonely hours throughout this harrowing childhood. Elizabeth could usually let her feelings be known, though she was not always able to express them rationally, but she was able to admit to having this friend when she saw Frieda for therapy one day, when some degree of trust had been built between them. Zillah in fact always came to therapy with Elizabeth – but only with Elizabeth.

MARTIN 4–5 YEARS

Martin, Bryony and Geraldine were the three devils, the personalities modelled on members of my own family, created firstly in order to help those members of my family to like and accept me more. They functioned secretly and were the most devious and cruel of all the personalities. They were unpredictable and perverse and, individually, became persecutors of Cordelia. Eventually, as I let them back into my personality in a more modified form, they again became protectors/helpers.

Martin was the first introjected personality of a family member, my second brother, who was an abuser. He gained autonomy when he was eight–nine years old. My second brother Martin was a terrifying abuser, sadistic and cruel, particularly to myself and my younger brother. He played practical jokes on us, and laughed at me all the time. In the introduction of this book, I have explained some of the emotional and physical abuse he subjected me to, but in fact he also experimented on me sexually, but usually only when his friend Maurice was with him. In some of the drawings I did in therapy, the memories were more easily accessible than I was aware of. These nine or ten-year-old boys urinated in a bucket in the garden shed and poured it over me, then they tried masturbating themselves and each other in my presence. They both sucked at my nipples and tied me to an old wooden garden bench, threatening all kinds of abuse.

As they grew older, their experimenting worsened. I remember the terror I experienced at being tied to a tree and threatened with an experiment they were going to try out on me, where all my blood was going to be drained from my body when they inserted a needle and tube in my arm. It didn't happen, but just being told they planned this, just being told they would burn me at the stake was enough, as it all seemed very likely to happen. Fear alone appeared to drain the blood from my body – as far as I knew, they were capable of horrific things. I was frequently terrorised by these two boys. Fear is an emotion I experience beyond normal proportions, even today when there is no real cause, I am still afraid of this brother and the lengths he might still go to to harm me in some way. This is not a rational feeling, but one many abused people continue to experience throughout their lives; one that is very difficult to deal with.

I now remember how one Guy Fawkes night the threat of being burned and being told I was mad, yet again, made me able to see some of my personalities as small children tied naked to wooden stakes. As the bonfire was burning with uncontrollable ferocity, I created Martin, a personality who firstly became a rescuer, since he was stronger than me and ran for help to a neighbour who called the fire brigade, but who later on changed into a persecutor. Indeed, the personality I created based on this brother of mine, in time actually took on the personality of my brother Martin. Hence, Martin my personality was far from normal. He deceived, he was angry, deeply tormented, clever, performed operations with knives and experimented on living creatures. He was cruel, selfish, paranoid and demanding. He would frequently, throughout his life, at times of extreme stress or any crisis he could not control, telephone the emergency services. It appeared to be a defence, a cry for help, as well as revenge on the abusers or indeed just revenge on the world we had both grown up in.

For the little girl who lived with terror, pain and abuse, the fear of her brother was told in this story I wrote in creative writing, early on in my therapy process with Frieda. Frieda told the group to write a story about Halloween:

> The wind rustled the leaves under the stalls in the market square as the vegetables were being laid out. It was the last week in October and half term for some children, Halloween and bonfire night were priorities in the children's minds. One small turnip whispered to a swede that had rolled over into the wrong section of a vegetable stall. 'I'm hoping some kind housewife buys me today, I'd rather end up in a stew than my inside cut out to make a jack-o'-lantern.'
>
> 'Same here,' said the swede.
>
> 'Oh God, here comes a young lad, I hope he thinks I'm too small to make a lantern with.'
>
> The swede had a good idea and said, 'Try and roll over and look unsteady, as if your bottom is all uneven, they look for flat bottoms.'

The turnip began to tell the swede about a turnip friend of his who was sold to the same boy the week before. 'This boy told the lady at the stall that he buys turnips and swedes every year, makes them into lanterns and has them glowing in his bedroom. He lies under his bed and calls his little sister into the room to frighten her. He ties her to his bed and terrifies her with ghost-like noises and stories of what he will do to her. She said this boy's face lit up as he told her of the things he did to his sister as a special treat, really some of them I could not repeat. I think someone should know about this, so this cruelty could be stopped...' Just as the turnip was finishing the sentence, the boy snatched the turnip and the swede from the stall without paying and shot off down the street. Unfortunately no one saw him and as usual this wicked boy got away with his evil pranks!

I didn't know turnips and swedes had feelings, did you?

This, we now know, was my internal observer trying to reveal the truth that I was unable to voice even to myself.

In the third chapter of the book, I mentioned briefly the attempted female circumcision, as my brother called it, which he performed he said for research and was therefore an important experiment. In fact, both my mother and brother seemed unable to make proper human relationships and had total disregard for other people's feelings, or their well-being. My brother, moreover, spent all his spare time experimenting in his school laboratory, and I imagine, that is where he took the chloroform from. That awful day, one summer, I was forced to walk into the garden shed and take my clothes off. I watched my brother sharpen his knife, pour the contents of the bottle onto a rag and press it over my face, warning me not to scream. This was the day that Martin, my created personality, became autonomous, thereafter, once I had switched into my personality Martin, my brother could not hurt me anymore. I was too much like him, and I was a boy anyway.

Martin (my personality) became the only member of my class at senior school who was prepared to perform vivisections on the animals and prepare them for class study with the laboratory assistant. He never felt squeamish, and when training at the hospital, he enjoyed laying out the dead, visiting the mortuary and performing surgical procedures of the most gruesome nature – which was hugely satisfying. Amputations in the operating theatre or drilling burr holes in a patient's skull for brain surgery gave him a thrill just to watch or assist. Thus this personality, one could say, assisted my chosen career, but has also caused me a lot of grief and often sabotaged my therapy sessions; stopping me revealing the truth and my hidden pain, sometimes causing others to avoid me, and staff even to be afraid of me. My personality Martin did not relate to anyone. He was totally isolated from the other personalities, except for the similarity in his character with Geraldine (who was based on my grandmother). They nevertheless, still worked independently.

ANGELA 6 YEARS

When I was six years old, my mother had another child, a boy. My father and my mother told me I had to look after this child. When he was born, I was taken by my father, who died soon after, to the hospital where he was born. I was so disappointed, because I was told by the nurse that I had to look into a blue cot, not a pink one – I so hoped for a little sister. He was a big baby, and I was told my mother was unwell because she had had a difficult birth, and I had to look after her as well as the baby. I felt so little, and the responsibility of all this seemed too much. My father told me on the way home that he would be proud of me if I could look after them, as he might not be around to help. I know now he was ill, and maybe he knew his condition was serious. I remember the look on his face as he told me he was in pain. I was too young to know what this might mean. Before we left the hospital, my mother and father had a terrible argument. I put my fingers in my ears and my mother shouted at me to stop it; they were the only words she spoke to me that day.

When my mother returned home, she seemed weak, and the baby cried a lot. I had no idea how I was going to cope, so I created Angela, who was a coper. She was older and sensible and learned a lot from the lady next door, who was her saving grace many times. Angela gained autonomy when her father died, one month later, and her mother gave her full responsibility for the baby, handing her two bottles and announcing that she was too ill to do anything. Somehow, Angela did cope, with the neighbour's help, and others rallied around when they knew of the tragedy that had befallen our family.

When Angela became an adult, she trained as a nurse and was a good one, achieving the high standards that were required of her. She can remember her first day on the maternity unit, being flung a newborn baby who appeared to be choking and blue, and was told by the midwife to 'suck her out'. She asked a few more questions and did as she was told and filled her own mouth with amniotic fluid – not quite what should have happened – but at least the baby seemed better and survived, as indeed my own brother survived, despite being cared for in a somewhat haphazard way. This caring for him was not just while he was a baby. I became his little mother, taking him to school, teaching him to read, and speaking to the teachers on open evenings. On one occasion, when my brother was only two years old, he fell from a height on to some glass, severing an artery in his wrist. My mother screamed and screamed as I tied a handkerchief tightly where the blood was spurting out and applied pressure. I then summoned a lorry driver, sitting at the end of the lane in his lorry eating his lunch, to quickly take us to Casualty. I knew my brother needed emergency treatment, I knew it was serious. This was dealt with during an anaesthetic and I sat with him all night. The next day, I carried him home in my arms with no transport or adult help. No doubt I would have refused it if it had been offered, which it might have been. I was eight years old in reality, but older as Angela.

I equally visited him in hospital, following a tonsillectomy – he was five years old. I was refused admission when visiting him but I firmly told the nurse that my mother was too ill to come, so I had to come. I was eventually allowed in as I stood my ground. I can remember, how angry I felt with my mother, when my brother asked, 'Where is Mummy?' I was not my brother's sister. I was his mother until my mother decided she could take the role from me, when my brother reached the age of ten years. I now realise, of course, that his childhood was far from normal – although not abusive, certainly, to this day I know my younger brother venomously hates our second brother – and although a very successful businessman (and workaholic), somehow you can sense the searching and the loneliness.

As an adult person, I found the responsibility of babies and children quite frightening, consequently wanting them to grow up faster than they do anyway, almost wishing their childhood days were over, which was very sad indeed, for them and for me. As I look back, I now wish I could have that time given back to me, time to enjoy my children and find fulfilment as a mother. The child I lost seemed to be only what I deserved – and an escape at the time, from what seemed to me to be the hardest task I could be given. I was given this task too young in life, spoiling, what should have been total fulfilment for a young female adult desiring to be a mother – and the loss of a child should have been felt as loss. I now enjoy my grandchildren, which is an enormous privilege and pleasure.

The Self Returns

It is often said that truth is stranger than fiction. I'm certain that any reader having stayed the course so far will surely agree with me that the account of Cordelia's therapy journey endorses this point of view. For sure, Cordelia's real life was indeed far more involved and far more complex than any of the stories Cordelia used to write whenever she joined me in the creative writing group – as the following example will illustrate.

Once upon a time, there lived a little girl who belonged to two loving parents. They lived in a cottage, which backed onto the river bank. Ducks would waddle up onto the bank and into the garden. The little girl's father took her for long sailing trips down the river every day. She learned to sail on windy days and how to use the motor when necessary. She swam with her father on sunny days and her mother taught her the names of the wild flowers, even their Latin names, and she knew all that there was to know of the countryside, the riverside, about boats, about doing things together, having fun and what belonging meant.

As she grew older, she knew on the days she went out alone in the small sailing yacht, that she had to be careful which bend she took in the river, because one way led her to danger, into reeds and undergrowth. But she had been taught well to protect herself, and she always knew that someone was concerned back at home and would be there for her on return.

At the dividing of the four ways to the river stood the biggest tree she had ever known. It had large red juicy apples on it, and her father told her that if she ever picked one and ate it, she would have all she ever longed for in life. But if she picked it and dropped it into the river, she would have a life of misery.

She made various attempts at mooring on the bank and learning to climb, which seemed like an impossibility. As she got bigger, her confidence grew and she made a crook out of a stick on the bank and carefully pulled the nearest branch into reach. She reached for an apple. She tried many, many times, and almost grew tired of the struggle and task her father had set her.

One day, when she had grown into a slender attractive teenager, she met a young, good-looking man and told him of her task. He offered to help and sat her on his shoulders. She then could reach for the biggest apple she could see, but as she held one apple in one hand, all ready to eat, the other apple attached to the same stem fell deep into the water and then floated downstream. The young man assured her that good things would and could be available to her, but life also brought its miseries to everyone.

Once upon a time indeed there was a little girl who, just like the girl in the story, trusted her father implicitly, believing that he had her best interests at heart. However, just like the father in the make-believe story, the real father did not tell his little girl the whole truth. He did not explain to her that life is not a question of either you are a good girl and love me or else you are bad and don't, either the apple will fulfil your wishes or else it won't, but rather that life consists of bewildering and absurd paradoxes and that good things and miseries indeed go hand in hand. Instead, the real father just sang beautiful songs to the little girl, such wonderful melodies as, 'Only make believe I love you... Only make believe...' Or else he sang, 'If I hurt you, I will die. If you love me, I will cry,' and asked her to, 'Console me, you precious one,' even though he hurt her, which totally confused the little girl and left her with no choice but to opt out and begin to live in a real make-believe world.

Luckily enough for both girls, they each met a good-looking young man whose genuine love guided the way to the truth. And thus began another story – a tale of pain, of sorrow, of betrayal, yet also a tale of abiding love, of courage and determination to unravel fact from fiction, once and for all. Indeed a veritable real life story, which at this point of the book, I have to inform the reader was far from finished!

On the fourteenth of June, three weeks after returning from holiday, Cordelia in fact finally confirmed that she now knew for certain that her father had sexually abused her. As soon as we had both returned from our holiday, about the end of May, we naturally returned to the exploration of why Cordelia had created the bluebell children in the first place. Since returning from her holiday in Tuscany, Cordelia had been very distraught. Certainly, the good feelings the bluebell children had given her when she had visualised them forming a circle and holding hands in the bluebell woods had just disappeared. Nonetheless, Cordelia confirmed that she had coped with being away from her therapist better than ever before and that she had been 'aware of all her parts', 'aware that some kind of integration had taken place', which had felt so very strange. Indeed, as I recorded in my notes that day: 'Cordelia said: It felt strange because it is new – even though there were times she did split and became just one of the personalities.'

The reason for her distress, Cordelia explained, had been the sudden realisation whilst she was on holiday and made love to her husband, that the rape at the age of thirteen had not been the first time she had experienced a similar situation. The low ceiling, the rafters and the general decor of the hotel room had reminded her, Cordelia said, of the room she had shared with her parents until she was six years old. Sudden flashbacks had subsequently made her feel unable to walk or talk, and her husband had later on told her that she had in fact curled up, changed into a very little girl, and had even begun to suck her thumb.

The implications of the flashbacks, however, were far too big. Could her beloved, ideal father really have done something so vile and evil to his 'precious' little girl? And what about her other family members? Cordelia felt that her mother knew and wondered if it could explain why her eldest brother left home and why he once told her that he hated their father. But could she be mistaken? She needed to be sure before she made such an accusation! Yet Cordelia also told me that certain parts of her know that the flashbacks are for real but that there are others who tell her, 'It's a huge lie, ignore it.' Since then, a true battle of words had been raging inside her, with each camp arguing its case for or against. If she revealed the truth, it could eventually lead to complete health. But it would of course also mean that certain parts could never achieve the independence and total control over the system they would like to have, and hence they were very adamant that the secret should remain a secret. Then again she was told that others would simply reject her, i.e. Victoria argued that she should not reveal this abuse because others such as her therapist would not be able to cope with it, and would drop Cordelia like a dirty rag. Over the weekend, however, notwithstanding her internal dispute, Cordelia had been able to get in touch with Peter. He is the one who knows, Cordelia said, who the person is who sexually abused her when she was a very young child. But as yet she felt unable to reveal this person's name because if she did so, it would all be real, and she must be certain of her facts first.

On Tuesday, Cordelia was very tearful and yet also appeared timid, whereas normally when she cried, Elizabeth would never be very far away, making sure that her tears would not go unnoticed. That day, however, we were in fact in a different therapy room. Building work in the clinic was disrupting regular routines, although I still made sure that paper and crayons etc. were available. Anyhow, this particular room was much larger and certainly a lot more clinical (it was in fact a standard porta-cabin). Hence I at first attributed Cordelia's different demeanour to the change of rooms. But as we talked, I also noticed that she was rubbing her legs as though she was in pain. As I observed her doing so, it suddenly dawned on me that Cordelia was in fact introducing me to yet another child part of her, who must have worn the callipers when she was very young and who periodically would experience numbness in its legs. Way back, Cordelia had in fact told me that she once wore callipers, though she had never been able to tell me precisely why she had needed to do so.

When I told her that I had noticed that she kept rubbing her legs, and asked her whether there was something wrong with them, Cordelia introduced me to Peter (the boy who came to help Cordelia cope with the sexual abuse from her father). Peter then confirmed that it had indeed been Cordelia's father who had been the one who had sexually abused her; that her father was the one who had caused her legs to be pushed out of the sockets, resulting in Cordelia being admitted to hospital, which is why she had needed to wear callipers for a number of months – a whole year to be precise. The secret was out! Cordelia cried, tears of distress but also tears of relief, saying that suddenly all the mysterious events in her life now seemed to make sense, including the hatred of her mother and the dislike and abuse by her brother. When the time came to end the session, Cordelia was still very distraught and I naturally encouraged her to stay in the hospital and once again suggested that she became an in-patient and get some respite from her relentless distress.

Although I hugged and held Cordelia and encouraged her to cry, as I had done many times during her therapy, this was never enough. As usual, Cordelia refused to accept my concern for her and declined to become an in-patient and take a well-earned break, because I did not comply with her request to continue her therapy whilst she was an in-patient. Despite her obvious distress, despite the enormous step she had taken to reveal the abuse by her father. I did not believe that it would be advantageous this time to consider lifting the boundaries, after which it was of course no use explaining to her that continuing her therapy as an in-patient would not give her the respite she needed. All Cordelia heard was that I would indeed not go that extra mile for her. Thus she left, though still clearly distressed, after recovering somewhat, having spent some time in one of the bedrooms, leaving me to nurse my concern and my anxieties. She did, however, return to the hospital later on, but went home again with her husband after his own therapy had ended.

Throughout Cordelia's therapy there were many, many painful moments like this, and frequently I used to worry and wonder whether it would indeed, as Cordelia often feared, be too much, all too demanding for her to cope with. There was such distress, such sorrow, such earth-shattering realisations, such heartache that I found it difficult at times to comprehend that anyone could tolerate such pain. I often used to feel that being a therapist was a cruel profession; having to twist the proverbial knife so to speak and dislodge established patterns, misguided beliefs, familiar behaviours and that ever-crippling, ever-beguiling false hope. How could she ever repair such violations, such damage to her self-esteem, I used to ask myself. Then again, despite Cordelia's frequent desperate behaviour, despite her belief that she was unlovable, bad, ugly, caused more harm than good etc., Cordelia nonetheless had a very stable, loving core which the abuse and deprivation somehow had not been able to tarnish, as indeed all abused people I used to work with seemed to have. In fact, I very much believe that it was often their very naivety, their unquestioning belief in the goodness of others, their very sensitivity, which made them so vulnerable to abuse and exploitation. Every time, therefore, it would have been very easy to wholeheartedly give Cordelia the love she so desperately craved for and go that extra mile, as Cordelia used to call it. Surely giving her what she needed so badly could not harm her, I reasoned at times. However, as usual, I also had to remind myself that it would not be in Cordelia's best interest to do so. I just knew that any such 'extra mile action' would merely entrench Cordelia in her transferences and eventually, when substitution no longer worked, would only have succeeded in fortifying her longing for something she could never have: the love of a mother, thereby effectively condemning her to go on searching and searching and searching. As usual, Cordelia found her own way of protecting herself giving herself that much-needed breathing space, and by the next day she had duly switched into

Geraldine (unlike her therapist, who could not switch and had to stay the course and somehow carry on).

Anyone who has worked with MPD (see also Kluft, 1989b and Watkins, 1984), would I'm sure, agree with Bloch (p.45, 1991), when he wrote 'Treating MPD is arguably the most demanding, complex and draining endeavour that a therapist can attempt!' Anyhow, Geraldine was the one who does not feel. She was also the one who insisted that the abuse was 'not worth making a fuss over'. And she was also the one who very much wanted to be the only personality and therefore sorely regretted that Cordelia had revealed this secret. However, even here a change had occurred. Geraldine used to believe that she was indispensable; expecting to be treated as a doormat, and that her function in life was to be used by men, (hence why she found it difficult to feel anything about being abused by her father). Geraldine had recently become aware, Cordelia said, that she in fact represented a third generation of women who had been abused by men, and that she was therefore just as much 'in need of understanding and love' as the other children. Thus she had decided, explained Cordelia, that she was now prepared to work together with the other parts.

For the rest of the week, however, Cordelia continued to be Geraldine, although she also switched back and forth into Elizabeth, who naturally was very angry about the boundaries, shouting at me, 'I hate the boundaries. Dr C said they will never be lifted, but just wait and see. A little freedom would not go amiss.' Thus once again it seemed that the system was in turmoil. An hour later after her therapy had ended, Cordelia phoned in to say that she did not remember having been in the clinic that day. Still, whereas in the past such drastic switching would have gone on for days, this time, Cordelia seemed to regain her control quite quickly, and in the next few days worked very hard on herself. As a result, Cordelia apologised for leaving yet another angry note on my car; 'I now know why Elizabeth has always been so angry,' she said. 'Previously she had just been angry, but she never really knew why.' She finally also accepted that her angry, irrational, often misdirected behaviour could and did indeed upset others – as I had previously pointed out to her on more than one occasion.

During the next week, Cordelia painstakingly drew the images and wrote down in huge angry accusing letters how the abuse by her father had caused her to split into two – into Rosalind who represented the music part of her father, and into Peter who represented the hurt her father had caused her. In addition, Cordelia also talked about how she now realised that she had wasted her love trying to get her family of origin to love and care for her, and that her father's betrayal, especially the unforgivable act of disguising sex as love and making her feel responsible for what had happened, saying to her, 'Stop me – this is wrong,' had left a huge hollow within her, which she had filled with a substitute family of her own. It was a very precious family nonetheless, which she now would have to lose, as the reason why this substitute family had been created – to help her deceive herself – was no longer valid. Cordelia naturally expressed her concern as to how she would achieve this and feared that without the personalities, there would in fact be nothing to her!

And yet, notwithstanding the fact that the awareness that her father had abused her was a shocking and painful revelation, it did not really cause Cordelia to feel as desolate as she had feared it would. Instead, it felt as though at last she could begin to heal for real! Indeed, by the end of the week, Cordelia had actually begun to cry on behalf of herself, on behalf of this 'poor little girl'. In fact, when we looked back over Cordelia's therapy, there had been many clues that something was very amiss. Not just because Cordelia had at one time shared a dream with me in which her father had injected a can of worms into her abdomen, without leaving any visible scars. Nor because Cordelia had indeed mentioned that she would not be able to cope with such devastating betrayal. But because we had tried many times to grieve the loss of this wonderful father, and every time we just seemed to come to an inconclusive end. Cordelia would either sidetrack herself, or else her excessive anger would prevent her from feeling anything and seemed way out of proportion. Thus, when Cordelia eventually remembered that her father had sexually abused her, it did not come as a great surprise.

Doubtful, I hear the anti-repressionists reply! Such traumatic memories simply cannot be repressed and then suddenly remembered. Why did she not recall that she had been sexually abused by her father before – for instance, the very first time she made love to her husband? Surely, such an important event would have stimulated her to remember? The patient must have had an ulterior motive to disclose such details now. Sexual abuse would of course guarantee that her therapist would continue to be interested in her. Sexual abuse would provide a convenient explanation for all manner of irrational behaviour. Sexual abuse is a modern ailment. Sexual abuse makes the patient special. Sexual abuse is supposed to be the main reason for someone developing a multiple personality disorder. Anyone who reads any book on MPD would know this for a fact, etc., etc. The truth is that Cordelia did not so much repress her traumatic memories but rather compartmentalise them. But what does that mean and how did it help Cordelia to manipulate her memories?

Again, if we take trance logic into account (which I enlarged upon in the previous chapter), and reason in the same way a child would think, it becomes obvious that whenever Mary Magdalene made love to Cordelia's husband – as she was meant to do (she was after all the designated personality to engage in sexual behaviour) – it would not be possible for her to recall her father's abuse, because Mary Magdalene came into Cordelia's life only after Cordelia was thirteen. If Mary Magdalene did remember the abuse by the father it would mean that she was a fraud, that she was not real. In fact, it would be quite illogical for Mary Magdalene and Victoria, in fact, for any of the older children to remember the early abuse, because Cordelia's father had died before they came. If it were not so, the whole precarious house of cards would simply tumble down.

But how then, one might ask, was it possible for Cordelia to remember the abuse this time? True, the setting and decor of their hotel room in Tuscany could have acted as a trigger. However, the reader might remember how Cordelia had decided prior to going on holiday that she was determined to allow Delia I and Delia II to work together. Thus, for most of the holiday, she had in fact felt as though all her parts were as one. Besides, since Delia I and Delia II were an amalgamation of all the internal children – this time, logically speaking, it had not just been Mary Magdalene who was engaged in making love to Cordelia's husband in Tuscany, but all the internal children had become involved. Taking trance logic thus, squarely into account, it had now become feasible for Cordelia to remember the earlier abuse, since Cordelia could now legitimately claim to have access to the memories of those children who never forgot what their father did to them.

Of course, none of this was as conscientiously thought out by Cordelia as I have described it. But some part of her would nevertheless have kept track of it all. Indeed, as I have expressed before, the organisation of a multiple system is rather unique and has a peculiar self-serving logic of its own. However, I'm glad to say that despite its mind-blowing and boggling machinations, I never lost sight of why it had been created in the first place. Moreover, once Cordelia had begun to dismantle the secret world, it soon became quite evident that the same dogged determination with which the system had safeguarded the Self in the past was now being used to direct a steady healing from within, which often used to leave me feeling that I too should and could trust the system, as I frequently urged Cordelia to do herself. Be that as it may, having remembered and revealed the abuse by her father in itself did not appear to prevent Cordelia from dissociating. She continued to switch from Elizabeth to 'this other Delia' (as Cordelia had so succinctly observed), although Elizabeth, according to Cordelia, 'no longer felt like the old Elizabeth because she was no longer as angry'.

At least something was changing and what's more, Cordelia subsequently told me, there was yet another personality whom she had not talked about. Her name, said Cordelia, was Alice, like *Alice in Wonderland*. And just like Alice who was able to change her size in the stories her father used to read to her, Cordelia's Alice could equally make herself smaller or larger in order to evade her jailers and abusers. Of course, my immediate reaction was a cautious one. Certainly, according to the books (Bloch, p.44, 1991), many MPD patients can find the unravelling of their system and the intrusive 'uncovering therapy' far too demanding, and can only cope with it by creating new alters, or suffering an iatrogenic deterioration. Thus I wondered, was this Alice a new alter? Was I in fact witnessing Cordelia relapsing? Or did Alice indeed belong to the established system as Cordelia had implied, even though the role she seemed to have within the system was somehow quite different from the others?

As it turned out, Alice was in fact the very first 'assistant' Cordelia had created. For unlike Cordelia, who could not disappear, by pretending to be Alice, Cordelia could disappear; dissociate herself and pretend that the games her father wanted her to play in the bath were not for real. After all, as everyone knows, Alice could verily go through the looking glass to another world, where everything was different and everything was make believe. Cordelia's Alice then eventually came of age, became autonomous, the day her father died and her mother told her that she must stop crying and look after her. Alice that day duly became a real person, and as Cordelia has already described, with the logic of a child promptly made herself six years older (six years – into the future), so that she would indeed be old enough to be able to look after her mother and comply with her mother's command never to talk about her father ever again. Consequently, when Alice was asked to give her date of birth, she was always six years older than Cordelia. Very confusing when it came to filling in forms, since the actual date she used to give would of course be six years into the past. Many times, Cordelia explained, I used to cover up this apparent mistake by saying I must have written down someone else's date of birth and try to turn it into a joke.

Although Alice was the very first alter personality Cordelia's Self had created, surprisingly she was also one of the last of the internal children Cordelia revealed. But as a result of having done so, Cordelia consequently was able to write an updated list of her personalities – this time describing their qualities as well as their appearances and their ages: i.e. Cordelia herself had fair, short, curly hair up to six years, whereafter it grew very long except for the period when she was in the asylum. She had short, fair, slightly darker waved hair at nineteen years. One or two characters have no hair. Two of them are boys with short to medium-length fair hair.

1. Young Cordelia – two years old: sad child not appearing to be here. Very alone, weak smile, secretive, introverted, no emotion.

2. Zillah: shadow friend – like young Cordelia age two years.

3. Alice – eighteen months old: very, very small, almost disappears like Alice in Wonderland (dissociation).

4. Stephanie – two years old: very sad, despairing, frail, always ill, wants to die.

5. Rebekah – three years old: loves stories, books, Bible and Sunday School, and church.

6. Elizabeth – three to four years old: behaves badly, screams, hurts herself, feels trapped, panics, jealous and angry, loves deeply.

7. Rosalind – two to three years old: gentle, musical, sang well when she was old enough, played piano.

8. Peter – two to three years old: kind, caring, pale, worn out. Legs dislocated at the hips. Wore callipers on legs.

9. Felicity – five years old: extrovert, daring, passionate, flirtatious.

10. Angela – six and a half years old: carer of little brother (a baby), looks after mother, everyone. Kind.

11. Bryony – six and a half years old: cold, indifferent to others, cruel, abuses, demands. Hair shaved off.

12. Esther – six and a half years old: loves outdoor life, swimmer, dancer, strong and brave.

13. Geraldine – seven years old: paranoid, strong, aggressive, argumentative, abuses, cruel.

14. Gillian – seven to eight years old: laughs in a serious situation, giggly, plays jokes, clown, naughty.

15. Martin – seven to eight years old: kills, experiments, inflicts pain, sly, critical, sarcastic, abuses, shouts, cruel, cold, no friends, viciously strong in word and deed, academic.

16. Mary Magdalene – thirteen years old: feels injured, dirty, dislikes herself intensely, full of guilt and shame. Doesn't eat. Bald head. Abuses herself.

17. Victoria – fourteen years old: confident, academic, dressed smartly, loved company, achiever. Hair long but pulled back in a pony-tail.

20. Delia I – nineteen years old: strength and courage. Short wavy hair, slim. Nurse in uniform, met future husband, who called her Delia, instead of Cordelia.

21. Delia II – nineteen years old: despairing hopeless. Shortish wavy hair, slim, met future husband – out of nurse's uniform.

I'm sure that the reader has not failed to notice that Cordelia in fact skipped from seventeen to twenty. At the time, when I asked Cordelia why, all she could tell me was that she must have made a mistake. Of course time would reveal that it wasn't! Indeed, as usual, in this apparently nonsensical system when it was put under the microscope, its structure and its logic made perfect sense; the sudden appearance of Alice at first threw me somewhat, and made me feel quite suspicious as to why she had appeared at this stage of Cordelia's therapy, taking into account the fact that most of the personalities by now had indeed told their individual stories. We had consequently also begun to discuss the prospect of reducing her therapy sessions to four times a week, a tricky proposition which in the past would have been enough to upset Cordelia's fragile balance. But when I considered Alice's place in the hierarchy and structure of the system, revealing her to me at this late stage of course made sense. After all, once the secret of her father had been disclosed, there was no longer any need to maintain the secret of Alice and her particular Wonderland.

However, letting others enter into this secret world did not come without a price, and during the weeks following the disclosure of the sexual abuse by her father, Cordelia literally went in and out of grief. One minute, feeling relieved that the secret was out, then again, feeling overwhelmed with the implications of it all, scared that her brothers would accuse her of lying, fearful about what they might do to her. Moreover, Cordelia also complained that she felt as though she was dissolving, becoming one, which scared her, even though it also made her feel 'very much alive and different'. However, she continued to switch from one tearful personality to another. Thus, she cried, she was angry, she was disgusted, she was devastated and she was out for revenge and wrote a letter to her father, which actually began and ended as follows (the rest of the letter has been included by Cordelia in the chapter entitled My Father).

Dear Father,

You are lucky you are already dead, because if you were still alive, I would want to beat you to a pulp, hang you up by your penis and shoot it at close range – whether I could actually do this or not is another matter! Instead, all I can do is write this honest, very frank letter, spit on your grave and burn your photographs. You took advantage of my need for love and nurturing. I returned nothing but love and trust. Yes, I trusted you and you betrayed me, but I went on adoring you.
   I never ever thought I would say: thank God you died when you did.
   Goodbye Dad,
   Cordelia

PS Never was love like mine – never was grief like mine.

In fact, Cordelia was very distressed and very sad. She was also quite clearly traumatised by it all, complaining that her arms and legs had gone numb whilst she was reading this letter to me and requesting to sit close to me for comfort. But, when she did not feel wholeheartedly encouraged by me to do so, she went and sat on the floor, pushing herself into the corner of the room, allowing the walls to hug her as she used to do as a child. Nevertheless, after a while she responded to my questions and subsequently was able to resume her therapy and conquer the numbness in her arms and legs.
   However, during the next few days Cordelia also became very, very angry, and as a result she not only accused her husband of deserting her – since his own therapy was helping him to 'stand back' – but she made many, angry phone calls. She also rampaged through the garden in the nude with knives, chopper and an axe; chopping, sawing, trying to cut down a small dead tree. She dug the soil into a grave shape, she exhausted herself, she drugged herself, she did not feel. She even missed her appointment with me – the first time ever. Although we tried many times, we simply could not reach her by phone, and when she came the following day for her therapy, Cordelia said that she had spent the day in a wonderful garden. She had neither heard the telephone ring, nor had she been aware of time passing!

I drifted off... not into sleep, but into an escape world. I became unaware of my surroundings, of time – even the sound was mostly blocked out. I occasionally thought I heard a phone ringing in the distance. It was like having a light anaesthetic or a drug. I seemed only semi-conscious. It was like a journey to a different place, a place where I wanted to stay.

I found myself on a long garden bench, situated in a high position overlooking terraces of rock gardens. These were steep and at the bottom was a long, winding stagnant strip of water that appeared from nowhere, though it led into a larger area of still water; a pond with water lilies and all kinds of ducks. There were fish darting in and out, occasionally startling a passing duck by the intrusion.

There was an old rustic bridge that passed over the narrow strip of water. On one side there was a woodland area, with trees just about to break forth in bud. Primroses, celandines, violets, wood anemones, fading snowdrops and crocuses carpeted the ground, even bluebell leaves were beginning to poke through the leaf mould – it was Spring in the woods and the birds were singing. On the other side of the bridge was a summer meadow of long grasses; red poppies, blue harebells, white and blue Canterbury bells, white and yellow tall daisies, blue wild scabious and cow parsley gracefully decorated the banks of the meadow, as if all the rest needed a delicate white frill to round it off. It was beautiful. It was Summer in the meadow and butterflies were dancing.

Where I was sitting there were deciduous trees all changing colour and dropping their leaves. I kicked my shoes among the build-up of leaves around the seat, as they rustled they told me it was Autumn. The gold, yellow, bronze, brown and reds of the turning leaves on the trees made a picture to move any artist. Conkers and their shells and the spiky sweet chestnuts were crisp and cracking beneath my feet as I walked about, enjoying the lazy low sunshine. It was my birthday. It was Autumn.

Where I sat, the view was inviting. I walked down through the terraces, stopping to look as I went.

I went to gaze at Spring and Summer, the promise of new life and happiness.

Behind the bench the view stretched for miles and miles. Frozen glistening lakes looking as if their life had stopped. Coniferous trees weighed down with heavy snow, frozen where it dropped. Crisp frost and sparkling icicles dripped from the branches of cold bare deciduous trees. Ranges of mountains drenched with snow, towered above and enveloped the scene.

The silence and stillness were unaffected by the echo as I looked back at the vastness, the expanse, the grandeur of the past and hurled pain down the valley – back down the years.

I screamed for as long and as hard as I could – but not for real, that is yet to come.

I started to come round, as I heard my husband talking to me and mentioning Frieda's name.

Indeed, as events unfolded and as Cordelia predicted, the 'real scream' was yet to come, although at that stage neither Cordelia nor I were aware of the significance of her words. But then again, perhaps Cordelia was. Nothing it seemed, in this amazing system, ever happened without a reason! Anyhow, despite the fact that Cordelia continued to go in and out of grief, by the end of June, she was able to write an honest and moving appraisal of how the abuse had scarred her, whereas knowledge she asserted, had 'grounded her'.

My father – 30 June 1995

I imagined he loved me. I imagined he cared. I imagined I was safe with him and that he protected me from every harm. I imagined that if he had lived much longer he would have given me all the love I needed to feel secure, he would have gone to the ends of the earth for my sake, and no one else mattered as much as I did. I imagined that I was the most precious possession he had ever had or ever wanted to have – I imagined he adored me and I could have anything I ever wanted, if it was just the two of us together.

I imagined a lie, a falsehood. I was not only deceived, I deceived myself in order to survive. It has shattered my dreams. The one perfect reason for living was my father's love – I thought. There must have been something good, or a moment of truth, to give me the courage to go on. Even the love I have held in my heart all these years is false, it makes me feel my love is worth nothing, and I am worth nothing and never will be because of all this. It has made me doubt my capability to love as others love, it has made me want to run miles away from those who are so important to me, those I think I love, in case I've got all that wrong too!

Yet, the love I have experienced over the past four and a half years was born out of connecting with another human being, seeing myself through her, gradually learning to respect and understand myself more, growing into a whole, feeling person. If this had not happened, I could not have faced the whole horrible truth of my father and why I felt so abnormal and deeply sad, why I felt false and my life was false. There has never been a sense of anything being real. My life didn't ring true and I felt unreal. I could not hold in my heart even moments of truth, nothing lasted very long except a deep sadness.

Deep, deep in my soul, I must have known my whole life was a lie and that none of my human emotional needs were ever met. This gave me an intense longing and a constant searching for something intangible.

Knowledge has grounded me, but it has been earth-shattering.

Thus, after the storm came the calm – at least for a week or so. However, it would turn out to be a week in which Cordelia did an awful lot of growing and an awful lot of learning. In truth, from then on, my role would often become a mixture of therapist and teacher-parent; helping Cordelia to discover new ways of relating to others and the world; assisting her to live with 'continuity of memory' and feeling responsible for her actions. Consequently, not only was Cordelia actually able to discuss the ending of her therapy without getting unduly upset, we had in fact agreed to reduce her therapy to four times a week after I returned from holiday in September. But she was also able to turn to her husband for guidance, who confirmed that, like her, he had been devastated by the actions of her father, but that seeking revenge would not give her the peace of mind she craved. In addition, during one of her therapy sessions, Cordelia also drew up a genealogy of her family of origin and quickly realised that she was indeed very different from certain members of her family, whereas she had always feared, that the same 'mad, abusive streak' might be lying dormant within her. Hence, she also accepted that it was pointless asking 'why' questions as she would probably never get an answer as to how it all went so drastically wrong. Finally it seemed that Cordelia was beginning to feel able to look at her past without feeling instantly overwhelmed.

Then again, after drawing the moment she created Martin – which of course helped her to understand why she would dial 999 whenever she felt out of control – Cordelia said that this particular drawing, called 'Martin's terror' (depicting a bonfire on the moors, of people dancing and three naked girls tied to stakes) disturbed her, as it appeared to portray ritual abuse. Naturally, at the time it would have been very tempting to follow Cordelia's lead, but as I have explained elsewhere, instead I allowed time to reveal the true meaning of this particular image. Moreover, I could of course not help wondering whether this new slant was perhaps too much of a coincidence – once again taking into account the fact that we had just been discussing the end of her therapy.

However, when all stories were told, all details collated, we were in fact both wrong! Cordelia was not trying to prolong her therapy as I had suspected. Cordelia felt disturbed, because a child-part of her knew why the children were naked, and she felt ashamed. There was no ritual abuse. True, it was a yearly event. But the mysterious bonfire which threatened to get out of hand, the people dancing etc., were in order to celebrate Guy Fawkes night. And the girls tied to the stakes? They were in fact Cordelia's internal children! But why were they tied up, and why were they naked? Again, the answer was quite logical, once Cordelia had complete access to her memories: Cordelia's brother Martin had threatened Cordelia, saying he was going to burn her as a witch. Felicity, as was her wont, came to help Cordelia, and tried to draw attention to all this abuse in the only way she felt she could, by taking off her clothes as she had done before, whereafter her brother tied her to a tree. Elizabeth, remembering being tied up in the loft by her mother, then took over from Felicity and of course fought back. After this, Cordelia created a brand new person to help her when she feared that the fire might indeed burn her, and a substitute Martin (the loving brother she would like to have had) ran to get help, asking their neighbour to dial 999. Thus, the three girls tied to the stakes, were Cordelia, Felicity and Elizabeth.

At the time, of course, neither of us had access to these details, so we left the drawing for what it was and silently we each nursed our doubts. In any case, Cordelia also reported that although there were still times when she felt as though she had not been to see me on a certain day, she now knew that she had indeed been to see me, 'which felt very new'. And she now also knew, Cordelia said, that feelings did not last; hence she was able to begin tolerating them. What's more, she could now feel, for instance, sensible and sad at the same time, without needing to switch in order to do so. Nor did she feel any longer compelled to displace her feelings by going shopping on the way home from her therapy and buying yet another card to send to me, expressing her longing and hopes. In fact, Cordelia beamed proudly, she had 'not switched for several days now!'

Yet, the emotions of jealousy, suspicion and fear of abandonment were of course never very far away. Indeed, by the end of this productive week, they once again raised their head when Cordelia was confronted with the fact that she had to share me with other patients. Although this time Cordelia said, clearly maintaining her progress, she had been able to talk herself out of feeling jealous by confronting her inner people and getting them to admit that they were all sad. For the first time, Cordelia added wistfully, the feeling of jealousy had felt like a change of mood, rather than that she had 'switched into a specific personality'. For sure, a far bigger achievement than it actually sounded! But what then does it mean to switch?

Switching (between personalities) first and foremost meant that Cordelia was able to maintain her trance logic: her self-deception. In fact, every time Cordelia was one of her internal people or dressed herself in their specific clothes, it simply reinforced her belief that they must be real! 'They have to be real – otherwise, I couldn't be them – I wouldn't be able to see them!' Indeed, every time she wrote a letter in their peculiar handwriting, created a work of art in their special style or behaved outrageously, out of character or contrary to her moral code, it would be translated as further proof that they must be real (like being caught in a self-perpetuating, self-deceiving feedback loop).

Secondly, it also meant that Cordelia was able to control and distribute her feelings around the system, as well as delegate responsibility, compartmentalise her memories, avoid reality and manipulate the truth. Indeed, switching allowed her to dissociate herself from life, or any unpleasant event. Switching, moreover, especially when she was a child, allowed her to endure great terror and utter pain, both physical and emotional – in short, switching saved her life. It has, however, also severely complicated her adult life.

Imagine for instance, driving along in your car, feeling fairly happy and content. You are on the way to meet up with some friends. Suddenly, the strains of haunting music invade your thoughts – such soulful music as the 'Wings of a Dove'. Instantly you are transported back to the past, when you believed that seagulls tapped on the window of your bedroom in order to comfort you and invite you to fly away with them. You change, not just your mood but everything about you – who you are, what you know, where you are at. You suddenly don't know any more why you are driving along; why you are on this particular route, where you are going, whom you are going to meet – if you are meeting someone? All you know is that you are in pain, hurting, whilst pictures of the past crowd your head. They are too huge, too real, too painful! You change again. If you are lucky you change back into whosoever you were when you set out. If you don't… well, the rest I leave to your imagination.

Because that is in fact all we can do; imagine what it must be like to know one minute who you are, and the next, be a different person altogether.

In fact, it is just because we can't imagine such a state that most people find it so difficult to accept the truth of Cordelia's accounts. It just is not logical to be many different people. Until that is, you take trance logic into account. And yet, any visit to the cinema, a museum, the theatre, or a bookshop will confirm that the right side of our brains can create the most vivid scenarios, the most improbable virtual reality you can imagine, far better than any computer ever could! And certainly so, when your very life, your very survival and precious sanity depends on it.

In Cordelia's virtual reality, most of the children did not know each other. Only some did, and would actually assist each other whenever they were in trouble. Elizabeth and Felicity, for instance, tended to help each other out, because they were both created in order to fight back. Elizabeth kicked and screamed and tried to help Stephanie fight her mother whenever she tied her up in the loft, whereas Felicity tried to help Peter reveal the abuse by their father by taking off all her clothes at his place of work. Peter's father had in fact taken him for his first walk since the callipers had been removed. He actually took him to the recreational lounge at his work, in order to show him off and demonstrate that his daughter's legs were sound again. Peter, on seeing all those other men grinning, laughing, and hearing them say, that she was 'a gorgeous little thing; a real catch', became convinced that these other men, just like his father, would want to abuse him, whereupon Peter duly left his body and heard Felicity trying to reassure him, saying, 'Don't worry. I'll show them what they really want. It doesn't have to be you this time!' She promptly took off her clothes.

Yet, all the children knew about Victoria but did not know her – in the same way, that we all know that there are a queen and a prime minister in charge of the country, who periodically will issue guidelines and directions but whom we will of course never really know. Delia I and Delia II of course knew all the children, though mostly denied that they existed. The children, however, knew all about Delia I and Delia II and bitterly resented the constraints imposed on them by these two. Hence, they frequently used to break free in order to live their life as they saw fit: going on sudden trips to the seaside, going on expensive shopping sprees, because they just could not believe, what they were wearing. As for the others, they each did their bit and did not associate with any of the 'naughty, wicked children'. And as for Martin, Geraldine and Bryony, since they believed that they actually lived inside a different body altogether, they certainly would not be able to help.

In fact, Cordelia often used to describe that sometimes her life felt as though it was a 'blind beggar's muddle', each part of her groping in the dark as to what, where, why, when, how she was going to proceed. I'm sure that if her husband had not acted as her daily prompt, reminded her to go there, go then etc., Cordelia would have missed many more appointments. He in fact often acted as Cordelia's link with reality, her focus on the real world. Nonetheless, Cordelia was definitely gaining ground, assisted I'm sure by the fact that one day whilst sorting through her wardrobe, she had indeed discovered that over the years she had actually accumulated a set of clothes for each personality. This was a most devastating realisation, which of course confirmed all she had revealed so far but also highlighted the extent of her self-deception. As I recorded in my notes that day, 'Cordelia said it was as though she was seeing her past life for what it was, having lived a lie, by taking on these various roles – but without a Self.'

For the next six weeks Cordelia would continue to work very hard on herself. First of all, we did some very painful work on exploring why getting a hug from me was so important to her. As Cordelia was able to explain, being touched made her feel real; the lingering smell of my perfume helped her 'to stay real'. Touching me meant that I must be real. Indeed, just like a child learns to recognise its mother's and father's faces through touch, Cordelia learned to accept that I too was for real, and with time, would also learn to accept that I would remain real, even when she could no longer see me. Being touched, getting a hug, meant that I did not shy away from her because I thought she was dirty or felt that it had sexual connotations. Any embrace she did get from her mother, was of course in order to abuse her sexually. Getting a hug meant she could return the hug and meet me as an equal – yet it also allowed her to furtively stroke my hair and momentarily be the child she was never allowed to be. Getting a hug also meant that she was not treated differently; that she was as important as other patients; as special as her brother had been to her mother. Being hugged thus was a vital aspect of her therapy, even though over the years it became a balancing act between not feeding Cordelia's transferences and healthy re-parenting!

Needless to say, many angry tears were shed whenever she did not get the expected hug. Or else, whenever she felt that no one would want to hug such a dirty, ugly person anyway, she would go missing for hours, invariably causing her husband to fear the worst. Then again, counter-transference did not always make it easy; to be readily available as a substitute mother to another mature woman – naturally adding its own brand of confusion. I'm sure that we both felt at times that this therapeutic relationship was like walking on a tightrope – make the wrong move and you end up in the sawdust! Which we did of course, quite frequently, especially in the beginning, though we always dusted ourselves off and climbed back on again – stubborn as we both were. For more information on transference and counter-transference when working with MPD patients, see also Beahrs (1982), Greaves (1989), Kluft (1989a, 1989b), Putnam (1989) and Wilbur (1988).

Secondly, Cordelia also came to terms with being powerless – powerless to prevent the abuse, powerless to turn her mother and father into loving parents, and accepted that in trying to defend herself against these devastating feelings of powerlessness, she rather thought that she was omnipotent. She had always believed, that if she had tried harder, her parents would have loved her for real!

As I explained to her (in my teacher's role), with sexual abuse especially, because it is so invasive, so disabling, so degrading, so shameful, so belittling, in trying to defend the Self, one will often end up convincing oneself to feel all powerful, all liable instead. But in doing so, these narcissistic, grandiose feelings will often ensnare the abused person in a permanent victim role, effectively taking away free will, the right to make mistakes, the right to learn, the right to be human, the right to love and be loved. As a result, Cordelia not only drew the pictures and wrote down the words which described how the abuse began, but was also able to place this 'defiled child, this horrible child which no one could love' within her own heart. It was a very cathartic moment indeed! And consequently, Cordelia reported that Young Cordelia was now a part of herself for real and described that she felt as though she had 'come together like a set of Russian dolls'.

Thirdly we tackled loss – always a stumbling block in the past. Cordelia drew yet another sunset depicting the loss of the ideal father, the loss of the real father, the loss of the ideal therapist, the loss of the real therapist, as well as the loss of her internal children. Throughout her therapy in fact, the very idea of loss, the thought of an ending, had always been an instant trigger to send Cordelia into dissociation. Although, bit by bit, she had come to realise that the end of a therapy session did not mean that I would die, or that I would leave without ever returning, as her father had done. Indeed gradually, Cordelia had begun to feel a lot more at ease whenever the subject needed to be discussed. However, any potential loss, real or imaginary, still had the power to upset her new-found equilibrium all too easily. And certainly so when it involved several of her insurance policies! For instance, Cordelia had talked about her husband's depression (he once again, according to Cordelia, had proposed a suicide pact because he felt unable to cope with Cordelia's distress) even though she had previously tried to explain to her husband that her many tears were in truth progress, as she now no longer felt that she had to hide them, she naturally agreed that from his point of view it would of course seem as though she was going backwards, but when I subsequently also confirmed that I would be away for two weeks' holiday, whereafter therapy would be reduced to four times a week, as we had agreed, Cordelia said it was all too much to cope with and duly dissociated. Stephanie, however, obliged, as usual and promptly stepped into the limelight, and once again Cordelia reported in her next therapy session, that she felt 'half dead'. But in comparison with the past, Stephanie did not stay in the foreground for very long, and Cordelia, in due course, was able to resume her work on coming to terms with loss; learning to be content with what she could have, rather than going on pining for what she should have had, effectively beginning to tear up the IOUs, as Dr C called it.

Week twenty-seven. We had both returned from holiday, and as we had agreed prior to going on holiday, therapy was indeed reduced to four times a week. Cordelia, however, informed me that she had become quite ill whilst she was on holiday, and that she had been admitted to hospital. She was also due to have further keyhole surgery to remove her gall bladder in two weeks' time. Illness it seemed, had intervened again at a crucial time. It certainly always appeared to do so, whenever any kind of loss entered the picture.

Naturally, there were times when I did wonder whether one of the side effects of all this abuse was a kind of Munchhausen's Syndrome', and Cordelia and I actually discussed this aspect being within the bounds of possibility, as I remember. Certainly, the following piece of creative writing by Cordelia, clearly endorses the fact, that Cordelia's body was quite often the battleground where abuse, sorrow, stress, despair, and longing all found their resolution – somehow.

Creative Writing: Conversation between the liver and gall-bladder, before the operation of Cholecystectomy takes place.

Colonel Liver: Now Choley my friend, I hear you are leaving me after nearly 52 years of faithful service. Can you give me a reasonable explanation for this sudden and totally unexpected desertion? Haven't I been a faithful friend, protecting you, giving you work, purpose and status? What about all the years we have shared our sorrows, our disappointments, our sickness, our hardships? We've stuck together through thick and thin, and now, when things are looking a bit brighter, you've decided your time is up. Well it won't do. Fancy giving up on an old and faithful friend like me!

Choley: Sorry Colonel Liver, but I'm tired and worn out. I am full of sludge, gravel and a great big stone, 2.5 cms in diameter and weighing 25 grams. I don't want to leave you, but when your time is up, you have to go. There's nothing more I can do for you or anyone else. I've taken a lot of kicks in life, and I'm not as strong as you.

Colonel Liver: I know I am a very important chemical factory, and I'm very strong. I repair myself better than any other organ in the body, but we all have a different job in life and it's no good being a weakling and giving in too easily. Come, come, my friend, pull yourself together.

Choley – crying great big tears: No one has ever heard my story or heard my pain. All I've ever been good for is to store, in a concentrated form, all the waste products of your worn-out blood cells and the bile salts, used in the digestion of fats. You'll just have to take on my task for me and work overtime as necessary. It won't kill you, you are always telling me how wonderful you are.

Colonel Liver: Wonderful, yes, of course I am. What about my equally wonderful network of a drainage system, that of course starts with me. Is that going with you too?

Choley: Yes, I'm afraid so, Colonel.

Colonel Liver: My bile ducts! This is preposterous. I cannot allow this to happen!

Choley: The body we have worked for all this time has survived many serious illnesses, tragic and traumatic life events beyond belief. We have taken the brunt of all this, because secrecy, deception and fear has ruled this body's life, now we are paying the penalty and some of us have to leave the ranks. I'm not the first to go, after all.

Colonel Liver: The others didn't affect my function or well-being, you do. This is a hard blow, and one that will leave me catastrophically in hell.

Choley: What do you mean by hell?

Colonel Liver: Hell, my dear Choley, is a permanent sense of loss. It would be much easier to die with you on 2 October than to go on living without you. But as always, I am going to face this bravely, and instead of storing all the bitterness and hatred of our body in you, Choley, I'm going to let it go.

Anyhow, when we resumed regular therapy, Cordelia said that at first, she had missed our therapy sessions dreadfully, but all things considered, she felt that she had coped remarkably well. A new person was emerging, Cordelia said, who was beginning to use the personalities, rather than be one of them, and though it scared her 'to feel so different', she had also been amazed at how she had begun to care for herself and ensure that she no longer had to suffer unnecessary stress. For example, when visiting the dentist, she had informed the dentist that she found it very difficult to lie back, because she had been sexually abused as a child. Nonetheless, Cordelia also wanted to know whether I wanted to continue her therapy, as she no longer had 'interesting events to talk about'.

During the next two days Cordelia in fact did yet another very important piece of work. She had described how the children-parts and the adult-parts of her are very separate, and that whenever she looks in the mirror – which she tended to avoid – she sees a little girl and not a grown woman. 'I just see my eyes!' She subsequently also told me that when she does look at herself, looks at her body in the mirror, she sees her mother. Hence, Cordelia said, the children allow her to hide. They keep the adult hidden, because she cannot cope with the idea of being like her mother (which is why she saw her internal children instead).

Some time prior, I had in fact requested to have a mirror installed in the therapy room, which I used primarily in order to enable certain patients to engage in vital Self descriptions. When I consequently encouraged Cordelia to draw a self portrait, based on what she remembered seeing in the mirror, she drew a detailed head, carefully depicting her hair, her mouth and other features, and patiently coloured in the eyes. Then, on the same piece of paper, next to the detailed head, she drew the outline of a round, headless body which did have a belly button and two breasts. She had, however, attached the arms to the hips. After which, I asked her to draw a second set of pictures, depicting her mother as she was now and also how Cordelia saw herself with her mind's eye. After some hesitation, Cordelia drew a decomposed body, a skeleton in fact, to depict her dead mother, ending by writing the name Bryony underneath it. Thereafter, on a new piece of paper, she drew a tall, slim, fairly young person to portray herself and called it Delia. However, the head in this particular drawing, although it was in the right place, was still not attached to the body (in the same way, she had always separated her father's head from his body). We naturally explored the implications of these drawings, and Cordelia consequently was able to realise that her mother is not only 'dead, cold, lifeless', but that all that is left are 'remains, bones' which are 'rotted' and 'can't hurt me' and have 'no power...'

Cordelia suddenly also recognised that she was indeed separate from her mother; that she herself was very much alive, and that she was a person in her own right. On reflection, Cordelia then corrected the drawing of herself, adjusting the shape of the body to depict her as she is today, and after due encouragement, she eventually also decided to connect her head to her body.

And yet, on the drawing of the skeleton, Cordelia had also printed the words 'gone, empty, alone'. These few tell-tale words, these apparently incongruous words, should have warned me. They should have told me that being separate from her mother was one thing, but the fact that all her internal children were now aware that their mother had died was bound to reverberate.

The following Monday Cordelia described, that she had looked at herself in the mirror at home. She at first saw nothing but a bag of bones, but briefly had also begun to see an amoeba shape – aware that she was in fact acquiring her own individual shape. However, the next day Cordelia also reported that she had seen all the cars in the car park turn into hearses. And what's more – each one, had also contained a coffin and flowers. They were all exactly the same coffin. They were exactly like her mother's coffin. They were exactly the same flowers as those Cordelia had chosen for her mother's funeral. 'How could this be?' Cordelia demanded to know. 'It surely could not be normal!' Cordelia then continued telling me that she was not certain how long this image had lasted but that she had been brought back to the here and now, she explained, by seeing a young man hiding in the bushes by the car park behaving rather strangely, brandishing a milk bottle, whereupon she discovered that she was in fact standing by the wrong car, 'which was no longer a hearse but just an ordinary car, like all the other cars in the car park!'

Nevertheless, despite her distress and concern about what she had just experienced, what she had just seen? Cordelia had decided not to return to the hospital and inform the reception staff that someone was behaving suspiciously in the car park because, Cordelia insisted, she was certain that when she left the hospital, the deputy clinic manager had looked at her in a hateful and hostile way, and hence, she had not wanted to take the risk of meeting her again. Obviously it was quite clear that Geraldine had once again appeared on the scene, and that she had been rather busy creating her own particular chaos and confusion.

Still, the positive outcome of all this distraction was that prior to going into hospital for surgery, Cordelia was able to welcome Geraldine to the fold and realise that she was not mad after all, as she had indeed, frequently feared that she was. Although Cordelia had never felt able to talk about it before, she had in fact experienced many such hallucinations and they had always felt so very real. For instance, she would often see her family of origin sitting round the table in the hospital dining room, although Cordelia reassured me that they had been far less frequent recently. 'Geraldine was not bad, or mad, but just sad,' Cordelia had consequently realised, after Geraldine had felt encouraged by me to draw the images depicting the abuse and trickery Cordelia had been subjected to by her mother, grandmother and especially by her brother, who was always trying to get her diagnosed as mad.

One time, Geraldine recalled, Cordelia's brother Martin, very much encouraged by his mother and grandmother, had actually tried to make Cordelia believe that her mother was dead, going to such extraordinary lengths as making the water in the bath look like blood, and ordering a hearse, which had indeed turned up at the house, and as expected had totally freaked Cordelia out. After that, the events of the previous few days were of course no longer quite so weird and bewildering. Indeed, taking Geraldine's experiences into account, as well as the fact that the previous therapy session had undeniably confirmed, that this time, their mother was dead for real. No wonder then, that such devastating realisation, such deception, such truth, would have caused each one of the children to see their mother's hearse and coffin in the car park.

Cordelia was not insane – indeed, as each personality had now revealed their particular piece of the jigsaw puzzle, it all began to make sense. It all had a logical explanation. There was a reason as to why she behaved as she did, there was a real event as to why she saw such pictures with her mind – there was a real need for her to have become so many people!

Two weeks later, Cordelia's surgery went without a hitch, though obviously not without physical pain, and yet, a week or so later, she was able to resume her therapy. However, despite the fact that Cordelia was now quite certain that she was indeed not mad or insane, she still did not seem to have any real say as to which part of her would be in conscious control. Even though they all had confirmed that they now wanted to live and they all had agreed to try and work together for the greater good of Cordelia, each part was still seeing the world very differently and would react to people or events according to its particular brief. In fact, Cordelia was still maddeningly and uncontrollably switching from one personality to another. So something was still very wrong. Yet, as the books predicted, there certainly had been 'spontaneous fusion of alters/ego states' indicating a willingness to be a whole person. For instance, one day Cordelia had reported that Martin and Peter had recently decided to work together. (See Bloch, p.68, see also Kluft, 1982 and Putnam, 1989.)

What's more, Cordelia had also clearly agreed with the notion that the long-term aim, as some authors advised, was now to achieve unification of personality: 'the blending of alters into a single non-dissociative personality structure', duly arrived at via the process of a functional integration; the promotion of increased harmony, cooperation, communication and respect amongst ego states, whilst initially, still maintaining the ability to divide, switch and dissociate, which, for some dissociative clients, is as far as they are prepared to go! (Bloch, p.69; see also J & H Watkins, 1979, 1981, 1984, 1988, and Beahrs, 1982, 1983.) However, as far as Cordelia and myself were concerned, we had in fact both come to the same conclusion, that only by encouraging all parts, every other-self, every separate personality to actively seek togetherness, seek unification, would we arrive at Cordelia's true personality. Furthermore, we both had certainly also endured more than our fair share of what the books called 'abreactive working-through of traumatic experiences', or so I thought! (Bloch, p.68) Indeed, every drawing Cordelia had made, every letter she had written and read out to me, had been a cathartic moment, resulting in some very painful awareness. In addition, we certainly also had our fair share of confronting the abusers within and without, via role reversal, sculpting, trust exercises, etc., and whenever we translated feelings into dramatic actions, such exertions as Cordelia repeatedly bashing an old, rotting, mouldy tree stump in the grounds of the hospital. At the time, Cordelia said that was exactly what she would like to have meted out to her mother – for real. And yet Cordelia still did not seem to have any real control over which one of her many different other-selfs she was going to be next.

So, what was missing? 'The self' was the obvious answer! The Self, who had been the architect and creator of these other-selfs in the first place! The Self, who was meant to be this metaphorical conductor, who would allow these other-selfs, these talented musicians, each very skilled in their particular craft, to play and work together. The Self, who would ensure that the right and the left side of Cordelia's brain worked in unison. The 'Observing Self' as Deikman (1982) called it, whose two modes of consciousness, the 'manipulative, controlling, thinking Object Self', and the 'passive, letting go, relaxing Receptive Self', when working as one, would ensure creative problem solving. The Self, who was meant to be the mediator who would improve internal communication, help to resolve conflicts, and reach compromises between conflictual ego states (rather than the therapist, who in the absence of the Self had to take over this role). The Self, who henceforth would help Cordelia's internal system to achieve what Bloch described as the goal of therapy, 'a synthesis of new styles of internal diplomacy that allows increased acceptance of the disparate motivations and specialised functions of various ego states' (p.72). Or, as I tried to explain it to Cordelia – in plain English:

> When the Self is once again involved – prepared to be in overall control, and when these other-selfs, (each separate personality) have renounced their self-status (their separateness) and are prepared to function as the ego; accept the authority of the Self, yet, are nevertheless able to remain idiosyncratic; negotiate with each other, contribute their unique knowledge, their specific insight, their

ambitions, their beliefs, their feelings etc., and share their individual skills, share dominance, share consciousness and when necessary, shift (rather than switch) into the appropriate mode of responding to the world. Then, Cordelia will be able to function as a united, whole person!

Thus, the task ahead was clear. The Self, who until now had been concerned solely with survival, who had opted out in self-defence, needed to be enticed, needed to be motivated to come back and take its rightful creative place within the system, within the personality, and facilitate all its ego parts to work as one! But how? I asked myself at the time. Today, writing with hindsight, I can of course see, how the return of the Self had actually been facilitated, step by painful step throughout Cordelia's lengthy therapy – even though there was an actual moment during her therapy when the Self did return – for good, as it turned out! Indeed, week by week, I had diligently listened to Cordelia and fed back to her what I had heard. Week by week, I had also observed, explained, contained, hugged, laughed and told stories. I had also stood my ground. I had even preached.

I naturally had used dramatherapy, but also used hypnotherapy, NLP, cognitive therapy, behaviour therapy, stress/anxiety management, systemic family therapy, transactional analysis, dream analysis, Gestalt, art therapy, creative writing and bereavement counselling. In short I used anything, any method, any technique, everything I had learned, in order to set the Self free from its self-made prison. Truly one can say that I have used a very varied bag of tools! In fact, as a result of working with MPD, I have realised that the therapeutic relationship is greatly enhanced by the application of a mixture of skills and can only benefit from the versatility, which comes from expanding our knowledge in many different directions. As it is, as therapists, we are certainly not spoiled for potential tools. Indeed, according to Griffin and Tyrrel (1998) there are at present over 400 therapies on offer worldwide. Enough choice for sure, provided of course, we dare to be eclectic!

However, irrespective of whichever tool I have used, the guiding principle I followed throughout Cordelia's therapy has been a solid belief in the integrity of the Self, as well as due acceptance that the Self is quite prepared to learn new ways, but that first and foremost it will always act in the perceived interest of the person, no matter how bizarre or avant-garde its methods might appear to you or anyone else, including self-imposed incarceration in a black hole.

Nevertheless, as the following collection of arguments and strategies will illustrate, enticing Cordelia's Self to trust and once again engage with the real world has been a most painstaking task. To begin with, I frequently used to assure the Self that, despite its elaborate defences, I could see the Self in the same way that Cordelia could see my own Self – in those unguarded moments when the person behind the therapist mask became visible. For instance, I explained, how else would she be able to tell me that she knew that the death of my sister had upset me more than I could tell her?

Secondly, I also assured the Self that it was now safe to open its eyes and come back; that its abusers, in truth, were either dead or could no longer inflict pain, although I equally assured the Self that I would respect its fear and accept that it would only feel able to show itself in its own good time. (In any case, as experience has taught me, you can only work at the pace of the patient. Push too hard and it all comes to a sudden halt anyway! This of course applies to any therapeutic encounter. (See Chu, 1988; Putnam, 1989; Strean, 1985 and Wachtel, 1982.) I nevertheless also reminded the Self how it felt when it did come back – those special moments when it felt at ease in nature, at one with God, or when Cordelia experienced the love of her grandchildren. Indeed, I very much reinforced the message of Cordelia's own story: 'You cannot have good apples without taking the risk of dropping some in the water.'

I naturally also used Cordelia's drawings, the photographs I took of her drawings, her diary and creative writing, as well as my therapy notes, in order to demonstrate that the secret was out and there really was no need to remain silent any longer. Moreover, I also made it quite clear to Cordelia's Self that in the meantime, the child had grown into an adult, and hence was now capable of taking care of itself. In fact, Cordelia could now rescue herself, although whether she chose to do so or not was another matter.

This might seem a rather obvious statement to make, but as I explained before, the Self did not experience, the Self did not engage in life, and therefore did not grow. In fact, Cordelia would often indicate that she was still firmly convinced that she was a tiny child in danger of being killed or maimed. Consequently, I also made a special point of recognising the enormous sacrifice involved, deciding to opt for Self preservation, rather than madness, badness or death, and encouraged Cordelia to say thank you to the Self for suffering such isolation, such nothingness in trying to avoid her father's and mother's warped attention.

However, I also encouraged Cordelia to use her imagination wisely, and not feed her fears or distort reality, and appealed to the Self's sense of responsibility and pointed out that Self preservation was indeed a noble choice, but that today it was no longer appropriate to turn a blind eye to the world, or deny the existence of a substitute family system which in the absence of the Self had evolved into an autonomous structure. Rather, that the Self needs to learn, grow, and accept its rightful place: being in charge of its internal family, as well as feel at ease about being a part of a real family. This meant caring for others in a realistic way, and allowing others to care in return. Indeed, by reminding it that, as the primary entity, it had in fact created each one of the other-selves for a specific function. Also, that it was now imperative to question whether the actions of itself, and the other-selves were still in the best interest of Cordelia.

Thirdly, I naturally also reminded the Self that it was unable to be untruthful to itself and its moral code. After all, had Cordelia not herself told me that even at such a young age, she knew what her father was asking her to do was wrong, and hence had chosen to pretend and become Alice rather than partake in her father's deception and compromise the Self. Yet, paradoxically, I also encouraged the Self to return by reminding it that it was in fact untruthful to itself the moment it replied 'I don't know!', when the nurse asked the young Cordelia who had injured her legs. However, I also encouraged the Self to accept that, at the time, it did not have any other choice.

It goes without saying that I also regularly used to assure Cordelia that neither myself, Anne or her consultant rejected, judged or held Cordelia to blame. I also recall that I used to explain, that excessive feelings of shame and guilt were not really a reliable guide, since they were in essence narcissistic feelings, designed to make us feel wholly responsible, in a desperate attempt to negate the feelings of powerlessness which we all, but especially an abused person, have got to come to terms with. Nevertheless, during many a therapy session, I also had to confront Cordelia's pride, shame and omnipotence and help her to understand, that she is only responsible for her own actions, and not the deeds of others. I remember that I explained this vital step to Cordelia by borrowing an image from the ancient Egyptians (Wasserman, 1994), and pointed out, that at the end of the day, it would be her heart being weighed and judged whether it was lighter than a feather, and not her father's or her mother's, or her brother's!

In fact, looking back, I used stories all the time, and duly allowed the metaphor to do its work. (Gersie, 1997; Shah 1991; Taylor, 1996) Moreover, I also used to encourage Cordelia to translate her dreams and reveal their messages, rather than rely on the therapist to interpret them, since any such interpretation will always be contaminated by the therapist's frame of reference, no matter how careful one tries to be! (Griffin, 1997) You could say that I tried to boost Cordelia's self-esteem by affirming that the Self knows what's good for it, knows when to reach out to others, and that most of the time, it can cope, without experts/insurance policies or ideal rescuers! Then again, I also used to talk directly to the Self, telling it quite clearly 'I want to talk to the part which disappeared', inviting it to share its opinions, beliefs, observations and enter into a dialogue, not just with its therapist, but also with the rest of the system. In addition, I also used to reinforce its importance and due place in the system, as well as highlight the harm it does by remaining absent and aloof and allowing the personalities to fight amongst themselves. Consequently, I frequently also used to appeal to its logic and its common sense, and encouraged it to reason things out and not just rely on feelings or indeed trance logic. In fact, to wake up; to wonder and look at reality in a multi-dimensional way, rather than the primitive one-dimensional view it had employed so far.

As a result, you could say we effectively became scientists together. Not only did we explore this phenomenon of dissociation and multiple personalities during many a therapy session, but I also tried to explain how the mind works, how trance was keeping the Self a prisoner, and shared the knowledge I had gleaned from a collection of books such as *Emotional Intelligence* (Golman, 1996), *Frogs into Princes* (Bandler & Grinder, 1979) and *The Family Inside, Working with the Multiple* (Bryant, Kessler, Shirar, 1992). (See also Andreas & Andreas, 1987; Bandler, 1985; Gregory, 1987; Grinder & Bandler, 1987; Fezler, 1990; Sanford, 1985; Singer, 1981 and Wolinsky, 1991 – as well as Goulding & Schwartz, 1995; Ross, 1989 and Yapko, 1992.) We naturally also explored what the books had to say about what it means to be sexually abused as a child. Consequently, discovering that she was not alone, that others would understand, brought Cordelia a measure of comfort, even though it was a very painful part of the process. Moreover, by sharing such books as *The Drama of Being a Child*, (Miller, 1992) and *A Life Worth Waiting For* (Wolter, 1989), Cordelia was able to discover like souls. (See also Bettelheim, 1965; Gil, 1981; Hall & Lloyd, 1989; Levine, 1990; Muller, 1992; Parks, 1990 and Sanford, 1991.)

In time of course, I also urged Cordelia to try and control her environment in a different way: no longer withhold love and affection, instigate rejection or escape into illness; no longer behave as a victim, but instead, become actively involved in achieving physical and psychological health. Including no longer using medication as a means to manipulate or inflict self-harm. Today, I'm glad to say, Cordelia is indeed no longer a victim – because the Self did return. One auspicious day, I effectively used Cordelia's ability to travel in time; I went back to the moment it all went awry, back to the moment the Self disappeared, and assisted her to promptly act it out and rewrite the script. (Jennings, 1992; Jones, 1996) However, I'm running ahead of myself.

In the meantime, Cordelia had retreated once more, or so it seemed, into the victim role. Whilst recovering from her gall-bladder operation, she had in fact taken the phone off the hook, and thus effectively had prevented anyone from inquiring after her health, including her son, who naturally grew most concerned. As before, Cordelia believed that no one could care for her, or would be worried about her. What's more, Cordelia said, that being loved would mean a whole new set of rules and responsibilities, and it was far easier, to just take care of herself, rather than allow others to care for her.

Yet, when we practised role reversal, she was able to empathise with her son and of course gladly accepted his love and due concern, now painfully aware of the distress her misguided thinking caused others.

However, her refusal to allow others to care for her had a much more sinister origin than just wishing to avoid rules and responsibilities. Cordelia recalled that, as a young child, after she had recovered from the operation to reset her legs, (the pressure of her father's body had caused them to be pushed out of the hip sockets), her father had in fact become very angry with the nurse who was taking care of her. He was adamant, Cordelia said, telling the nurse, that he would take care of his little girl and that she 'did not need anyone else'. After which, as Cordelia described it, her father had picked up yet another little girl – 'out of Peter' – and had promptly taken her home. This other little girl was of course Rosalind, so named, Cordelia duly explained, because this particular little girl – just like her sister Rosalind once used to be – soon became her father's favourite child.

As per usual, when Cordelia experienced a traumatic event in the present, she would go back to the past and relive a similar event as though it was happening right now. Hence her reluctance to allow others to care for her after an operation takes on a very different meaning when we consider that she was only following her father's order: she did not need anyone else! Indeed, since her recent operation to remove her gall bladder, Cordelia had been switching back and forth between being Peter and Rosalind for quite some time now, and she consequently was able to recount Peter's painful story; describing that the first thing he saw was the operating lights of the theatre after which he woke up in the hospital with splints on his legs. Cordelia grieved for this little boy, painfully aware that he had in fact been the main carrier of her father's abuse. Yet, the following day, Cordelia complained that it was all right to feel sorry for a little boy, but what about the little girl? This little girl, who deserved to be loved just as much as all the boys in the family had been loved – especially by their grandmother! – this little girl, who had been promised so much by her father and had ended up with nothing but two rotten apples!

By now it was once again late September, about the time of Cordelia's birthday. It had been nine months since we had started to work together five days a week, and in that time Cordelia had achieved so very much. On 17 October, we once again looked through all the various drawings Cordelia had produced – although she remarked that it felt as though she was seeing them for the first time. Two days later she revealed that she had in fact remained in a bubble throughout the previous days, because she had not really wanted to admit that those drawings depicted her life. Yet she also went on to describe how Peter and Rosalind had each helped her to cope with the abusing father by splitting him in two: Peter just saw his body and experienced the pain whereas Rosalind saw only his head and enjoyed his singing and walks in the country. Cordelia furthermore also confessed that she had been able to embrace such parts of her as Victoria quite easily, but that she found it difficult to consider incorporating such sad parts as Peter because she feared that she would not be able to cope with it.

Over the weekend, however, Cordelia had begun to cry and scream, and as a result was beginning to lose her voice. Nonetheless, during her therapy time, she was able to draw in sequence the details of the early abuse. Truly a major achievement, considering that previously, each aspect had been an isolated fragment which did not really make any sense on its own. Together, they told their sad tale and clearly depicted how it all began; how the sexual abuse by her father led to an argument between her parents... From then on, things just went from bad to worse. Her mother was furious. She held Cordelia to blame for what had happened, and started beating her. At that stage, however, Cordelia was still very able to defend herself, and loudly remonstrated with her mother that it was not her fault, that her father had done this. Yet, when her father took her to the hospital and told her that it would never happen again, that he was so very sorry and asked Cordelia to keep it a secret, Cordelia believed him. Thus, when the nurse holding Cordelia in her arms asked her, 'Who did this to you?' Cordelia lied and said she did not know. 'Ask my daddy.' However, the moment those words were spoken, Cordelia of course realised, that any hope of rescue was now gone for ever. Her father did not really love her as he said he did, and would never speak the truth. And as for her mother? Cordelia knew that she would equally never defend her. And now, this last chance – her last possible rescuer, the 'kind, warm nurse', was also gone.

She was well and truly trapped, acutely aware that pretending to be Alice, was no longer going to work! Just like a fragile animal caught in the glare of a poacher's lamp, she could neither fight nor flee, and hence Cordelia took the only option left available to her – she froze. Outwardly she became very still, very passive, very cooperative, and allowed herself to be placed on a stretcher. Yet inwardly she converted all that fear, all that anger, all that survival energy into a very different kind of escape: into dissociation, determined to preserve her free will at any cost. Cordelia floated out of her body. 'She' was no longer here. Whatever was about to happen, in the immediate future or in the long-term future, it was not going to happen to her!

Cordelia then saw herself being wheeled into the operating theatre, and distanced herself even further by seeing a little boy lying on the operating table being stitched up. The little boy whom she would later on call Peter, and who was in fact the first of the other children who from then on would live Cordelia's life for her. And the Self? The Self promptly retreated into nothingness, into the abyss, into the black hole. Into self-preservation – into exile. The Self – apart from continuing to create other-selfs, as and when events in the real world dictated – unpretentiously ceased to be involved. Indeed, as the reader is already aware, the series of incidents which were to follow, fully ensured that self-preservation, instead of a passing solution, would become a permanent state. To begin with, when eventually Cordelia came round after the anaesthetic, a man in a uniform asked her again, 'Who did this to you?' But Peter had in fact become mute, and would not speak again until Cordelia went to school – which is why Cordelia so often did not speak whenever she phoned the hospital. And when her father in due course came to collect Cordelia, he was so very sorry, so full of remorse and promised to look after her and said, that he would never hurt her again. In order to cope with this perplexing and confusing paradox, Cordelia simply split herself in the same way she had split her father into a good part and a bad part, which is why she saw her father take yet another other-self, this time a little girl, out of Peter, after which the new girl, who would eventually be called Rosalind, went happily home with her beloved father. And when, the following day, Cordelia asked a kind neighbour who came to look after her what had happened and why did she have these splints on her legs, this kind neighbour told her to forget all about it, and pretend that everything was all right, then, the pain would go away. Cordelia duly obliged, and from then on, as Alice would say, life just got curiouser and curiouser!

Thus, these many years later, and though Cordelia was now able to describe these painful events in detail to me, she nevertheless complained that she still did not feel as though she was talking about herself – despite understanding why she had indeed always felt so different and dead! As Cordelia explained, she felt separate from it – it had happened to someone else – it felt as though she was talking into a dark tunnel, not sure of being heard. She felt afraid to feel – scared it would make her ill again, though agreed with me that maintaining the secret of her parents had made her ill for years. She wished she could have outside confirmation, then she would have to believe it. The stigma was too great – it was all too terrible – she could not accept it was the truth.

Cordelia, nonetheless, decided to try and write down everything she could remember, in detail in her diary. Little did she know how significant her brave decision would turn out to be, and although Cordelia has in fact already included the following excerpt from her diary in the chapter entitled, My Father, I have nevertheless decided to repeat her words here. Precisely because they proved to be so very important, and because they became the key, which has allowed her to unlock the past.

Am I ever going to smile again? I feel such despair inside.
I am in a dark black pit, it smells like a sewer, and I cannot see the light of day.
Why did I remember all this?
It's like coping with an army of demons inside me, an army of horrific
    memories,
one goes and another comes to haunt me.
I feel angry with myself for opening up this huge can of worms that I don't
    know what to do with, except to deny myself the truth and run away.
I know the anger is about the truth, and the grief will heal my deep black hole.
'Never was grief like mine.'
Grief for the little girl who never was.
Grief for the little girl who was not to blame.
Grief for a lost childhood and the loss of a whole life.
To be a healthy adult I have to find Cordelia. I need to be this child again. I
    have to feel like Cordelia, to find the softness, gentleness, and innocence of
    this small child. I have to cry the tears this little girl was unable to cry. I
    have to feel what happened to her.
She feels separate from me, even when I've told my therapist as much as
    Cordelia can remember. I want to remember what it felt like to have a little
    body, to be vulnerable, trusting, dependent and then full of fear.
I want to get under her skin if possible.
I think it was autumn, I think it was near my birthday, it might have been the
    very day. I remember my father telling me, I would have a big surprise…

This in fact, is how Cordelia began her therapy session on 25 October 1995, by reading her diary. But how, I wondered, listening to her sad words, could I help her reach this child? It was quite clear, that even though it had been imperative to confront her trance logic and engage her rational mind – which Cordelia had done so successfully – this alone was not enough. In truth, the child part of her was still very much trapped in its make-believe world. Somehow, I realised, I had to help her breach the gap between her rational mind and her emotional mind, between the logic of her heart and the logic of her intellect. Somehow, I realised, Cordelia desperately needed to feel, as well as understand. Indeed, as Cordelia so rightly described, she 'needed to be this child again; cry her tears; feel what happened; get under her skin – if possible!' Suddenly, whilst listening to Cordelia describing the very details of the first rape and the subsequent dash to the hospital, the brief encounter with the nurse, and hearing Cordelia describe how she had denied that she knew who had done this to her, I suddenly realised that I had to create a magic 'as if stage' which would allow Cordelia to go back in time. I just knew that the very moment she lied was the very moment she had turned her back on herself, and the only way the Self was going to come back, I feared, was via the truth. Somehow, I had to enable Cordelia to tell the truth – for real. Maybe, I reasoned, maybe I could use this peculiar ability of hers to relive the past as though it were happening now. Maybe this time I could use this fringe benefit of auto hypnosis to her advantage. True it involved risks – Cordelia could get stuck in her imaginary world for ever; the looking glass might shatter and Alice might never be able to cross over. Should I take that risk? What were the options? Ruefully I realised that Cordelia was stuck in Alice's wonderland, anyway, so what did she have to lose?

I then also reminded myself, how a previous patient of mine, many years before, had actually taught me to trust this amazing aspect of the recovery process, when, without apparent effort, he had managed to travel back into his past; right back to the moment when life became all too painful, all too unbearably real, and for the first time in his life he had felt able to confront his internal father about the sexual abuse he had so callously inflicted upon his son. At the time, I had been truly amazed to discover how potent and healing such a journey back into the past can be, as the adult man literally became the little boy again, screaming with the pain of it all. I also reminded myself that we had achieved this remarkable journey into the past by reassuring the man that I would accompany him and help him to face whatever truth he needed to see. As a result, I'm glad to say, my erstwhile patient eventually felt empowered to successfully 'kill' his long dead father and finally banish him from the present.

I therefore asked Cordelia to stand up and sit down on the floor. I then sat next to her and held her in my arms. I told her that together, we would go back in time, to when she was a young child, to when she could remember being held by the nurse in the hospital. I then asked her to tell me, 'Who did this to you?' Who had injured her legs? As I had anticipated and hoped she would, Cordelia seemed able to go back to the past almost instantly. I could literally feel her becoming this young child again – vulnerable, confused, in pain, in distress and desperate to be understood. Once again, Cordelia tried to make sense of what had happened to her – her father's betrayal, his painful birthday present, her mother's refusal to see the truth, believing that her daughter could be such an evil child. I repeated the question. 'Who did this to you?' I could feel how Cordelia was reliving the fear of abandonment. How she again felt the surge of hope that her father meant it when he said he loved her and would never hurt her again. Perhaps she should believe him?

I again demanded she tell me, 'Who did this to you?' And I could feel her beginning to doubt! Could she really take the risk to trust a stranger? What would happen if she told the truth, would everyone abandon her? Yet this time, this stranger was obviously not going to let go – this substitute, kind, warm nurse, insisted that Cordelia tell her the truth!

Again I repeated the question. 'Who did this to you? Who injured your legs?' And to my surprise, this time I could feel Cordelia begin to struggle. I could feel her fighting back. I could feel her defy her father and her mother. All the energy, which once upon a time she had converted into dissociation, seemed to flood back into her and suddenly, fully engaged, she blurted out, 'My father did it! He did it! He hurt me. My father did it!'

It was a tremendous cathartic experience, and the Self literally in that moment came back from its self-imposed exile; it had told the truth, it could be itself again, be proud of what/whom it was. Indeed, just as effortlessly as the Self seemed to have disappeared on that fateful day, it simply returned. It was such a significant moment that even as I write these words, I cannot help but be transported back to my therapy room and once again experience the feelings of love and joy that this child had found its way through the 'sewer' and was finally meeting up with itself; meeting the adult Cordelia for the first time.

I remember just holding Cordelia whilst she sobbed and wailed, how could you do this to me? How could you injure your precious little girl? How dare you do this to me? These angry sobs and angry words, however, were clearly relaxing the long-held tensions within her body when suddenly Cordelia sat bolt upright. The child was gone, and in its place was a calm mature woman who suddenly had discovered 'who she was' – even though she felt quite sick and wanted to 'vomit her father out of her system'.

I vividly remember her look of amazement, when all of a sudden Cordelia seemed to know everything, seemed able to remember so many more details, as though all the personalities had revealed all there ever was to know about her – as though she now had access to the whole of her life.

I can still clearly hear her say, 'How can this be?' Quite non-plussed by it all, as indeed I was! In truth, I could not answer her question, for I equally could not explain how it was possible to suddenly gain access to all your memories – other than accept that the Self had indeed returned. The session ended. Cordelia left, and duly was sick, finally getting rid of the bad father; getting rid of the pain of betrayal she had carried all these years within her stomach. Finally, getting rid of these nonedible objects for real, and for good. I stayed behind in the therapy room, wrote up her notes, and simply recorded that Cordelia was able to connect with the moment in time when Cordelia denied her true Self! I was strangely aware that no manner of words would be able to do justice to what had just occurred.

And the next day? Cordelia's long suppressed and overdue anger came through with a vengeance, and as she had predicted, when we went for a walk in the hospital's garden in the late autumn sun, she was able to scream for real.

The Personalities... continued
Before the Death of My Mother

ESTHER 6–7 YEARS

As a child, I loved the beach and water but I could not swim properly at this stage. The only lessons I had were the few occasions when my father had taken me into the sea. He encouraged me to trust the sea to hold me up and made an attempt to teach me the various strokes. One summer's day, my two older brothers took me to the beach; my mother had requested time alone. My second brother had taunted me with threats of teaching me a few more lessons, as I needed to be tamed, and today, Martin said, was 'taming of the shrew' day.

I set off with them as the angry Elizabeth, very fearful of what may be in store for me, yet strangely excited too, as the prospect of being taken out by my brothers made me feel a little bit special. Such mixed emotions were a daily experience for some of my personalities, particularly Elizabeth, but they caused me such confusion and anxiety. These mixed emotions sometimes, even today, are a common denominator in my life and the extreme anxiety has to be constantly addressed. Some days I still experience total lack of trust in anyone and then again, I can equally throw all my trust in almost any direction. I so wanted to trust my brothers this day, but the threats were the cause of my anxiety and fear.

The day ended with my second brother pushing me off some high rocks into the swirling sea below. My brother hated the water and could not swim, yet he said, 'Now swim for it.' I came to the surface, struggled and hung on to a nearby rock. I could not scream; I could not get enough breath to scream but I could see one or two people rushing across the rocks to help my eldest brother. I was eventually pulled to safety but I remember very little more as Elizabeth, because as I sat on the rocks, I became Esther, after the film star Esther Williams I had heard so much about; she was of course a beautiful swimmer. Esther, having regained her breath, became full of confidence; she got back into the water to try and swim, and prove to her brother that she was not afraid and could do something better than him. I remained afloat but as I grabbed an easier rock nearer the shore to climb on to, Martin's boot was hard and fast on my fingers. He stamped on them to make me let go, then ran away as he was being watched. Esther became immediately autonomous after what seemed like an enormous achievement.

I can remember one dreadful day in the clinic. Frieda was off sick and I felt as if all my problems were too much and there was no one who could help. I was facing my big black hole. I knew for the first time it was the black hole, and it felt as if I was drowning in a sea of despair; everything was too much and I was sinking fast. This time when I pulled myself out, there was nowhere else to go except up, and with the encouragement of others, I drew from myself all the courage I needed to go on. Even when it felt as if someone had stamped on my fingers and knocked me back, I knew I had to carry on. God's promise was that I would not drown in the waters or be consumed by fire. I could do it; someone was beside me, however alone I felt. Never will I forget how devastating the aloneness was throughout this long and painful journey. I hate to be reminded of this feeling but Esther was my champion within.

Maybe Esther, along with other parts of me, who were strong fighters, were the parts that saw me through the struggle of life and the struggle of therapy. This kind of strength can only be tapped into when the going gets though, and Esther was a happy, pleasant personality, easy to get on with and fun to be with. She enjoyed and achieved a good standard at tennis and hockey, playing for her school first eleven, as well as being a strong swimmer. My second brother was the only member of the family not at all interested in sport of any kind. He loved breaking the strings of my tennis racket, but my mother was a good tennis player so there were always plenty of rackets to choose from. Perhaps Esther was the only child personality that my brother could not trample on, apart from Victoria, who appeared in my teens. Somehow, I covered every need; every possible scenario had a solution; I took care of myself, albeit in ways that trapped me for nearly a lifetime.

BRYONY (MOTHER'S NAME), 6½–7 YEARS

This child personality appeared around the age of six years, after the death of my father. It all started with my mother in the kitchen, boiling crabs and lobsters in an urn on the stove. The squeaking of these creatures and the steam made me identify with the pain that I believed they were experiencing, which made me feel numb. I was Stephanie that day, because I only had my mother for company. She sent me out of the home to play and I returned to the old stone wall which surrounded our property, where I would often sit and dream in my trance-like state. The evening shades were drawing in and I felt cold, and on returning to the house I ran upstairs as I heard what sounded like crying, and found my second brother and mother in bed together. What was happening I do not know, but my mother had cut her hair very short, and I experienced fear and horror numbing my body.

I could not think, I could do nothing, except almost instantly create in my mind Bryony as my internal mother; just as I knew her before this episode, with long flowing brown hair. She instantly became autonomous when my brother demanded I made him his next meal, when he insisted that I thus had to behave like my mother.

Bryony (my personality) acted out my mother's character to some degree; she did not abuse anyone to the same degree as my mother, and never abused sexually. She would, however, frequently, physically kick out at others as my mother did, deny the truth, lie, deceive, be suspicious and ridicule at every opportunity, but mostly she hurt herself. I am ashamed to admit that I have on one or two occasions been physically cruel to my own children, but my husband always stopped me and I learnt to control these outbursts. They only happened when provoked or at times of extreme stress.

The sort of cruelty my mother displayed each day was regular beatings, and force feeding me if I didn't feel like eating. I remember vividly her telling me that I would bleed to death when I first menstruated, and deliberately crushing my fingers in her sewing machine. Collecting me from hospital after the mutilation done by my brother, I know hospital staff questioned her. She made me walk a good two miles home after being in hospital a month, with the added complication of a kidney infection. If I stopped, or just felt unable to go on, she pushed me hard from behind, demanding I walked quickly. I was no longer to be a 'weakling or cause any more trouble'. My uncle in fact said of my real mother, 'If there was anyone around to hate, she always hated them with such ferocity.'

Just when I thought my mother had changed and improved her attitude towards me, I remember another sad Christmas. My own children were young and she invited us as a family for Christmas day. She had told me to buy nothing; she would provide it all. On Christmas morning she telephoned to say she was going to spend the day with a friend after all. It felt so reminiscent of the Christmas she wrapped up the house brick. Christmases are to this day always tinged with fear and disappointment, but this time she had rejected my children, and for the first time I told her what I thought of her, and I called her a bitch. I remember, I felt sick and frightened all day for having spoken to her this way. And yet, after my mother's death, I experienced the deepest, blackest depression for very many years, just as I think she did.

Bryony, the personality, also experienced deep depression at Christmas. She wore my mother's clothes as she became older, and remained a slave to my mother and brother, as indeed my real mother became a slave to my second brother as he became more adult.

Bryony, my created personality, was used in every way possible to look after my real mother and she became her own persecutor. She was a mirror image of my own mother; she was deeply depressed, presenting unexpected irrational behaviour. If she spoke at all, her words were cruel and unreasonable. She avoided meeting people if possible, or answering the telephone. She hid behind the four walls of the house, often taking to her bed during the day, even sometimes going as far as lying under the bed. She did not eat, sleep or communicate properly; she saw the world as threatening and always unfriendly. She unintentionally caused situations with others so that the outcome was rejection of her, which is what she expected and almost wanted. She lacked vitality, felt dead inside and wanted to be dead. She felt unloved and hated herself and others.

This personality, consequently, grew into a woman with a harrowed facial expression, and like my mother, she wore dark clothes, often brown, that covered every contour of her body. There was, however, another side to Bryony, as she could switch from this depressed state into a very manic state. Her laugh was false and her pretence at happiness fooled some people but not everyone. My mother could equally be two different people, and I split the personality of my mother into two as well. There was a part of my real mother that could show the outside world that she really cared about her daughter but alone with me, it was always a different story.

ANNA 6½–7 YEARS

I created Anna at around the same age. Anna was the good part of my mother who only appeared very occasionally. I so wanted to be like this good part; I tried hard to model my own mothering on what I saw could be possible, hopefully not just the face to the world. I did not see this good part of my mother until after my father's death. I didn't settle at school and eventually my mother sent me to an expensive independent school. At the initial interviews before the examinations, my mother spoke lovingly of me, the difficult time I had since my father's death, and said that she wanted me to have a good education. It was hard to take in or believe. Anna became a personality who gained autonomy when my mother at the second interview, praised me for passing the examination, and when she took me shopping afterwards to buy the uniform, I remember the smell of the newness of the blouses and the blazer as I tried them on. At last I knew my mother must have loved me just a little bit. I remember, I dared to feel happy until she kicked me so severely outside the shop for humming a tune. My second brother received a scholarship to an excellent public boarding school but my mother could not part with him when the time came. I weekly boarded for a while until she decided I was to be at home and help with the cooking and household chores as she was constantly unwell.

I became a day girl who was so many different children; I confused and deceived everyone. At home the using and abusing continued. The personality Anna appeared as infrequently as the kind mother did, but I hope I have been able to incorporate kindness and some sort of expression of love in my private life as well as my public one.

When I was waiting for a bed at my very first admission to the hospital, my primary care nurse Anne would telephone to ask how I was. I did not want admission to hospital, yet I longed to be cared for. I felt comfortable with Anne and I was able to tell her more than I had anyone for a long time, she seemed so understanding. She was indeed more kind than the good part of my mother in the personality system, my own Anna. Bryony saw Frieda not as a very cruel therapist but as a person with a great deal of feeling and kindness for mankind.

When I was only nineteen years old, nursing in a training hospital, on one of the maternity wards, I nursed a mother who was emigrating to Australia with her husband and two teenage children. The application to emigrate had been made before she realised she was pregnant, and she decided to have the baby and leave it for adoption. The baby was a little girl; she cried so much, and my heart went out to her. I could think of nothing else except this awful abandonment and I nursed this baby with all the love and tenderness I could muster, which could never be what she really wanted or deserved. I begged my mother to adopt her and look after the child until I was free to be her mother. I thought she would love any baby more than she could love me. Of course this did not happen, but to this day I still think of that abandoned child and hear her cries. I never will forget that sweet, helpless little soul that wanted her real mother more than anyone, and until now I did not realise how I unconsciously identified with her rejection and desperate need for mother love. Hence, I now fully understand why, when it looked as though my mother had disappeared, when she cut off her hair, I instantly created Bryony to take her place. Likewise, when she died, I created yet another personality in order to maintain the illusion that my mother was always there for me. The concept of losing my mother was too big; any mother, even an imaginary one, was better than no mother at all.

I wrote a letter to my mother in therapy that I think explains the enormous struggle I had to accept she could not love me unconditionally, and how outraged this made me feel.

Written in therapy – April 1993

Dear Mother,

The instinctive love of a lioness for her cubs is the kind of primal love I needed and still long for; something I felt cheated out of. That fierce, clear love is what I have craved for all my life; instead I was offered something that was either smothering or abandoning, manipulative or controlling. A love that didn't take into account my needs as a child and as a young adult, a love that required me to compromise my integrity and my values. Yet it was – until now – terrifying to say no to any kind of love. Closeness is a basic human need, and I craved that closeness even more after my father died. I need to start saying no to the kind of love that you offered, which drained me, and say yes to nourishing love. I need to give up on you. I need to feel who I am, and do, and be who I am. I don't have to have your approval on anything any more. I know I'm not the daughter you wanted, I've always known that but now I can see you're not the mother I wanted either. I wanted a mother who was all loving, all giving, all protective. I am finding my courage to grieve for what's been lost. I can stop striving for what I'll never have and find room in my heart for those who can give me some sort of good love. I stand back, separate from you now for the first time ever; you cannot touch me anymore. I've crouched in a corner all my life; I can move, stretch and reach and remember what was denied, what never was there to begin with.

I've had to tear down a false assumption that mothers must love their children and replace it with reality – I am giving up a little girl's longing for security and protection but I find it excruciating. I am finding it difficult giving up the fantasy of what my family could have been. In reality, my needs have never been met but my child inside has sustained a hope that maybe, maybe someday, my family would come through for me. This had kept me alive.

I realise I was furious when you died because I could no longer hope that you would one day love me. I then experienced deep depression for many, many years. I now feel like a speck of dust floating all alone in a big empty universe. I have no emotional foundation, I have tried to build on a hole filled in a bit with sand, but it should have been rock formed out of real unconditional love which you were unable to give me.

I am now trying to say goodbye to you for ever, but I am also trying to be angry, but my anger is the denying and twisting kind. I didn't know I had the right to feel outraged, I always felt I had to protect you. I have stuffed my anger with food, drowned it with alcohol, stifled it with drugs and made myself ill all my life. I blame myself, I am angry with the child within, the child who was vulnerable, who was injured, who was unable to protect herself, who needed affection and attention and could not let go of you. The struggle to do this seems impossible but one day I hope I will find peace.

Cordelia

GERALDINE 7 YEARS

She was the fourth introjection of a family member, my maternal grandmother, whose name was Geraldine. I remember so well walking down the path towards my grandmother's house on a visit to see her. We had moved to be near her now my father was dead. I hoped and prayed my grandmother would help my mother look after my brother; life seemed such a burden to my mother and to me. I did not remember my grandmother that well, because I believe it had been sometime since I had seen her. My father didn't like her very much, I was told. I was so excited, I had in my mind a picture of what I imagined her to be like; a kind, warm elderly lady who knitted all the time and would show me lots of love.

I carried my baby brother in my arms; he was by then quite big and rather heavy for me. My mother was with me but she carried nothing and neither did she speak. We arrived at the gate by taxi; I stepped out of the car clutching my brother, whom I had looked after since he was born. I was so full of hope as my grandmother rushed down the path towards us. She took my brother from me, pushed me away, and as she looked back she glared at me, saying she preferred boys. She even ignored my mother.

Yet again, disappointment, sadness and rejection filled my already over-burdened heart and I instantly created a personality called Geraldine, who I thought then would like and love me, but she eventually turned against me as a persecutor, as I will soon explain. My grandmother from that day ignored me, apart from putting her fist into my face and half closing her eyes in a hard glare as she looked at me, because, like my second brother, she found the sight of me distasteful. My brother and grandmother, I realised, were so alike.

My grandmother's garden was very large and rambling and at the bottom she had chickens in a large hen house with outside runs, also rows and rows of hutches with lovely rabbits in. I remember the first time she made me watch how she killed my favourite chicken, and afterwards threw it into my face. I could not eat the dinner of roast chicken that night but I was force fed by my mother until I was sick. Every so often a rabbit was made into a pie and I had to watch her kill those too. It was the expression on my grandmother's face that I remember, as if she enjoyed her task. Geraldine, my personality, learnt to enjoy all her grandmother taught her to do, but only Geraldine copied her grandmother; the other children could not have done the things she did.

My grandmother did not treat my mother very well; she spoke harshly to her and could be difficult with her. I often expressed to her and others my fear of losing my mother, always asking her if she was all right and where she was. My mother spent a lot of time resting in bed and my grandmother always seemed to spend a lot of the day with my mother, either at her home or ours. On my return from school one day, there was a funeral car with darkened windows outside my mother's home, and fear overwhelmed my heart. I thought it surely must be for my grandmother; I secretly hoped it was, because although she never physically hurt me, she was very mentally cruel. Then horror struck me as I saw my grandmother through the window. She opened the door and said, 'Your mother's dead, go and see her.' Trembling with shock, I bravely went into her bedroom. There was blood on the floor and on the sheets, and she was covered over. My second brother was standing by her cackling like one of my grandmother's chickens. Then my mother sat bolt upright and everyone laughed, I believe I fainted as I later woke up in my mother's bed. I have no idea how I got there, but my personality Geraldine instantly became autonomous and I never again said, 'Please, Mummy, don't die.' This was a hugely funny practical joke I heard them discussing and laughing over later that evening. I heard my brother say that he had to tell the undertaker someone had played a joke on them and made a hoax call to him. My brother was still laughing.

Geraldine, my personality, became as cruel, as paranoid and as anti-Cordelia as her own grandmother was. She now had a life of her own and acted independently of all the other personalities. In fact, Geraldine, like her grandmother, tried to rule the roost; she influenced the other small personalities, never displaying sadness or need of others, often behaving in a bizarre manner. She displayed her anger coldly or cruelly and she always carried a knife. She hated others, as they seemed to hate her. Her words cut as sharp as a spear. One would normally say 'this side of my personality', but I have to say that this separate part of me kept control over the other personalities and enabled me to give the impression to others that I was self-sufficient. No one took liberties or the risk of crossing me, or even approaching me with a suggestion or request. Geraldine was a protection in the enormous and painful struggles of my life.

One day, I saw my grandmother steal a gold watch and lovely opal/diamond ring from my mother's dressing-table drawer. These two items my aunt had left me in her will to wear when I was older. I never saw them again. I can only assume my grandmother took them in order to hurt me and maybe she was jealous. Ironically, many years later when an elderly patient I had nursed left me a gold watch and opal ring, I had to tell her husband I could not accept them. I didn't feel I deserved them or could have such lovely gifts given to me. When I met my husband I had to learn that I could and should have the pleasure of beautiful things, but by then I had tried to control the personalities, which I explain later. However, it comes as no surprise that my personality Geraldine also stole. They were just small things I wanted in order to pretend I was receiving gifts from others, for example, the musical box I told Frieda about. I found that having a few things in my possession, even though they had to be hidden, were a form of comfort, but I stopped myself doing this as I grew older. It is remarkable that I can own up to this when it was the part of me that trusted no one, and I am now, trusting the reader to understand.

In therapy, Geraldine hated Frieda, hated therapy; she hated everyone at the clinic and claimed she did not need anyone, least of all them. They were all idiots, none of them knew what they were doing, except they were experts at playing games with patient's emotions and enjoyed doing so. I often used to wonder, Why am I here allowing these people to abuse me? They definitely could not be trusted, as Geraldine never trusted anyone throughout her life; she was suspicious of even a kind act. She sabotaged relationships all her life; she sabotaged therapy sessions many times. Geraldine of course eventually learnt to trust in therapy when she became aware Frieda could cope with her mind filled with bizarre irrational thoughts and confusion. This happened the night I turned up at the clinic saying I hadn't seen Frieda for six months and apologising for missing an appointment. Geraldine was intelligent and intuitive, she knew that Frieda was aware that there might be much more going on beneath the surface than she was able to disclose. She eventually trusted enough to show her true colours, which could be frighteningly dangerous and out of control. As she grew into an adult, she drank alcohol quite heavily, as indeed Martin did too. All three devils greatly affected my life, causing undesirable situations; all three fill me with fear as I write about them, and they are parts of me I am not proud to own. I am pleased to say these parts are now very tame compared to the control they operated when separate personalities.

GILLIAN 8–9 YEARS

My brother Martin, only thirteen years old, and his friend Maurice, who was two years older, enjoyed terrifying me with threats of blood transfusions, cutting me open and removing parts of my body and using them for their experiments. Both these boys were brilliant chemistry students, and occupied an old garden shed for concocting their potions and cutting up small animals during school holidays. The shed was laid out like a chemistry laboratory with

Bunsen burners, chemicals and instruments of various kinds. Jars of formalin or formaldehyde were preserving small animals or parts of them. There was an old work bench where my brother chloroformed his own cats when he felt they had lived long enough or he thought they were ill. I used to watch him through the window until he yelled at me to go away. One summer's day, my brother invited me in to see his laboratory. He had that certain cold blank look on his face and his eyes stared long and hard at me; he was also laughing in his usual horrible way, an evil high-pitched cackle. My heart raced and fear immobilised my body, so he pushed me through the door, told me to take my clothes off and to climb up on to the workbench which, he said, was his operating table. He said he was going to perform a very necessary operation that every girl should have. He told me African tribesmen performed this operation on every girl before they could marry. I learnt later in my life that it was called female circumcision.

I was Elizabeth, who screamed with terror until he tied a scarf very tightly round my mouth and head, then, tied my wrists and ankles to the slats of the workbench. I struggled, trying to free myself, having desperately switched into as-if Martin (the boy I had created who could get the better of my brother), but Maurice held a cloth soaked in chloroform over my nose and mouth until I stopped screaming and I became sleepy but not unconscious. I instantly created another personality called Gillian, who watched what he did to me, cutting me with a bone-handled sheath knife until I bled so profusely he went to the house to telephone my mother at work to say I had had an accident.

I was rushed to hospital where I stayed for many weeks, having developed a severe kidney infection. My brother never touched me again from this day. Gillian remained perfect and intact, while Elizabeth always believed that she had injured herself on a bicycle and become ill. My brother Martin had cut my flesh, but he wasn't completely successful in his venture. In my adult married life, after a difficult childbirth, I had expert repair work done both on the inside and outside, making everything look normal again.

Gillian spent her time in the garden recovering from her illness, sitting on her swing fantasising about what could happen to other little girls, but not to her. In a child-like way they were sexual fantasies; she had after all seen and experienced too many sexual acts not to imagine seeing her mother and brother do outrageous things. In her own imagination she therefore created scenes of sexual abuse which took place on the garden swing. Elizabeth was naked and her legs were tied upwards to the sky while her mother inserted plastic hosing from a tank with garden manure flowing through it into her body; sticks of rhubarb and runner beans were inserted into her vagina and were left to rot. When all that was over, her brother placed the prickliest of roses in her hair, daisy chains around her nipples and a garland of poisonous ivy and laburnum between her legs. Gillian enjoyed these fantasies and laughed at the thought of them.

As Gillian grew older, she found safety in the company of girlfriends and at the age of fifteen, she and her friend Linda talked about sex and experimented a little with each other. Both finally decided they wanted to have boyfriends. Gillian, after the age of sixteen onwards for a few years, was only attracted to homosexual boys or young men, as they were safe friends to have. The other parts of my personality hated my female body and were frightened to let the games teacher see me under a shower, which she seemed to delight in. I was also very afraid of growing into a woman.

This child personality was not mutilated. She remained untouched and untouchable by any boy or man throughout her separate existence. She was proud of her body that was perfect in every way – the only part of me who did see her body this way. So proud of her body was she in fact, that towards the end of my therapy when we began sorting out the various clothes worn by each personality and took photographs of myself wearing those clothes, I actually gave Frieda a photograph of myself standing in front of a mirror, the camera neatly obscuring my face but clearly showing that the top half of my body was naked, long before I would have been able to voice why I had done so, or realise how incongruous this picture was.

The little girl who watched the child's body being mutilated by her brother was not her, and she saw this act like an apple being cored and the bad cut out. The bad was her brother Martin. She laughed always in the face of adversity, being separate from it and copying her brother's laughter. She was the one who played pranks at school on the teachers and giggled a lot. Her giggling could be uncontrollable when faced with the worst events in life. When as an adult I was excessively and dangerously haemorrhaging before losing a baby, I could only ignore what was happening and drive to the hairdresser's as if I was still going to the ball that night. I laughed with the doctor when all around me looked like a slaughterhouse. I apologised at the hospital for my large abdomen and for weighing ten stone, still laughing and joking. Now, when I think back to the event in the garden shed, both the chloroform and the attempt at circumcision were both potentially dangerous acts from which I could have died. Somehow, again I continued my struggle to maintain life. As I said earlier, I spent a long time in hospital, because they found other medical problems as well as the kidney infection, which were of some concern. My mother didn't visit me in hospital but she was asked to collect me and to see the doctor. She did this, but she was very angry after seeing the doctor when she arrived at my bedside and told me that I was too much of a worry and responsibility for her. She made me walk home, and when I lagged behind with tiredness, she pushed me so hard she caused me to fall, exclaiming that I was a wicked, stupid child and I was not to be ill again. As a result, Gillian became autonomous and just laughed at her.

MAD CORDELIA (CORDELIA II) 10–13 YEARS

As with other personalities associated with my mother's abuse, I saw my mother's face as I wrote about Mad Cordelia, which coloured the truth; trying to let it fit my expectations of my mother. Each time, I had to abandon the inevitable denial and instead, accept that she did not protect me from my brother and grandmother, nor from herself.

From the ages of ten to thirteen, these three years were very painful and disturbing. I was told so many times by my brother, mother and grandmother that I was mad and bad, that eventually I gave them what they wanted. It was like some sort of revenge on them that I could be even madder than they thought. I could be very mad indeed, but I didn't create a real other personality. The mad Cordelia or Cordelia II was like an extension of the original personality. I couldn't give her a name because she was so mad and I didn't want her as part of the system, although in fact she was. I had no role model for her; she was just a little sad person with huge behavioural problems.

I felt so mad, yet a part of me knew I wasn't really, I was just completely out of control. In truth, since having created Gillian I was losing control over the personality system, which is another reason why I had to create a separate mad part, somehow almost to get the control back, if that makes sense. I couldn't create any more separate persons while I was completely out of control, yet I somehow preserved my core and the madness was a sort of protection to my core or centre. Being in an extreme state of dissociation, which I explain later, was like protecting myself and healing myself in a mad way. In a strange way the mad Cordelia kept me sane.

The (psychotic?) dissociative experience I had when I was in the clinic; an incident I remember so clearly and have mentioned before in the chapter The Clinic, was in actuality, a repeat of a childhood illness when I was sent to a mental hospital at the age of ten years.

I was locked in a bedroom because I had behaved so abominably, and during the time I was in this room, I went, what my family called, completely mad. I was told by my brother Martin I was going to be left alone and the family were all going away, which in fact they may not have done; after all, the adults were too clever to open themselves to such a potentially dangerous situation. I was, however, very afraid of being left alone, which my brother Martin knew. My mother had often left me alone or disappeared for long periods in my short life, hence I feared abandonment more than anything else. In fact, my eldest brother, whenever we were indeed left alone, in order to deceive me into thinking she was at home, would make certain noises that my mother would have made – noises such as turning the sewing-machine handle – until I was asleep, or the radio left on with her favourite programmes in progress faintly in the background, though I was always suspicious. My eldest brother would always help because he couldn't cope with a distressed sister, but my second brother, if alone with me, would delight in causing me unnecessary distress.

On this particular occasion, my brother Martin was left alone with my grandmother and they decided to board the windows up and leave water and bread in the room with me because, he said, I was going to be left and I couldn't get out. How long I was left I do not know, but I reacted very badly to these threats by breaking open feather pillows, stripping the wallpaper off the walls, turning the room upside down, screaming until I was exhausted. How long I lay on a wet bed in total chaos, I will never know, but when my mother returned the door was unlocked, and after her usual ranting and raving which I could only hear faintly as if I wasn't present in the room (it felt as if I was some distance away), she then called the doctor. I was so afraid that I really was mad, that my family was right, I created Cordelia II. I was really only a very frightened little girl who was treated with such bizarre cruel behaviour by my family. How could I behave any differently when pushed to the edge?

I remember sitting on the edge of the bed, waiting for the ambulance the doctor had ordered, and thinking, as my internal observer would have done, that the mad people were outside me; my family were the mad ones and that I had to protect myself, by making just a small mad part of me, that could react to the cruelty but keep the rest of me sane, as well as safe. I looked at myself in the cracked mirror, which I had smashed during my frenzy, driven out of my mind by fear, anger and despair, and saw in my face for the first time, the pain and brokenness of a little girl I didn't recognise. I brushed my long hair and as I did so, I stared into the mirror and saw a child whose mind was blown into a thousand pieces – just like the glass in the mirror. I saw the same picture again much later in my life, driving home after therapy when I thought the task was too big and too impossible to put right. The shattered mirror symbolised my shattered life.

I was sent away to a mental hospital, resigned and relieved for a while, but I have no idea for how long, though I remember I was locked in a small room. I also remember clearly the noise of the wind in the rigging of ships in the harbour but I wasn't then anywhere near the sea, I discovered later. I also remember wash time, when we were hosed down with warm water following a good scrub with a long-handled brush. I thought the nurse who washed us in the communal shower rooms was abusing us all when washing our genital areas, but it may have been my expectations of any woman in a caring role. It was Bryony who went into the hospital, where the carer cut Bryony's long flowing hair so short that she looked like a boy. Mad Cordelia became autonomous during this ordeal and she became very physically ill as well. I was eventually sent to an isolation hospital for some time before returning home, having gained a degree of control over the personality system during that time.

I repeated the severe dissociative experience in the clinic, hearing the wind in the ships' rigging again and not recognising anyone until I heard Frieda's voice outside when I had locked myself away in an en-suite bathroom. I had been in the bathroom for some time; I felt so cold and the bathroom was warm. I thought I was dying but I did not mind as I began to realise that those I loved were already dead. The children inside me were crying as I was giving birth to them. I had had strong labour pains all day; a pain in my chest that paralysed me followed this. Then everything seemed far away, almost like looking through the wrong end of a telescope. I lay emotionless on my return to bed and coldness crept over my body again, especially in my legs, which I could not feel at all. They were heavy and paralysed again, as they had been many times in my childhood and adult life. I felt different by then, distant from everyone to a greater degree than ever before but it wasn't frightening, it was comforting in a strange kind of way.

I suppose to try and explain the experience, it was as if I had given up on fighting and decided flight was a safer option, like a TV's power turned on but on standby. No life but frozen in time, having made a journey to a different place where feelings didn't hurt any more. I was alive but not living, where nothing from the inside or outside can affect you. It was like a journey to my mother's womb. Mad Cordelia gave me such respite on many occasions, I could slide up the scale of dissociation very quickly or stop where I needed. I could make Frieda disappear, see shapes and colours to distort other people, and my vision of the four seasons, which I have described elsewhere, even allowed me to forget my appointment with Frieda.

Looking back at my seemingly (psychotic?) strange behaviour, I now realise and firmly believe that I was actually healing myself, but I upset the progress I was making by having a weekend at home, against my doctor's wishes, to attend my husband's leaving party, which proved too much for me. At this party, my husband revealed my secret and treatment to everyone present but the people there either did not react, or reacted with disbelief. Being left alone and not being believed were always the two triggers for Mad Cordelia to appear, which resulted in me taking a harmful overdose of drugs on my return home.

I saw my mother's face so clearly at the window before and after the overdose. I thought everyone in my life had died, including the children inside me, my husband, my children, everyone I loved had gone – the aloneness transported me to a desolate place.

I was discharged eventually from the Accident and Emergency department of a general hospital because my husband told them I was being cared for at the clinic. I went back but I was treated just like my family treated me. They were all angry with me, even Anne, which hurt so much. I interpreted this as anger at my not being successful at killing myself; they would have preferred that I had died. No one showed any kindness at all or help for my husband as I have explained in the chapter The Clinic. I cannot describe the blackness and despair I experienced; trust of anyone went right out of the window and I had to start again. I did start again, I don't know how, but it amazingly eventually worked to my benefit. I had an amazing survival system, which began to work overtime as I committed myself to regular therapy. The chaos inside me told me I had to trust and reveal the truth.

In my childhood, when I eventually returned to some normality, the behavioural problems continued, but only at school. I played tricks on staff and pupils, leaving white mice in a teacher's desk, itching powder in the sports outfits in the games room; water pistols, stink bombs and the like were used on a daily basis. I stole small things from shops like Woolworth's. I told lies about my wonderful home life and caused chaos at lessons and on the buses. Eventually I was expelled from this school for breaking a statue of Mary, the Mother of Jesus, in the entrance hall, an unforgivable sin. This event, however, immediately followed the holiday on the Continent when I was raped at the age of thirteen years. After this my behaviour drastically changed and I became mostly ill and withdrawn, having created a new personality to cope with the experience. I started to switch personalities continually, to gain some control over Mad Cordelia, but I felt deeply unhappy and very alone.

MARY (MAGDALENE), 13 YEARS

Mary was the ultimate of self-hatred, who abused herself daily from the day she became autonomous. I was sent off for the duration of the Easter holidays – my mother and brother had told me they wanted me out of their sight. I heard them plotting to send me abroad, to stay with a foreign family on a holiday for fatherless children, arranged by this certain town. I started to imagine from that day on that I would be loved and welcomed into the bosom of a new family. Maybe, I thought, they might even want to adopt me. Although very inexperienced in travel and very frightened, I became excited, in spite of my fears. I knew my body was changing into a woman's and that frightened me more; I did not want that to happen. I used to stuff my food to please my mother, then make myself vomit afterwards – I didn't know that I was becoming ill with bulimia. I had started to menstruate just before this holiday and asked my mother what I should do, what was happening to me, and would the bleeding stop? She laughed and said, 'No, you will bleed to death.' I remember tearing up old bath towels, underwear, anything I could find to stuff into my knickers, and then storing the soiled pieces in a bag, hiding them at the back of a large cupboard in the laundry room, I was so frightened about what was happening to me.

It was one faithful older school friend who supplied me with sanitary towels when I asked her what I should do; she explained that it happens to all girls – but that if I stopped eating the monthly periods might not happen. She was very thin at the time and confessed to me sometime later that her father, who was a bank manager, regularly had sex with her, but I still did not tell my secrets. My friend changed, she became very fat and left home as soon as she was old enough and went to live in America. We lost touch of course, but in her I found a kindred spirit and I missed her so much. I hope she found help and finally peace.

It was Elizabeth who went off on holiday. The family I stayed with were not quite as I had hoped for. The father, who I called Monsieur, was warm and welcoming at first and the only one who spoke English. I tried to converse in French with the mother and three children, but they were not very responsive. The older daughter was totally aloof and seemed frightened of her father. The house had several floors; it was large and austere. My bedroom was huge; there was a single bed near the window that I slept in, and also a large four-poster bed with ornate tapestry drapes and a wash-hand basin in the corner opposite my bed. My days there felt lonely, as I spent all my time only with Monsieur. He took me out almost every day in his Jeep but I was never shown the sights or played with the children. He drove me miles and miles through flat pine forests and I was taken to his place of work or some sort of recreational club, where all the men stared and laughed at me. It reminded me so much of my experiences of being taken by my own father to see his colleagues, so it was Felicity who came to cope with this male behaviour. Very quickly, Monsieur started to leer at me and touched me inappropriately on the trips through the forest and I became quite terrified of him, but as always, I still kept this longing in my heart to be cared for. Monsieur started to enter my bedroom every night; he kissed me and tried to fondle my body. I pushed him away, he got angry and sulked all the next day, saying he thought I would love him for his care and kindness to me. I wondered, what he thought care and kindness were. He made me feel guilty and under pressure to let him have his way, but I still resisted his demands.

One fateful night, one I will never have any difficulty remembering, he burst into my bedroom, tore my nightdress and... As I write, I am stopped in my tracks to explain the strange pictures that flash in front of my mind's eye; feelings in my body that indicate I might have somewhere in my unconscious mind memories of an experience of gang rape, after being fondled in the Jeep one day. Many times the vehicle stopped while he fought with me to put his hands where he wanted to, but I struggled every time, which made him angry. He eventually stopped and carried on with the journey, muttering as he did so.

The faces of men keep appearing in my mind's eye, and they lurch towards me before they disappear again. The recurring dreams of being pushed from behind down a long dark tunnel with a chink of daylight at the end. Not being able to turn round and go back, the tunnel was so narrow I could only continue in the direction I was being pushed. Then, the bedroom, the four-poster bed had something that looked like cameras on three corners, I could see them only slightly from my bed – but sometimes I was able to look down and see them more clearly below me. I now know this was a dissociative experience of leaving my body and watching myself being raped. I cannot remember for certain, although I now know that pictures which flash across my mind and the feelings evoked by these pictures are real – but maybe I don't want to remember any more pain, and maybe it is not necessary to remember everything. I do, however, remember the details of the rape, after which Monsieur never touched me again; neither did he speak to me, or take me out in his Jeep.

To return to that scene imprinted on my memory, when he tore my nightdress I also clamped my legs together and shouted, 'No!' He yelled at me to keep silent; anger, shame and agony filled my being. I didn't want any of it to be happening, I wanted to be somewhere else. This hairy, heavy monster demanded I opened my legs. 'No, no, no,' I yelled, he hit me hard across my head and face. He then told me, he was going to take what he wanted, what he deserved, and I owed him for his kindness. He pushed hard against me, pumping hard, and my skin felt as if it was being beaten; my frail, thin body seemed bludgeoned to death. His body fiercely slapped against my own; I felt as if I was going to die because all the air had been pushed from my lungs and a red hot poker was burning my inside. Heavy breathing filled the room as he panted and exclaimed obscenities. I left my poor broken body and watched him raping another child on the bed. It felt as if it wasn't me – although it looked like me; it was then I created Mary. The pillow was soaked with tears, the body on the bed had been contaminated with the steamy, horribly smelly, slick semen which burned her inside all the way through, and her legs were covered in trickles of blood.

Mary rose like a corpse from the grave to find him gone and she staggered to the basin and tried to wash away the stickiness and the blood. She felt so numb, she felt dead – being dead meant it didn't hurt any more. When a dead person is washed, Mary knew, they looked as if they were only sleeping, and if she was dead, then to touch and to wash herself meant it hardly hurt at all. She tried to convince herself that the monster was not real, and if she did tell anyone they would think she was crazy and put her in a loony bin!

Then Mary changed into Alice, the external observer part of me, who left the room and rushed bare-footed in her torn nightdress to the friends of the family, a little way down the road. She burst in and told them everything and pleaded with them to help her, but they did not understand English and looked at her as if she was mad, which she knew in her heart would be the case, and she left, feeling the whole thing was her fault and perhaps she was mad after all. The next day, Monsieur and all the family seemed angry and even more distant from Mary. She was punished by being locked in her room and meals were brought to her there. Alice then wrote a letter to her mother in England but Monsieur the rapist read it and tore it up. It was a good letter too; explaining everything as Alice was well able to do. Alice was my observer part, who reported information correctly and explained her feelings well, but she became used to being ignored and misunderstood.

I do not know what I did with the time I had left on this holiday, except I bought a small crucifix which I carried in my hand until my return home; it felt like a symbol of protection. On my return home, I plucked up the courage to tell my mother what had happened to me. I felt I had to tell someone and it was one of those rare occasions she showed me a degree of kindness which gave me some comfort. It was later, when she talked about my experience again, that she told me I was a dirty, filthy slut to let it happen and I probably asked for it, so it was my entire fault. So yes, I became a dirty filthy slut for real. I began to put on weight and my breasts enlarged, which my mother noticed one day as I dressed in her bedroom. I was sent away to my uncle, who was a doctor; he arranged an abortion in a private clinic in London. Abortion then was illegal he told me, but he would help me. At first, I had no idea of what was happening to my body and why I needed to have this abortion, but my aunt explained that girls who have been naughty need to learn a lesson. My aunt travelled with me on the long journey to the clinic, to an event that changed my life even more; it felt as if another part of who I was really meant to be was yet again lost for ever.

I cannot describe the fear, humiliation and shame that I experienced when I was told I was pregnant and treated with such unfeeling coldness by the nurses, who expressed their disgust in no uncertain terms. I remember, when I regained consciousness after the operation I was disappointed that I had not died completely; although I felt dead, I could still think and experience fear. From that day on, I always welcomed an anaesthetic as an escape from life, always hoping it would be the end of me. Mary became autonomous when she regained consciousness, her self-loathing increased. She felt from that day on that what she represented was stamped all over her and everyone knew her disgrace, she was Mary Magdalene and it was all her fault.

My aunt and uncle kept me in their home and nursed me back to some sort of normality but I eventually had to return home and to school. I remember one of the nuns asking me if I had enjoyed my holiday. I could not answer her, I just sobbed and sobbed uncontrollably until someone took me home, where I hid at the bottom of the garden until I felt able to face my mother. The self-loathing turned into self-abuse; frequent washing and cleansing in disinfectant baths, swallowing TCP antiseptic and drugging myself, all manner of harmful behaviour. This behaviour by Mary continued throughout my life until my healing process began in therapy. I sometimes still feel, even today, that everyone knows I have been abused, it feels as if it is stamped indelibly into my flesh and that I smell of semen and blood. When I feel vulnerable in this way, any rejection or being forgotten, left out of a gathering or such like, I end up feeling quite ill for several days. I no longer abuse myself in any way whatsoever, and the feelings of self-loathing are so much less – I now can value who I am.

The personality Mary did not weep, but I believe it was one of the other children who did so on her behalf, maybe Elizabeth or even the forgotten child. Mary had learnt a little Arabic from her scripture teacher and spoke in this tongue when her self-loathing was at its peak. During therapy she would ring the clinic and speak in Arabic, seeking help, yet never able to ask for it, and more often than not was totally ignored which is what she had come to expect throughout her life. I can remember, after an unproductive call to the clinic, in desperation I swallowed some TCP and cut myself with a sharp kitchen knife. This was the part of me called Mary. Anyone mentioning the TCP or any self-abuse, I would not be able to explain the reason, or how it happened.

Writing about Mary seemed to be releasing, until a day or two later when I quickly realised clinical depression was fast consuming me. It became impossible to cope with the pain of this life event, which had never really been absorbed by me until now, and the shock of it was fully experienced for the first time, thus making it necessary to seek medical help.

VICTORIA 14 YEARS

Je suis Victoria, j'aime beaucoup les belles tenues et j'aime être attirante. J'ai plusieurs amies et j'ai bien travaillé au lycée à mes études; j'aime beaucoup la musique et le sport. Je ne supporte pas bien les gens qui se plaignent de leurs douleurs, je me débrouille avec n'importe quoi, et ma vie va bien, ma devise est: 'Souriez et le monde sourira avec vous.'

Je me suis appelée comme la Reine Victoria que ma grandmère a beaucoup admirée. J'ai parlé couramment en français souvent quand j'étais jeune, ma mère m'a parlé en français.

Je me suis toujours assurée et j'ai aidé à maintenir tout en ordre à la maison, surtout de diriger les autres enfants. Je les ai bien connus mais ils ne m'ont pas connue. J'ai toujours essayé de rendre ma mère contente, parce que c'était l'essentiel et je crois qu'elle était fière de moi quand je devenais jeune femme qui semblait prendre contrôle plus grande de sa vie.

J'avais le visage fort et joyeux pour le monde qui devenait plus facile avec mon deuxième frère qui était à l'université et n'était plus à la maison. Alors, c'était mon frère plus jeune, ma mère et moi, et la vie devenait plus supportable.

The English translation:

I am Victoria, I love good clothes and I like to look attractive. I have many friends and I enjoyed and worked hard at my studies, music and sport at school. I do not have a great deal of time for those who dwell on their troubles, I can cope with anything and all is well in my life. My motto is 'Smile and the world smiles with you.'

I was named after Queen Victoria, whom my grandmother admired greatly. I frequently spoke fluent French as a young person, my mother spoke to me in French. I have always been confident and helped to keep things in order at home, especially to control the other children. I knew them well but they did not know me. I always kept my mother happy because that is how it had to be and I think she was proud of me as I matured into a young woman who appeared to take greater control of her life.

I was the happy, strong face to the world, which became easier with my second brother away from home at university. So it was just my younger brother, my mother and I, and life became more tolerable.

Victoria was created following the abortion. My mother told me I had to forget the past and put on a brave face to the world; she would be proud of me if I could do this and not let her down. I was to tell no one of what had happened to me over the last year, it was to be our secret – I was to lie. She, however, expected me to go on sleeping with her – this was to be our secret too. This secret is the one I found most difficult to tell Frieda about and even more difficult to write about for everyone to know. I have not disclosed details to anyone. I was fourteen, I should have said, No, but I couldn't. I so wanted my mother's love at any cost, but the cost was too great. I felt repulsion every time I saw her, every time she came near me, the smell of her body, her face, her breath and, even worse, her touch. I feel nothing but shame, but to say no to her would have meant total rejection. I would not have had a home; she threatened to throw me out. Frieda said, I was after all still only a child, I had no alternative, but I hate myself for just being there to receive her demands.

The detail of our relationship I cannot express but I felt caught in her web of vile deception. She used my body to satisfy her sexual needs but I did not participate or respond except to feel dirty, guilty and shameful because it produced some kind of sexual feeling in me. When I reached a certain level of closeness with anyone in later life, just learning to ballroom dance for example, I would panic so much I couldn't breathe. At the same time I could throw my trust at anyone because it became too intolerable not to trust. I only knew extremes; I had no role model to show me who or how to trust. In my opinion the mother and daughter incest was the most damaging to me in the long run – more so than the abuse of my father – consequently I have always had trouble trusting any woman. I know some people refuse to believe incest of this nature ever takes place. Victoria coped by convincing herself none of this happened and she actually made quite a few female friends, although she never allowed real closeness.

Although Victoria had to do all these things for her mother, I actually liked her because she was all that I wanted to be for real, not just a pretence. The rest of me seemed to be so mixed up, and Victoria conducted herself properly, but I was always aware that Victoria was acting. She had to sleep with her mother in order to look after the system, the other children. Martin the personality, was jealous of Victoria but the battles between them were often won by Victoria. Martin was her only threat because he had a special relationship with his mother. It would be Martin for instance (depicted on one of my drawings), who kicked the door open and split the wood, but Victoria was the one who dealt with the problem, explaining to her mother that it was purely an accident. Victoria, however, took a back seat when my mother found a new girlfriend and I got my own bedroom at the age of sixteen years. At the age of nineteen years, Victoria became part of Delia I.

I am aware that with the personalities Victoria, Martin and Geraldine particularly, I have only been able to write objectively for the most part, for the following reasons; firstly, Victoria was able to cope well and always appeared pleasant and outgoing, but she fooled herself and everyone else. I cannot do that anymore, because I know the truth of my life, but her existence depended on pretence. The reality of her life was denied and as I wrote about her I again went into denial. It's so much easier to be Victoria who can cope with anyone or any situation, and she coped extraordinarily well.

Secondly, with Martin and Geraldine, it was indeed very frightening to write about them, and consequently I found it very difficult to explain just what it felt like to be them. Martin and Geraldine guarded the door, so to speak, and let no one into their lives; they lacked total trust in everyone. They were both strong defence forces. At the same time, I still remain very afraid of my brother Martin. These two strong personalities, Martin and Geraldine, who were part of my defence system, joined forces in the young, adult Delia, as Victoria did, when I was nineteen years old, which I explain later. However, I feel cheated by the fact that I did not have time in therapy to fully get to grips with some of the personalities and allow them to go inside themselves and really feel. I have only done that to a certain extent by writing about them, but there is a sadness too, because they served me well indeed.

When Frieda tackled me on being in denial and not able to progress in writing this book, I screamed at her and asked her if she would like to have her head stuck down a sewer all the time with the stench of one's own pain and sadness permanently in your nostrils, which is how my life would have been if I had not created the personalities. I would have died from a broken heart. I needed a break, I needed to try and forget, but the truth is, I didn't forget, I just made myself depressed – I will never forget. I think it is important to explain just how difficult life is after therapy for a multiple personality – all the coping skills and defence systems have virtually been destroyed.

I want to try and help the reader as well as myself understand that at a conscious level I was not aware of what I was doing or what was happening – although a part of me knew. The part that knew was indeed in the unconscious mind, even without the personality system in place – but reinforced when it was. This applied to every moment of deceit, denial or harm to myself. For instance, even though I remember, I knew I was opening a bottle of paracetamol and counted the tablets, I did not know I really wanted to kill myself, as Stephanie did. Today, I don't think I could regress and reinstate the personalities even if I wanted to, because of the knowledge I have gained and the truth that has been revealed. However, I am left with an adult, who has to relearn, to live a different life as one person. That is harder than anyone can imagine, and I feel totally alone in it most of the time, although in reality I do get some support – no one can do my journey with me.

It's the beginning of May and the bluebells are out early this year. April is always a difficult month; the rape on holiday was during April. May now brings hope for a better future, and I am reminded that the bluebell children joined hands in May, but it is a month that brings back feelings of sadness and excessive loss. There are times, even now, when the sadness is just too much, and my heart feels it will burst wide open.

Integration

The long guarded secret was well and truly out in the open, especially so after we had spent most of the next therapy time in the gardens of the hospital, as Cordelia had requested. Cordelia had explained that she wanted to scream her awareness and accusations to the sky, hoping that the vibrations of her anger and pain would reach the soul of her father and her mother, wherever they might be. Having been silenced for so long, having finally found her voice again, she wanted to let the whole world know, wanted the truth to travel on the winds to the far corners of the earth and achieve some kind of retribution. However, she also hoped that God might be listening, and that he would finally decide that she had suffered enough. 'Maybe after this,' Cordelia added thoughtfully, 'I might perhaps find God again, and make my peace with him, when all the anger has left my heart.' Yet, as time would reveal, just now we might indeed be able to see the trees but we were definitely not yet out of the woods.

First and foremost, the sudden return of the Self naturally caused us both to wonder and speculate. As Cordelia quite rightly had demanded to know, how can this be? Indeed I replied, can the Self – this mysterious part of the soul, of the mind, truly just opt out, and just as easily re-engage again? What then I queried, was this something called consciousness? We take it so very much for granted but we do not really understand its mechanisms or potential. In fact, according to Steven Pinker, exploring the very idea of consciousness in his book *How the Mind Works*, the concept of consciousness actually presents us with puzzle after puzzle. Although he adds, 'Unfortunately, many of the things that people write about consciousness are almost as puzzling as consciousness itself.'

For sure, most of the books I read at the time only confused me even more, and were not able to explain what had occurred; how it was possible that Cordelia could suddenly have access to details of her memories which hitherto had been left vacant and had not been available? And yet, as Pinker clarifies, most of the confusion the various authors have created is the result of the different meanings the ambiguous word 'consciousness' tends to provoke, as well as how it is used. For instance he explained, at times the word consciousness is used as no more than a 'lofty synonym for intelligence' (1998, pp.131–134). Nonetheless, Pinker has identified three specific meanings which I have decided to include. Even though they do not provide an unequivocal answer, they nevertheless confirm that the mind truly is a wondrous thing!

One definition of consciousness, wrote Pinker, is 'access to information'. When we search our minds, we can in fact share our thoughts, dreams, memories, experiences and sensations. We can indeed access our internal world. However, this access tends to be rather selective. Not only are we unconscious when it comes to the inner workings of our heart, the spleen, the varied hormones dashing around the body etc., but we also experience bottle-necks, states Pinker, which constrict the flow of information from either coming in or being released. The storing of information, Pinker continues, depends very much on the way our senses react, the level of our attention, the emotions attached to an event, and whether we have been able to 'funnel the control to an executive process; something,' describes Pinker, 'which we experience as the Self, the will, the "I".'

Contrary to the popular belief of the psychologists who were convinced that information fades with time, the brain in fact can record indelible memories, such as the content, details of the place and time when we heard shocking news. It just follows its own peculiar rules when it comes to making the information freely available again – to many different areas of the mind; to 'a large number of information processing-agents' (p.137), who will each assess the information accordingly. Hence, we will not just see a ruler for instance, asserted Pinker, but we will also work out its various uses and associations. Furthermore, 'items' (fragments of memory), writes Pinker, 'drip into awareness one at a time'. Yet they are also frequently impeded from doing so, especially when the information is 'old or uncommon' or when the cost outweighs the benefits. Storing and retrieving information, he explained, is governed by the amount of space available in the brain, the time it takes to classify material and the energy required to do so, and whether the item is in fact relevant.

The second discrepant meaning then of the word 'consciousness', according to Pinker, is 'self-knowledge'. Being concerned with 'building an internal model of the world that contains the Self' (p.134), as opposed to being alive, awake and very much aware, which is how most people would translate the idea of consciousness. Self-knowledge – seeing oneself in a mirror, recognising oneself; being able to state categorically, that's me, according to Pinker is certainly no mystery, nor a miracle as some authors, attests Pinker, tend to describe consciousness (p.132). 'If I have a mental database for people,' asserts Pinker, 'what's to prevent it from containing an entry for myself? A robot that could recognise itself in a mirror would not be much more difficult to build than a robot that could recognise anything at all' (p.134). Quite so, but taking Cordelia's experiences into account, when I read Pinker's clarification, I could of course not help but wonder, what happens when the database of someone cannot sustain the allotted entry for a Self, or there simply is no one available who is willing to program the robot?

On the other hand, the idea of a Self in charge of the mind is not necessarily accepted by all. For instance explained Pinker, according to the artificial intelligence pioneer Marvin Minsky, the mind is 'a society of agents' (p.143). However, if this was indeed the case, needless to say when a multifarious, speechless, angry, immature, rebellious, autocratic and autonomous 'society of agents' is calling the shots and the 'I' is indeed not playing ball, information gathering or releasing it again, must be sorely affected. Certainly, it would not have been considered relevant by Young Cordelia, Victoria, Delia I or Delia II, to remember certain details when the whole raison d'être was in order to forget. But could this then be the actual reason Cordelia suddenly got access to her memories? When the Self returned, when it again assumed its executive position, did it perchance dislodge the bottle-neck? Did it perchance reassess which memories were indeed relevant?

The final meaning of consciousness Pinker described is 'sentience: subjective experience, phenomenal awareness'. It is the ability to know what it feels like to eat an ice cream, what it means to have toothache, to catch a snowflake, watch a sunset, or feel confident enough to reply as Louis Armstrong did, when a reporter asked him what jazz is, 'Lady, if you have to ask, you'll never know' (p.60). The *Oxford Dictionary* actually calls it 'having the power of perception by the senses', from the Latin word *sentire* to mean *feel*. To me, it is the one faculty which makes artists of us all, since harmony, artifice, love, beauty, symmetry and representation truly are 'in the eye of the beholder'.

Access and sentience, Pinker explained, tend to go hand in hand: we experience, we feel – end of story. However, the way Cordelia and others have reported how they could experience pain, for instance, without actually feeling it, would seem to indicate that we can keep the two very separate. Pinker, however, does quote some possible scenarios envisaged by Ned Block, which might well illustrate, he wrote, that there is indeed a distinction between access and sentience. In the strange syndrome called blind sight, when a person who has a large blind spot due to damage to his visual cortex, this person is nevertheless able to guess correctly where a certain object is, even though he will argue that he cannot actually see it. Or else, someone might hear a jackhammer out in the street but not register it. Although, Pinker added, Block admitted that his examples were rather strained and hence suspected, 'that in reality access and sentience go together' (p.145).

I believe that access without sentience, experiencing without feeling, is something we are probably all familiar with. We can suddenly become aware that the traffic has been roaring outside the office window, the baby must have been crying for some time, the music has been blaring, a pneumatic drill was indeed ripping the street apart, and the ever-present television was churning out unwanted adverts in the background but we did not really hear any of it. In fact, I do wonder whether modern man could in fact survive in this buzzing world without this ability. Indeed, how could I spend my time typing this manuscript, if I truly heard the constant hum of my word processor? Moreover my own experience of access without sentience, intellectually registering the death of my parents but not really feeling it until many years later, has taught me that we can so very easily be fooled in assuming that one implies the other.

Sadly it was this last aspect of Cordelia's consciousness which tended to be so very much impaired. Again it is not difficult to imagine the effects of not feeling, not seeing, not smelling, not tasting, not hearing what is being done to you, in order to preserve your sanity, to get an idea of how debilitating such an escape clause can be. Dissociation certainly comes at a costly price! Indeed, so often Cordelia would bemoan the fact that she knew it had all happened to her but could not feel any of it; that she knew she was alive but always felt dead; that she knew she had been a beloved wife, a special mother, a cherished friend, a valued colleague, an esteemed nurse, but had never felt loved or appreciated by anyone. Thus, was this the spark which allowed the Self to return? Did sentience and access touch and become connected and give her back her life, her selfhood? Who knows? However, what I do know is that since that day when the Self had returned, Cordelia seemed to be experiencing and feeling what it meant to be herself, the person she used to be, whom she had become and whom she could have been.

It is one thing to cerebrally know yourself, it is another matter altogether to also sentiently know yourself. The only way I can explain the difference between the two is by describing how it felt when I went to Egypt and saw my first temple. I had seen so many photographs, watched so many various films, but nothing had prepared me for the awesome beauty and immense achievement standing there forlorn in the desert sands. Apart from the sheer scale, what impressed me also was the fact that I really did not have a clue as to how grand and imposing the temples were despite the photographs and the many books I had read on the subject. Only by standing by the side of those columns, feeling the smoothness of the stones, seeing the alignment, the perfection and dedication of the masons, did I truly understand the miracle of Egypt. Perhaps the reader may likewise get an idea of how immense the return of the Self actually was for Cordelia. She now truly understood what it meant to be abused, what it meant to dissociate yourself from life, what it meant to be fragmented. However, whereas my awareness in Egypt was a joy, Cordelia's sudden insight brought mainly anguish and despair. Yet such was the fortitude of Cordelia that it also brought her relief and the hope that one day, she would be one person, no longer need to be the personalities and be able to lead a better life, beyond therapy and the hospital. But, as I described at the beginning of this chapter, although we certainly could see the trees, we were far from home and dry.

For the time being we had decided to continue her therapy four times a week. We had both agreed that Cordelia needed to say goodbye to each of the personalities as a real person before she could truly incorporate them as parts of herself. However, we had also discussed the fact that at some time, we needed to reduce the sessions and work towards an ending of her therapy, since the time I intended to leave was getting nearer. As usual of course, whenever Cordelia was reminded that her relationship with me was but a therapeutic one, it would invariably bring Elizabeth to the foreground. Elizabeth, who had been the keeper of the secret hope that one day her mother would love her, that one day her therapist might return her love, and who was not only very cunning, so Cordelia had informed me, but was also quite determined, and did not easily accept no for an answer. Hence, we began the session on the second of November (but nine days since Cordelia's Self had so impressively returned), by discussing Cordelia's anger – because I had failed to give her a hug the previous day. She also tore up a belated birthday card a member of staff, recently returned from her holiday, had given her, saying it was 'Too late, too little', and when I subsequently retrieved yet another hastily scrawled note she had left on my car, Cordelia was still in the car park and screamed after me at the top of her voice, 'I hate you,' as I walked back up the drive.

Although I had of course witnessed Elizabeth in action before, I was nonetheless rather surprised at the level of her aggression. It was as though there were no longer any holds barred, and Cordelia was now letting me see the true extent of her rage. However, by the end of the same day, Cordelia had in fact phoned the hospital, desperate to deliver her apologies and to seek my reassurances that I would not reject her, saying she had realised that she had been shouting at her mother and her father, instead of at me.

Yet she missed her next appointment with me, and later on her husband phoned in to inform me that his wife was very depressed and that Cordelia had decided not to attend until the following week (two sessions hence). Naturally I was surprised. In due course, however, Cordelia confessed that she had decided not to attend because I had 'bunked off' on a training course and she felt like doing likewise. She had continued her therapy at home, and had written a revealing letter to her mother, which Cordelia has included in the chapter entitled Frieda. Cordelia furthermore also described that, since that day when the Self had returned and she had confronted the truth about her father, she had experienced a range of emotions, but without switching from one personality into another, and that she felt 'one person'. But so far, Cordelia added, it all felt so very strange. Exciting and scary at the same time, and as yet she felt unable to tell her husband that she was one person, in case she switched again and 'it all came back', though she had tried to switch but to her surprise had discovered that she couldn't.

By the end of the week, Cordelia also expressed that she would like to reveal to me some of the desperate actions Geraldine had undertaken over the years, even though, Cordelia said, she was aware that I might not be able to keep them a secret as they might prove to be criminal acts. Although the therapeutic relationship is usually one, where all information can be shared, I nevertheless felt that I needed to point out to Cordelia that she had to think this through. I did not really understand where my reluctance was coming from, but by now I knew all too well that it would not be wise to ignore my misgivings, and hence I encouraged Cordelia to recognise that I have a clinical duty and a code of ethics to which I have to adhere, and that, therefore, she would have to be the judge as to what she feels she can safely tell me.

I naturally also informed her that I would discuss her request with Dr C, who subsequently reinforced my decision to encourage Cordelia's reticence, and pointed out that we were not priests, nor that we were able to give absolution. He agreed with me that patient and therapist alike, need to have an equal share in the responsibility to safeguard the therapeutic relationship. But all was not well. As well as encouraging Cordelia to shoulder the responsibility for her past actions, I also had to tell her that I would not be available for certain sessions during the coming week. As a result, Cordelia phoned the hospital and demanded to be given a different appointment. A total of nine calls were recorded that day, each one more abusive than the previous one, with Cordelia angrily insisting that we treated her unfairly and that priority was given to other patients. Again, it was as though Cordelia no longer cared whether we saw her anger or not. For sure, she was certainly no longer disguising her voice. What I wondered was happening. Only a week or so ago, Cordelia had been so full of hope that she was finally going to achieve the peace of mind she so desperately craved.

The following Tuesday, Cordelia arrived for her usual appointment and began the session by stating that she had decided that she no longer wanted to continue her therapy. She had also brought two knives with her, a rather fearsome looking cleaver and a large bread knife, which she placed on the desk in front of her. At first I was of course quite taken aback and again could not help wondering what was happening. I asked Cordelia to explain the reasons why she had brought the knives with her, and she replied that she used to keep them in her car for protection. But when I pointed out that it did not seem appropriate to bring knives with her to a therapy session, Cordelia of course, became quite defensive, saying that I need not be scared; that she would not stick them in me; and that to her the knives were a mere extension of herself; just as her clothes were, and I surely did not object to her wearing clothes to her therapy sessions? Whereupon she removed the knives from the desk, and hid them underneath her coat.

What indeed was happening? If, as Cordelia had claimed, she was no longer switching, who then was it, sitting here in front of me arguing with me that carrying knives in your car for protection was an appropriate way of behaving. Who indeed had screamed at me in the driveway, who had made the abusive calls, who had decided to 'bunk off', and who had decided to end her therapy? Who indeed wanted to reveal all the doubtful deeds of Geraldine, who was no longer concerned that I would discover the extent of her pathology? Who had felt able to scream her distress to the sky, who phoned in to apologise, who had become so acutely depressed, and who wrote such an insightful letter exploring her transferences?

On the other hand, the books had warned me that the integrative process creates distress for the client. So, was this what was happening? Was the pain of truly feeling her past life too much for her, was the experience of being one person too demanding? Was I witnessing what the books called 'a relapse to dissociative coping strategies', or was Cordelia 'regressing into further dissociation and forming new alters or fragments?' (Bloch, pp.67–70)

But like Cordelia, I also felt convinced that she was no longer switching – though I was aware that my conviction might well be influenced by wishful thinking. Nonetheless, something was telling me that the different parts I had witnessed these past weeks were not the personalities of before – nor did they feel like new people. What then was occurring? Listening to Cordelia defending herself – accusing us all yet again that we gave priority to others, etc. – it suddenly dawned on me that Cordelia was being each part in turn, as though she was in fact discovering them for herself. But because she was being them without the trappings or veneer of Victoria, each part was therefore in its raw state and was duly behaving according to its original make-up. As such, I suddenly also realised that the true cost of dissociation, of experiencing life without feeling any of it, meant that every part had not developed a conscience, nor felt able to empathise with others, and hence could quite easily make abusive phone calls, carry knives, or scream their hatred for all the world to hear. Since the Self had not been involved and each part acted their way through life: correctly portrayed the character they were supposed to be. Their separate performances on life's stage were nothing but mere acts, totally devoid of any meaning. Indeed, whereas in dramatherapy for instance, based on 'the assumption that the Self can assume different, fictional identities' (Jones, 1996, p.197), we might boldly step into a role and gain insight and understanding from doing so. In Cordelia's case, stepping into role simply meant putting on the clothes of the character and behaving according to its script, but without being able to interpret or feel what it meant to be such a person or perform a certain action.

According to Sue Jennings (1999, p.4), dramatic development, the establishment of the imagination, the entrenching of our preferences and subsequent potential lifestyle, occurs in three specific stages. The first stage is called Embodiment, and influences 'our capacity to form attachments' (the manner in which the infant is held, sensory stimulation etc.). The second stage begins towards the end of the first year and is called the Projective stage, when the child begins to organise the world beyond the body, projecting itself into characters, stories, toys, for example talking as a monster through a toy rhinoceros. The third stage, when the child is about four years old, is called the Role stage, when the child will begin to play the characters: the child is the monster. A stage 'which then continues to develop through dramatic play'. A stage where we 'learn about the outcome of our actions; learn about con-science'. Needless to say, faulty navigation of any of these stages can have dire consequences. In fact, Cordelia's recent performances confirmed that, as a result some people may well require a fourth stage: Reabsorbtion – meaning that whatever the Self projected first needs to be allowed to become a modified part of the Self again, or else the ensuing role will remain just an act, a fictional identity, an as-if characterisation, without any strings attached, without meaning. Repossession of projected parts, however, as explained in the chapter, Objects Relationships, is not an easy task, since the ousted parts originally were unwanted parts and their exclusion served a very real need. As far as Cordelia was concerned, leaving these unwanted parts safely deposited into a make-believe person meant that she was not involved. It, however, also meant that she could go on reasoning as a child and go on believing that she did no harm, no matter how badly she behaved. She was a nobody as her mother so frequently told her. How then could a nobody harm others or be concerned about them? Whatever she did could not have any impact on anyone. She did not matter, so nothing she said or did mattered. Indeed, Cordelia concluded, she had no conscience because she could always justify her actions and convince herself that others hated her. Yes, she followed certain rules because they were to her advantage, and in the case of her children, she had instinctively trusted her husband to show her the way.

Here then was the answer as to why I had felt so reluctant to allow Geraldine to offload her past behaviour! It would simply have been a story without meaning; it would simply have meant that she could distance herself from it all without having to feel responsible, without it stirring up her conscience. But how, I wondered yet again, could I help Cordelia acquire a conscience? On reflection of course, I knew that I would simply have to confront her reasoning and make her realise that whatever she did, whatever she had done in the past, certainly did matter. In fact, I realised, I would have to step out of role myself and no longer be the reasonable therapist who understands all behaviour in terms of transference; no longer be the osmose substitute mother. In truth, I had to become an unreasonable mother for real, and hence, just as I might have lectured my own children on their bad behaviour, I proceeded to lecture Cordelia on hers, informing her that the abusive phone calls had not only upset the reception staff but that they had also very much upset me. I also told her that I considered it to be extremely irresponsible to have such dangerous knives in her car. How would she explain it to the police if they ever stopped her car and searched it? Would they believe her if she told them they did not belong to her but to Geraldine, Bryony or Martin? And how would she explain to them who Geraldine, Bryony or Martin were? Furthermore, I added, I was not prepared to continue her therapy until she had in fact clarified it with her husband whether it was worthwhile for her to do so. Nor did I intend to argue with her or discuss other patient's requirements with her. What's more, I concluded, she could no longer go on excusing her behaviour on the basis that she was 'a nobody', that whatever she did did not matter – it did. After all, did she not have proof to the contrary? Did not the fact that her grandchild was alive to day, due to her timely intervention, tell her that her actions mattered, that her actions had saved a life?

The session ended on time – even though Cordelia was naturally very upset and had requested some extra time to try and explain everything. For the next ten minutes she remained outside my office door, crying, before she left. Consequently, some days later, we actually held a meeting between Cordelia, her husband and myself, in order to bring him up to date and discuss the future of Cordelia's therapy.

Once Cordelia had explained why I had insisted on this meeting, Cordelia's husband acquiesced, saying that he could now recognise how he had in fact unwittingly assisted Cordelia in not developing a conscience about her behaviour. Usually, he explained, he had tended to ignore it all, believing that it was safer not to say anything or antagonise Cordelia. However, on a more positive note, Cordelia's husband also confirmed that Cordelia had indeed not switched these past weeks, and that she appeared to be far more stable. Thus, after due discussion we all agreed to continue with her therapy until such time as I would be leaving, which I envisaged would be in about six months' time.

By now it was December, and conscious of time, aware of the need to begin a leaving process, I accordingly proposed that we should read through her notes again. As well as being aware that time was getting precious, I also had an inkling that the Self might not have been paying too much attention when I read through my therapy notes the first time round. Indeed, as I had suspected, Cordelia soon reported that it was as though she was discovering herself all over again, 'like finding a deeper layer of the onion'. For sure, she was not only discovering her memories of the recent past but also of the distant past. For instance, when I read out my notes, which described how she had told me that her father had given her a music box, she corrected me and told me that she had made it all up. As Cordelia has described, she had in fact stolen the music box and given it to herself! Naturally, we both also expressed our surprise that it would be via a music box that the personalities first began to reveal themselves and allowed themselves to be found out. Truly the unconscious works in mysterious ways!

Then again, as a result of reading through the notes, Cordelia was also able to describe where Alice belonged into the structure as well as remember why she had always felt so worthless and self-conscious in the presence of her brothers. At first, she had felt unable to place Alice anywhere, until she remembered the sequence of the early abuse by her father: the sexual games in the bath where Alice learned to alter her size, and then how her father later on had used her tiny body to illustrate and teach his sons about sex.

The shame of it all had made Alice go very small indeed, and had resulted in Felicity becoming a real person, although this aspect of this degrading memory would be a piece of the jigsaw puzzle which we would not be able to slot into its rightful place until much later. Nonetheless, as Pinker had so aptly described, it seemed that my therapy notes were certainly stirring up her memories, and items were subsequently, steadily dripping in one at the time. Quite sensible really, such drastic memories would surely be enough to drown anyone if they gushed forth.

Although Cordelia was naturally upset when this memory came into her consciousness, especially since it implied that her older brothers must know the truth of their father, she did not dissociate, switch or relive the event as she would have done in the past. Instead, when she felt herself beginning to dissociate or go into a trance, she stopped herself – feeling of course very pleased that she had been able to do so. Moreover, during the next week she also reported that for the first time she had actually felt concern for another person, which was so very new. But as yet, she was scared to love or be loved. Self-hatred, she realised, had in fact protected her against being hurt by others.

As each personality seemed to become a part of herself for real, Cordelia literally was developing before my eyes, though not without a few hiccups along the way. One day, she came knocking on the door of the therapy room – twice – during a session with another patient. She had done so, she subsequently confessed, because I had made her feel jealous, and because she wanted to ensure that I would notice her. (I had of course seen her running away down the stairs on the second occasion, when I investigated the disturbance.) However, when I tackled her on her impulsive behaviour, Cordelia initially tried to get away with it by making me believe that she had switched! Yet another lecture was called for – though I could not help smiling to myself whilst I delivered it, for it seemed that the erstwhile child was indeed fast becoming a teenager!

For sure Cordelia was growing – but it was a very painful growing, many, many years too late; a growth that should have happened gradually; a growth that should have taken place within a secure setting, amongst loving, nurturing people who would have helped her come to terms with 'ugliness', and taught her how to love herself in a healthy way. Yet despite it all, as Cordelia described, she was changing; she was steadily climbing up the spiral to yet another level:

My healing is like layers; the more I work, the more they keep coming around, but I don't come back to the same place. I come back at a different level. I suppose it is like one massive grief process; a spiral. Some personalities have gone through their own memories of abuse, they reach the level where the tears, fears and terrible fatigue are, but I have to trust that where I am now is where I need to be in order to heal. Some personalities have not reached any stage, perhaps they don't need to.

I now feel a whole person, feeling perhaps more fully the difference in night and day, of living in hell or living here on earth. Everything in me is changing, my perception of myself, of others, of my power, of my strength, of my abilities, of my sanity – just everything.

For so much of my life, I have fought death wishes. Now I feel grounded most of the time, and I feel determined to stay and see this through. My strength and energy to deal with the terrible pain and anguish are returning, but today, all the power I had didn't seem enough to handle the sheer terror, shame, revulsion, rejection, rage and total violation that possessed my whole being. I felt caught, trapped in my body, as I heard the messages from my body, which has not been the case all my life.

I was sick and staggered, my legs ached until I cried with the pain. I've often felt like this in my life but if I had listened, then I would have heard the worst and not survived. My inside ached, I could not breathe. My father's penis was in my mouth and I was choking. I could not get my breath. I tried breathing into the pain and as I did, I just vomited until my inside felt sore with the strain of it all. I sat in the toilet and cried with the pain that shot up both openings like red-hot pokers, then throbbed and throbbed, so much so, I could not sit in a chair because it hurt too much.

I realised that today, I had to accept myself through all this pain and agony and pride, of being that survivor, just in the same way I had to accept myself as a victim first and then not wanting to be a victim, but a survivor. I had a sense, even when I was in the deepest hell, that something inside me said, 'I'll get you out of this – trust me.' It seemed like a spiritual awakening but it didn't last, because I went back into my 'hate' mode. I hated, I hurt, I hated myself, I hated the mess I was in – I wanted to run away.

There is a reason why I need to keep facing what seems to be the same thing but I believe from a different position. My domination and cruelty are connected to my fear of feeling. It feels disgusting and degrading to want sex, for example. My husband, a gentle man, makes me feel destructive. I say to him, 'Don't love me, don't you know I'm poison?' I scream and beat him and say, 'Can't you see how ugly I am?' Loving someone seems more humiliating than being raped or tortured. Now I understand why I get angry with myself for intense loving feelings.

I hear voices, before I see the pictures of the memories, this is often why I think I am crazy or even possessed. There isn't a part of me I like really... I keep the light on all night when I feel like this. I try to be just an observer because that takes the fear away of being really crazy. Believing another human being could do these things to a child, a human being who should have loved and protected, is where the doubt comes in. I wish I had someone, like a brother, to share these memories with; it seems like an insult on top of terrible injury to be denied that. I would heal so much quicker if someone close to me, could share my experiences. It was a way of life and my personalities accepted it. Today, the reality seemed to properly sink in. Everyone is afraid of the rawness of pure human need, so I've always said, don't let anyone see – but today I wanted someone, just one person, to see me, someone to hear me in a way I've never felt before – but shit, that was not possible.

Knives were my favourite playthings. I would carve an opening in my skin, to see the blood, so I would know I was real and alive. This gave me tremendous release. Can anyone accept the ugliness in me, the ugliness I try to hide? I am a carrier of all the tremendous atrocities that were done to me, that is why I feel so alone, and that I have no right to be alive; ugliness and shame are an abomination to God and to mankind. I want to sit in a pile of smelly shit and rub it all over myself and risk letting somebody love me in spite of it. But I doubt whether I could risk this much.

A demonstration really of how I feel inside: I want someone to see how I feel. I wanted, today, someone to see all the pain, filth, dirt, ugliness and shame, but I wanted them to love me so I could start loving myself properly.

Round about this time, we had also begun to talk about the possibility of writing about her therapy journey and her multi-faceted substitute family, which prompted Cordelia to disclose to a close friend that she had multiple personalities. This friend consequently told her the story of Sybil (Schreiber, 1974). Cordelia, however, was quite rightly alarmed about the similarities. Sybil's mother also used to wash her out, hang her upside down, and fill her vagina with water. Sybil had sixteen personalities, one of which was called Victoria, whose many brothers and sisters, mother and father lived in Paris, and who equally – just like Cordelia's Victoria – was a capable, confident person who knew everything about the other personalities, and tended to take care of them all. Although Cordelia had initially felt relieved that another person had likewise been able to create such an internal world, making her feel 'less mad or strange', she had nonetheless felt quite disappointed, because she had wanted to write her own story first, without having read similar accounts or having talked about others who equally had experienced a multiple world. Now she was convinced that if she wrote about her own experiences, everyone would say she had just copied Sybil.

Christmas came and went and was fairly uneventful, even though Cordelia had been aware of her sadness and was deeply worried about her husband, who was due to retire that year, and had told her, she said, that he was going to die during the coming year. Nonetheless, come January, Cordelia reached yet another milestone. She had discovered, she told me, that she was a person in her own right, regardless of whether others would be with her or not, whereas in the past the only time she had felt remotely real, Cordelia confessed, had been during her therapy session. This was truly a major revelation which made her feel wonderful.

Of course, reading through the early notes stirred up her feelings about how she had been misunderstood; how she had missed out on the right kind of treatment from the very start, whereas if she had been treated in America, Cordelia suggested, she might have been recognised as having multiple personalities much sooner. Yet she also expressed how she now understood how the various personalities had often sabotaged her revealing the abuse by her father by ensuring due admission to the hospital for the wrong reason. She even said that she now could see how necessary the boundaries had been, and that she truly had not realised that she had been so demanding. In addition, Cordelia also affirmed that she could now distinguish the difference between reality and imagination, and that she now knew that the various personalities had been but images in her mind, which she had imitated and acted out, even though she insisted that the children especially had always, been very, very real!

During every session, it seemed, Cordelia was discovering more and more about herself, and hence we both felt very optimistic for the future. Perhaps, I ventured carefully, the end of her therapy, feeling okay about leaving me, was in sight? But I spoke too soon!

One section of my notes talked about the difficulty Cordelia had in using the phone in an appropriate manner. When I read out this observation to her, yet another memory 'dripped' into place, and Cordelia recalled how her mother had insisted that she phone her every day, though when Cordelia did, her mother would invariably not answer her or acknowledge the call. That evening, Cordelia phoned me at home, but after two rings and before I could answer her, she stopped herself and replaced the phone, arguing with herself, 'What are you doing, you are not even meant to know her number.'

When I asked her during her next therapy session, if she had in fact called me up, Cordelia agreed that she had done so and explained that she had become scared, because Dr C had told her she said, that she was still splitting at times, whereas Cordelia felt that she no longer did. I naturally advised Cordelia to confirm with Dr C, what he meant by 'splitting', as it might not mean the same to Dr C as it did to Cordelia, and queried whether she had in fact understood him correctly. However, Cordelia subsequently confessed, that after listening to her notes and remembering how her mother had insisted she phone her every day, she had once again begun to talk in French and Arabic, although she was adamant that she had definitely not switched into a different personality. Naturally, in view of this disclosure, I could not help wondering whether this time I was indeed witnessing Cordelia relapse? Perhaps, as she had hinted, she was indeed still splitting?

Nonetheless, Cordelia seemed able to sidestep this blip quite quickly, and hence we continued to explore the notes. But two days later, when Cordelia requested a joint session with her husband and I had to inform her that I would only be able to see them for a short time on the day she had suggested, things went awry again. Cordelia there and then wanted to know whether I had been joking about her with another male patient, and a few days later, whilst she sat waiting in reception, she was seen drinking from a bottle of gin. When challenged, however, by the staff nurse, she agreed that it was not acceptable behaviour and put the bottle of gin away. Had yet another part of her made its debut in its original state? Or was something far more serious happening?

Nevertheless, despite it all, the session with her husband (on a different day) was again very encouraging. He reassured Cordelia that the abuse by her father had not affected his affections for her, and that he was in fact glad that she had now told him everything, as it gave him answers to so many unexplained questions and behaviours. However, a sour note clouded the meeting, for when I asked Cordelia's husband for feedback about Cordelia's behaviour at home, he reluctantly confirmed that during the past week Cordelia appeared to have switched. All was definitely not well! What's more, during her next therapy session, Cordelia also confessed that she had once again dissociated, because she did not get the extra time she had hoped for when they both came for the joint session. Dissociation, she had duly discovered that weekend, had helped her to get rid of the pain. What, I wondered yet again, was happening? Something else was surely afoot?

In the meantime, however, I had become aware that reading through the notes appeared to be rather counter-productive. Instead of learning from the past events, Cordelia seemed to just regress, and had clearly started acting out again, reliving her past distress about not being heard. Furthermore, I was also conscious that we were in fact avoiding the main issue, the end of her therapy! Thus I requested to know whether reading through the notes was helping her, and proposed that instead of going over the past, we should concentrate on ending therapy; not just because I might leave, though I confirmed that I definitely intended to leave before June of this year, but more pertinent, because Cordelia had come to the end of the road herself.

I explained that I considered this last stretch to be as important as everything else which had gone before, since it presented her with a unique opportunity to part in a healthy way, voice her distress and say her goodbyes. Much to my surprise, Cordelia agreed with me and said that likewise she had been avoiding the issue and was actually relieved that I had brought it up. Hence we decided that we would indeed continue exploring the notes, but on the understanding that it was a part of the leaving process. In addition, I would also try to sort out her various creative writing and her drawings in chronological order.

During the following week, Cordelia seemed to settle down again and truly benefited from analysing the notes. And, as I had promised, on Friday we looked through the drawings she had made during her first year in therapy, mostly on her own in the art room (I tended to keep all my patient's work unless they decided otherwise), and to her surprise, recognised how consistent her artwork had been. Naturally they contained yet another sunset. All seemed well again – but as before and unbeknown to us both, Cordelia's early drawings had acted as a trigger to upset the status quo yet again. Although Cordelia quite clearly had come to grips with her multiple system, the following weeks would show that the real battle was far from over: she still had to relinquish the search for the all-loving mother! Indeed, all too soon, we would in fact discover that transference was still very much alive, thriving and as intense as it ever was.

Cordelia in fact began the following Monday session by wondering whether her mother, likewise, had been a multiple personality, because, as Cordelia explained, she was always changing and being different people when friends or neighbours would call. She then continued, by saying that she had not made any of this up but that she had found another three! Another three personalities! She described how, since Friday after we had looked through her art work, she could not remember what she had done, where she had been, and that on Sunday she had found a new swimsuit in her bag. Moreover, the swimsuit was wet, but she had no recollection of having bought it or having used it. What – she wanted to know – was going wrong? Cordelia had relapsed for sure! Or had she? I recalled having read somewhere – in Ross (1989, p.306–307), that it is in fact possible to discover a 'new layer of alters'. And, that according to Kluft (1986) discovering such another layer of alters is not a true relapse, even though it can be very discouraging to do so: 'When there are many layers, it can begin to seem like an infinite regression. The therapist starts wondering if he is being conned and whether the new layer really has been there since childhood.' Patients, wrote Ross, can relapse for a number of reasons, and the five most common ones are:

1.   Discovery of a new layer of alters (not a true relapse),
2.   Re-emergence of previously fused alters,
3.   Creation of new personality states,
4.   Feigned integration (also not a true relapse),
5.   Recurrence of dissociative symptoms short of emergence of a full alter personality.

Patients furthermore, asserted Ross, may feign integration because they want to please a therapist or 'attempt a flight into health'. In addition, dissociation might simply be a habit, whereas other patients might not feel able to face life as single people and deliberately relapse with no intention of doing any further work. Such a decision, however, concluded Ross, should be regarded as a partial treatment success, with which I most certainly agree – after all, who are we to say how someone should conduct their life! But in contrast, Ross also pointed out yet another reason for relapse might be the fact that not enough work was done in therapy.

Then again, integration certainly is no easy option, as Ross described: 'The first year following integration is tough' – tougher, say many patients, than actually having MPD and so very different. Indeed, no longer can problems be distributed around the system. No longer can responsibility be delegated.

For sure, having reached oneness for some is just the beginning and often the point where many other patients begin their actual psychotherapy. Naturally, when Cordelia told me that she had found another three personalities, I was at first quite disappointed – but then, in fairness, so was Cordelia. However, in response to her question, 'What is going wrong?' I duly explained how the demands of therapy may cause an 'iatrogenic deterioration', and encourage the patient to create new alters in order to cope with the therapy coming to an end. Although it was also possible, I continued, that she was not experiencing a relapse but that the so-called 'new' personalities were in fact another layer? And if so, I remonstrated, it was surely no longer acceptable for her to say that she did not know where she had been or what she had been doing, or who had bought the new swimsuit, since by now she knew how to access her internal system, and hence that she would be able to work it out for herself as to why she had dissociated again.

Today, as I type out my words, I can of course recognise that I must have been far more disappointed than I let myself register at the time. However, notwithstanding, my rather abrupt appraisal and the fact that my explanations about the iatrogenic aspects of MPD initially caused Cordelia to doubt herself; caused her to wonder whether she had invented the three adult parts. She had always been aware, Cordelia told me later on, that she had created these three particular people, whereas she knew that the children were real. She was nevertheless able to identify several triggers and reasons for her apparent relapse. First of all, Cordelia divulged, she had become extremely jealous again when I had confirmed that her therapy was not the only experience I had of working with MPD, and that I might therefore want to write my own book about it all – though I had affirmed that I would assist her with writing hers. Secondly, Cordelia's early drawings, and especially the scene depicting yet another sunset over the sea, had reminded her, Cordelia said, of the last wholesome memory of her father; how he had in fact taken her for a walk by the seaside on the day he raped her, and how they had both watched the setting sun dip into the glistening sea. Cordelia consequently remembered that she had gone to the seaside, had bought a new swimsuit and had gone swimming in the sea – cold as it was in early February... brrr! Thirdly, Cordelia asserted, the three new personalities were adult personalities, two of which, she added defiantly, did not even belong to her, but to her mother.

Naturally, we explored the meaning of this rather strange statement and concluded that it appeared as though these three new personalities were in fact a separate system altogether, which of course would explain why they had not been integrated along with the children. Cordelia then described that one of the personalities was called Davina and that she came into being when Cordelia was about forty, at the time when she experienced a religious conversion; when Cordelia in fact believed that she had become a Christian. Davina, however, had disappeared again, Cordelia said, after she stopped believing. The other two personalities were respectively called Raza and Riva. Raza, so Cordelia informed me, could be especially secretive, and it was she who encouraged Cordelia to make the phone calls to me – in the same way, she had often urged her to phone her [dead] mother (Cordelia in fact, frequently still dialled the old, now disconnected number of her mother).

Riva was the manic part of her, and it was she who had bought the new swimsuit, gone for a swim in that cold sea, and had a coffee in one of the local hotels afterwards.

At once, Cordelia's reported switching and apparent relapse over the past weeks made sense. For sure, when the notes had triggered the memory of how Cordelia's mother had insisted that Cordelia phone her every day, Raza and Riva had both duly re-appeared on the scene, not only had Raza subsequently persuaded Cordelia to phone me at home that same evening but more than likely she had in fact done so, in order to assist Cordelia and seek a solution for her feelings of envy and jealousy which my reticence about joining her in writing her book had provoked. Three weeks later then, after we had looked through the early drawings, Raza had equally tried to comfort Cordelia when she remembered her last walk with her father by the sea, before Cordelia split herself into Peter and Rosemary. Thus, Cordelia suddenly also understood why she had so frequently yearned to be by the sea in the course of her life or during her therapy. Obviously, as well as being a source of pain, the sea had nevertheless also been a place where Cordelia could find solace; where she could remember a time when all was still well; a time when her father truly appeared to love her, which is why Raza had persuaded her to go to the seaside – as she had indeed done so many times before. In fact, as I was listening to Cordelia telling me how she had driven to the seaside, bought the expensive turquoise swimsuit, etc., I actually recalled that Cordelia had wistfully told me on the Friday whilst we were looking through her drawings that she might well take some time off and go to the sea on Saturday. Raza and Riva, it would seem, had indeed not only been very present during that particular session but had not wasted any time in trying to console Cordelia.

Much to my relief, I must confess. Cordelia's apparent relapse, therefore, turned out to be just another layer of personalities. But why, I queried, had Cordelia created them in the first place? When did they come into being, and why had Cordelia revealed them to me at this stage of her therapy? Having subsequently explored some of the answers, the session ended on time, much to Cordelia's disgust, who felt that I was imposing yet another boundary on her. Admittedly, in the past, due to the abreactive process of her therapy, I had been more flexible, and the precise time when a session would end tended to vary according to whatever had occurred within a given session. I usually managed to direct the work, so that we could safely conclude it within the hour, or within the next half hour at least. But, because we had actually begun a leaving process, I had suggested that we needed to be more precise about our time keeping, and to regard it as a rehearsal for when therapy ended. Although Cordelia had agreed with the logic of it all, it nevertheless rankled with her since it once again clearly reminded her that this relationship had its limitations, and finally had to end.

As a result, we began exploring what it means to lose a therapist, and also how it felt at the time when she lost her own mother. Cordelia consequently explained that whenever a therapy session ended, she felt as though she was leaving a dying relative. It was easier to think of me dying, Cordelia said, than accept that I would leave her. Transference, it seemed, was indeed still as intense as it ever was. However, in order to prove to herself and to me that she trusted me, Cordelia there and then decided to stop wearing a watch. She was determined, she said, to trust me, and hence wanted to prevent herself from checking up on how much time she actually got!

Over the next four to five sessions then, as well as continuing to explore the loss of her therapist and her mother, we also discussed the why and wherefores of Raza and Riva. And drip by drip, Cordelia was indeed able to tell me that first of all she had created them when her own mother died, and secondly, that they were meant to be a substitute mother. Together, Cordelia explained, they were meant to give her the unconditional love she could never have from her own mother, as well as help Cordelia pretend that her mother was still very much alive and had not left her. Which is why they had popped up at this stage of her therapy, because her therapist was leaving her. However, since Raza and Riva were based on her real mother, with time, and of course following suit with all the other personalities and duly becoming a person for real, they became oppressors instead (although they were of course never as vindictive as the as-if Bryony, which is yet another reason, asserted Cordelia, why they had not appeared in her therapy before. Not only had she 'tried to disown them' but she also believed that they were in fact a split personality, schizophrenic (as she rather believed her real mother had been), which is why there were two of them, and why they were so secretive. Raza, so Cordelia described, was in fact 'the voice inside of Riva', and it would be she who usually persuaded Cordelia to make the anonymous phone calls and thus get the comfort she craved, whereas Riva tended to indulge Cordelia by encouraging her to be a spendthrift and follow her desires.

During these same sessions, we naturally also discussed the implications of maintaining a make-believe mother, and how it had effectively prevented Cordelia from grieving the loss of her real mother. This painful work, however, caused Cordelia a lot of emotional distress, since she was convinced that she would not be able to live without mother love. But gradually she began to accept not only that the kind of mother love she craved was not available, but also, that the artificial love of Raza and Riva only served to fool herself. Hence, one day, Cordelia resolutely declared that she had realised that she had lived in order to take care of her mother, but that from now on, she wanted to live for herself. And, what's more, that if she could live without her mother, she could equally live without her therapist. Thus once again the intention to live an independent life, be free of her insurance policies had been clearly stated. But, as so often seemed to happen in this therapy, a parallel event would usually occur which always provided that extra nudge which tended to reveal the true state of affairs. This time, it was a rather innocuous fire lecture which duly ensured that transference became, once again, very visible indeed.

By now we were halfway through February, and on the Monday of the second week, I duly informed Cordelia that on Thursday of the coming week, I would have to finish five minutes earlier in order to attend a fire lecture, or else (conscious of providing value for money), that we would have to forfeit the session, since I could not offer her an alternative appointment. Cordelia there and then insisted that she wanted to talk to the hospital manager about this, and considered that it was not right. Her therapy time was surely more important than a fire lecture! Cordelia then wrote a hastily-written note to the hospital manager, asking if I could be released from attending this fire lecture, since there was still so much work to do before I left. Although I had of course informed my colleagues that at some stage I intended to leave, as yet I had not been able to confirm the exact date, and hence Cordelia's note came as somewhat of a surprise to the hospital manager, since it created the impression that my departure was imminent. When I, however, explained the background, the need to inform certain patients long before others, in order to ensure a meaningful leaving process, etc., the manager decided that she need not intervene as Cordelia had requested, and duly informed Cordelia that she had passed on her note and letter to me, confirming that her normal appointment was indeed available, minus five minutes.

I naturally tackled Cordelia on this note, and wanted to know, what she had hoped to gain from it, since it could well have landed me into trouble? Cordelia was amazed, shocked even, to think that I would consider that she might have had an ulterior motive. However, later on, she again confessed that she had hoped that I would have to leave sooner, rather than later, since my leaving her was causing her too much pain and she wanted it to be over. If I was going to die on her as her mother and father did, if, I was not going to go those extra miles for her and stay until she could let go of me, then she might as well do without me now. Although at the same time, she was desperate to continue seeing me as long as she could. Losing even five minutes of her time was too much! After this, Cordelia hurriedly wrote a second letter to the hospital manager, trying to make amends, and undo any possible harm or repercussions.

In the past, we had of course explored transference many times. However, the evidence of her positive transference, the many, many cards, the poems, the letters expressing her love, the presents and flowers she bought for me every birthday, of course far outweighed the evidence of her negative transference, the angry letters, the hastily scrawled notes, the angry outbursts, the one bunch of nettles left on my car etc. Hence I realised that it was of course quite easy to ignore or be lulled into accepting transference, and disregard its true power to distort and enthral. For instance, I was aware of how easy it would be for Cordelia to reason that transference could not be so very wrong, since it gave her at least some kind of loving feelings, allowed her to please me, receive pleasure in giving, find acceptance, etc. Indeed, Cordelia herself has since described how loving me, not only felt like the only thing in her life that was real, but also that it was 'like a diversion from the complete horror and awfulness' of her life.

I was of course always delighted and very touched whenever Cordelia bought me flowers for my birthday, and truly appreciated her fond wishes – but as her therapist, I was naturally also very much aware of its hidden agenda. As such, it was a veritable catch-22. If I had refused her flowers as most of the how to do books advise, she could not have experienced a caring, loving, nurturing relationship. But by accepting them, I was of course in danger of helping her to avoid reality; helping her to live in yet another make-believe world. At the time, however, I gambled on the first, instinctively knowing that Cordelia needed to be allowed to experience her transferences first (the positive ones as well as the negative ones), and that it would be counter-productive to insist, right from the beginning, that she take responsibility for having 'redirected her childhood emotions onto a new object' (as the *Oxford Dictionary* describes *transference*), hoping of course, that one day I would be able to assist her to do so. That one day, I had realised during these past weeks, had arrived. And what's more, the incident of the fire lecture was to give me the necessary means with which I might indeed be able to assist her.

The hastily written note to the manager, Cordelia's subsequent letter to try and make amends, and the fact that she might have caused problems, not just for me, but also for herself, (the manager could after all decide to send her a bill for the times we went past her allotted hour) were in fact proof of her negative transference. Directing Cordelia's attention to the effects of her negative transferences, as opposed to the effects of her positive transferences, I felt might prove to be the necessary jolt which might well release Cordelia from this entrancing *divertissement*. Once again it would seem, it was time for the unreasonable mother to interfere, and I must admit that I made rather a meal of it (although talking with hindsight of course, I'm sure that having to justify my actions to the hospital manager as a result of Cordelia's negative transference might well have had something to do with it!).

Not only did I inform Cordelia that I had felt aggrieved, that she might have got me into trouble, but more importantly, I felt that I did not deserve her anger or hatred. I also reassured her that I was aware that she had needed to experience transference, and that I fully understood how, whenever she felt insecure or believed that no one cared, she consequently experienced a negative transference and would then treat me as though I was her punishing mother. By now, I had hoped that she would be able to keep the two quite separate, and be aware that most of her reactions and feelings, especially during her therapy, were no more than either a negative or a positive transference. She simply could not go on transferring her anger or her love onto people in the present without a real cost to herself. Furthermore, I added, she could either say goodbye to me as the loving/punishing mother, or else she could also say goodbye to me as her therapist who has allowed her to act out her distress and needs. I then also informed Cordelia that, in my opinion, she had better do something about her transferences, or else, when her therapy ended, she would need another therapist for sure. For a while, I ventured, she might make do with Raza and Riva, but sooner or later she would find yet another therapist/mother to help her live out her fantasies.

At the time, my words must have sounded pretty harsh, but although I was rather embroidering my lecture (in the role of unreasonable mother of course), I was nevertheless truly concerned that Cordelia might get stuck in the twilight zone of transference with either Raza or Riva for company or else with an ongoing string of substitute mothers. However, at the same time I also realised that the eventual outcome was in fact very much out of my hands. Only Cordelia could decide whether she could give up on searching for the illusive mother love. Only Cordelia could decide that the love she could have from her husband, children, grandchildren and friends was worth so much more than the inert desires she held in her heart. All I could do from now on, I had ruefully realised, was encourage her to take this vital step. The following day, Cordelia brought me a card, wishing to atone, saying she had not really wanted to get me into trouble. What's more, Cordelia said, she had also realised that whenever I do become her mother, she stops feeling connected to me. Much to her surprise, she added, this painful realisation was in fact helping her to keep us very separate, for she had never felt remotely connected to her mother.

Cordelia then drew the pictures of when Raza and Riva came into being, remembering how on the day of her mother's funeral the distress of her younger brother and the bewilderment of her daughter had made her create a new mother, when Cordelia heard herself say, 'You've still got me', duly mixing up her own words with her longing for an ideal mother, one she might equally be able to grieve over herself. Cordelia then drew a second picture depicting yet another memory, which had obviously made it through the bottle-neck, and recalled how she nearly lost her life as a young child of ten whilst swimming in the sea. She was rescued Cordelia described, by a man who dived into the sea off the end of the pier, after she had kept on swimming and swimming towards the setting sun. Her mother had in fact been with her that time, and had actually bought her a new turquoise swimsuit, but had also told her 'to swim away into the sunset', and that she no longer wanted to see her. Perhaps a harmless enough as-if phrase, which many exasperated mothers might have exclaimed, but a phrase which of course became deadly serious when a certain child part of Cordelia, present at the time, was unable to decode its as-if meaning and took it literally as indeed most children will tend to do, until they learn otherwise.

Cordelia in fact recalled, that she had felt exhausted. She had also asked the man to let her drown, not only because she was so tired of living, but also because, despite it all, she would have done anything for her mother, including killing herself, and hence had fully intended to 'swim away into the sunset'. But why, Cordelia wanted to know, had she remembered this now? She had not remembered it before. And why had she re-enacted this scene at the seaside during the previous weekend? It must be connected, Cordelia answered herself, with the fact that her therapist is leaving, and she is having to face up to the fact that there never was and never will be a loving mother, even though her mother might have, once upon a time, taken her to the seaside, and bought her a new swimsuit!

Then again, Cordelia wondered out loud, had my hammering away at her about transference tipped the scale, and was that the reason why she had suddenly also remembered the few positive aspects of her mother? Was transference perhaps losing its hold over her?

During the following three days Cordelia did a lot of soul-searching, trying to fathom out how transference had indeed ruled her life. For sure, Cordelia had arrived at a very important and painful watershed. Whereas she had been able to negate the effect of her positive transferences, she had found it impossible to deny the repercussions of the negative ones, and thus had become acutely aware of a real need to resolve her transferences. But as courageous as ever, as the notes I wrote at the time so clearly illustrate. Cordelia did not shirk from the struggle ahead – ultimately emerging as the victor though not without paying a certain price.

19/20/22 February 1996

Cordelia said she wants to sort out this transference, because it had shocked her to realise the amount of damage she does to relationships when she feels others behave as her abusing mother.

We explored the need to think it through, i.e., when I am two minutes late, it does not mean I have forgotten her, the way her mother used to forget about her, though the feelings can be the same.

Cordelia also talked about how she has been able to let go of her mother, because she never did put her on a pedestal anyway (in the way she did put her father on one). Cordelia agreed that she still avoids the real truth of her mother, that she did not love Cordelia, because it hurts too much, and hence why she still 'needs Raza and Riva' since they are the mother she did not have.

On Tuesday, Cordelia continued to try and understand why she finds it so difficult to let go of her mother, and hence we looked through the various drawings she has done over the past year, to help her realise the real extent of the abuse and the futility of trying to 1) get her mother to love her, 2) find substitutes.

On Wednesday, Cordelia described how, on Tuesday evening, after looking through the drawings, she felt as though she wanted to die; that giving up on her mother was the one thing she could not do. Cordelia said she took a larger dose of her medication, but before going to sleep she prayed to God to help her find a way to end this longing for her mother. Cordelia also said that her husband had been quite concerned about her, and had also (again) suggested that they die together. But, Cordelia said, 'I realised that longing for my mother's love was not a good reason to die for, so I reminded my husband of the distress it would cause the children and grandchildren.' Cordelia said that on Wednesday morning, however, she woke up knowing what to do: say goodbye to her mother and symbolically bury her again, by burning the wedding dress she had made for Cordelia's wedding.

Cordelia subsequently was able to do so, as well as burn a photograph of herself and her mother depicting them both looking very happy, as though everything was all right. Cordelia said she hoped that the longing could now stop, and that she had accepted that the kind of love she should have had from her mother, can never be hers. Afterwards, Cordelia said she felt very free, and that she saw her husband and myself differently! She also said that Raza and Riva appeared to have disappeared and she no longer felt separate. 'I don't need to be them any more,' Cordelia said. 'I now know I had to say goodbye to my mother (and the mother part of you), before I could say goodbye to my therapist.' And the price Cordelia paid for this freedom? The price had been a life-threatening pneumonia.

At first, after burning the dress, Cordelia had continued to report that she was experiencing a real sense of feeling free of her mother, as well as describing how she had recognised that she had verily been under a 'transference spell'. For instance, she explained, she had never truly allowed me to see the individual personalities, in the same way she had always tried to hide them from her mother. Only her husband, she now realised, had seen her walk in a doubled up way, the way Elizabeth used to walk – holding her stomach/protecting herself from another beating. Although, Cordelia said, sometimes she would walk that way, following me up the stairs to the therapy room, but at the time, had not known why she did so. Cordelia in fact felt elated. She had actually experienced times, she reported proudly, when she had been without longing for her mother or the ideal therapist. And in addition, she added, she had also been able to inform Dr C that she had torn up her IOU. No longer was she intent on seeking revenge, no longer did she feel the world owed her a living. Yet, come the end of the following week, Cordelia's husband phoned in to say that his wife had developed labyrinthitis and would be unable to attend her therapy.

Labyrinthitis usually indicates some kind of infection of the delicate hearing canal, which means that the person may well experience vertigo – loss of balance. Considering the recent revelations and major decisions Cordelia had taken, feeling off balance would seem to be a rather appropriate response to what had occurred. However, the labyrinthitis quite quickly developed into pneumonia, and Cordelia became very ill indeed, enduring a near-death experience: her lungs had collapsed and she had stopped breathing.

Cordelia, however, had fought back, responding to the young doctor who urged her to breathe, suddenly aware that she wanted to live, suddenly conscious, that she felt connected to her children.

Needless to say, the symbolic burning of the wedding dress and all it represented had been far more traumatic than either Cordelia or I had realised.

At the time, Cordelia had been very calm, and certain of taking the right step. The hospital gardener usually tended to have a weekly bonfire, and together Cordelia and I had stood watching the flames consume her wedding dress and the smiling faces on the photograph. It had been a strange sensation to say the least. It was a fairly cold, but clear and silent day. The huge beech trees along the drive were beginning to wake up from their winter frost, and perhaps it was just my imagination, but it felt as though they too were watching, waiting, being sensitive to how significant it all was. Although I knew that Cordelia was very much aware of me standing next to her, she nevertheless felt very remote, as though this sacrificial burning was something she had to do by herself, for herself. Both of us, however, had the same kind of thoughts, reflecting on the mythical phoenix rising from the ashes, and when eventually we turned our back onto the smouldering bonfire and returned to the therapy room, we both also felt the sorrow of an end and the joy of a new beginning.

For the next three months, however, the sorrow of an end would of course overshadow any beginning as we continued to read through the notes and say goodbye to each other, though naturally not without some surprises. One morning, after we had discussed the fact that Geraldine never liked me because I always threatened the system's status quo, Cordelia had actually contacted the undertakers, and had ordered a hearse for me, though she had also managed to cancel it in time – once she had become aware of what she was doing – before it had left on its way to the hospital. Cordelia subsequently explained that she had ordered the hearse for me because ending, leaving and dying were all mixed up in her mind, and also because we had actually been talking about a similar incident involving her mother and grandmother. After reading about it in her notes, Cordelia said she had been particularly affected, when she had realised just how bad some of her parts could be. 'I couldn't believe that I would have acted like Geraldine.' However, she had also reluctantly agreed with me that the struggle to accept these 'bad' parts of her, as well as her 'good' parts, would probably continue long after her therapy had actually ended. I naturally also confirmed that most of the human race would probably be in that particular boat with her. Indeed, I reassured her, coming to terms with all aspects of one's thoughts, desires, actions and behaviours is a shared burden of what it means to be human.

The other surprise of course was the fact that Cordelia arrived one day wearing a pair of jeans, and was intent on creating a new image for herself. Proudly she exclaimed that she had never dressed like this before, and that in contrast, her wardrobe was full of clothes which actually belonged to the different personalities. Cordelia furthermore explained that the clothes in her wardrobe were the kind of clothes her mother would expect her to wear. Those clothes, Cordelia added, were in fact relics of the past, and had been an attempt to gain approval from her mother. Although Cordelia professed, that she would like to be rid of those clothes, that she wanted to forget all about the personalities, she nevertheless found it difficult to do so, simply because, regardless of the fact that they indeed belonged to the various personalities, they of course also held many memories, both good and bad, of her present-day life. Moreover, still very conscious of being believed, Cordelia also pointed out, that those clothes were of course the only evidence she had which reassured her that the personalities had existed, and that she had not invented them. Then again, Cordelia also wondered whether she had in fact been reacting the way someone reacts after a funeral and throws away all the clothes of the deceased, only to regret it later.

Thus, rather than dispose of them indiscriminately, I suggested that, for the remainder of her therapy I could in fact help her sort through them; help her select the kind of clothes which would suit her new image, and in the process of course, thereby also assist her to say goodbye to each personality as a real person.

Cordelia was at first rather apprehensive about doing so, fearing that I might laugh at her. As she explained, 'some of those clothes were quite outrageous!' However, during the remaining weeks, Cordelia henceforth, would not only bring her clothes along, but when I encouraged her to do so, she subsequently also tried them on. And as a result, Cordelia discovered many more aspects of herself which hitherto she had just accepted as part and parcel of it all. For instance, she usually only bought certain clothes because they looked good on the hanger in the shop, but she had no idea whether they either did or did not look good on her, or how she appeared to herself or to others, since she never really looked at herself. Hence, Cordelia's image had not only been very changeable but had also been very typical, very incarnate – and very much influenced by how a certain character would have been perceived in her mind's eye.

In addition, Cordelia discovered that Stephanie must have been in evidence far more frequently than Cordelia had suspected, because of the amount of grey, ghost-like, fairly insignificant dresses in her wardrobe. In fact, Cordelia remarked, she now understood how Stephanie 'who always felt dead, whose head was permanently in a fog', had always tried to go unnoticed, which is why, she had mostly worn see-through clothes. Then again, the clothes of Bryony (which Cordelia did not remember buying), taught her that whenever she had been in the presence of her brothers, she had always ensured that she wore older-looking clothes, usually brown, which completely covered her up. 'I could not let them see me having a woman's body, because they had seen too much of me.' In addition, putting on the clothes of Bryony stimulated Cordelia to remember how her mother had made Cordelia wear her mother's clothes before she abused Cordelia sexually. Most surprisingly, Cordelia had in fact, unwittingly, portrayed this in her drawings, by always selecting a brown marker whenever she depicted the young Cordelia being abused by her mother.

When Cordelia subsequently also dressed herself up in the clothes of Martin (which was of course a male outfit – a black morning suit in fact, which had actually been worn by her brother when he abused her), she also realised that she had invariably put on these clothes after making love to her husband, in order to regain a sense of being in control, a feeling of being as important as the men in her family of origin had been regarded as – which prompted her to exclaim that she could not understand how she could put on the clothes of an abuser; feeling that it was a 'sick thing to do'. Likewise, she did not really understand how she could have worn the clothes of Peter, usually khaki-coloured shorts, clothes which camouflaged him, as well as wearing thigh-high boots, resembling callipers, without having been aware that something was very amiss.

Nevertheless, as Cordelia continued to bring in the various clothes of

Felicity, Rosemary, Esther, Angela and Elizabeth, her sense of Self grew, and much to her delight, she was also beginning to establish her identity; becoming much more assured about the kind of clothes which suited her, and certain about which ones she actually wanted to wear. For sure, even though she found it difficult to come to terms with the behaviour of Geraldine, she did, however, like her clothes, bright flowery clothes which ensured that she, would not go unnoticed. Likewise, Cordelia expressed that she would like to wear the bright, younger-looking clothes of Elizabeth much more freely, and not feel that she needed to conform, and live up to the standards which she suspected her brothers expected of her. Moreover, she had also recognised that she had worn the black clothes of Mary in order to hide her femininity and feel safe from men, whereas in contrast, she had actually tried to defy her mother by wearing the blue and white clothes of Riva – clothes which her mother would of course never have worn, but which actually represented the mother Cordelia would like to have had.

Although the initial suggestion to help Cordelia with her clothes had been made, in order to help her decide which ones to throw away, as well as help her say goodbye to her internal people, the very act of dressing up in their clothes and then sharing this image with her therapist was having a much more profound effect than we had both anticipated. By putting on these various clothes in my presence, then removing them again after we had both scrutinised them in the mirror, Cordelia was not just 'saying goodbye' to the different children. Cordelia was in fact shedding the personalities, her other-selfs, as real people, yet she was also absorbing them in a style of her own. Truly a remarkable achievement.

By now it was the end of April. The end of her therapy was approaching fast, and after some painful negotiating, we had in fact agreed that her last day would be on 20 May. In the meantime, we had actually been reducing the sessions gradually over the past two months (we were down to twice a week), and we had also re-read most of her therapy notes. I had also given her copies of my notes, and returned all her drawings and creative writing to her, including the photographs I took of her artwork. Cordelia, equally, had given me the photographs her husband had taken of her wearing the various clothes of her different people, which had caused her to exclaim that she had been truly amazed to recognise how 'bonkers' she had been, and how far she had come since she had begun to accept the truth.

She also reported feeling pleased when Dr C told her that he regarded her recovery as 'quite remarkable', and that she had overcome many obstacles, which should have meant that therapy should never have started in the first place. Gratified, she added that he had always been very fond of pointing out to her that she had suffered a great deal of deprivation. Yet she was also desperate to leave with as clean a slate as possible, and hence she tried to fill me in on as many details of her multiple system as she had discovered since being one person, or had not yet revealed, such as more precise details about Angela,

Esther and Rebekah. For instance, I recorded the following on 26 April:

> Cordelia confessed that on her list of personalities was someone called Rebecca, who tended to read, write, acquire knowledge, but usually in secret, i.e. 'I would go to bed in order to read, until my husband reassured me that it was all right to read in public.'
>
> Cordelia feels that Rebecca had been with her for a very long time – came when she was told there was nothing for her in the toy cupboard – so she learned to collect her own toys, shells from the beach, and read books an elderly neighbour would let her borrow. 'But I had to do it all in secret.' Hence, Rebecca is very secretive. 'It is Rebecca who always seemed to know what was happening to me – she did not seem to have loss of memory as the others.'
>
> Cordelia agreed that Rebecca could be described as her internal observer – the one who tried to tell Cordelia the truth about herself – which would explain the many different letters/stories she wrote over the years hinting at the multiple system and the many secrets.

For sure, right to the end, Rebecca had maintained her secrets! Thereafter, Cordelia told me that the complete list of personalities should also include three imaginary friends, which Cordelia had created during her days as a student. Two were called Dawn and Denise, Cordelia explained, and they had each been inspired by two fellow pupils, whereas Freda, Cordelia told me rather sheepishly, had been modelled on her music teacher. Needless to say that this rather late admission supplied us with yet more answers, as well as provided me with extra ammunition to expose the clever ramifications of transference.

But I suppose the most remarkable aspect of this last stretch of Cordelia's therapy journey was the fact that Cordelia was grieving. She was not dissociating, becoming depressed, or psychotic, she was allowing herself to register what it meant to lose her therapist, and consequently she was able to put her distress into words, and share them with me:

> To Frieda
>
> I have found my true inner self through gradually seeing myself in and through the person who listened to my pain for so long. The person who helped me unravel the awful mess I was in. I discovered myself through you, Frieda, through the risk I took in trusting and loving you. I discovered how I protected myself over the years. I discovered such wonders to behold, it set my own mind in a whirl. Could all this really be me, for so long the imprisoned me? To lose you, Frieda, feels like losing a part of who I am.
>
> In my near death experience, you were there encouraging me to live. To me it felt as if you were going to die because you are leaving – but whatever happened, I had to write my book and live in honour of the hard work and successful achievements we've made together over the last five and a half years. It felt as if I was saying no to death because you gave me life and because now I had a reason for living.
>
> Of course it feels as if you are going to die. To me, you will be dead, because

I can no longer see your face, your smile or touch your hand or hear your voice – what memories I have will be all that I can hold on to – and those are associated with pain.

I try to reassure myself that I really don't mind so very much but I am fooling myself. I mind very much indeed. I feel as if I am drowning, my lungs are filled up with tears of grief.

I'm angry you are leaving me for ever, angry that your friends and all the people in Ireland you know or will get to know, will share in your life, while you leave me behind so full of sadness. You have been talking about leaving for so long and now it's really happening, it's hard to take in what it really means to me. I am full of unexpressed grief and anger, now it has come, it's too awful to bear.

Five sessions left! Cordelia arrived dressed in the clothes of Victoria – a very smart suit – but she did not feel like Victoria, because Victoria would not be able to show her feelings, and she felt so very sad. She had also begun to feel as though she was floating, Cordelia informed me, and wondered if she was experiencing what Dr C, had called 'false health'. The following day, a distraught Cordelia appeared in the hospital, saying that she was overwhelmed with grief, but left after she was seen by Anne. Several notes, however, were left on my car, each one detailing her distress and voicing her doubts about whether she would indeed be able to cope. But all was not as desperate as it seemed, because in due course, Cordelia would actually be able to own up to having panicked after she had an argument with her husband, fearing his loss as well as mine had been too much! Naturally we subsequently explored dependency, and how it will probably always continue to rear its desperate head, although we also agreed, that it would be quite understandable and appropriate for Cordelia to seek help with grieving the loss of her therapist after I had gone. Cordelia, however, said that, ideally, she would prefer to contain her grief herself, with the help of her husband, though she would of course continue to see Dr C.

20 May, the last therapy session was here. Cordelia observed that she had thought that this day would never come. She gave me a painting she had made of the children in the Bluebell Wood, saying that somehow it felt as though they now belonged more to me than to her. She felt sad, but she also felt very well. Her daughter was expecting her third child, and it would help her to put her grief to one side, allow her to concentrate on giving love and attention to her family. She did not intend to neglect herself, and she was determined to allow herself to grieve, as and when. Although she still felt that she should have been allowed to write to me in Ireland, she would settle for her letters being sent on to me, via the hospital, and hoped that I would write to her in return. She also hoped that I would help her with writing her book, though confirmed that, regardless, she fully intended to write about her suffering; to write about her struggle to uncover the truth and explain how she had managed 'to climb out of the goldfish bowl' – and what's more, she had every

intention of staying out! Cordelia then remarked that she could not under-stand how she could be so calm and composed. 'I expected to be screaming the place down for sure,' Cordelia added, 'I must have grown up!' – and then decided that she had.

Time to leave. So we ended this last therapy session and this remarkable therapy journey with how it all began – with a hug – but with one difference. Whereas all these years ago I had given Cordelia a hug, she now hugged me. Perhaps there is not a lot of difference between the two, a hug is a hug after all – but we both knew that a whole new world had been created in the space of these years – for both of us. Cordelia briefly touched my hair, the way she used to do at times when the needy child was too desperate, remarked that she must have been the only adult patient who probably treated me as a mother, said goodbye, said I will miss you, and left. Her therapy days with Frieda were over – what now? What could sustain her now? But as usual, in this most unusual therapy, Cordelia had of course, already discovered the answers:

What gives me hope.

I had a dream last night that gave me hope. I was in this long dark tunnel, like the long dark tunnel I sometimes look down and see scenes from the past relating to the abuse, as if from a distance. Last night I saw pictures of two men removing my clothes in the recreational lounge and then I couldn't look any more. But I did look again and I was back in the tunnel, facing the open end with blue sky ahead. I rushed ahead to get out into the blue sky, but I fell, someone was pushing me from behind. I shouted, 'Don't push.' I want to get there but in my own time, I was trusting that something was happening, there was hidden growth going on.

1. When I feel I'm really crazy and need locking up, I remember what my therapist says. She gives me hope, she tells me I'm not mad, not crazy, she tells me I was a remarkable child to cope the way I did, the only way I could. I believe her, because I love her.

2. When I want to die I remember my grandchildren, their eyes meeting mine with love returned. They give me hope and a reason to live.

3. When I'm full of fear and afraid of the future, my own inner strength gives me hope.

4. When I feel totally unloved and unlovable, I look across the room to the one adult in my life who truly loves me and is totally dependable; my husband gives me hope.

5. When I feel confused and very alone, music, poetry and literature have become a source of hope.

These are all new discoveries.

The Personalities... continued:
The Adults

THE FRIENDS 16–18 YEARS

At the age of sixteen, my brother Martin had already been at university for quite a while and away from home. My mother was working and had met a younger divorced lady with a daughter a few years younger than myself to whom she showed much kindness. My mother and her friend became very close and I saw very little of them. She also at this time gave me my own bed, which I had always longed for, my own wardrobe, dressing table, and in my own room. During this period, I was working harder at school than I had ever done. I was freer to study at home or stay after school, as long as I had a meal ready for my mother and brother. Life became more tolerable, although I felt desperately lonely and unwanted. I found I still did not make friends easily. I created three more personalities modelled on two pupils at my school and a teacher.

DAWN

She was American, friendly, kind with a lovely smile. Attracted many friends. Had a strong voice of her own with an American pronunciation.

DENISE

She was wildly attractive to look at, quite stunning in fact. I suppose I envied and admired these real people and made them mine.

FREDA

She was like my music teacher who I thought was wonderful. This music teacher took a special interest in me, and as it happened, was a niece of Vaughan Williams. I wanted to be like her and to be a relative of someone famous, talented and good that I could model my life on. I did not want to belong to such sick people. I longed all my life to belong to someone I could trust and who could value me. I internalised this teacher but she became split off into another personality who could stay with me for ever.

DELIA I AND DELIA II, 19 YEARS

At the age of nineteen years, I met my future husband whom I fell passionately in love with. Determined to keep this kind and dependable man, I took a conscious decision to put the past behind me. I thought that all I had been would disappear, now that I was really happy. I was new, someone else, called Delia. My husband-to-be shortened my name to Delia, the first person to do so. This in itself set the scene to be different, or so I thought. I knew I had to contain my deep sadness somewhere, so the dark inner pain was put into Delia II. This part was a secret; no one, I thought, would know about her except me. The face of the world and this new person in my life would only see Delia I.

After I married, with the responsibilities of being a wife and a homemaker, struggling with work and becoming a mother early in the marriage, the cracks in my personality started to show, but I tried hard to keep everything under control. I was very ill after the birth of our first baby, physically as well as suffering from depression. As a full-time mother, I found it even harder to cope and I felt very alone in a new area with no friends. My husband was kept busy with work and all his musical engagements. What could I do, where could I go for help, were my constant thoughts. How I kept going, pretending that all was well, I do not know. The aloneness and deep gnawing inside pain would not leave me. As my family increased, we moved house, and life for a while became a little more tolerable. I made more friends and started work again when the children went to school and enjoyed life a little better – until my mother died. She had been a constant problem to me even though I was married; the emotional blackmail was crippling.

I became deeply depressed after her death and had to give up work for over a year. I received drugs, and later ECT, but no one ever talked to me. Work was never the same after this; I only coped with part-time for a while and then not at all. Relationships were difficult and life seemed full of problems. We constantly moved house, making new starts. I always felt I was running away from myself. I can remember that for about ten years, I felt dead inside and life was at times totally intolerable, but there was, however, the strong side of me, that would occasionally bounce back and cope. This part of me, Delia I, did not feel and pretended to be happy. Even losing two babies, a twelve-week pregnancy and a much more advanced one, didn't seem to really matter at all. In fact, I find it hard to remember the details of the more traumatic birth, because at that stage I did not care what happened to me, and I encouraged the haemorrhaging by taking a large dose of laxatives and did not call an ambulance until I was in danger of losing my life. As a nurse I knew the dangers of uterine haemorrhaging. Even though the blood loss and pain started in the hairdressers, I insisted my hairdo was completed. I was still going to a ball that evening. I had no regard for myself and quite enjoyed the drama that followed. A crisis in my life was the norm for me, and I was more comfortable with an ambulance, flashing lights, a bell and all the attention in A and E. I didn't want to see the baby; I didn't want to recognise any sort of loss.

I was very physical and psychologically ill afterwards, only accepting the physical weakness when attempts to carry on life as usual failed. The day of discharge from hospital, I attended speech day at my son's school and collapsed completely. I was still too unwell to be going anywhere following such blood loss and replacement by transfusion. The anaesthetic and the sudden change of hormones, let alone the loss of the life that had been growing inside me, were totally ignored by me.

Delia I deceived herself as well as others, Delia II remained a secret. Although my husband saw frequent and dramatic changes in my personality, he still seemed to think I was always the life and soul of any party and thought I was basically a happy person – I had deceived him too for a very long time. The so-called depression worsened and my husband found all medical services failed him when he asked for help, and I would not accept the only help offered, which was admission to a psychiatric hospital. I felt I had to be at home for my children. I just took drugs, which kept me going for a bit longer. Whether it was true depression no one seems to be sure but I am sure that it was a deep sadness, a complicated grief that had poisoned the centre of my being and festered over a long time. I was numbed but still imprisoned in my goldfish bowl.

My husband could not cope with this sadness and became more intolerant of the changes he saw in me. As always I found a way to help myself, I let all the personalities take over again; this brought a degree of relief to the situation and helped me to cope again. My husband preferred me unpredictable to the constant depression. I then went through a lot of physical health problems, which might have been caused by the constant internal stress. No longer was I just Delia I or Delia II, I was twenty-three other personalities, and the new one was Davina, who came in my late thirties. She made me feel happier for a while but the chaos inside me was stirring and as I explain under the personality Davina, this was almost a conscious beginning of the longest and most painful journey of psychological recovery, to my knowledge, ever written about in this country. I needed Davina; I needed this spiritual experience which was very real, to set me on a hazardous but correct path to wholeness.

RAZA AND RIVA 25 YEARS

Raza and Riva were personalities who came after my mother died. They were forms of my internalised mother. Raza is an Arabic name, meaning secretive. Raza was a 'voice' who told me what to do, she was very compelling and obsessive. She used her voice on the telephone or in my head, otherwise never revealed herself to others. She was a depressed and deeply unhappy personality.

Riva is an Italian name, meaning coast or shore. She was energetic, daring, almost a manic part who became a spendthrift to pacify her craving; her need to buy clothes, things for the home, presents for others, for her children, which made her feel good. Often, she would take the clothes back to the shops the day after, feeling guilty she had spent so much and decided the clothes didn't suit anyway.

Both these parts would leave me anxious, exhausted, depressed with a great deal of internal conflict.

DAVINA 38 YEARS

Davina is a Hebrew name meaning 'beloved by God'. I believe she was the adult version of Rosalind, the child personality (none of the children in fact aged: they all remained whatever age they were, when first created). She came in my late thirties and was the part of me that split off from the rest; the part that was able to be loved by God. I could only allow a tiny part to be this special and Davina was the Christian who had a very real spiritual experience. She spent all her time at prayer meetings, Bible studies, talking to groups, her own family group that led music worship in church, she read the lesson, led the prayers, counselled and helped, as well as prayed for healing of others; led a home group, youth group and shared her family home with others.

Davina was completely genuine. She remained a strong part of the system for seven years, the part that lived a completely different separate life, again as an escape from reality of other things. Davina disappeared slowly when the buried pain started to emerge. Most of her friends at the church disappeared too, very few remained. I believe this spiritual experience was God's way of stirring up the chaos inside me so that it could eventually be sorted out. I had let Him into a heart so full of pain.

Evaluation

As a budding dramatherapist, I remember writing an essay on the need to evaluate a therapeutic encounter. However, I also recall that my tutor was not exactly impressed by my erstwhile composition and made me rewrite certain parts of it. Consequently, I soon realised that I had in fact omitted to include one of the most important reasons as to why we should indeed evaluate: to be wise after the event. Perhaps this seemed so obvious a fact that I had not considered it worth mentioning. Nevertheless, it sure set me thinking. Would not the experience of a life event alone, I queried, automatically make a person wiser? Did we not all, inevitably, learn from the mistakes we made, the achievements we had, the perils we had overcome, the patterns we repeated? The answer of course was a resounding, 'No, we do not.' For sure, a life event, a mistake made, a positive outcome achieved, even a glaring replication, will not make the person instantly wiser, unless the lessons of the life event, the value of the mistake, the benefits of the risks involved and the never-ending circles of behaviour patterns are analysed and evaluated. Contemplation of how, why, when, etc., stringing answers together like so many pearls of wisdom, I concluded, was the only way we could truly be called wiser after the event. In this, my last chapter, I have attempted to do just that – to try and string even more answers together; to evaluate precisely how and why Cordelia and I had arrived at a certain point, bearing in mind of course, that future events may always shed more light.

First of all, putting transference under the microscope, it becomes even clearer that certain incidents were not just random reactions, irrational behaviours, or a sign of 'illness', but that they had in fact been triggered by events and people in the present – whereafter they took on their special meaning by evoking situations and certain people from the past. As such, they should not have been ignored or simply accepted (as they usually are) for what they appeared to be, 'yet another patient acting out'. In fact, when we place our first encounter squarely under the same microscope, it becomes all too clear that a first meeting between a therapist and a patient can be highly significant – irrespective of whatever may follow in the next few weeks.

Cast your mind back if you will, to when Cordelia first ran out of the stress management group after meeting me for the first time. And remember also how she left it to the last minute, the final days of her therapy to tell me that she had a make-believe friend called Freda. How then are these two events connected? To begin with, the following two aspects of our first meeting may well go a long way to explaining why Cordelia felt safe and at ease with me right from the start, and why she thought that she had met me before, (although, stranger coincidences have occurred). Not only did I behave more like a teacher than as a therapist during the stress management lecture, but since I used to introduce myself at the beginning of the session in an attempt to make any new patients feel at ease and very welcome, Cordelia was of course aware that I shared the same name as one of her internal people.

This particular part of Cordelia was in fact called Freda. And, as Cordelia has described, since her schooldays, Freda had been a treasured substitute for her music teacher, who had always taken a special interest in Cordelia. Thus the scene was set for a positive transference and for Cordelia to feel indulgent with this other Freda who appeared interested in her, talked sense, and who knows, might even become her own special therapist. However, when I subsequently distributed a set of handouts to everyone, there was my name clearly printed at the bottom – but spelled with an 'i'. Frieda was not Freda and what's more, since I then also proceeded to involve every member of the group in exploring questions and answers, Cordelia was confronted with the fact that, even if I was to become her own special, ideal therapist – just like her mother, she would have to share me with others. The previously enhancing scene then shifted to a negative transference, to a more familiar abusive relationship – one which Cordelia had felt compelled to repeat over and over. This Frieda was bound to hurt her, just like her mother, the other therapist, and everyone she had ever dared to love.

She deftly left the group and ran out of the door. But lo and behold, here comes Frieda, and with a hug and good intentions, she managed to make the ideal Frieda real; real enough, that is, to ensure that Cordelia would faithfully keep the secret of this other Freda until it could no longer do any harm. Indeed, the reader may remember how Cordelia had in fact skipped certain places on the list of personalities she gave me, when we first started to unravel them all. Cordelia would in fact continue to do so, right to the end – as the following list illustrates, although the empty spaces would of course always clearly indicate that the list was far from complete. (Extra descriptions Cordelia gave me later on, are also included.)

Cordelia –the observer:

1.   Young Cordelia, sad child, alone, secretive, not appearing to be here.
       Totally introverted.
       (No voice.)

2.   Zillah, shadow friend.
       (Loft, shadow friend to Elizabeth)

3.   Alice, 18 months.
       (Bathing with father. Started to dissociate around 18 months–2 years.
       Makes herself small enough to disappear; makes others disappear.
       Hallucinates.)

4. Stephanie, very sad, despairing, frail, ill, wants to die. Hospitalised many times.
(Dead twin. Sister's name – Bath/mother. 2–3 years.)

5. Peter, kind, caring, pale, thin, worn out. Legs pulled out at hips. Wore callipers on his legs.
(Father's abuse.)

6. Rosalind, gentle, musical, sang, played piano.
(Father's goodness, loves dancing)

7. Rebekah, loves stories, books, Bible.
(Loves books, learns in secret. Became the observer, writes letters. But cannot communicate verbally.)

8. Elizabeth, behaves badly, screams, hurts herself, feels trapped, panics, jealous, angry. Loves deeply.
(Loft.)

9. Bryony, cold, indifferent to others, cruel, demands, abuses, cuts her hair. Went to asylum, schizophrenic
(Rejection by mother – wears mother's clothes.)

10. Felicity, extrovert, daring, passionate, flirtatious.
(Reaction to abuse, needing love.)

11. Esther, loves outdoor life, swimmer, dancer, strong and brave.
(Thrown into sea.)

12. Angela, carer of little brother and mother, kind but firm.
(Birth of brother.)

13. Geraldine, paranoid, strong, aggressive, argumentative, abuses, cruel. Can be vicious in thought, word and deed.
(Hated by grandmother.)

14. Gillian, laughs in a serious situation, giggly, plays jokes.
(Brother's abuse, a clown.)

15. Martin, kills, experiments, inflicts physical pain, sly, critical, sarcastic, abuses, shouts, cruel, cold, no friends, viciously strong in word and deed.
(Became a protector.)

16. Mary, feels injured, dirty, dislikes herself intensely, full of guilt and shame, doesn't eat, vomits, abuses herself badly, shaves her hair sometimes.
(Rape and abortion, speaks Arabic, abuses herself in many ways.)

?

?

19. Victoria, confident, academic, dresses well, loves company, achiever.
(Mother's sexual abuse until age sixteen years, speaks French.)

20. Delia I, 19 years. Strength and courage, nurse in training.
    (Good in a crisis.)

21. Delia II, 19 years. Despairing hopeless.
    Both met future husband. (Depressed.)

?

23. Raza, 30 years. Arabic name, secretive, voice tells her what to do, compelled and abuses.
    (Telephone.)

24. Riva, 30 years. Italian name, (meaning coast, shore), energetic, daring, almost manic, buys lovely things, spendthrift.
    (Internalised mother after her death, both leave me anxious, internal conflict, exhausted, depressed.)

25. Davina, 40 years. Loved by God.
    (Became a committed Christian after spiritual experience, but she disappeared when the buried pain started to surface.)

Although after our first meeting, I initially set out to try and discover why Cordelia had left the group, somehow, that particular question was simply hijacked along the way by tales of abuse, and never received an answer. Today, we can of course only speculate on how different Cordelia's therapy might have been if Cordelia had been able to tell me precisely why she had left the group. But as it was, Cordelia's hasty departure was in due course, simply filed away under that all accommodating label of 'just acting out'. Of course, Cordelia had indeed been 'acting out' but unfortunately – as labels tend to do – why, or what she had been 'acting out' was not explored at the time, and hence failed to be utilised until much later. What's more, looking back it now becomes all too clear how quickly and effortlessly I had in fact become involved in Cordelia's drama.

Again we can but speculate on the actual outcome if I had just let it be, if I had decided not to ask Cordelia why she had left the group. Indeed, how different her therapy might have been if I had taken due notice of my apprehension and had sat down in the vacant chair, instead of sitting down next to Cordelia on her bed, which proved to be such a vital decision (the precise reason why will be explained later on). Then again, what if I had equally decided to resist the impulse to demonstrate to her that, unlike her brother, I could cope with mental illness; that being admitted to a psychiatric clinic was nothing to be ashamed about, or had denied my feelings to comfort her, and had refrained from giving her a hug? But since I did not resist, since I in fact, somehow, also managed to create the impression that I had all the answers; since I somehow managed to pick up this 'dirty, wet, screaming baby from its cot', no wonder then that Cordelia became determined that I should be her therapist. Unreservedly, it seemed, I had stepped into the vacant role of ideal rescuer with both feet.

During the following week then (unbeknown to us of course), not only would Cordelia experience yet another positive transference, when I took her swimming as her father used to do, but during the following stress management lecture, she would again experience all the painful negative feelings of rejection when I again shared my attention around the group and when I again appeared to ignore her, as her mother used to do. Whereupon, Cordelia duly complained to Anne, her care nurse, that she was concerned about 'Frieda avoiding me'.

As we now know, the inevitable outcome (aided and abetted by counter-transference, as I described elsewhere) was the merging of me, father and mother into an ideal therapist; a highly prized 'insurance policy', which would remain in force until Cordelia would finally feel able to reveal to me how this ideal Frieda came into being. This, however, should not be read as meaning that the ideal therapist from that moment on has somehow miraculously disappeared. Striving after an ideal, whether it is the ideal Self, the ideal relationship, or the ideal life, is part and parcel of what it means to be human. Somehow, we all seem to need this kind of healthy dependency – which is why the role of Anne has been so vital. Indeed, the belief that an ideal exists; the certainty that an ideal other, such as a father or a mother will always be there for us – no matter what we do – makes us feel secure and connected to others, even though for most of us, we will of course never really know for certain, as such a belief is not usually tested out. Of course, such dependency ceases to be healthy when the ideal can no longer be distinguished from what is fact. In Cordelia's case, in addition to longing for ideal parents, an ideal family, and the ideal long-term therapeutic relationship (which she was determined to have), she was of course also convinced that an ideal Frieda was bound to rescue and love her, and that an ideal Anne would indeed always be there for her, regardless of commitments or personal needs.

Certainly, the belief that an ideal rescuer was out there, the hope that someone, one day, would take her away from all this sorrow, had been a crucial aspect, which had ensured Cordelia's survival. Then again, did she not have proof that ideal rescuers did exist – had not a 'kind warm nurse' been prepared to defy her father, take her away from him? The fact that Cordelia had blown her chances of being rescued by her did not mean that she had not been for real. It was no good, this Frieda arguing with her that ideal rescuers did not exist, Cordelia knew better! The fact that today, apart from the occasional blip, Cordelia can now keep the ideal very separate from what is real and available must surely be considered an enormous achievement, and would certainly place her on a rung above many others, which leads me on to yet other aspects of transference, now clarified by this process of evaluation.

What Cordelia's therapy has so copiously highlighted is the debilitating aspect that whenever transference is severe, there is at first little or no insight that transference is distorting facts. As far as the unhappy victim is concerned, the therapist is the abusing parent, the therapist is the ideal mother, is the ideal father. And therefore (as my vampire dream urged me to recognise), it can of course be very easy to end up 'being left holding the baby', meaning that the therapist/patient relationship never moves on from parent/child, to adult/adult. The needy baby, the rejected child, the difficult adolescent never really grows up, and the ideal therapist is simply replaced by another, as and when needed. Sometimes, this process of replacing an ideal therapist/parent with another is already in evidence whilst the first therapist is still safely in place. Indeed, Cordelia so graphically illustrated this with the phrase, 'safety in numbers', when she described, how she wanted to continue seeing both Dr M and me, even though she meant it in terms of not wanting to be dependent on anyone ever again. And yet, Cordelia was eventually able to break free from this enchanting spell! How then has Cordelia achieved this?

On reflection, it becomes clear that the concentrated focus on coping with loss, and the many sessions we actually spend on exploring the ideal versus the real, writing many lists of wished for attributes versus what is available, have been highly significant. Furthermore, the lengthy leaving process, reading her notes, and surprisingly enough, even the fact that we maintained some form of contact after her therapy had ended, and certainly the writing of this book, have all contributed to the demise of the ideal therapist. For sure, analysing the ending of Cordelia's therapy has revealed that certain conditions are in fact essential in order to secure a healthy dethroning of the ideal therapist. First of all, it has to be understood that the end of the therapeutic relationship has to mean the end of the special relationship which existed between the therapist and the patient, in the same way a mother would not return to breastfeeding once the child has been weaned. Secondly, this vital emancipation then can be made easier when the vacant space can be filled again with an ex-therapist who becomes available to evaluate the preceding therapy, who makes her/his notes accessible to the patient, who helps the patient to strengthen the bonds with a partner and her or his immediate family, who may allow the ex-patient to write to the ex-therapist, who may even answer her or his letters – might even help the ex-patient to write a book – but above all, is an ex-therapist who gives the therapy back to the patient, takes her/himself down from the pedestal and is not above scrutiny nor reluctant to share her/his special knowledge or insight with the patient.

Although most therapists will in fact give due importance to a leaving process, the role of the therapist tends to be set in stone. The therapist does not de-role, frequently because the patient might well need to come back for further therapy. Needless to say, the very idea of having such a breast on tap has certain attractions and dire consequences.

Then again, therapists, despite their best intentions, are of course handicapped with the same unconscious motivations, and hence may find it just as difficult to actually let the patient grow away! However, this should not be translated as meaning that all we have to do is to de-role towards the end of therapy. In fact, a therapist who suddenly starts behaving as a potential friend, for instance, can be in danger of making the ideal therapist an even more permanent fixture than it had been before. Moving from therapist to ex-therapist is a gradual process whereby the therapist, bit by bit, hands over the reins, and puts the patient firmly back into the driving seat. In Cordelia's case, this process in fact began the very day I started reading her therapy notes to her.

So what then, have I learned from putting counter-transference under the microscope? Certainly, that health professionals can unwittingly help the patient to re-enact a past drama, whether it is via a mix-up over appointments, lack of communication, or by duplicating treatment. I have also come to the conclusion that we need to utilise counter-transference more; be direct and share our misgivings with the patient; be prepared to defend our point of view; trust the inner voice and do not explain discrepancies away, but ask for clarification; insist that the responsibility for maintaining a healthy therapeutic relationship is shared equally between the therapist and the patient, and finally, that we need to stay alert, and avoid being hoisted by our own petard. But I had better explain what I mean. Again, cast your mind back to the early days, to when I began to feel, increasingly, more and more reluctant to work with Cordelia. What my own supervision, as well as the writing of this book, have made abundantly clear, is that I simply resented being manipulated by Cordelia into being this 'ideal therapist'. Yet, when Cordelia subsequently began sending me all those abusive letters, it gradually dawned on me that she was just repeating patterns of old; that although she very much wanted to have an ideal therapist, she equally felt compelled to manipulate this therapist into rejecting her, so that she could safely remain a victim. If I resented being manipulated into being an ideal therapist, you can bet that I certainly resented being manipulated into giving up on her – and the rest is history!

The fourth aspect placed under the spotlight are the books – without the books I would have been lost completely. They helped me to stay on a true, albeit at times invisible and perplexing, path. For instance, the book *Multiple Personality: An Exercise in Deception*, by Aldridge-Morris, encouraged me to stay on my guard and question the meaning of Cordelia's disclosures, instead of just blindly believing her and accept the accuracy of her reasoning, which would have trapped us both. The book by Bloch: *Assessment and Treatment of Multiple Personality and Dissociative Disorders*, gave me facts and symptoms gleaned from other patients with MPD, which in turn enabled me to trust the often demanding and bizarre machinations of a multiple system, and to believe Cordelia and assist her by feeding back informed opinions about what I saw and heard. However, since the books were my only source of information on how to unravel a multiple system, they have made me realise how limited their teaching actually can be. One of my patients in the creative writing group once wrote the following, 'Understanding is a hard-earned treasure that no book can impart.' On reflection, I most certainly agree with this observation. For sure, even though I had read the descriptions of how malevolent alter egos, for instance can cause havoc and dread, it still had not prepared me for the face to face confrontation with Martin, who was bent on revenge. Nor did it teach me how to stay one step ahead of Elizabeth, or negotiate with Geraldine, or win over Victoria so that they would work with Cordelia, rather than against her. I literally had to learn it the hard way – by simply using common sense, by just trusting my instincts and recalling everything I had learned, recollecting everything I had read. And, by remembering all I had experienced, especially the bad times, and letting myself feel again how these varied life events had affected me, though none could of course compare with the stress and sorrow Cordelia had suffered. On the other hand, regarding the books as the only expert in the field can prove to be an even bigger handicap, and therefore, my advice to anyone who happens to find themselves in a similar situation is naturally to read the books first but then to persevere and find like practitioners who can at least tell you – in plain language – what to expect, and what to do about it. Unfortunately (maybe because the concept of MPD has had such a chequered career?), some books in fact appear to have been written in order to impress, rather than just impart information, which can make them extremely difficult to read (religiously keeping in line with so many other textbooks). Then again, all textbooks are written with hindsight and therefore predict the known – but what can you do when a particular twist or unexpected event is not covered in the books? The answer of course – if indeed no one can advise you – is to learn it the hard way, through experience, through perseverance, and hope that your patient will literally 'survive the operation'. A precarious situation, to be avoided for sure!

In my opinion, as well as employing an eclectic approach, it is also important at times, to widen the search for answers. Indeed, to my surprise, I have found confirmation of my theories in such diverse books as *Child Abuse, the Educational Perspective*' by Peter Maher (1987), and *A Handbook for Tarot Prediction*, based upon Qabalistic methods written by Emily Peach (1991). The first book in fact described how one particular child, when drawing about the abuse she had suffered, had depicted herself with 'her eyes on top of her head', and was thus unable to see what was being done to her. Likewise, Cordelia's first drawing of herself, depicted her with her hands before her eyes. Whereas the second book enabled me to understand even better how the use of trance logic could indeed lead to 'cumulative and self-perpetuating errors': how not seeing oneself in the mirror being abused – could lead to seeing many other-selfs being abused instead. For sure, trance logic, by allowing the conscious part of the mind, the observing tabulating part of the mind, to dabble in a spot of conscious deduction – which is actually, 'the prerogative of the subconscious,' wrote Peach (1988, p.215). Notwithstanding the fact that these dabbles are usually rather ingenious deductions, these conscious deliberations, however, could leave the subconscious with no other choice but to come to the wrong conclusions, since it has effectively been fed false information.

Recall the hapless, duly hypnotised student, helping his lecturer to demonstrate trance logic. He was instructed by the hypnotist to cross the room but to disregard the table in the middle of the room, to believe that the table was in fact invisible. When the student was subsequently asked why did he not walk in a straight line across the room, if nothing stood in his way, he fabricated the following false information: 'I walked in a circle... because... I saw a penny on the floor!' Thus leaving his subconscious with no other choice perhaps, but to assume that the table must indeed be invisible – even though it knows it isn't. Likewise, once Cordelia had given her subconscious that first falsehood: 'the girl I can see being abused in the mirror by my father is not me.' It had no option but to uphold the lie! As described before, some can tolerate trance logic better than others, and certainly so, I presume, when your very life and sanity depends on it.

So, what of this particular book? Both authors simply hope that its pages and printed words will make the process of acquiring this precious treasure, aptly called 'understanding', a little bit easier for anyone; the reader, the therapist, the patient or the patient's relatives alike. However, apart from the opportunity to foster understanding, the writing of this book also served as a means to truly complete the therapeutic journey – though it was not intended as such. As I explained in the second chapter, the main reason for joining Cordelia in writing this book, had been in order to share my memories of her therapy with her, so that Cordelia would be able to complete the picture. However, as a result of sharing this information, the book has in fact allowed Cordelia to engage in what Colin Ross has called a 'post unification process', a means to 'incorporate new structures and non-dissociative coping skills' which my leaving at the particular stage of therapy Cordelia was at had of course prevented. Moreover, whenever any discrepancies occurred (such as the mix-up about deciding not to take Melleril) they tended to be woven into the next chapter, and thus provided Cordelia with the means to gain even more insight, overcome denial, or make amends.

Then again, the writing of this book, as well as being a valuable postintegration tool, has also been very cathartic for both of us. Speaking for myself, the opportunity to put the many years of therapy down on paper, to clarify my thoughts, to clear them out of my head and translate them into words, has been very healing and of course revealing. I certainly feel that I have benefited a great deal from doing so, irrespective of whether the book was ever going to be published, which has always been Cordelia's decision to make. As for Cordelia, apart from writing about her enduring struggle to be heard, writing about each one of the personalities, and putting it all down in black and white, has been a most impressive achievement, although it has of course also been very painful and indeed 'mind-blowing'. Some histories were certainly more involved than others, some histories were best forgotten, some histories were too distressing to contemplate – yet others seemed too outrageous, whereas others would make you sad, or mad, or ill. Cordelia nevertheless stuck with it and, personality by personality, she has put her past life into words – even though, at times, it was touch and go, and certain pages consequently went up in flames – literally!

Indeed, the reader might remember how Cordelia in fact gave the bluebell children to me when her therapy ended, in the form of a painting (as shown on the cover of this book), feeling as though they belonged more to her therapist than to her. By writing the sad tale of each personality, Cordelia has claimed them all back, has effectively reabsorbed what was projected, and has truly now made them, warts and all, her very own – although some she would rather still have kept safely in limbo. A truly remarkable achievement, considering she did most of this by herself, via her writing.

The fifth aspect this microscope has made all too clear is the fact that MPD raises more questions than it gives answers. For instance, is it really possible that one can truly leave one's body and observe what might be happening to it? Certainly, descriptions of near-death experiences by soldiers in battle, and those who have suffered a heart attack, for instance, would seem to indicate that we can. Moreover, according to a TV programme called The Mysterious Universe (on the Discovery Channel), those pilots who were exposed to a centrifugal force, and consequently would almost certainly have been hyperventilating, thereby reducing the flow of blood to the nervous system (in the same way an anxious person in extreme danger or in excessive pain would respond), likewise reported that at the point of losing consciousness, they had experienced travelling through a tunnel and saw a bright light which made them feel euphoric. They also described how it had all felt so very real, and how afterwards, they were able to observe themselves whilst walking behind themselves along the corridor.

Furthermore, MPD naturally also raised a number of questions about abuse. Why, for instance, is a certain child disliked or abused in a family, whereas the other siblings are not? Is it because these children were often struggling for survival, even before they were born? Is it because some were a replacement for an older sister or brother who recently died? Is it because they became a victim of the secret longing, the despair, the guilt feelings and the inevitable stress which can often follow such a life event? Are the very cries of the baby reminding the mother about her loss; reinforcing the belief that she is not a good enough mother? Or is it because the experience of sharing the womb with a twin, for instance, could make the growing foetus become aware of itself and others long before it is born? Certainly, Michael Fordham has suggested that the process of deintegration and reintegration might well start before the baby is born. Moreover, what then is the effect of losing such an other-self? Is it indeed, as Dr Hambling described in the foreword to this book, because some mothers do hate for the wrong reason? Or is it simply that some children are born at the wrong time, to the wrong parents, in the wrong family? Sadly enough, it is a fact that so many of the parents who do abuse their children did not have an easy life themselves, were equally abused, or did not really want this particular child. Besides, many of the mothers were often ill after the birth, were dominated by their partner or tended to become bizarre themselves in later life. And yet some parents, despite experiencing quite severe abuse themselves, as Cordelia's case so aptly illustrates, do not continue the pattern, do not pass on the sins of the father to the next generation. Still, why do some children who are abused, develop multiple personalities, whereas others in similar circumstances do not?

Is the experience of sexual and physical abuse the vital aspect, or is it the fact, that so many children who go on to develop MPD actually endured a near-death experience: they lost consciousness – thinking they were going to die, either at the moment their father almost choked them to death with his penis, or when the mother tried to smother them? And therefore, is it because they subsequently so often feared for their very life? Or is it because so many of these children were usually left on their own, for hours on end, without attention, without stimulation, so that they had no choice but to turn inwards, and find diversion inside their own mind? Undoubtedly, being left to your own devices at a very young age, and suffering a near-death experience into the bargain, must surely prime such a child in the art of dissociation. Dissociation in this instance meaning that at the point of losing consciousness, the subconscious (which I believe is the internal observer) interchanges with the conscious and for a while, becomes an external observer instead. In fact, I believe that we are never truly unconscious – only when the body has died, are we without any form of consciousness.

Be that as it may, dissociation, as I explained before, is a skill we can all achieve. Observing ourselves, leaving our bodies, seems to be just another step along this continuum. Indeed, when I first started to use a specific NLP exercise which requested the patients (prior to going into a deeper trance) to float out of their body and observe themselves sitting in the chair, or else watch themselves from an imaginary projector booth in a cinema, sitting in a seat in the cinema, watching themselves on the screen (in order to find a solution to a certain phobia), I duly expected most of my patients to tell me that they could not do so, and that I was the one, who needed therapy! But to my surprise, none of the patients ever said that they were unable to comply, and afterwards, when the observer had once again been duly reunited with the body, they all reported that they had indeed been able to observe themselves, whilst they completed the exercise. However, although it might indeed be a natural skill, it surely follows that when a child employs a form of dissociation at the extreme end of the scale, interchanges consciousness quite frequently, that the boundaries between what is real and imagined must become very permeable, making the creation of an internal world peopled by other-selfs not only feasible but also a lot easier to maintain. For sure, reality testing, along with logical thinking, ceases to be used, and what is internal becomes external, and the external becomes internal!

Then again, are excessive feelings of shame, guilt, perfectionism, being inordinately self-conscious, self-aware, self-centred, having a narcissistic inclination or a superior self-esteem the reason why one child will develop MPD, and not another? Are they the necessary ingredients, which promote the fabrication of such an elaborate smoke-screen? Or is it indeed, as Dr Hambling has so succinctly explained at the start of this book, the fact that there is a personality type which is inclined to be, not hysterical but histrionic – an 'entirely theatrical contrivance that adapts continually to circumstances with a view to manipulation, advantage, attention, dependency and control' – meaning, someone with a highly developed sense of drama, able to play any role required, who likes to impress and who 'lacks integrity, is double faced, and ignores the cost of duplicity'?

I am not convinced about the lack of integrity, etc. However, I could certainly subscribe to the notion of a 'dramatic personality'. Indeed, both Cordelia and I often used to joke together, that she should have been a 'diva, a prima donna, or a tragedienne'.

In any case, MPD certainly seemed to have brought out the scientist in both of us, in Cordelia as well as in her therapist, and as a result, the book is strewn with theories. How valid are these theories? Time alone might well be able, to answer that question. However, what these theories have highlighted is that the quest to understand the mind is far from over. Nevertheless, every detailed account of the struggle to be one person must add to the collective knowledge, even though it is a bit like donating your body and your mind to science whilst you are still alive; not a proposition many of us would be prepared to accept!

The most important benefit of the varied theories is the fact that they each endorsed the undeniable truth, that Cordelia had been the architect and builder of the multiple system, and that therefore, fundamentally speaking, she was no different from anyone else: we all create our own ego; we all have to learn to balance 'the children within' (the primitive 'id'), with 'the others' (the mature 'ego'), and with those ever-present, relentless critical voices, 'the persecutors' (the introjected 'super-ego'). Although, Cordelia was at first rather reluctant to consider herself as 'no different from anyone else!'

The obvious drawback of course of searching for answers, of reducing everything to a theory, is that it can all become so very remote, so very scientific, and no longer has anything to do with life, with sorrow, with pain, with distress, with abuse. Consequently, the message of these courageous books is in danger of being missed altogether; namely, that any abusive environment hurts people far more than we allow ourselves to realise – even though our everyday language clearly illustrates that we in fact know better. Indeed, such phrases as turning a blind eye; going through the motions; opting out; behaving like a robot, like a zombie; lives in a world of his own; he is always play-acting; she is a drama queen; lives on another planet; out of this world; lives in cuckoo land, on cloud nine; he is for the birds; there are no lights on in the house; is anybody home? She hasn't got a full deck; he's got a screw loose etc., would seem to indicate that the concept of living in a make-believe, internal, secret world is not only familiar to us, but also, that those who do so tend to be viewed by society as rather mad or eccentric – which in turn can of course ensure that the secret world becomes a hidden world, and hence is never challenged.

Then again after reading through the previous chapters, it became all too clear, that in the process of trying to get some answers we had in fact created our own language, as well as borrowed some jargon which might actually prove to be a handicap rather than facilitate understanding. Hence, we decided to include the specific meaning of certain words. It is a rather imposing list, one, which the reader might well wish to skip and read afterwards, though it does highlight how complex and demanding it all was.

When we used the word switching, for instance, we meant that a certain personality, after being in conscious control of the body, had stepped aside and allowed another personality to take its place - in the same way we can all switch from one social role to another. However, switching in this instance meant that the new personality was amnesic, had no knowledge of what had been said or what had been happening prior to the moment he or she stepped into the limelight. Being amnesic is probably the most difficult and certainly the most unbelievable aspect of MPD for most people to accept. Yet when it is viewed in terms of the internal world, when you approach it with the same kind of closed feedback loop, with the same [child] logic the patient uses, it does make sense. In fact, amnesia is a most crucial aspect and appears to be the mechanism which allows each personality to 'isolate their specific unpleasant memories from the rest of the personality' something that, according to Freud, we can all achieve.

As far as Cordelia is concerned, it certainly enabled her to maintain the individuality of a certain personality and reinforce their separateness and truly believe that they were real. Separate personalities imply real people. Real people meant they could have their own names, they could make independent decisions. Moreover, certain other-selfs could not know what another personality had been up to, or what he or she had just revealed. They had to be amnesic; ignorant of each other, or else they were a fraud, they were not real. Amnesia on the other hand, can of course also be induced by hypnosis. What's more, amnesia is not uncommon. Indeed, we can all forget, at times right in the middle of a sentence, or why we went all this way upstairs? The following list explains how we both understood and utilised the varied (jargon) words:

Original personality: the original child – before Cordelia began to split herself into separate other-selfs.

Personality: one other-self, displaying its own characteristics, with its own set of behaviours, pertinent history and specific memories. Personality could of course also mean the united person: all parts working as one. (We all have many parts.)

Non-edible objects: the introjected parts of the important others which the Self was unable to stomach or refused to acknowledge as a part of its ego. Consequently, the Self spat out/projected; turned these Self reflections, these non-edible objects into other-selfs.

Trance logic: the conscious creation of a falsehood, thereby feeding the subconscious the wrong information, which in turn would of course produce cumulative and self-perpetuating errors: i.e. in Cordelia's case, not seeing herself reflected in the bedroom mirror when her father abused her meant that another person was being abused. And if this other person was real, then all the following other-selfs were also real. Trance logic thus, motivated by narcissistic feelings such as shame, guilt and perfectionism, was the mechanism which ensured that the other-selfs became real people, each one becoming a person, with its own name, history, memories, characteristics and specific function. Trance logic consequently also meant isolation: the unacceptable world is permanently shut out, and the person becomes sensitive only to stimuli from within.

Topsy turvy world: whatever the imagination has created becomes a fact; the imaginative right side of the brain is left in sole charge to produce certain ideas, perceptions and guidelines (allowed to produce its own brand of magical/logical thinking), whereas reasoning, logical deduction with the left side of the brain, literally goes out of the window. For sure, a very creative means to dissociate oneself from the real world.

Dissociation: switching rapidly from one personality to another without being aware of doing so, so that nothing in fact would make any sense. It could also mean being spaced out, going into a trance: looking at others and the world from 'within a goldfish bowl'. However, it could also mean 'literally expanding in the bath; becoming one with the bath; filling the bath' – and 'floating out of the body; floating up to the ceiling' and observing what is happening, interchanging consciousness, or else it could simply mean, to 'fly away with the birds'. Dissociation, however, could also mean distributing pain, sadness and unbearable memories around the various parts, or retreating into a blind spot: not seeing anything; closing your eyes; no longer being present, retreating 'behind the mirror'.

Blind spot: shelter from internal and external stimulation, safety from memories; no longer hurting, no longer remembering, no longer seeing the pictures of the past.

Trance, thus, or auto hypnosis: escape strategy; a phylogenetic mechanism of defence: a third alternative to fight or flight – to freeze, to remain immobile, in the same way animals used to do in order to avoid being killed. Auto hypnosis, in addition, also meant, an 'unconscious mental process' – a means to produce altered states of consciousness; a means to interchange consciousness. Interchanging consciousness: the subconscious (the internal observer) has switched places with the conscious and becomes an external observer instead; able to leave the body.

Leaving the body: conscious awareness of observing oneself, especially when experiencing unbearable physical or emotional pain; feeling utterly powerless; scared of being killed; scared of being left alone; being abandoned, or when reliving the past. An extreme form of dissociation. A psychological response to demanding conditions, possibly achieved via hyperventilation.

Psychosis: 'going into a psychotic state', going into a safe place, or being sucked into the black hole; becoming disconnected, the world becoming distant, imploding or travelling backwards through a tunnel. It could, however, also mean being mad; travelling back in time or into the future; being locked up in the asylum; being pulled into the abyss, which could swallow you up so that you no longer existed at all.

Going into a psychotic state, however, should not be confused with the psychotic experiences of schizophrenics or manic depressives – although they will closely mimic the condition and may well present themselves as such and thus influence a potential diagnosis. The temporary psychotic states experienced by MPD are yet another form of dissociation; a means to get some respite, a means to remain sane. Mad Cordelia in fact would often act as the safety valve on behalf of the system; by allowing only a small part of Cordelia to be mad, to enact the madness of her internal and external world, her core or centre would remain unaffected. As Cordelia has described elsewhere, she needed a sound mind to maintain the system.

Black hole: being really ill, having lost it, being insane. Yet it could also mean the bottomless pit, the 'fruitless search for love'.

Being crazy: seeing things, hearing voices, being possessed. Although once amnesia had been exposed, it also meant still seeing the other-selfs; still believing them to be real – rather than just images created by the mind's eye.

Being sick: doing weird, bizarre things.

Splitting: keeping the head of the abuser, as well as one's own head, very separate from the rest of the body. It meant splitting the person into either a good or a bad person.

Splitting the personality: isolating the other-selfs from each other, thereby ensuring that their specific memories could be compartmentalised.

To act out: behaving according to the script and the designated role ascribed to a certain other-self; to speak and dress according to how the mind had perceived a certain personality, a certain character.

A character: the way society would generally envisage a certain kind of person, and how such a person was meant to behave.

As-if people: another name for the other-selfs, which highlighted the fact that they were not real people, but perceptions, make-believe creations of Cordelia's mind.

Hallucination: fabrication of Cordelia's mind; 'neurotic falsification of reality'. Negative hallucinations: no longer seeing oneself; the Self had disappeared (behind the mirror). Positive hallucinations: seeing other children reflected in the mirror instead. However, seeing the children in the corners of the room for instance, were also wish-fulfilments, duly achieved by having abandoned reality testing.

Coming apart: rapidly switching from one part to another – but now being aware of doing so.

Falling apart: 'being smashed into a thousand pieces', becoming consciously aware that all the parts are separate, had become unglued. Falling apart thus meant that the dreams, the nightmares, the flashbacks were for real and that the self-image, 'the jigsaw puzzle' Cordelia saw in the sky that day after her therapy and in the cracked mirror all those years ago before being admitted to the asylum, were all true, and hence that 'the carefully constructed life' had been no more than an artful deception.

Relapsing: returning to dissociative coping strategies, including creating new other-selfs.

Dissolving: all the parts were coming together, no longer being separate, becoming just one person.

Being one: no longer being able to switch without conscious awareness; no longer employing amnesia, no longer being able to delegate pain, feelings, memories around the system – in short, being responsible for one's actions, thoughts and behaviour, no longer deceiving the Self.

Deception: the employment of trance logic; not questioning, not testing reality, 'not being consciously aware, that a multiple system is ruling your life'.

The System: the internal make-believe world; the internal organisation of the self and the other-selfs, including the three devils and the internal and external observer – its primary aim being the survival of the person. The system moreover was also visualised as a precarious house of cards, held together with deception, trance logic, amnesia, shame, veneer and denial.

Bluebell Children: all the other-selfs being present at the same time; belonging to one person; visualising the system as one family with many members, each one exercising its voice, each one contributing to the overall welfare of the person.

The Self: the primary unit, the original person. The one who created the other-selfs. It is nonetheless also the 'part that disappeared'.

To disappear: incarceration; the Self is locked away for safe-keeping; it is in exile; no longer plays a vital role in the day to day life of the person. 'The part that disappeared' actually refers to the moment when the Self realised that rescue by others, such as a father, a mother or a nurse, was no longer a viable option, and that there was indeed no other choice left but to rely solely on oneself in order to survive; although in Cordelia's case, hope ensured that 'it' kept popping back, testing out the waters to see, if it was safe to return (a peculiar aspect of MPD it seems, which I have encountered in various biographies).

The child within: the young Cordelia, the original child, before she split herself into Peter and Rosalind.

The helpers: passive obedience, parts such as Peter, Rosalind, Angela, Mary, Gillian and Anna, who assisted Cordelia to endure the reality of her life.

The defenders: aggressive disobedience, such parts as Elizabeth and Esther who tended to fight back.

The friends, the adults: wish-fulfilment, rite of passage or a developmental stage.

The persecutors: the three devils. They were the introjected important others such as the mother, grandmother and brother (introjection meaning the 'unconscious incorporation of external ideas into one's mind' *Oxford Dictionary*). They were also the parts that were 'spat out' twice. Not only had the Self projected them, turned them into other-selfs, but when they subsequently turned into persecutors and became copies of the original role models, they were duly banished from the personality altogether, and thereafter were perceived as living in the body of the mother, brother and grandmother. They were the voices who constantly berated the parts that were borderline.

Borderline: a part in a raw state that prefers to be on the edge of the personality, which enables it (luckily enough, usually only temporarily) to take complete control of the personality, utterly dismay the other-selfs and the Self; becoming paranoid, defensive, blinkered, narcissistic, superior, vain, cruel, and destructive; parts which do not relinquish their fringe position without a fight or a good reason, and mostly need to be kept firmly under control for the sake of the personality, and the welfare of the person.

Raw state: primitive, without veneer, without sophistication, without conscience; evil, but not in a religious sense, more the kind that can pull the wings of butterflies (a state we all to some degree might well have lived through when we were children).

Victoria's veneer: glossing over the abuse, maintaining outside appearances, paving over the cracks beneath the surface; providing guidance for the children within; the 'glue' keeping the system together; defying discovery; securing normality (at any cost). Behaving like an adult; the mask hiding the raw state. Main agent preventing the person from having conscious awareness, that he/she is in fact a 'multiple'. Victoria was effectively the one who controlled the information from coming in, or from being released.

The observers: Rebekah was the internal observer; the one who watched over the system; she was the keeper, the guardian of the secrets; the one who ensured that Cordelia would in fact never forget what had happened to her. She was the voice of the subconscious, who tended to write poetry/stories/letters in order to let Cordelia herself and the real world know the truth about the abuse and the complex way in which Cordelia coped. But since the subconscious could not openly contradict the information (the falsehoods) it received from the conscious, she tended to do so in secret, or via indirect means. (A crucial aspect, which I believe, is the fundamental reason, why a multiple system is so enduring. A conscious lie, means a shackled subconscious; one which is unable to expose the as-if quality of a given situation; one which has no choice but to go along with the make-believe world, even though it knows, that it is a lie.)

Alice, however, was the spokesperson, the external observer. Like Rebekah, she equally watched over the system and tended to write letters, invariably reporting fairly accurately on how she perceived a given situation, although she would usually not pursue the matter if her letters were not acknowledged. Instead, she would rather take action on behalf of the system, such as securing admission to the hospital whenever Cordelia could no longer cope, or had once again tried to kill herself, so clearly illustrated by the wrong dates duly recorded by the nurses on her admission forms and the letter of the Casualty officer, where Cordelia was admitted for that ill-fated overdose in September. They all record her age as six years older (Alice in fact, always believed, that she was six years older than Cordelia).

The protectors: Geraldine was the paranoid protector, the one who mistrusted the world and ensured that Cordelia was forever on her guard. Martin on the other hand, although he was also a protector, helped the system by being ruthless and unforgiving, whereas Felicity, yet another protector, kept the other children safe by flirting and encouraging sexual overtures in order to try and control men. Each part of course created more problems than they solved!

The mad part: Delia II was the unacceptable schizophrenic part; the one who was mad; the child who was sent to the asylum and therefore needed to be kept hidden as much as possible. Consequently, she also endured long periods of clinical depression on behalf of the system, when memories were pressing to be heard or threatened to overwhelm Cordelia.

The person: the competent face to the world. Delia I was the part who had been in conscious control of Cordelia's body and mind most of the time; ever since the day in fact, she had been created; ever since Cordelia had met her future husband. She had been the face to the world; the one who had lived Cordelia's adult life for her. Although Delia I was of course fooled herself by Victoria, most people who met her would nevertheless confirm that she was wholly convincing, wholly persuasive, and the main reason why others – including her husband – would not suspect that anything was so dreadfully amiss. Delia I fooled them all – including herself – most of the time!

Other words such as the ideal rescuer, ideal therapist, ideal father, substitute mother, real father, make believe mother, etc., of course speak for themselves. Whereas, some words were action words, describing the therapeutic process; yet others simply depicted specific aspects of Cordelia's unique system – such words as:

Magic mirror: mental mechanism which allowed Cordelia to close her eyes, and see the other children; means to cope with the feelings of shame. Effectively representing Bion's 'object' which indeed assisted her so convincingly, to 'un-think, mis-understand, and establish lies and hallucinations'.

Assistant: (Alice) first imaginary helper; means to allow Cordelia to pretend that she was not a 'dirty child', means to allow her to disappear; means to keep self-esteem intact. Alice in Wonderland could make herself small, could pretend she was not there. Cordelia, by pretending to be 'Alice', could do the same.

The very first thing: the beginning of the pertinent history of one of the other-selfs; the very first experience – anything – a smell, a taste, a touch, a sensation, an image; the very first thing, 'it' can see, or hear. Either at the moment of creation when the other-self came, was invented by Cordelia, or the moment of birth, when the invented personality ceased to be 'make-believe' and became a real person, an autonomous structure, separate from the others, acquiring its own name and specific function.

Conscious control: one part being in charge, in control of the body, directing the actions, what to do, how to behave, what to say.

Turning: becoming a persecutor, behaving like the original person on whom the personality was based; turning on oneself. For example, Geraldine becoming as vindictive as the original grandmother used to be, and inflicting the same kind of distress on certain other-selfs (thereby of course also harming herself). Turning, however, could also mean turning back into a helper, working with the rest of the system, instead of trying to remain independent; no longer claiming to be the true self, the true personality, in sole charge of the system; the only one who is living in the body; no longer trying to kill the other personalities.

Flashbacks: sudden vivid memories; not just seeing the pictures of the past, but actually re-experiencing them; feeling again the penis inserted in the mouth, choking, vomiting; feeling the cushion being pressed over the face, smothering, fainting, yet knowing that the experiences belong to the past.

Scenarios: re-enactment of past events, as though they are happening for real, triggered by a name, a similar aspect (i.e. a haircut); past and present merging; time becomes distorted, no longer certain where the event belongs.

Homework: analysing the day's therapy; writing a daily diary, recording thoughts, sensations and observations.

Narrations: reading the diary, letters, therapy notes out loud, for the benefit of the children within; to inform the internal system; means to upset the status quo; means to awaken the left side, as well as the right side of the brain: to promote reasoning and confront the many discrepancies and anomalies; means to reinforce the authority of the therapist.

Found out: one part revealing itself in an indirect way, usually via the telephone.

Going inside (confronting): accessing the system; going into a light trance and asking the various personalities a set of questions; encouraging them to draw the internal pictures; getting answers (light trance meaning turning the attention inwards, in the same way we might perhaps do whilst listening to music, or when daydreaming).

Status quo: maintaining the internal organisation; preventing outside information from disrupting the established order.

Sabotage: resistance, side-tracking: certain parts (usually the borderline parts, or Victoria) disrupt the therapy either by seeking admission or via illness, in order to safeguard the secret and maintain the status quo: literally keeping the Self out of harm's way (which can of course be interpreted in different ways).

Turmoil: a cycle of behaviours which tended to manifest itself whenever a painful truth had surfaced, or memories were pressing to be heard, including sabotage, denial. 'The abuse was a figment of Cordelia's wild imagination'. Rapid switching; dissociation; retreating into the black hole; psychosis. 'I see the dead face of my mother, hear sounds coming from a jug.' Clinical depression; physical illness; self-harm; self-doubt; self-hate; overdose; using TCP – disinfecting herself; blinding headaches; anonymous phone calls; pleading notes, etc., usually followed by paranoia; excessive anger; angry letters or angry phone calls, etc., which tended to break the cycle and led to acceptance of the truth. A truly exacting cycle of behaviours, which of course also included due manipulation of her varied 'insurance policies' in order to test out their loyalty and reliability, usually by giving selective or conflicting information about certain aspects of her treatment and medication, invariably resulting in Dr C once again, having to engage in clarifying correspondence with, for instance, her GP and myself. For sure, turmoil was a very demanding, often frustrating and bewildering part of treatment. Yet it was also a very necessary and salutary part of the process, giving Cordelia due time and space in order to incorporate some very unpalatable and earth-shattering truths, as well as enable her to give these life events their long overdue and rightly deserved mantle of drama and respect. Turmoil, thus, was effectively a roundabout way to allow Cordelia to declare quite categorically, to herself and the world, 'What happened to me, matters.'

Clicked: the sensation of feeling the switch from one personality to another.

Blank periods: loss of time – gaps in the day.

Compartmentalised: distributing sensations and memories amongst the various parts.

Illness: denial. As a child: escape from the abuse, as an adult: escape from the memories of the abuse; means to get extra care; means to silence the three devils.

Medication: illness, comfort, manipulation, self-harm, overdose, suicide, drugged state, sleep, forgetting; means to maintain 'insurance policies'; means to keep memories at bay and maintain the system; means to cause chaos since adult parts tend to react physically to certain medications quite differently from how a child part might react (i.e., anti-depressants are tolerated by one, yet can cause another part to have an allergic reaction).

Characteristics: idiosyncratic way of being, posture, tone of voice, mannerisms, clothes, handwriting, etc. (i.e., only some personalities needed glasses to read).

Consumed: swallowed up by her mother; believing that mother and daughter were one, not separate, but living in each other's body, which meant that the boundaries were very blurred.

Boundaries: restrictions, authority of the therapist, safety of rules, being separate from others, defining oneself, responsibility for one's own actions, reality of the real world.

Important others, such as the father and mother, were of course, the main characters in the drama of transference, whereas the significant others might be anyone involved in caring for the person. They were also called 'insurance policies', meaning, potential rescuers. Rescuers meaning, persons you can trust. Trust meaning, being predictable.

Power: apparent ability to call forth a certain personality, either by asking for it in person, or simply by mentioning its name (the power of the therapist, and I presume, the power of anyone, who happens to mention the right name).

Return: The Self returns! The Self reclaiming its executive position. The Self bridging the gap between the right side of the brain, and the left side of the brain, restoring the right order; the subconscious once again making logical deductions based on accurate information received from the conscious; information flowing from one to the other; sentience/feelings no longer kept separate from access/understanding: a united mind.

Sense of Self: recognition; able to recognise oneself; know oneself.

Real scream: knowledge, fully aware of all the truth.

And finally there is the word nothingness, meaning that the eyes of another can see you but do not recognise you – even though they have known you for a number of years. Nothingness, however, also means that a particular person looking in the mirror, looking at photographs, etc., does not recognise her or himself; inhabits a no-man's land where the soul, the Self appears lost, or is in hiding. In my opinion, nothingness means multiple personality disorder, or perhaps more precisely, dissociative disorder, which has become the preferred description. For sure, this baffling word, this scary word, which according to the *Oxford Dictionary* means 'non existence, worthlessness, triviality, insignificance', more than any other word in fact, sums up the devastation the condition of MPD can leave in its wake. According to Oliver Sacks writing in the *Oxford Companion to the Mind*, the very idea of nothingness is in fact inconceivable, and as soon as it does occur, it tends to be 'instantly banished from memory and mind', because the experience is so abhorrent.

Indeed, when I allowed myself to remember examples of nothingness, I wholeheartedly agreed with him and could not help wondering about how perplexing the experience of nothingness actually must be for a very young child. Who knows, I speculated, adding yet another theory to swell the ranks, perhaps this was the very reason why a child would begin to use a tangible something – a something which could give the child the necessary feedback that he/she was a somebody, and not a no-thing, since a nothing would not be able to hold and feel a something such as a blanket or a teddy bear, which the therapy books would normally call a 'transitional object' (rather on the lines of Descartes; I feel... 'therefore I am').

However, theorising aside, as Oliver Sacks points out, most of us at some time or another have in fact experienced nothingness, i.e. when lying in a certain position and one of our arms fell asleep. Even though we can touch the arm, know it is a part of us, it feels as though it is not there. Likewise, when a spinal anaesthetic is used, for instance in childbirth, the lower half of the body feels gone. Then again, as one of my own examples has taught me, a visit to the dentist can leave us feeling as though we no longer have a top or bottom lip, though we can of course still use them to 'have a rinse'. A most unpleasant experience indeed! Moreover, continued Sacks, anyone who has experienced a stroke, a tumour, or an injury, especially to the right half of the brain, can experience nothingness whereby the corresponding affected part of the body no longer feels as though it exists – yet it is still very much connected, still very visible.

When I first read this particular example of nothingness, it naturally made me wonder if there was a possible connection between the severe headaches Cordelia used to complain about on the right side of her head, and the fact that she equally tended to describe her body as 'separate, numb', as an 'inert, senseless nothing', as something which is 'non-existent'. However, what is more significant, I feel, is that she also used to experience her soul, her centre, her Self as 'being lost', as 'being nothing but a void'. This truly is inconceivable for most of us. And yet, as Cordelia 's drawings so graphically depicted, for some, such horror, such nothingness, is all too real: the head is divorced from the trunk; the Self is divorced from the other-selves, from its ego.

'Having a body,' asserted Oliver Sacks (quite rightly famous for his book *The Man who Mistook his Wife for a Hat*), 'having anything, depends on one's nerves.' The nervous system is the 'transformer' that converts reality into ideality, ideality into reality. However, if having a body meant nothing but pain and distress, it surely becomes quite understandable, that some children make the decision to tamper with this transformer. Indeed, as Cordelia and others have so graphically described, in a desperate attempt to shut down the neural traffic, they simply stop feeling; they stop seeing the body as one's own, and banish the Self to a 'dark place', duly replacing 'it' and the body with nothingness. Unfortunately, as the previous pages have highlighted, the price of such deception is high indeed, since opting for nothingness (in trying to avoid the reality, the pain, the truth of one's life), this 'terrifying transient annihilation', as Sacks calls it, this nothingness can so easily become a permanent fixture, duly resisting all attempts to banish it from the mind. Indeed nothingness, described Oliver Sacks, when it occurs, far from being transient, becomes 'endless – a most unwelcome part of its peculiar horror'.

For sure, creating multiple other-selfs may be an amazing solution. The 'manufacture of lies', as Wilfred Bion proposed, could indeed be called 'an employment of positive ingenuity', it certainly is no easy option in the long run, nor is the therapy which is needed to untangle it all – which leads me on, to yet other aspects to be clarified, i.e. such vital questions as, does therapy work, does it need to be such a lengthy process, and is it cost effective? Surely what the account of Cordelia 's therapy journey has highlighted is the fact that therapy not only can work but also, that the therapy journey could have been a lot shorter. Indeed, Cordelia 's therapy worked. But why? As well as drawing up a list of why therapy took so long, we naturally also drew up a list as to why it worked – although this particular list is a lot shorter, yet it speaks volumes. This is how Cordelia compiled it:

> Reasons why it worked:
> Desire: to get better – or change.
> Husband at home – support
> Stickability even when everything was against me
> Because of deep attachment to the therapist.
> 1 therapist immovable in every way.

Certainly, if it had not been for Cordelia's 'stickability', I doubt whether this therapy journey would have reached the ending it has. Working with MPD, as I have quoted elsewhere, might indeed be one of the most demanding endeavours a therapist can undertake, it can, however, not compare with actually having to live through the memories of abuse again – or having to own the abuse – or coming to terms with everything else, such ownership entails. 'Stickability', therefore, is indeed crucial – provided, of course, it is employed for the right reasons. It is quite a different proposition altogether when a patient is in therapy for years and years, and endures memories, flashbacks, pain and sorrow, solely in an unconscious attempt to maintain a substitute relationship with an ideal therapist/parent – although more often than not, transference tends to be the fly in the ointment, in this kind of therapy.

So, it worked! But, was it cost effective? It seems almost inhuman to talk in terms of money when we are discussing the treatment of people who have suffered such appalling abuse. However, the real world has its own rules, and hence monies certainly do dictate whether certain types of treatment are available or not. However, a study by Colin Ross and Vikram Dua seems to indicate that the diagnosis and subsequent treatment of MPD with 'specific psychotherapy appears to be cost-effective'. Be that as it may, the authors of this study also described that the usual prescription tends to be 'benign neglect', thus saving the 'unnecessary expense of prolonged "treatment" for a non-existent disorder'. And yet there are so many patients (usually diagnosed as a personality disorder) who come and go through the system, through the 'revolving door', who receive costly outpatient treatment; have many short admissions and expensive medication but never really benefit from any of it. Certainly makes you wonder, although it naturally does not mean that they would all suffer from a dissociative disorder. What's more, even if they did, it would still not mean that psychotherapy was the right option. Indeed, the treatment of MPD is not so clear cut. As well as the cost in terms of money, yet another cost needs to be taken into consideration, not just the cost to the therapist, although it is an important factor, but more precisely, also the cost to the patient and her/his family. 'Stickability', whether it is exercised by the therapist or the patient, does not come cheap, and may exact too high a price on all concerned.

Nevertheless, when a patient is prepared to unravel the truth and stay the course, when eventually he or she is able to unveil the other-selfs, feelings of awe, amazement, as well as feelings of relief, hope, appeasement, and gratification, are all in evidence. In fact, despite the years of pain these other-selfs have in store for the patient, there is no better word which will describe this mix of emotions than the one Melanie Klein used when she talked about 'the pleasure… of discovering little known parts of oneself, repressed, split off, or not realised in one way or another'. Although she was obviously not talking about other-selfs, but presumably, about parts of the ego. Moreover, if the patient thereafter is able to allow the other-selfs to tell their particular tale, to share their precious secrets, to unite and let the true Self return from its self-imposed exile, there can be no bigger reward than knowing that it has indeed all been worth it!

How then could Cordelia's therapy journey have been shorter? With hindsight of course it is easy to say, if only Cordelia and I could have been more honest with each other right from the beginning. If only the boundaries had been clearer. If only she had been able to answer her consultant's questions instead of delegating it to Zillah! If only she had picked a therapist, a consultant, a hospital which specialised in MPD. If only there was no stigma attached to MPD, Cordelia might have been able to let her internal and external observer insist that others listen, hear the truth and procure for her the right kind of treatment, etc. However, such 'if only' observations now seem rather perverse, and yet they also describe how the lengthy process, could have been reduced.

First and foremost, previous experience of MPD is obviously a major asset. However, if there is no previous experience, being alert to the possibility of MPD, and when in doubt, insisting on a second opinion from an experienced practitioner, must surely be a second best. Secondly, due recognition of the fact that a multiple system operates in rather complex and confusing ways, often contradicting itself, may well shorten the therapy journey by many years. For instance, a multiple system will invariably protect the patient by withholding information about the secret world, and sabotage the patient's conscious awareness; literally keep the patient in the dark. At the same time, however, the patient may also demonstrate to the therapist that sometimes he/she is aware and knows that something is very amiss; knows that there is indeed 'a deeper level of disturbance'. A most peculiar aspect of MPD, which in itself could of course inhibit due diagnosis, since it tends to create the impression, that the patient is trying to con the therapist. And yet, within these contradictions lies its resolution.

The realisation that MPD in essence is but a deception, that initially it was but a conscious act to manipulate and conceal the truth, a deliberate falsification of reality rather than a true belief or a true state of affairs, ultimately makes it possible for the patient to correct his/her thinking. Indeed, if there was no level of awareness at all, if the patient truly was oblivious, such realisation could not occur; healing would not be possible. Nevertheless, as I have explained elsewhere, the use of trance logic may well prevent the patient from confronting many anomalies and could make it impossible for the patient to tell the whole truth. Hence, the therapist, may well have to be the one who breeches the defences. The therapist may well have to be the one who makes it feasible to explore the possibility of other-selfs. Such a decision by the therapist, however, requires due awareness of potential iatrogenic dangers, and something Harold Merskey called prior preparation: the widespread knowledge about how to fake a multiple system, gained from the dramatisation of certain books such as *Sybil*.

In Cordelia's case, we finally achieved this all-important breakthrough, by reading her early notes, which clearly highlighted the lack of progress.

The third aspect which could considerably shorten the therapy journey is the manner in which the therapist is able to relate to each personality. Some books advocate that it is necessary that the therapist gets to know each person in detail – some even suggest that it is important to allow the children to play, and hence will provide toys for them should they appear during a therapy session. However, I believe that it is imperative that the therapist in no way whatsoever colludes with the frame of reference of the patient. Indeed, providing toys should not be confused with using toys in order to enable a child personality, finally, to reveal its secrets. The personalities are as-if people, they are not real, even though they feel very real to the patient. Providing toys, sweets, trips to a fairground, a birthday party, or a birthday card etc., for a specific child, I believe, can only succeed in making this as-if child be perceived as even more real than it already was, and could ensure that the patient stays firmly attached to its own particular wonderland, or else remains a victim of transference.

It surely follows that if the therapist in the act of catering for a child personality succeeds in providing a measure of the kind of childhood, the kind of love the patient has missed out on, that the patient is going to be loath to give up believing that its internal people are real. Besides, I also believe that when the therapist relates to the personalities as 'real people', it is extremely difficult not to reinforce the original split and deepen the gulf between the good parts and the bad parts, thus ensuring that 'being one' becomes a truly difficult goal to achieve. For sure, some personalities are easier to love than others, and rightly or wrongly, those who feel less loved, less valued, will not give up their acquired position within the system without a very good reason. Coming to terms with the fact that the carefully constructed life has been nothing but an artful deception is not an easy task, and the patient will gladly embrace anything, will use any reason, any excuse which will prevent him or her from having to do so. Eventually, the therapy might indeed enable the adult to reason like an adult; might succeed in getting the patient to test out the reality of its inner world. And the patient may well allow the Self to return to its rightful place. However, it could take many years to do so. The answer, as I have explained elsewhere, is to respect each part, give them each their due recognition, but relate to them as though they were real whilst reinforcing the fact that they are perceptions, make-believe people with a specific function, a specific role to play, who each have a story to tell – a rather impressive kind of make-believe at that, but one that is not real. In contrast, Cordelia 's therapy has certainly demonstrated that coming to terms with the reality of a multiple system, once it is revealed, need not take years and years, bearing in mind of course that no two cases of MPD will ever be the same.

Moreover, in my opinion, the following aspects are just as vital for reducing the overall length of time; such provisions, as finding a way around the stigma, debunking dissociation, and engaging in a journey of discovery together; setting precise boundaries of course; letting all parts of the patient know what the rules are. This will not only make the therapy journey shorter, but will certainly make it safer for all concerned, as well as establishing the authority of the therapist. For sure, asking the patient to 'go inside' and confirm whether all its parts agree with a certain rule or decision, may prove to be most enlightening. It also goes without saying that regular supervision is essential. Then again, Cordelia's therapy seems to indicate that a time limit may also be required, in order to motivate essential risk-taking; a deadline acting as a 'now or never' stimulus to reveal all.

Naturally, confronting amnesia is a vital aspect, which we achieved in Cordelia's case via her drawings, diary, and my therapy notes. Likewise Cordelia's homework proved to be a safe short cut. I am of course also well aware that the fact that we were able to work together five days a week is a facility which is not usually available, yet it ensured continuity, thus avoiding repetition and blatant memory loss. Of course, due medical care by a GP or consultant is needed, certainly if medication is involved; preferably someone who has a working knowledge of MPD, since it is a unique feature of MPD, as James Bloch has explained, that adult parts and child parts will in fact react quite differently to certain medication. Hospitalisation may also be a necessary option and could give the patient some respite, provided due communication takes place between all involved. Likewise, regular feedback sessions with the patient's partner or main support is a vital aspect. So is the provision of a life line, a telephone link which the patient can use when he or she is in extreme danger.

Then again, Colin Ross, in *Multiple Personality, Diagnosis, Clinical Features and Treatment*, has devoted a large part of his book to describing how to conduct a dissociative disorders interview and has included several check-lists for patient and therapist alike.

Why then is it important to try and reduce the length of time? Apart from the rather obvious reason, to avoid going round and round in circles, as

Cordelia's therapy has highlighted, a shorter therapy journey will make treatment of MPD less of an ordeal for patient and therapist alike, and of course less costly, thus making it a viable option. Reduce the length of time, reduces the cost. Reduce the cost, and treatment becomes affordable. Affordable treatment means more practitioners who could gain the necessary skills. More skill means more patients may get the right diagnosis and specific treatment. Specific treatment means better treatment. And so on...

However, since this last chapter is an attempt to be wiser after the event, it needs to be said that the aforementioned aspects which are designed to reduce the length of treatment will of course only be effective provided the practitioner is indeed able to recognise that he or she is dealing with a potential diagnosis of MPD. What Cordelia's lengthy therapy has in fact aptly clarified is that initially, my training as a therapist, rather than assist me, actually handicapped me. In fact, looking back, I can now see how I doggedly stuck to the conventional rules governing a therapeutic relationship, even though I was aware that I was somehow stumbling along in the dark. And yet the intense transference, the inordinate fear about being abandoned, and the fixed belief that I would be cruel to her once Dr M. had left, as well as the tales of the friend who made anonymous phone calls to the counsellor, or the strange phone calls to the clinic, etc., should have made me doubt what I had learned. Indeed, the fact that Cordelia disguised her voice whenever she phoned the clinic or else would speak French and Arabic; the mysterious notes left in her car by somebody else, her many letters, and the way she would jump from one topic to another, from an accusation to a declaration of love; the 'spacing out' during her therapy, the drastic changes in mood and behaviour, the interpretations which did not match the truth, as reported by the nurses, as well as the constant repetitions of the tales of abuse, and the sudden very knowledgeable and insightful observations about her dependency and transference, only to revert back to normal, I now know, were all symptoms of dissociation.

As it was, quite early on in the course of Cordelia's therapy (see the chapter entitled Boundaries), I did try to introduce the possibility that MPD might be the right diagnosis, and had informed Cordelia's consultant at the time of my misgivings. But since Cordelia once again successfully managed to produce her friend, the moment was lost. When eventually the light did dawn, by then transference was so acute that it became a case of 'better the devil you know', rather than change therapist, change to someone who has worked with MPD – even though it would have been the better decision. Since then, I have of course asked myself the question, why was I not wise before the event? Why, indeed, is MPD so neglected during training? Even if some patients may well attempt to fake it, this cannot be a good enough reason never to mention it at all? Should we not at least be taught how to tell the difference? But then, as Colin Ross described, if it is indeed the norm to neglect the patient, I suppose it becomes rather pointless to train a therapist in a non-existent disorder. Nothingness, so it seems, has yet another meaning.

Consequently today, it is indeed gratifying to be able to write that a positive outcome was achieved, although this in no way exonerates the mistakes that were made. They can of course never be made good. Still, at this point in time Cordelia is indeed well, and learning to be one person; learning to juggle a brand new ego! True, there might be some pieces of the jigsaw puzzle which will remain forever lost, there might be some pieces that we have probably put in upside down, certain dates will not be totally accurate, since they are but a rough guess, but gradually, this will cease to be important, as the past fades, and the present and the future take over.

Here then, is a final list: the pieces of Cordelia's jigsaw puzzle, those 'thousand pieces' she saw in the sky and in the 'cracked mirror' now as complete a picture – at least, as far as we both know – including yet another personality which had escaped detection, until Cordelia began to write down the specific history of as-if Bryony. In fact, the more Cordelia was able to describe as-if Bryony (based on the bad part of her mother), the more she began to be aware that something was missing, that there was in fact also a part of herself called Anna (based on the good part of her mother), which she had tended to ignore. Indeed, just as she had tried all these years to deny that there was a bad part to her father, likewise, she had tried to deny that there was a good part to her mother. She had of course not been able to totally disregard its existence and hence, as Cordelia has since described, she had been quite rightly alarmed when she first came to the hospital, and was subsequently introduced to Anne, the nurse in charge of her care.

As-if Anna, as Cordelia would in due course discover (after experiencing yet another period of turmoil), had in fact faded away into the background, which explains why she only emerged at this late stage. As-if Bryony, on the other hand, had remained very much a part of the prevailing system. However, the reason why as-if Anna and not as-if Bryony had been left out of the current system – and the various personality lists – I feel once again endorses the peculiar logic of a multiple system. When Cordelia's real mother died, as-if Anna was in fact replaced by Raza and Riva and thereafter duly relinquished her role (Cordelia could after all not have two substitute good mothers!). But there had been no need to replace as-if Bryony, Cordelia's bad substitute mother, because, quite simply, Cordelia's mother was not Bryony's mother! Indeed, since as-if Bryony regarded herself as quite separate from Cordelia, the death of Cordelia's real mother had not affected her in the least. This is how as-if Bryony was effectively able to continue operating as an active part of Cordelia's current system. Trance logic so it would seem, had once again won the day.

Cordelia's Internal System:

Cordelia's Self: primary unit, creator of the other-selves. Disappeared (2–3 years old) into self-imposed exile, when Cordelia denied herself/denied the truth, and split herself into Peter and Rosalind. Returned periodically, when it was safe to do so, especially at moments involving spiritual awareness. 'Popped out from behind the mirror' (6½ years old) when her father died. Returned for real (52 years old) when 'it' spoke the truth about the abuse. Now an active part of Cordelia's personality.

Cordelia (Cordelia I): Original child, her name was chosen by her father. Two elder brothers, elder sister (Rosalind, who died), twin sister (Stephanie, also died at birth), one younger brother. Slept in parents' room in a white cot. Always had a sense of being alone, wet, hungry, dirty; did not cry. First memory is the noise of the seagulls, but heard it as crying, '…as crying for me, as though they knew how I felt on the inside'. They used to tap on the bedroom window. 'I learned to fly away with the birds.' Cordelia knew Alice. When her father asked her to play sex games in the bath, Cordelia pretended that she was Alice, which meant that she would equally be able to disappear. Thus, with the logic of a child, she would duly dissociate herself from what was happening. To begin with, Cordelia knew that Alice was make-believe in the same way that *Alice in Wonderland* was but a story (her father had read the story to her). But in time, Cordelia's Alice would of course become quite real herself.

Cordelia remembers her father putting his penis in her mouth, telling her to pretend it was a bottle, just a big bottle. She did not know what was happening. 'In all innocence, I did not know what I was doing!' Cordelia lost consciousness, thinking she was going to die. Afterwards, the smell of her father's ejaculation made her sick; she was punished for being sick; she became scared of being sick. As a result, she was presented with a choice of two evils; if she asked to be taken out of the cot it meant potential danger/abuse, but if she was not, it meant that she was trapped. Eventually, she learned to distance herself from the abuse by going behind the mirror; 'I could see, yet did not want to see. I reasoned that if you can see it happening over there (in the mirror), it can't be happening here. I began to see what was happening to me from the back of the mirror, I could feel myself behind the mirror in my mind. I decided that it must be happening to someone else. From that day on, that is how I coped: I either went behind the mirror, or I floated up to the ceiling.'

Cordelia thus heard more than she saw. 'I had difficulty in seeing.' Sense of seeing went. Sense of sound and smell increased. In fact, Cordelia has been acutely sensitive to smell ever since. Always felt mildly drunk or concussed. Had severe headaches. She was also very confused: her father's face would change from a loving tender face to a leering, sneering face, hence she split her father in two: into a very nice, loving, adored father who reassured her about the abuse and the fact that her legs had come out of their sockets. He panicked! 'Don't worry, it should not have happened, we will put it right.' (Cordelia was always searching for this loving father.) And into a hated father who leered at her, desired her in a wrong way, 'loved my childish body, could not keep his hands off me'. This was the face of her father that frightened her, the side of her father that was sick and made Cordelia feel glad and relieved that he was dead.

Cordelia (2–3 years old) also remembers that she was taken to her father's bed after being bathed and then raped. She heard the argument between her parents. Her mother was angry with her and blamed her for what had happened. She was beaten by her mother. Cordelia argued ('I had a voice then'): 'He did it, I didn't do it. No. He did it. *He did it.*'

Thereafter, she 'lost her sense of self'. Her Self went away in the hospital when she lied to the nurse and they put the mask on her face (chloroform). The Self went to sleep, and Cordelia woke up as a boy; 'I lost who I was, I was like a frozen embryo, unformed, no longer here, no longer able to speak.'

Prior to 'going to sleep', Cordelia was taken from her father's arms by a 'big, warm, kind nurse'. But when the nurse asked her who had injured her legs, she kept the secret, she didn't tell anyone, as her father had asked her to do. Pain, however, made her faint. It became very foggy; great deal of pain; fog increased. People's faces became distorted. 'I was doing what Alice did: making them go small. I left my body, and floated up to the ceiling. I was looking down on Peter. It was important that I was a boy. Boys were liked, girls were not.' Afterwards, when she recovered consciousness, she heard her father tell many lies. She also saw him cry, and believed he was crying for her, which made it seem all right.

Cordelia's Self then 'popped out from behind the mirror' when her father died (she was 6½ years old), believing that it was now safe to do so. But since her brother took over from her father, his abuse and mutilation coupled with the ongoing neglect and abandonment by her mother, ensured that the Self had no other option but to disappear again.

Thus it seems just like every created personality tends to have a second beginning, it appears, as though the system as a whole is equally given a second chance, and depending on the conditions the Self encounters when it 'pops back again', the secret world will either be dismantled and the right order restored: the subconscious once again making logical deductions based on accurate information received from the conscious such as 'I was indeed the child in the mirror, I was indeed the child being abused by my father!' Or else the secret world will simply be strengthened, become all too permanent and very, very real – permanent that is, until all lies are revealed and duly acknowledged.

After her father died, Cordelia then slept with her mother until she was sixteen, when she finally got her own white bed. This white bed, as well as the garden swing (which the adult Cordelia took with her whenever she moved to another house), became synonymous with safety, and whenever Cordelia felt stressed or was in emotional pain, she would seek solace by lying or sleeping in her white bed. Cordelia only very recently, a year after her therapy ended in fact, has been able to part with this bed, and has given it to someone else, outside the family. Thus yet another piece of this complex puzzle falls into place. The reader might recall how I sat down next to Cordelia on her bed the very first time we met, instead of in the vacant chair. As a result, Cordelia the original child, duly appeared on the scene, and for the first time in her life 'felt the possibility of being cared for'. However, it would take her a long time before she would see me as anything else other than the ideal rescuer 'who took her out of the dirty cot, and gave her a taste of spontaneity'. In fact, it would be many years later. As Cordelia has since informed me, she saw me as Frieda and 'who I really was, for the first time', on the day her Self returned! Strangely enough, throughout the years of therapy, my initial apprehension about sitting next to Cordelia on her bed had always puzzled me. I knew my subconscious antennae had picked something up, something that was very important, but I did not know what it was, which of course now also explains why, even as I wrote down the account of our first meeting, I still felt compelled to give a reason for sitting on the bed next to Cordelia, and consequently wrote, 'It was indeed a small room.'

1. Cordelia II (Mad Cordelia): Reality of Cordelia's childhood; fear of abandonment, created (10 years old) by the Self/Cordelia. When Cordelia was about 10 years old, she was locked in her room by her brother and grandmother, which caused Cordelia to become distraught and hysterical. She was consequently sent to an asylum, where Cordelia not only became very physically ill indeed but also where Mad Cordelia became a real person, a separate structure, the other schizophrenic part of Cordelia, as Cordelia used to call it, her function being to contain the madness, since 'a sound mind was needed to maintain the system and its peculiar logic', and because deep down, Cordelia knew that she was not really mad, but was just acting out what her family said she was and expected her to be.

2. Stephanie: First wish-fulfilment (1–2 years old) the twin who died; loved by her mother.
   Cordelia pretended to be Stephanie, hoping that her mother would like her just as much as she said she liked this other little girl. She hated Cordelia, who was frequently asked by her mother, 'Why were you not the other one?' Stephanie consequently remembers being shaken quite violently by her mother and crying in her cot.
   Stephanie was created (4 years old) by the Self/Cordelia as a separate person when her mother began to wash Cordelia out in the bath (wash away the sexual sins of her husband, as well as her own?). Stephanie 'heard the creaking of the rope' as she was hanging upside down in the loft. Thereafter tended to feel 'half dead', her head permanently in a fog. Her function was to be the dead twin, and cope with the physical abuse by the mother as well as the sexual abuse which was to follow. Since Stephanie was 'loved' by her mother, allowing her mother to use her tiny body for sex and masturbation seemed a natural extension. After all, had not Cordelia's father told her that sex equalled love?

3. Alice: (18 months–2 years old) External observer who gave Cordelia the ability not to be there!

Alice could disappear. Pretending to be Alice meant that Cordelia could likewise disappear and pretend that the games in the bath with her father were not for real, and that her beloved father would not ask her to do such bad things. 'Alice allowed me to dissociate in the bath many times.' Cordelia, however, remained in conscious control, always aware that she was pretending to be Alice. Nonetheless, she would often feel quite mixed up, as her father would also sing to her: 'Only make believe I love you. Only make believe that you love me…'

Alice was born as a separate person, (6½ years old) when Cordelia's father died, and her mother told her that she was to stop crying, that she had to grow up, and henceforth look after her and her brother and not to talk about her father again: 'You are with me now.' Alice thus stopped being make-believe and became a real person, making herself instantly six years older in order to be able to look after her mother. After this, Alice took indeed great care of her mother – often to her own detriment – although she would delegate looking after her baby brother to Angela, and leave the cooking and cleaning for her brother Martin to Bryony.

Alice was the last of the internal children Cordelia revealed, since she did not really seem to fit in. In fact, Alice was the external observer, the spokesperson for the system, who took action on behalf of the system and reported to the doctors on what she perceived was happening to Cordelia. She knew all the other children, and like Victoria and Delia I, would usually present a competent face to the world. However, since Alice had made herself six years older than Cordelia on the day her father died (meaning six years hence), her actual birth-date (being six year before Cordelia's) would of course often cause her a lot of problems, needing a hasty explanation to cover up the apparent mistake. At first glance, Alice's decision to make herself older seems rather odd, yet once again, behind it all lies a certain [child] logic. Not only did it mean that Alice consequently never knew her father, which would make it a lot easier to comply with her mother's command never to mention her father again, but it also meant that she could not be held to blame for the death of her father, as her mother told her she was, which in turn helped Alice to come to terms with the conflicting feelings she was experiencing at the time: feeling relief that her father had died, yet fearing that it was indeed her fault, since she had obviously not loved him enough – as he equally used to sing to her: 'If you don't love me, I will die.'

4. Peter: First split. Little boy created (2–3 years old) by Self/Cordelia when pain and distress made her leave her body. ('I could imitate Alice for real!') Made herself into a little boy, thus could distance herself from

what was happening. (Yet another way of dissociating herself; another way of going behind the mirror.)

Cordelia observes what is happening to her body – from the ceiling. She watches the surgeon as he operates, and how with every stitch, he turns her more and more into a boy. Peter thus almost instantly becomes autonomous; a real boy, a real other-self. Peter then wakes up after the operation with callipers on his legs. The first thing Peter sees are the blazing white lights of the operating theatre and people leaning over him. A man in a uniform is asking him who did this to him, but Peter is unable to speak (he would in fact remain mute until Cordelia went to school). There was, however, a 'big, warm, kind nurse', who Peter recognised. He held out his arms to her, and she picked him up. Peter knew that he was safe with her. 'I clung to her as if my life depended on it.'

When his father eventually came to collect him, Peter clung to the nurse, but his father said he would look after him; he did not like the nurse looking after him and snatched him away from the nurse, whereupon Peter dissociated ('all the parts could in fact leave their body') and switched back into Cordelia, who watched how her father then took yet another young child, this time a little girl 'out of Peter'. Peter's first outing then, was a year later, when his father took him for a walk to his place of work in order to show his colleagues that Cordelia's legs were sound again. In fact, whenever Cordelia was alone with her father, Peter would emerge – take over the conscious control – his function being to contain the abuse by the father, and help Cordelia convince herself that she was not being abused. She was after all, a little girl, and her father only ever abused this other little boy.

5. Rosalind: First split. Created (2–3 years old) by the Self/Cordelia in order to cope with the dichotomy between bad father and good father. Rosalind is the beloved daughter. 'The one he did not abuse.' (Given the same name as Cordelia's older sister, who equally had been her father's favourite child.)

Cordelia watches her father cry. She sees him 'pick up a little girl' out of Peter. Likewise, the first thing Rosalind sees is her father crying. She believes he is sorry for what he has done, and that he is crying for Cordelia. Rosalind feels pity for him, she feels responsible. She blames herself. She hears him say there is no need to stay in the hospital, he will look after her. 'She does not need anyone else.' Her father then sang to her, all the way home: 'If you were the only girl in the world, and I was the only boy...'

Some weeks later then, Rosalind becomes a real older sister when she is sitting on her father's lap, whilst he is recounting his traumatic wartime experiences to her. She sings with him, adores him, and would keep him on a pedestal for many, many years to come. She believes that his face changes to a leering one because her mother makes him change, whereafter she would usually switch to Peter, and give him the conscious control. Rosalind always believed that her father would come back for her. She in fact always refused to believe that he had died. Rosalind's function was to become the perfect little girl, to be loved by her father.

6. Rebekah: Internal observer. Created (2–3 years old) by the Self/Cordelia.

Cordelia's father has taken her home after she spent a considerable time in hospital, acutely traumatised, ill with pneumonia and slowly recovering from the damage he did to her legs and vagina. On returning to the scene of the rape, her parents' bedroom, memories of the rape come flooding back. Cordelia screams with sheer terror, whereupon her father brings an old lady who lived down the lane, to look after Cordelia. Her mother has gone and Cordelia is left in the care of the old lady, who advises Cordelia 'to forget all about it'. Cordelia thus creates Rebekah, the part of her that will help her to do as the old lady suggests, by ensuring that the knowledge of what has happened to her is safely contained and stored away. Rebekah thus effectively becomes the keeper of the truth. The first thing Rebekah herself experiences is reading a story together with the old lady. Thereafter, Rebekah would read and play in secret. Her function was to learn and observe – be the voice of the internal observer; the subconscious. Rebekah, in fact, was always 'different from the other children'. She knew all the others, although the other children did not know her. She was also the last one of the personalities Cordelia described to me in detail, prior to the end of her therapy.

Rebekah, however, following suit, would in time of course become a real person, a separate child, when Cordelia was about 5–6 years old. Elizabeth is angry, having a tantrum and throws her brother's beloved cat on the fire (cat runs away). Mother and brother are very angry, they throw Cordelia's treasured encyclopaedia, which her father had bought, on the fire to punish her. Fire gets out of hand, sets chimney on fire; lots of smoke. Elizabeth is scared and dissociates, whereupon Rebekah walks into the room. She is, however, instantly banished from the room by her angry mother and brother and leaves, but not before she asks if there is a book she could take with her to read, convincing her brother and mother that Cordelia must be mad: 'She's mad. She doesn't even know what she has done. She is totally mad.'

7. Felicity: First defender – created (3–4 years old) by the Self/Peter.

Felicity is actually the first other-self who appears to have been created by an other-self; that is, by Peter. Indeed, by now, Peter is perceived by Cordelia as a real boy and as quite separate from herself, and as such (logically speaking of course), he, like all the other-selfs which were to follow, is thus quite able to create his own other-selfs, as and when needed. Having said so, however, Felicity's creation is different from the other children, as she seemed to appear out of the blue. Peter in fact hears her voice trying to comfort him – which might also explain why she always felt more unreal than the other children; she was aware that she was acting, and knew all the other internal children – they also knew her. Felicity, I believe, is the female side of Peter, or his twin. Cordelia after all, also had a twin. Rosalind was the little girl who had actually been created by Cordelia's father: 'he picked her out of Peter'.

Cordelia's legs are sound again, and she is taken for a walk by her father to the recreational lounge at his place of work. As per usual, whenever Cordelia is alone with her father, Peter takes over from her. Peter then hears his father's colleagues say that she is a gorgeous little thing... The men are grinning, laughing; Peter becomes scared, convinced that these other men are going to hurt him, just like his father. Peter dissociates, whilst hearing another voice say, 'Don't worry, I'll show them, it doesn't have to be you this time.' Whereupon another little girl takes his place: Felicity, who promptly takes off her clothes 'to give the men what they are after'. Felicity then becomes a separate other-self (6 years old) when her father uses her body to show Cordelia's brothers what to do with a female. Thereafter Felicity has many boyfriends, her function being to flirt with men, to try and control them, to keep the other children safe.

8.   Elizabeth: Second defender – created (4 years old) – by the Self/Stephanie. Likewise, by now, Stephanie is perceived by Cordelia as a real person; as yet another other-self; as a separate little girl – again meaning that, logically speaking, Stephanie can equally create new other-selfs.

Stephanie goes numb in the bath, she is being washed out by her mother and hung upside down in the loft/washroom. She leaves her body. She creates another girl to take her place: Elizabeth, who tries to express her anger, but she is trapped. The first thing Elizabeth sees is the tailor's dummy standing in the loft, but she sees it upside down, since she is hanging upside down herself. In her mind, Elizabeth then turns herself and the tailor's dummy the right way round, yet feels forever mixed up. Her mother clearly hates her, yet can show affection to her brother, and takes him on her lap. Elizabeth wants to kill her mother 'burn her at the stake'. Yet she is also angry on behalf of her mother and will forgive her anything. She is forever writing notes to her mother asking her to love her.

Elizabeth becomes a real girl (4½ years old) when her mother deliberately drops the top part of her heavy sewing machine on Cordelia's fingers. Cordelia is being punished by her mother for hitting her head on the sewing machine and getting blood on the pretty clothes her mother has made for her. Her mother, however, had pushed Cordelia, because she kept asking whether her father was coming home and whether he would bring her a teddy bear for her birthday. 'Elizabeth did not scream.' Instead, Elizabeth absorbs the injustice, the unfairness of it all, functioning as the other-self, who from then on copes with the topsy turvy world of her mother. Thereafter, she wreaks havoc and chaos in her own right, yet yearns to be loved.

9.   Zillah: Shadow Friend. Created (4 years old) by the Self/Elizabeth.

(Elizabeth at that stage is not yet perceived by Cordelia as a real, separate person, since she has only just been created by Stephanie – which might explain why Zillah would always remain just Elizabeth's 'imaginary friend', never becoming a real other-self, although Zillah would of course always feel very real to Elizabeth.)

Elizabeth is hanging upside down in the loft, hears a voice which says, 'Don't be angry, don't be sad. You've got a friend. I'm with you. I'm here again, I'll always be here.' Elizabeth has water in her ears, and wonders if she is hearing properly, 'but then knows it is real'. She hears Zillah speak again, who says 'I'm over here. It's all right.' Thereafter Zillah becomes the shadow friend of Elizabeth, and would often join her, whenever Elizabeth came for her therapy, usually sitting in the corner of the room, listening.

10.   Martin: Third defender. First introjection/wish-fulfilment – to be liked by brother. Created (5 years old) by the Self/Cordelia/Felicity/Elizabeth.

Whilst Cordelia's father is away, her brother Martin tends to give her a hard time. He especially delights in 'picking on Peter'. He is always threatening his sister, saying he is going to draw all her blood, etc., and together with his friend, he often tries out different sexual experiments on her, which invariably bring out Felicity in the role of protector; the one who is able to turn an unpleasant sexual experience into a pleasant one by making it into 'something they want, something she can provide, something she can offer and hence control'. Elizabeth, in the meantime, has been turned into a real little girl by Cordelia (see the description of mother dropping the sewing machine), and as per usual, comes to help Felicity and subsequently creates Martin.

It is Guy Fawkes Night, and the usual bonfire is being held. Martin once again is threatening his sister, saying she is mad, saying, 'We should do something about her.' Cordelia truly believes that her brother and his friend are building up to finally getting rid of her, and believes this is her last chance to let other people know about the abuse she has to endure.

Felicity then takes over from Cordelia, whereupon Felicity takes off all her clothes, trying to draw attention to herself in order to reveal the secret of her family. She hears her brother say, 'Let's burn her,' whereafter he promptly drags her by her hair and attempts to tie her to a tree. Elizabeth remembers being tied up in the loft by her mother, and takes over from Felicity, and just as Elizabeth could see Zillah in the loft, she can equally see the other little girls, Cordelia and Felicity, and of course also herself, 'who are all naked and tied to poles'. Elizabeth thus begins to fight her brother, but she is of course not strong enough. The bonfire, though, appears to be getting out of hand. Believing she is indeed going to be burned, Elizabeth dissociates and in the process creates a helper: a boy, as-if Martin (just like her brother Martin), who is of course stronger than Elizabeth, and hence quite able not only to get the better of her brother, but also able to run away and persuade a neighbour to phone the fire brigade. As-if Martin then becomes a real boy, a real other-self (7–8 years old) when Martin (Cordelia's brother) performs a circumcision on his sister. Martin has in fact enticed his sister into the garden shed, and proceeds to tie her to the garden bench. Cordelia in the meantime has switched into Elizabeth, who tries to fend off Martin. Feeling powerless, however, Elizabeth again switches into the boy she created at Guy Fawkes Night; hoping he will be able to set her free – and in the process, makes as-if Martin, a real other-self.

As-if Martin thereafter comes to the foreground whenever something untoward needs to be done, i.e. when Cordelia is watching a vivisection in school, as-if Martin takes over from her, since he is not afraid or squeamish – and just like Cordelia's real brother, has often dissected animals at home. In time of course, since he is based on the real Martin, as-if Martin, turns from a defender into a persecutor as he becomes more and more like Cordelia's real brother. Thereafter, on behalf of the system, as-if Martin will insist on getting help, but in an irrational and crazy way – as a defender and as an avenger. It would usually be as-if Martin who would either call all the various emergency services, or else he would play practical jokes on Cordelia.

11. Angela: Rite of passage: birth of a sibling. Created (6½ years old) by the Self/Cordelia. Cordelia is taken by her father to see the new baby. She feels very disappointed; she wanted a little sister. She hears her parents have another row. Her father tells her that she must look after this new baby. This message is reinforced by one of the nurses, who equally tells her that she must care for the baby. However, since Cordelia is only three years old (she stopped growing the day the Self disappeared), she is far too young to look after her brother; hence, she dissociates and creates another bigger girl, who will be able to do so in her place. Angela then becomes a real other-self (one month later) when her father dies and her

mother gives her two bottles to feed her baby brother with, telling her that she is far too ill to do it herself, and that from now on she must look after her brother. Angela in time of course becomes the nurse, who cares for others. Why two bottles? Cordelia never understood this, other than that the only way her mother knew how to care for her children was by overfeeding them – a fat baby meaning she was a good mother after all – at least in the eyes of the world.

12. Esther: Developmental stage: independence. Created by the Self/Elizabeth.(6–7 years old).

It is summertime. Elizabeth is behaving badly – as per norm. She is playing on the rocks near the sea with her two brothers. Her brother Martin suggests, that 'we have got to tame her', like 'taming the shrew'. He decides to throw her into the water. Elizabeth goes under and under, dissociates, believing she is going to die, and creates a little girl to take her place. Esther struggles up to the surface and clambers onto the rocks. Almost immediately thereafter, Esther becomes a real other-self, when she dives back into the water as Esther, to show her brothers that she is not afraid, can look after herself, can save herself. Esther thus becomes the part that is fearless and achieves – able to triumph over her brother Martin.

13. Bryony: Second introjection/wish-fulfilment – to be liked by mother – created (shortly after the death of the father 6½–7 years old) by the Self/Stephanie.

Stephanie was watching her mother, whose name is Bryony, put some crabs in a huge pot to be boiled. She identifies with the crabs. They remind her of the steamy baths when her mother used to wash her out. Her mother tells her to go and play outside. Stephanie sits and draws pictures for a while then returns to the house, goes looking for her mother. She can hear strange noises, and finds her mother in bed with her brother Martin. Her mother has cut off her hair; she looks like a man. Stephanie dissociates, believing her mother has disappeared and creates another girl to take her mother's place: as-if Bryony. Thus, the very first thing as-if Bryony hears, is herself screaming; she doesn't understand why her mother has cut off her hair; why would she want to look like a man? As-if Bryony almost instantly becomes a real person when she is told by her brother Martin, who is very angry about being found out, to get his tea ready, get their mother's tea ready, to light the grate etc., and be quick about it, or else something terrible will happen to her.

As-if Bryony from that day on not only becomes 'a slave to them all', trying to keep herself safe; pacify her brother Martin, but in the process becomes like her mother, meaning that instead of being a substitute mother (which is why Stephanie had created her in the first place), she turns into a persecutor instead, and gives Cordelia and the other internal children a hard time; progressively of course becoming more and more anti-Cordelia. And eventually, just like Martin and Geraldine, as-if Bryony actually ends up believing that she does not belong to the body of Cordelia, but that she is a part of the body of Cordelia's mother instead. (Cordelia never felt separate from her mother, believing that her mother had either swallowed her up, or that her mother lived inside her.)

14. Anna: Third introjection/wish-fulfilment – to be liked by mother – created (shortly after the death of the father 6½–7 years old) by the Self/Stephanie.

Stephanie is taken by her mother to visit a new school. She hears her mother explain to the reverend mother how her daughter has had a difficult time since her father died, etc., and that she would greatly benefit from being a weekly boarder. Stephanie cannot believe her ears. This is not the mother she knows, this mother seems to care for her, this mother is telling the reverend mother that she wants to help her daughter. Stephanie, bewildered, duly dissociates and goes into a trance whilst listening to the two adults, and creates Anna, the good mother, in order to help her cope with this confusing dichotomy. Anna thereafter becomes a real person when her mother actually takes her to buy a uniform, and for the first time ever, tells her that she looks very nice in it. From then on, Anna becomes the manic part of Cordelia, the one who is the very opposite of as-if Bryony, the one who tries to make her mother laugh in the hope that she might love Cordelia even more. Anna in due course, is replaced by Raza and Riva (by yet another substitute good mother), when Cordelia's real mother dies – which is why she was left out of the various lists Cordelia used to compile.

15. Geraldine: Fourth introjection/wish-fulfilment – to be liked by grandmother – created (7 years old) by the Self/Angela.

Angela is walking down the path towards the house of her grandmother, whose name is Geraldine. They are visiting her, having moved closer to her house. Angela is carrying her younger brother, and hopes that her grandmother will like her. But the grandmother takes her brother away from her, ignores her, and says that she prefers little boys. Angela dissociates, feeling jealous, and creates her own Geraldine, another as-if girl, who will like and love her. As-if Geraldine then becomes a real person (about six months later) when her brother plays a cruel trick on Cordelia. Since her father died, Cordelia has in fact become preoccupied with death. She is forever asking her mother not to die. As a practical joke, and with the full cooperation of his mother and grandmother, her brother then stages the death of Cordelia's mother, including ordering a hearse to come to the house. Cordelia of course freaks out, whereupon as-if Geraldine becomes a grandmother for real, in order to help Cordelia protect herself and try to control her brother – hoping that he will love the as-if Geraldine as much as he loves his real grandmother. However, once again, just like as-if Martin and as-if Bryony before her, as-if Geraldine becomes progressively more and more like the real grandmother, who is paranoid, cruel and very anti-Cordelia, and thus duly changes from a revered grandmother into yet another persecutor who from then on distrusts the world and everyone in it and proceeds to protect Cordelia in her own inimitable, mad and paranoid way.

16. Gillian: reality of Cordelia 's childhood/abuse by her brother. Created (7–8 years old) by the Self/Cordelia/Elizabeth/Martin.

Cordelia has been enticed into the garden shed by her brother Martin. She can hear her brother say, that she is not to scream. Cordelia then switches into Elizabeth the moment her brother attempts to tie her to the garden bench. Elizabeth of course struggles, trying to free herself, but she is not strong enough, whereupon she switches into the boy she created before, to help her fight her brother: as-if Martin. Her brother's friend, however, proceeds to put chloroform on Cordelia's face, which sedates her. As-if Martin consequently is unable to free himself, and has no choice but to dissociate; to leave his body, and in the process creates another little girl, Gillian, who watches Martin perform a circumcision on his sister. Afterwards Gillian, when the chloroform has worn off, begins to laugh in the same horrible way her brother and his friend used to laugh whenever they abused Cordelia sexually and physically.

Gillian then becomes a real other-self (six to seven weeks later) when her mother makes her walk home from the hospital, where she was admitted for haemorrhaging. Her mother is mad at her because she was told off by the doctors, who nonetheless believed the stories about a bike accident, given as an explanation to account for the injuries Cordelia had sustained. Gillian as a real person, however, is laughing about it all, 'in the same cackling laugh as her brother', and from then on will 'laugh in the face of adversity' – becoming a clown.

17. Mary: reality of Cordelia's life: abuse by a stranger. Created (13–14 years old) by the Self/Felicity/Elizabeth. Cordelia has been sent away by her mother on an organised holiday for fatherless children. Cordelia is naturally fearful that her mother might not want her back. Elizabeth, however, taking over the conscious control, hopes that the family with whom she will be staying might well adopt her. When the father of the family subsequently takes her for trips to the recreational lounge at his place of work, Felicity, reminded of the days with her own father, comes to the foreground in order to help Elizabeth achieve her dream, and begins to flirt with the father and with his colleagues. Consequently, Felicity is later raped by the father. Felicity, however, struggles

indignantly, she was aiming for adoption, not sexual abuse. Elizabeth then comes to help, but she is of course not strong enough to fend off this man. Moreover, by now Elizabeth knows all too well that switching into the as-if Martin as she used to do in the past will not really help her either, hence she is left with no other choice but to dissociate – she leaves her body and creates Mary to take her place. Mary becomes a real other-self (five months later), when Cordelia has to have an abortion. Thereafter copes with all the sexual demands Cordelia will encounter, including, eventually becoming the sexual partner to her husband.

18. Victoria: Developmental stage: Competence in life skills, establishing an identity. Created (13 14 years old) by the Self/Mary.

Mary is extremely ashamed. Her mother is very angry with her, and tells her that she should tell lies in school, that she must never tell anyone that she has had an abortion. However, Mary, whose complete name is Mary Magdalene, and who is in fact modelled on the prostitute who found favour in the eyes of Jesus, finds it impossible to tell lies. Yet feeling that she has no choice but to comply with her mother's command she promptly solves this moral dilemma by dissociating and creating yet another other-self; one who will indeed be able to behave as her mother wants her to: Victoria.

Victoria then becomes a real other-self some days later, when she does indeed pretend that everything is fine, and indeed tells lies in school – as her mother had told her to do. However, since Victoria is in fact pretending, she is not like the other children, and from then on is in fact put in charge of the system – acting as the glue which keeps them all together – duly acquiring the physical, intellectual and social skills necessary for a competent normal life in the real world, whilst keeping all those unruly children under control. Thereafter, Victoria actually models herself on her mother in the hope of being liked and accepted by her. However, in order to be truly loved by her mother, Victoria also has to take over the sexual function of Stephanie, which means that she has to make her body available to her mother until Cordelia is sixteen years old, when her mother in fact loses interest in her.

19. Dawn: First imaginary friend. Wish-fulfilment – establishing an Identity. Created (16–18 years old) by the Self/Victoria.

Victoria, in the role of student, creates a substitute friend, based on an actual classmate. When this particular girl joined her class, Victoria admired her smile, friendliness, and easy ability to make friends, and when she went away on holiday, Victoria made her into a permanent inner friend.

20. Denise: Second imaginary friend. Wish-fulfilment – establishing an Identity. Created (16–18 years old) by the Self/Victoria.

Victoria was very self-conscious about her body and admired a certain classmate for her litheness and grace, and when she was ordered by the PE teacher to undress herself and have a shower (in line with the other pupils), Victoria pretended to be like this classmate – and in time became Denise, in order to be able to stand naked amongst her fellow pupils.

21. Freda: Third imaginary friend. Wish-fulfilment – establishing an Identity. Created (16–18 years old) by the Self/Victoria.

Victoria created a special tutor, based on her music teacher, who took an interest in Cordelia, gave her lessons after school, and had a lovely singing voice. Cordelia had admired this music teacher; in fact, she had a crush on her, and hence, she had always wanted to be like her. Freda became a real person thus, in order that she could remain Victoria's special friend.

22. Delia I: Rites of Passage: Marriage. Fitting into Society. Created (19 years old) by the Self/Cordelia.

Cordelia has met her future husband whilst he was singing a solo in church. Cordelia, however, was very much aware that the system she had developed to cope with the world would scare him away. Hence she decided to contain the children by creating yet another other-self, this time an adult part which would literally begin to live a new life. 'Somehow, I realised, I would have to find a way of placing the children within, so that I could lead as normal a life as possible.' Delia I then becomes a real person, when her husband actually calls her by a different name than the one she was used to; having abbreviated her name. Delia I from that day onwards tended to be 'the competent external face', the one who was in conscious control of the body most of the time, and duly replaced Cordelia I, Rosalind, Felicity, Rebekah, Angela, Gillian, Esther, Zillah, Alice, Anna, Dawn, Denise, Freda and Victoria with just one adult person – indeed beginning a new life.

23. Delia II: Rites of Passage: Marriage. Fitting into Society. Created (19 years old) by the Self/Cordelia.

However, just as there was a Cordelia II, an unsound ('schizophrenic') child other-self whose role it was to contain the madness, when Cordelia started to go out with her husband, she equally created an adult version, Delia II, who was meant to help her contain Cordelia II (Mad Cordelia), Stephanie, Peter, Elizabeth, Martin, Bryony, Geraldine and Mary, effectively becoming 'the disturbed face within' whose function was to hide all the sadness, madness and degradation, a deception in which she obviously succeeded. In truth, Delia II only tended to emerge when Cordelia was feeling depressed – her depression in turn providing her with a very plausible smokescreen.

24. Riva: Rites of Passage: Death of her mother/wish-fulfilment – to receive unconditional love. Created (25 years old) by the Self/Delia I.

Delia I is distressed, feels confused about the grief others can display about the death of her mother. Hears herself say, 'Don't worry – you've still got me.' She instantly mixes up her words with her longing to equally have a mother she could grieve over, and proceeds to create Riva, the mother she would like to have had. Riva then becomes a real other-self, when she goes on shopping sprees in order to comfort herself – and like Delia I, who is the adult external face of Cordelia, Riva thereafter becomes the visible face of this new substitute mother.

25. Raza: Rites of Passage: Death of her mother/wish-fulfilment – to receive unconditional love. Created (25 years old) by the Self/Delia II.

Likewise, on the day of her mother's funeral, Delia II creates Raza – the other half of Riva, who duly becomes a real person, when Raza persuades Riva to phone her (dead) mother, as well as persuading her to make phone calls to friends and potential rescuers in order to receive support, Raza effectively becoming the compelling voice within Riva. Raza thus, like Delia II, who is the adult internal face of Mad Cordelia, becomes the invisible, unsound part of the new mother.

26. Davina: Developmental stage: Finding meaning. Beginning of the End/System beginning to release its secrets. Created (38 years old) by the Self/Cordelia.

Davina is the adult version of Rosalind. Since Rosalind was effectively created by the father, taken 'out of Peter' by the father, and became his special little girl, it follows that Davina, like Rosalind, would follow in the footsteps of the father and become a dedicated believer.

Cordelia is present in church, attending the service, and witnesses how it is possible to be healed by a spiritual experience. Consequently, she creates a part that can be totally separate from the system, in order to enable her to be healed and be loved by God. This part, however, slowly disappeared when Cordelia stopped being a church-goer, and after 'the buried pain started to emerge'.

Thus, many, many years after the child learned to hide the truth, the buried pain began to emerge. For sure, how wondrous is the mind of a child? And how courageous the adult, determined to unmask the truth, and relive such a horrendous childhood in order to be whole. It has been a tremendous achievement. It has been a most amazing therapy journey, and we can but admire Cordelia's tenacity to see it through to the bitter end. However, when all is said and done, we should not lose sight of the simple fact that Cordelia would rather not – should not – have had to go through it at all. A child should not have to endure such terror, such depravity, such sorrow. An adult should not be handicapped by such devastating memories. Indeed, just a few excerpts from Cordelia's diary will confirm that life for some children is all too painful, all too unbearable, and can leave an incredible mark upon the adult, and that in truth, none of us can ever truly comprehend such suffering, such betrayal, unless we have lived through it ourselves. Listening to their sad tales, however, is a beginning, a means to reach out and try to understand.

Stephanie's clothes:

Her clothes are grey – she is the ice maiden. Feelings blocked, all she wants and expects is to die to please everyone. She tried to fade into the background and be the person expected of a female child. She tried to please her mother by being dead. She liked floaty clothes, because she experienced such dreadful pain in her body; she loved floating up out of her body; this enabled complete numbing and total denial...

Bryony's clothes:

Brown, old fashioned, ageing and unattractive, dresses tied up to the neck. I remember how my mother made me wear her clothes before she abused me. I became my mother, she possessed me completely. I felt sick and unattractive as I left Frieda's therapy room. I hated what I was made in to, and could hardly believe I had bought or wore such clothes. It was as if I was covered up with my mother's wrapping. I had no soul, no heart, no spirit. I was dead and I've existed, not lived. Can I live, really live?

Pleasure and pain are linked – love and humiliation. I have to separate the fantasy from the feeling...

I wanted to feel love and joy on my wedding day. I could feel nothing. I could not even feel the love I knew I had for my husband, because I didn't know how to feel. I felt afraid to feel.

I have had to let go of the right to hate, to be confused and all messed up, because of what happened to me. Because I did have a right to those things! My personalities were treasures – but because I wanted to heal, I had to give them up too. I put prison walls around myself, because my parents put me in a prison of hell beyond belief. I have faced and I am still facing each aspect of myself. I needed to know where I have been in this life – who I am.

For sure, Cordelia's therapy has been remarkable – but the history of her life has been even more incredible. Against all the odds, without having a stomach; as my vampire dream so graphically depicted, her father had replaced it with a can of worms. And without having a heart; her mother had replaced it with a stone. The baby has not only survived, but today, the adult Cordelia is determined to claim back her birthright and be the individual she was meant to be.

It has been a privilege, to walk with her, and accompany her on a small part of her life.

Godefrida – December 1998

Learning to Live with Reality

I survived my journey of discovery, love, hate and excruciating pain. It is now four years since I stopped therapy with Frieda and I can say, I survived it well. In those four years I have written this book. The first chapters flowed without trouble or hesitation, but writing about each personality was much more difficult, and at times quite harrowing, confusing, embarrassing, as well as unbalancing – depending on which particular personality I was in the process of accepting as belonging to me. It seemed a necessity to give each of them time to be themselves again and let them act out their feelings and behaviour, so that I could write from my heart.

Having expressed themselves, I found each one integrated slowly but surely, until finally the broken pieces I saw in the sky as I drove home one day early on in my therapy had come together. Those pieces were the broken fragments of my inner self, and each one was a piece in a complicated jigsaw. The picture in front of me was the picture I have drawn in the pages of this book. Something miraculous happened as I wrote this book, it was as if a film was unreeling in my head and the doors of my heart were finally letting out the darkness and pain – and now the light can shine in! I can laugh, I can sing, I can love without fear, but the sadness still lingers and I will never forget.

I sometimes still feel angry, that I was cheated of being a well-balanced, happy, kind and caring person. I did not like the bad thoughts and feelings I had about myself and others, my lack of trust and suspicions. I would have loved to have blossomed in a childhood that had prepared me for a secure adult life, something many people take for granted. Moreover, I was also cheated out of my own creativity and had to borrow from others, sometimes to express my deep feelings as I was not secure enough to use my own words. Hence I sometimes used certain words from Eileen Soper's poems and Eddie Askew's poetic writings, which were imprinted in my memory and express his relationship with God. I of course quite often used my own words when expressing my relationship with Frieda, but equally as often, felt inhibited. Today, I no longer have to borrow life from others and this book has enabled me to believe in my own words. I now know, I could have achieved so much and made others happier, but I cannot make up for what has passed, I can only be myself today.

My husband has had to face the truth for himself about me and my past life, which hurt him and our children very deeply. Somehow, he found in his heart the capacity and love to cope with whatever life has slung at us, and continues to be a faithful, strong support through everything. Regretfully, the cost of my recovery has made him almost bankrupt and the only way I feel I can repay him is by letting him see that life for me can now take on a new look, with happier days ahead for us both. I also congratulate myself on the wise choice of a partner I made when I married, in spite of all my past. He has been the best thing that has ever happened to me and I pray we will have many more years together to make amends for the years the locusts have eaten. Even so, there are moments and days when I fail and old feelings return, especially when I experience rejection, but they pass in time and I try to replace them with understanding of the other person.

The pages of this book tell the truth, only small details may be incorrect. I have searched my mind and heart; there have been many days and months I have wanted, even now, to deny it all but I always come back to the truth. The truth that was too horrible, too terrifying for anyone to confront, a truth that Frieda helped me face. It hurt, that a consultant spoke such cruel and dismissive statements (see the chapter entitled Objects Relationships), and that other colleagues of Frieda's thought I was taking her for a ride. It makes me even more grateful for her belief in me. I cannot even imagine how anybody could or would create a story of such pain and trauma of this degree against those who had loved them. Perhaps, doctors, therapists and psychiatric nurses should trust their patients a little more – because so often, the patient is aware of what is going on at a deeper level and understands better than anyone. However, there were others who consistently stood by me at the clinic. Anne, whom I have mentioned several times, was a nurse who could cope with someone being dependent on her, and who did not back off when the going got tough. She believed in me and stood by me through everything. Her understanding of another human being in so much pain helped me to battle on. We are friends today, I don't see her much but I know she is there and when we meet, we greet like old friends and share together, her life as well as mine. The relationship now is quite different. I will never forget her as long as I live and I owe her a debt of gratitude for just being there; sometimes to support and hold me through it all. She is a very special person with a special gift.

Since Frieda left, Dr C has continued as my consultant, which gave me some stability in a difficult situation. He has supported me through the years I have been writing the book and will be there for me for as long as I require professional help, however infrequently. Unfortunately, life has thrown another crisis at me involving a loved one, a close family member, but I am coping well in spite of the heartache. Dr C is supporting me in this situation alongside the finishing of this book and the fears surrounding my story possibly going into print. Learning to live life in a different way with no more dissociation takes time and adjustment, and the sadness that can still overwhelm me needs to be shared with someone who completely understands. I could have so easily fallen into the trap of transference with Dr C but I battled against this from the start (certainly after Frieda had left) – never again did I want to experience the pain and humiliation of this phenomenon. I have been strong enough to succeed in having a more normal and good relationship with him, where I can tell him absolutely anything, but I have in my own time also gradually grown independent of him. In other words, I feel I have finally matured into a reasonable, well-balanced adult and grown out of the need for a substitute mother and father. I think I can quite confidently say that he too has wholeheartedly believed in me, if not from the beginning of his care, he certainly has for some time now. I learnt to trust him and it will be a very sad day for me, as well as progress, when I finally say goodbye to him. Very rarely in life can we find another human being as special as one who has the capacity to feel another's suffering, and even more so to admit it. I have never felt so accepted in my life as when I managed to take in the empathy he expressed with my intense sadness. He will always hold a special place in my heart and I want to thank him on the pages of this book for his support, his care and again his genuine belief in all that has happened and how I coped with it. He helped me to accept that I wasn't a bad person, bad things were done to me.

The whole process of growth, since my therapy ended, has not been easy. I was angry with Frieda for backing out before my therapy was finished, I felt abandoned again. I also had to grieve her loss as a therapist as well as a substitute mother. Her letters to me have helped. My letters to her, at first, had to go via the clinic, but eventually she allowed me to have her address and telephone number. She agreed to join me in my venture of putting my story down on paper after I had started, and occasionally we have met at my home during these last four years, to discuss our work. I think she will agree that I have not taken advantage of the knowledge of her address or telephone number. I've only used it for discussion or advice regarding the book, and sometimes about my feelings.

The day Frieda left the clinic, I switched into Victoria, who always pretended everything was okay, and I would not let her see it mattered to me more than I could ever explain. I walked from that clinic not believing I would ever see or hear from her again. I still felt I needed Frieda in order to survive – just as roses need rain – just as I had felt about my father. Those first months were agony indeed but I coped. My husband was a wonderful support and another grandchild was born on the day I said goodbye to Frieda, so my days were full and busy. I appreciated my own little family so much and gave them all the love and support they needed. Somehow, I have always managed to do this, in spite of the pain inside. I could put any pain aside and deal with the immediate. Thus, I put Frieda inside a box, and I put the box away in the corner of my heart, locked in a cupboard. I could then bring her out and deal with her when I wanted to. Like everything else in my life, anything painful had its own compartment or personality.

Frieda was just in a box, what else could I do at this stage but she kept popping out unexpectedly, so I got down to writing about her. I did my own therapy and grieving with Dr C's support. When I think back to the day, I had my last therapy session with Frieda, I left with a clear understanding of what had happened to me and why I created so many little people to help me. Although I could see clearly how the emotional maze had occurred, I could not yet see how I was going to get out of it. Everything was still so raw, and the personalities had not integrated. Without the safety net of being able to talk to Dr C about my feelings – alongside the writing of the book – everything could have gone horribly wrong. I could have been actually worse off than never having embarked on a psychotherapeutic journey. These last four years, with contact with Frieda and with Dr C's support, have proved invaluable. My original family had embossed in my heart and mind that I was worth nothing and therefore worth dumping. Now Frieda had left me too – far too soon. I had at least another three years work to do. Dr C was still around but how long for? I often asked myself this question. I expected him to tell me enough was enough; it was time I was better and able to cope. He never did, and he is still around. Whatever have I done to deserve this?

I look back on all my therapy and remember the pain, the fear, the confusion and the total despair – it was a potentially dangerous journey, one that could have ended my life, but worse than that, one that could have left me permanently mentally damaged. The risk was enormous and Dr C has often said that if he had been my consultant from the beginning, he would not have advocated psychotherapy as the treatment. I understand his caution only too well but I had already started down the road. However, I would say that maybe the guidelines for starting psychotherapy in multiple personality patients who have been severely abused should be as follows:

1. A deep desire within the person to sort things out and change.

2. A spouse or partner at home willing to support

3. A person showing strength from their inner core or centre. A fighter.

4. A person who has already achieved in spite of the damage done to them.

Those seeking to help adults who were abused as children, please allow my personal experience and understanding in consequence, to question the way forward. Tender loving care would have been wonderful and it was a necessary part of my care during admission, but I might have wanted it to last for ever. I chose the hard route, and as labour pains give way to the joy of birth, I embark on learning to live – and that is never easy, particularly with a handicap.

I'm sure the reader can see that my imaginary world was better than the real world. It was a better place inside my head, even the bluebells were more blue and more prolific than ever could be seen for real. Frieda was the catalyst for me wanting to be in the real world, so the transference was useful; otherwise, I could easily have continued backwards down my black tunnel. Frieda leaving when she did helped me break my deep transference. I could not go on with the intensity of this relationship, yet it will always remain in a class of its own.

She is still special and she will always have the power to hurt me, although I know she would not want to do this deliberately, but being a therapist at heart, who knows what she may do for all the right reasons? My relationship with Frieda is much more normal now, although there is a slight tendency for it to be on a love versus hate basis, as the relationship was born out of an enormous need. I shall always think of her with love and affection and it is a comfort as well as an embarrassment that she knows me better than I know myself.

It is a privilege I thought could never be mine, that she eventually was prepared to take the demands and challenges of taming this shrew – Cordelia with all her guises is at last free to be herself.

I want to express here my gratitude to God. He gave me the strength, He kept his promise, He was with me through all my suffering and still is today.

Some will ask why He allowed such awful atrocities to happen to a small child. I asked this question during some of my blackest hours. I don't know the answer, no one does, but I do know that He allows bad things to happen to innocent people and I do know I could not have survived without Him.

Maybe my experience will help others to trust Him and risk such a journey to wholeness.

Appraisal
by Dr C, Consultant Psychiatrist

I first met Cordelia in 1993 when she came under my care following the departure of her previous psychiatrist. It was clear from the beginning that the task ahead would neither be easy nor quick.

Cordelia exhibited a variety of challenging behaviours at times when she was most troubled. As her therapy progressed, she was dealing with some very disturbing material which, had she experienced it in ordinary circumstances, would have caused her great distress. But Cordelia had learned at an early age how not to experience distress and now that through therapy, the pain was again threatening her, these psychological defences inevitably and automatically kicked in.

To me, what one calls these defences is not crucial. In common with most European psychiatrists, I favour the term 'dissociative state' over 'multiple personality', but both essentially are referring to the same phenomenon. 'Dissociation' emphasises the separation of feeling from consciousness through a number of psychological manoeuvres. These include restriction of consciousness, as in 'walking around in a daze'. Another involves forgetting details of your past, your environment or yourself, such as in a fugue state, where the person may arrive at a Casualty department not knowing his name, address or any personal details. Occasionally a person may develop a symptom such as paralysis of a limb through this mechanism.

Cordelia's dissociation involved an extraordinarily complex set of personalities, each one with a specific purpose, allowing her to deal with whatever potentially painful situation or emotion she faced without having to feel the hurt she would have done as Cordelia. Because Cordelia's pattern of dissociative defences was so extraordinary, she was not believed. Many people, friends, family and even some staff at the clinic saw her actions when dissociated and experiencing herself as a different personality, as just wilfully bad behaviour. This isn't surprising. It isn't easy to be understanding toward somebody who seems to be manipulating you, pretending to be someone else or making it difficult for you to do your job. It is a lot easier to treat 'nice' people with courtesy and kindness than it is someone who is difficult and challenging.

Many of Cordelia's dissociative personalities were not 'nice'. How could they be? They were after all born to cope with an extremely hostile environment in which 'niceness' wins no prizes. As a result she attracted a lot of negative emotions. At the clinic we were only human and felt our share of anger, resentment and fear at the apparently anarchic person we had to manage. To be fair, I think most of the staff managed to separate out 'their stuff', from their therapeutic actions, but nonetheless, Cordelia did occasionally meet with less kindness than she needed. Hence her experiences of the world as a hostile place requiring her dissociative defences were confirmed and the personalities became further ingrained.

Many psychiatrists in the United Kingdom, looking at descriptions of Cordelia's behaviours over her time at the clinic, would have labelled her as 'personality disordered'. The categorical system of classification favoured at present encourages us to assign diagnostic labels and many of us have a tendency then to use these labels to explain our patients' actions. Thus, Cordelia might have been labelled then as having a 'borderline personality', an 'impulsive personality' or an 'emotionally unstable' personality. Once such a label has been given then it is easy to say 'she has done this or that impulsive or destructive act because she has this or that personality disorder'. This approach, of course, completely misses the point which is that people act the way they do for very good reasons and assigning a label does nothing to improve understanding of why the actions have occurred or the psychological basis for them. This is in my view one of the main ways in which what we call 'evidence based medicine' has led to us treating patients with complex problems of Cordelia's kind less and less well. In order to gain evidence one needs to categorise and in order to categorise one has to simplify, not to understand. Hopefully in due course we will move away from this reductionist way of viewing psychological distress looking more at behaviours and less at labels.

The other modern trend in psychiatry is away from an holistic approach to understanding psychological conditions. Psychiatrists tend to be either 'biological' or 'psychodynamic' in orientation. Thus argument is created: 'Should we treat with drugs or psychotherapy?' This again is missing the point. While there certainly is a chemical basis to many psychiatric conditions, this chemical disturbance happens because of psychological mechanisms caused by experiences through a person's lifetime. A person cannot benefit fully from psychotherapy if they suffer from a severe chemical depressive illness. Equally, treating a person's chemical depression and failing to deal with any of the underlying issues will only lead to them suffering from repeated episodes of illness. The textbooks tell us that depression tends to be a recurrent condition. This is of no surprise if psychiatrists are merely treating patients with antidepressants without dealing with any of the psychological problems or resultant behaviours. Cordelia does not enjoy a lot of happiness, as yet, though I still have my hopes that she will in the future. She realises that the work she has done in psychotherapy has been worthwhile and it has allowed her to be a great support to others in her family through some difficult times. Cordelia should not have gone through what she did. This unfairness in her life is very difficult for her to absorb. If only she had gained her present freedom to be who she is earlier on in her life. She feels the loss of this possibility very hard. However, she is now I think seeing that there are good possibilities for her to experience a full future and to be an important part of others' lives. The real Cordelia is a charming and considerate person; how wrong were those who judged her when things were at their worst.

In this book, Cordelia correctly quotes me as saying that I wouldn't have put her into psychotherapy had I been making the decision at the start of her treatment. Back in my training days, my first psychotherapy supervisor told me: 'If you ever meet a patient who you feel really, really needs psychotherapy, for goodness' sake don't give it to them.'

What he was referring to was the fact that people who have been severely damaged by early-life experiences often fail to develop sufficient resilience, confidence, tolerance of frustration and ability to accept limits, in order to be able to cope with the emotional rollercoaster which is exploratory psychotherapy. Psychotherapy can make people ill if the wrong type is used with the wrong patient; I have seen this happen more than once. A damaged person who has found some kind of stability and a means of coping through their defences can break down when these defences are challenged. Psychotherapy is a powerful drug, with powerful side effects which needs to be used with caution.

So how was I proven wrong? There is now, I am thankful to be able to say, no doubt that Cordelia has benefited from her therapy. The person who I see now still often suffers a lot but she is permanently Cordelia and she is free; free to suffer and enjoy, to experience her life spontaneously as it is, for good and bad.

Cordelia survived and emerged stronger from therapy against the odds for several reasons. Firstly, she had a therapist with all the necessary qualities: calmness, wisdom, patience, kindness and dogged determination. Secondly, for all its failings, the clinic was a good place, with some very good people who stayed with Cordelia when the going got tough. This was essential at times to contain the crises as they inevitably occurred. This role of psychiatric units as places of asylum for people in crisis is much neglected in modern times. Sadly, had Cordelia been treated under the NHS I don't believe that this 'bottom line' support in crisis would have been available when needed and the results could well have been disastrous.

Thirdly, she has a fine spouse, full of kindness, patience and love who has gone through the rollercoaster with her. The importance of a stable, loving relationship cannot be overstressed.

Finally and most crucially, Cordelia is a remarkable person with exceptional reserves of strength and resilience. She was terribly harmed by her childhood experiences, but not destroyed. Now she is able to accept the world as it is, warts and all, and can tolerate the sadness of the ending of her therapy occurring prematurely and the limitations of the type of work I am able to do with her.

This piece of work is, I believe, a very important contribution to the understanding of human distress and its psychic consequences. The awful clarity of Cordelia's account and the incisive rigour of Godefrida's analysis should inform those who read it and, hopefully, encourage more therapists and psychiatrists to take a risk and start off on the therapeutic road from which, had I been there in the beginning, I would have turned away.

Dr C

Bibliography

Aldridge-Morris, R, *Multiple Personality – An Exercise in Deception*, Hove, London, Hillsdale: Lawrence Erlbaum Associates Publishers, 1989

Andreas, S, & Andreas, C, *Change Your Mind – and Keep the Change. Advanced NLP Submodalities Interventions*, Moab Utah: Real People Press, 1987

Balint, M, *Primary Love and Psycho-Analytic Technique*, London: Hogarth press, 1952

Bandler, R, *Using Your Brain – for a Change*, Moab Utah: Real People Press, 1985

Bandler, R, & Grinder, J, *Frogs into Princes*, Moab Utah: Real People Press, 1979

Beahrs, JO, *Unity and Multiplicity: Multilevel Consciousness of Self in Hypnosis, Psychiatric Disorder and Mental Health*, New York: Brunner/Mazel, 1982

—, *Co-consciousness: A Common Denominator in Hypnosis, Multiple Personality and Normalcy*, American Journal of Clinical Hypnosis, 1983, pp.26, 100–113

Bettelheim, B, *Love Is Not Enough – the Treatment of Emotionally Disturbed Children*, London: Collier Books, 1965

Bion, W, *Learning from Experiences*, London: Heinemann, 1962

Bliss, EL, *Spontaneous Self-hypnosis in Multiple Personality Disorder*, Psychiatric Clinics of North America, 1984, pp.7, 135–146

—, *Multiple Personality, Allied Disorders and Hypnosis*, Oxford: Oxford University Press, 1986

Bliss, J, & Bliss, E, *Prism*, New York: Stein & Day, 1985

Bloch, JP, *Assessment and Treatment of Multiple Personality and Dissociative Disorders*, Sarasota, Florida: Professional Resource Press, 1991

Braun, BG, *Psychophysiologic Phenomena in Multiple Personality and Hypnosis*, American Journal of Clinical Hypnosis, 1983, pp.26, 124–137

Braun, BG, & Braun, RE, *Clinical Aspects of Multiple Personality*, paper presented at the meeting of the American Society of Clinical Hypnosis, San Francisco, 1979

Breggin, P, *Toxic Psychiatry – Drugs and Electroconvulsive Therapy: the Truth and the Better Alternatives*, London: Harper Collins Publishers, 1993

Bryant, A, Kessler, J, & Shirar, L, *The Family Inside – Working with the Multiple*, New York, London: WW Norton & Company, 1992

Caplan, W, *A Good little Boy*, The International Journal of Infant Observation and its Applications, Tavistock Clinic Foundation, 1998, vol. II, no. 1 October

Casey, JF, & Wilson, L, *The Flock*, Abacus, 1993

Chase, T, *When Rabbit Howls – The Troops for Truddi Chase*, London, Sydney, Auckland: Pan Books, 1989

Chu, JA, *Some Aspects of Resistance in the Treatment of Multiple Personality Disorder*, Dissociation, 1(2), 1988, pp.34–38

Confer, WN, & Ables, B, *René Multiple Personality: Etiology, Diagnosis and Treatment*, Human Science, 1983

Deikman, AJ, *The Observing Self*, Beacon Press, 1982

Eagle, NM, *Recent Developments in Psycho-Analysis; A Critical Evaluation*, Cambridge, Massachusetts, London: Harvard University Press, 1987

Fahy, TA, *The Diagnosis of Multiple Personality Disorder. A Critical Review*, British Journal of Psychiatry, 1988, pp.153, 597–608

Fenichel, O, *The Psycho-Analytic Theory of Neurosis*, New York: Norton & Co, London: Kegan Paul, Trench, Trubner & Co, 1945

Fezler, W, *Imagery for Healing, Knowledge and Power*, New York, London, Toronto, Sydney, Tokyo, Singapore: A Fireside Book/Simon & Schuster, 1990

Fordham, M, *Children as Individuals*, London: Free Association Books, 1994

Freud, S, *Formulations on the Two Principles of Mental Functioning*, 1911, Standard Edition, vol. XII, pp.218–27

—, *Fetishism*, International Journal of Psycho-Analysis, IX, 1928

—, *Outline of Psycho-Analysis*, Standard Edition, 1939, vol. XXIII

—, *Splitting of the Ego in the Defensive Process*, International Journal of Psycho-Analysis, 1941, XXII

Gersie, A, *Reflections on Therapeutic Storymaking – The Use of Stories in Groups*, London, Bristol: Jessica Kingsley Publishers, 1997

Gil, E, *Outgrowing the Pain – A Book for and about Adults Abused as Children*, New York: Del Publishing, 1981

Golman, D, *Emotional Intelligence*, London: Bloomsbury Publishing, 1996

Goulding, RA, & Schwartz, RC, *The Mosaic Mind – Empowering the Tormented Selves of Child Abuse Survivors*, New York, London: WW Norton & Company, 1995

Greaves, GB, *Common Errors in the Treatment of Multiple Personality Disorder*, Dissociation, 1 (1), 1989, pp.61–66

Gregory, RL, *The Oxford Companion to The Mind*, Oxford, New York: Oxford University Press, 1987

Griffin, J, & Tyrrell, I, *The 'Human Givens'. The Future of Psychotherapy*, The Therapist, 1998, vol. V, no. 1, Winter

Griffin, J, *The Origin of Dreams*, The Therapist Ltd., Henry House, 189 Heene Road, Worthing, West Sussex BN11 4NN, 1997

Grinder, J, & Bandler, R, *Trance-Formations: Neuro Linguistic Programming and the Structure of Hypnosis*, Moab Utah: Real People Press, 1987

Hall, L, & Lloyd, S, *Surviving Child Sexual Abuse – A Handbook for Helping Women Challenge Their Past*, New York, Philadelphia, London: The Falmer Press, 1989

Hawksworth, H, & Schwarz, T, *The Five of Me*, Chicago: Henry Regnery, 1977

Herman, N, *My Kleinian Home – A Journey Through Four Psychotherapies*, London: Free Association Books, 1988

Hilgard, ER, *Divided Consciousness: Multiple Controls in Human Thought and Action*, New York: Wiley, 1977

—, *The Hidden Observer and Multiple Personality*, International Journal of Clinical & Experimental Hypnosis, 1984, pp.32, 248–253

—, *Professional Scepticism about Multiple Personality*, Journal of Nervous and Mental Disease, 1988, pp.176, 532

Jacobson, E, *The Self and the Object World*, New York: International Universities Press; London: Hogarth, 1964 65

Jennings, S, (ed.), *Dramatherapy, Theory and Practice for Teachers and Clinicians*, vol. II, London: Routledge, 1992

—, *The Traveller: Healing Theatre in Magilligan Prison*, Journal of the British Association of Dramatherapists, 1999, vol. XXI, no. 2 Autumn

Jones, P, *Drama as Therapy – Theatre as Living*, London, New York: Routledge, 1996

Karle, H, *The Filthy Lie – Discovering and Recovering from Childhood Abuse*, London: Hamish Hamilton, 1992

Keyes, D, *The Minds of Billy Milligan*, London: Penguin Books, 1995

Klein, M, (1932), *The Psycho-Analysis of Children (The Writings of Melanie Klein, 2)*, London: Hogarth (1980)

—, *Some Theoretical Conclusion Regarding the Emotional Life of the Infant. (The Writings of Melanie Klein, 3)*, London: Hogarth (1975)

Kluft, RP, *Varieties of Hypnotic Interventions in the Treatment of Multiple Personality*, American Journal of Clinical Hypnosis, 1982, pp.24, 230–240

—, *Personality Unification in Multiple Personality Disorder: A Follow-up Study*, in Braun, BG, (ed.), *Treatment of Multiple Personality Disorder*, Washington, DC: American Psychiatric Press, 1986, pp.29–60,

—, *On Optimism in the Treatment of MPD: A Status Report by a Participant Observer*, Trauma and Recovery, 1989a, April. (A Newsletter of the Ohio Society for the Study of Multiple Personality and Dissociation; Appendix, pp.85–86)

—, *The Rehabilitation of Therapists Overwhelmed by Their Work with Multiple Personality Disorder Patients*, Dissociation, 1989b, pp.2, 243–249

Lacan, J, (ed. JA Miller), *The Four Fundamental Concepts of Psycho-Analysis*, The Hogarth Press, 1977

Lancaster, E, *The Final Face of Eve*, New York: McGraw-Hill, 1958

Lazar, RA, Ropke, C, & Ermann G, *Learning to be: on the Observation of a Premature Baby*, The International Journal of Infant Observation and its Applications, Tavistock Clinic Foundation, 1998, vol. II, no. 1 October

Levine, HB, *Adult Analysis and Childhood Sexual Abuse*, Hilsdale, New York, Hove, London: The Analytic Press, 1990

Lowenstein, RM, *Practice and Precept in Psycho-analytic Technique – Selected papers of Rudolph M Lowenstein*, New Haven, London: Yale University Press, 1982

Ludwig, AM, *Altered States of Consciousness*, Archives of General Psychiatry, 1966, pp.15(3), 225–234

Maher, P, (ed.), *Child Abuse, the Educational Perspective*, Oxford: Basil Blockwell, 1987

Mayer, R, *Through Divided Minds – Probing the Mysteries of Multiple Personalities. A Doctor's Story*, New York: Avon Books, 1992

Meltzer, D, *The Kleinian Development*, Clunie Press, 1978

Merskey, H, *The Manufacture of Personalities. The Production of Multiple Personality Disorder*, British Journal of Psychiatry, 1992, pp.160, 327–340

—, *Multiple Personality Disorder and False Memory Syndrome*, British Journal of Psychiatry 1995, pp.166, 281–283

Miller, A, *The Drama of Being a Child*, London: Virago Press, 1992

Mitchell, J, *The Selected Melanie Klein*, Penguin, 1986

Muller, W, *Legacy of the Heart – The Spiritual Advantages of a Painful Childhood*, New York, London, Toronto, Sydney, Tokyo, Singapore: Fireside; Simon & Schuster, 1992

Ogden, TH, *On Projective Identification*, International Journal of Psycho-Analysis, 1979, pp.60, 357–73

Orne, MT, *The Nature of Hypnosis: Artefact and Essence*, Journal of Abnormal and Social Psychology, 1959, pp.58, 277–299

Parks, P, *Rescuing the 'Inner Child' – Therapy for Adults Sexually Abused as Children*, London: Souvenir Press, 1990

Peach, E, *Tarot Predictions – An Advanced Handbook of Images for Tomorrow*, The Aquarian Press – Imprint of Harper Collins Publishers, 1991

Pendergast, M, *Victims of Memory – Incest Accusations and Shattered lives*, London: Harper Collins Publishers, 1998

Pinker, S, *How the Mind Works*, Great Britain: The Softback Preview, 1998

Piper, A Jr, *Multiple Personality Disorder*, British Journal of Psychiatry, 1994, pp.164, 600–612

Prince, M, *Christine Beauchamp: The Dissociation of a Personality*, New York, London: Longmans, Green & Co, 1906

Putnam, FW, *Diagnosis and Treatment of Multiple Personality Disorder*, New York: Guildford, 1989

Racker, H, *Transference and Counter-Transference*, The Institute of Psycho-Analysis, The Hogarth Press, 1968

Ross, CA, *Multiple Personality Disorder – Diagnosis, Clinical Features and Treatment*, New York, Chichester, Brisbane, Toronto, Singapore: John Wiley & Sons, 1989

Ross, CA, & Dua, V, *Psychiatric Health Care Costs of Multiple Personality Disorder*, American Journal of Psychotherapy, vol. XLVII, no. 1, Winter 1993

Rycroft, C, *Imagination and Reality*, The Institute of Psycho-Analysis, The Hogarth Press, 1968

Sacks, O, *The Man Who Mistook His Wife For a Hat*, Picador, 1986

Sanford, AJ, *Cognition & Cognitive Psychology*, London: Weidenfeld and Nicolson, 1985

Sanford, LT, *Strong at the Broken Places – Overcoming the Trauma of Childhood Abuse*, London: Virago Press, 1991

Schreiber, FR, *Sybil – The True Story of a Woman Possessed by Sixteen Separate Personalities*, London: Penguin Books, 1974

Segal, H, *Introduction to the Work of Melanie Klein*, Hogarth Press, 1973

Shah, I, *World Tales*, London: Octagon Press, 1991

Singer, JL, *Daydreaming and Fantasy*, Oxford, Melbourne, Delhi: Oxford University Press, 1981

Sizemore, CC, & Pittillo, ES, *I'm Eve!* Garden City, New York: Doubleday, 1977

Spiegel, D, & Scheflin, AW, *Dissociated or Fabricated. Psychiatric Aspects of Repressed Memory in Criminal and Civil Cases*, David Spiegel, MD, Department of Psychiatry and Behavioral Sciences, Stanford University, 101 Quarry Road, Stanford, CA, 94305–5544, 1994

Spiegel, H, *The Grade 5 Syndrome; The Highly Hypnotisable Person*, International Journal of Clinical and Experimental Hypnosis, 1974, pp.22, 303–319

Strachey, J, *Transference and Counter-Transference*, The Hogarth Press, Institute of Psycho-Analysis, 1937

Strean, HS, *Resolving Resistances in Psychotherapy*, New York: Wiley, 1985

Taylor, D, *The Healing Power of Stories: Creating Yourself through the Stories of Your Life*, Gill & Macmillan, 1996

Thigpen, CH, & Cleckley, HM, *The Three Faces of Eve*, New York: McGraw-Hill, 1957

Wachtel, PL, (ed.), *Resistance: Psychodynamic and Behavioural Approaches*, New York: Plenum, 1982

Wasserman, J, *The Egyptian Book of the Dead – The Book of Going Forth by Day*, San Francisco: Chronicle Books, 1994

Watkins, JG, & Watkins, HH, *Ego States and Hidden Obervers*, Journal of Altered States of Consciousness, 1979, pp.5, 3–18

—, *Ego-State Therapy* in RJ Corsini (ed.), *Handbook of Innovative Psychotherapies*, 1981, pp.252–279, New York: Wiley

—, *Hazards to the Therapist in the Treatment of Multiple Personalities*, Psychiatric Clinics of North America, 1984, pp.7, 111–119

—, *The Management of Malevolent Ego-States in Multiple Personality Disorder*, Dissociation, 1(1), 1988, pp.67–72

Wilbur, C, *Multiple Personality Disorder and Transference*, Dissociation, 1(1), 1988, pp.73–76

Wolinsky, S, *Trances People Live*, Connecticut: The Bramble Company, 1991

Wolter, DL, *A Life Worth Waiting For!* Minneapolis, Minnesota: Compcare Publishers, 1989

Woodward, J, *The Lone Twin; A Study in Bereavement and Loss*, New York, London: Free Association Books, 1998

Yapko, M, *Hypnosis and the Treatment of Depressions*, New York: Brunner Mazel, 1992